# RETHINKING OPEN SOCIETY

D0858750

# RETHINKING OPEN SOCIETY

## New Adversaries and New Opportunities

Edited by
MICHAEL IGNATIEFF
STEFAN ROCH

Central European University Press
Budapest–New York

© 2018 Michael Ignatieff and Stefan Roch

Published in 2018 by

Central European University Press

Nádor utca 9, H-1051 Budapest, Hungary
Tel: +36-1-327-3138 or 327-3000
Fax: +36-1-327-3183
E-mail: ceupress@press.ceu.edu
Website: www.ceupress.com

224 West 57th Street, New York NY 10019, USA

All rights reserved. No part of this publication may be reproduced,
stored in a retrieval system, or transmitted, in any form or by any means,
without the permission of the Publisher.

ISBN 978-963-386-270-4

Cover design by
STEFAN ROCH and ÉVA SZALAY

Library of Congress Control Number: 2018945713

Printed in Hungary by
Prime-Rate Kft., Budapest

# Table of Contents

# Acknowledgements

The editors would like to express their gratitude to the contributors to this volume for standing with CEU, for delivering such insightful talks and then for working with the editors to turn their lectures into enduring contributions to the debate on open society.

We are deeply indebted to Kinga Ágnes Páll for her invaluable work both during the lecture series and the production of the book. Her administrative support was essential to our work. We are thankful to CEU Press for providing crucial editorial and publishing support throughout the production-process of this volume, particularly Linda Kúnos for providing publishing support, Ilse Josepha Maria Lazaroms for copy-editing and Éva Szalay for helping with the cover-design. We are grateful to all the people at CEU that were involved in the Rethinking Open Society Series and made it such a success. This includes the CEU Communications office and their excellent promotional work, particularly by Adri Bruckner, Colleen Sharkey and Peter Lorenz; it includes Zsolt Ilija, Réka Bálint and Andrea Csele from CEU's Event and Space Management office for providing crucial event support, as well as all the student transcribers who helped us turning talks into manuscripts. Considering all this, we are proud to consider this publication a CEU community effort.

# Introduction

*Michael Ignatieff*

"We are becoming more and more painfully aware of the gross imperfections in our life, of personal as well as of institutional imperfection; of
avoidable suffering, of waste and of unnecessary ugliness; and at the same
time of the fact that it is not impossible for us to do something about all
this, but that such improvements would be just as hard to achieve as they
are important. This awareness increases the strain of personal responsibility, of carrying the cross of being human."

Karl Popper[1]

The values of an open society—free minds, free politics, and free institutions—have been constitutive of Western civilization. Since the Greeks, these
values have been under attack from authoritarian and totalitarian competitors. Karl Popper's *Open Society and Its Enemies* was published in 1945 as a
defense of these values against the twin totalitarian enemies of Nazism and
Stalinism, the one heading towards ignominious defeat, the other rising in
the ascendant. What was wise about Popper's analysis, now that we look back
on it eighty years later, was his awareness that the open society ideal cannot
exist without its enemies. An open society depends for its very definition on

---

[1] Karl Popper, *The Open Society and Its Enemies, Vol. I: The Spell of Plato* (London:
Routledge, 1945), 199–200.

the presence of a persuasive counterexample. Even in our own times, the disgrace of Nazism and Stalinism has done nothing to dim the lure of closed society to those who live within open ones. Instead, closed society has shed its totalitarian form and assumed new authoritarian guises. Closed societies are tempting because open societies are difficult to live in and their ideals are hard to practice. Upholding open society means accepting the "strain of personal responsibility, of carrying the cross of being human." Popper's language here may be overheated, but the thought is clear enough. An open society is very demanding. It asks us to respect the dignity of others, especially of those with whom we may disagree and to make choices for ourselves and our community. It offers us no readily applicable solutions, no straightforward recipe for a better world, but demands that we make reasoned choices, often in perplexing, uncertain, and frightening times. Moreover, open societies frequently fail their citizens. Freedom is easy to abuse. Oligopolies and monopolies distort markets; elites confiscate political power and use it to entrench their privileges; demagogues secure votes through distortion of the truth or the cultivation of hatred. In these and other ways, the freedoms of open society can be betrayed from within. Small wonder, then, that a closed society in which the burden of freedom is taken off the shoulders of citizens by charismatic leaders at the head of single party states, remains a seductive temptation, even for democratic peoples.

Defending open society has been vital to the mission of Central European University (CEU) since it was established in 1991. The institution's founder, George Soros, had been a student of Popper's at the London School of Economics, and CEU was created to further these ideals in former communist societies undergoing the arduous and uncertain transition to democracy and a market economy. CEU's task was to provide advanced education in the social sciences and humanities for societies whose universities had been shackled by the closed society thinking of official Marxism. Since then, and under a variety of political regimes, it has consolidated its reputation as a serious research university. This has not prevented it from coming under attack, most recently by the current Hungarian government. The core of the attack is the claim that the university is a political institution masquerading as a university. The claim is false, as the accrediting agencies who inspect our teaching or review our research have attested, but the attacks are inevitable, in a sense, since the university's mission—to promote the values of a free society—is bound to create suspicion and criticism when governments encroach upon those values. CEU, like any university worthy of the name, can never afford to allow its mission to politicize its teaching or research. It must stand for values without allowing itself to become a prisoner of politics or ideology.

In CEU's case, the duty to promote the open society ideal comes with an obligation to subject the ideal itself to constant re-interpretation and critique. We need to ask difficult questions: whether the ideal, as articulated in 1945, remains relevant in a world changed beyond recognition, why the ideal is under attack, and why single party regimes, promising the certainties and reassurances of the closed society, are now so much in the ascendant, including in the country, Hungary, that has been our home for 27 years. So in 2017 and 2018, CEU invited scholars and thinkers from around the world to join us for a sustained series of lectures and debates under the title *Rethinking Open Society*, the results of which are presented in this volume.

To begin, I would like to raise three basic questions. The first is: Who were open society's old enemies, when the idea first took shape in 1945 in Karl Popper's work? The second is: Who are the new enemies of open society, the ones we confront today? And then, the most difficult question of all: Has the open society ideal outlived its usefulness? I cover the first two questions in this Introduction; the third question is one we answer collectively in this volume.

## The Open Society and its Old Enemies

Karl Popper came from a liberal assimilated Jewish family in Vienna and did pioneering work in the philosophy of science before fleeing Austrian Fascism in the mid-1930s.[2] Open society thus is an idea whose deepest intellectual roots are in Central and Eastern Europe. The book *Open Society and its Enemies*, published in Britain in 1945, represents Popper's "war work," his contribution to the anti-totalitarian struggle. As such, it belongs in a lineage that includes works as various as Orwell's *Animal Farm* and *1984*, Karl Polanyi's *The Great Transformation*, J. L. Talmon's *Origins of Totalitarian Democracy*, Arthur Koestler's *Darkness at Noon*, Raymond Aron's *Opium of the Intellectuals*, and Hannah Arendt's *The Origins of Totalitarianism*. All of

---

[2] Karl Popper, *Logik Der Forschung* (Tübingen: Mohr Siebeck, 1934); Karl Popper, "Das Elend des Historizismus," 1936.

them sought to trace the roots of the totalitarian temptation into the recesses of human psychology and the origins of the European intellectual tradition, in Popper's case, right back to Plato. This is the family lineage that Jan-Werner Müller has called "Cold War liberalism."[3]

These figures, writing between 1945 and 1950, identified the dangers of the totalitarian vision embraced by Hitler and Stalin and defended an anti-utopian politics based on a gradualist defense of freedom. Popper speaks for all of them when he writes: "How can we organize political institutions so that bad or incompetent rulers can be prevented from doing too much damage?"[4] Hannah Arendt, another Jewish refugee from Nazi tyranny, also belonged to this "war work" generation. Her *The Origins of Totalitarianism*, first published in 1948, echoed Popper in his critique of determinist theories of history, chiefly Marxism, as a legitimation of a coercive politics. As she writes: "Caution in handling generally accepted opinions that claim to explain whole trends of history is especially important for the historian of modern times, because the last century has produced an abundance of ideologies that pretend to be keys to history."[5] Marx had said that Marxism is the key to history and knows itself to be such. Open society thinking was an active rebellion against the coercive arrogance that this idea brought to politics.

A third Jewish refugee from totalitarianism, Isaiah Berlin, born in Riga, came to Oxford in the 1930s and played a key role in developing the third distinctive feature of open society, namely, its commitment to liberty. By freedom, Isaiah Berlin meant freedom from interference above all, freedom from enslavement to ends not freely chosen by oneself. Open society's conception of freedom is negative, the liberty of human beings to choose their own ends, as they see fit, as opposed to a positive vision of "freedom to," in which a society shapes collective ends and individuals achieve freedom by serving those ends. Open society is anchored in a passionate belief that each of us must be sovereign in the choices we make in our own lives. This moral individualism was the core idea of open society.

It is important to notice that each of these thinkers prioritized liberty over equality. The totalitarian temptation sought to level, to equalize, and to

---

[3] Jan-Werner Müller, "Fear and Freedom: On 'Cold War Liberalism,'" *European Journal of Political Theory* 7, no. 1 (2008): 45–64.

[4] Popper, *The Open Society and Its Enemies, Vol. I: The Spell of Plato*, 107.

[5] Hannah Arendt, *The Origins of Totalitarianism* (New York: Harcourt, Brace & World, 1968), 9.

forge individuals in the same mould. For open society thinkers, this was a cardinal reason why, when choices had to be made, priority had to be given to individual freedom over equality. If today we are looking for a critique of the tendency of capitalist societies to generate inequalities that threaten the freedom and equality of voice necessary to make a liberal democracy flourish, we will look in vain through the works of the founding generation of open society thinkers. They had other problems in mind.

These thinkers had their differences, but they shared the same opponents: the totalitarian tyrants, their apologists, and those on the European and American left who sought to salvage a revolutionary alternative to open society from the totalitarian temptation. Popper, Berlin, and Arendt were in critical, sometimes embattled dialogue with western apologists of communist totalitarianism like Jean Paul Sartre and western Marxists such as Eric Hobsbawm, Edward Thompson, and Christopher Hill in Britain—brilliant academic radicals who, having rejected totalitarianism, remained attracted to the ideal of a revolutionary alternative to the open society.

In addition to enemies on the left, there were enemies on the right: conservatives—Michael Oakeshott in Britain comes to mind—who were repelled by what they took to be the moral individualism of capitalist society and who feared that capitalist modernity would destroy valued traditions and collective ideals. Popper conceded more to these conservative misgivings about modernity than one might assume. He gave much thought to what he called "the strain of civilisation." Open society thinkers were anti-utopian in the sense that they did not want to persuade anyone that liberal democratic freedom was paradise. They all wanted to say that it was disorienting to live in societies where we have the responsibility of personal freedom and political choice, and where we live in a hurricane of what Josef Schumpeter called "the creative destruction" of the capitalist order.[6]

Open society's final enemy was what both Popper and Berlin called "historicism," the attempt to think that history could provide a reliable scientific guide to political action. Their attack on historicism had a metaphysical implication that should be emphasized. Living with "the strain of civilization" meant being reconciled to uncertainty, to accept the future as the open horizon line of a free society. Open society thinking has a tacit meta-

---

[6] Joseph A. Schumpeter, *Capitalism, Socialism and Democracy* (London: Routledge, 2003), chapter VII.

physics, the idea that to live in liberal freedom is to live in a world in which we accept—to quote Alexander Herzen's wonderful remark—that "history has no libretto." We have to be reconciled to the limits of our knowledge and our predictive judgments. It is better to live in ignorance, Berlin and Popper believed, than in tyrannous certainty.

These refugees from Nazi and Soviet tyranny did not have very much to say about the institutional order of an open society. They simply took it off the shelf. As they arrived in Britain and the United States, they adopted the liberal democratic constitutionalism of their countries of refuge as their tacit institutional framework. So, if contemporary liberal democratic constitutionalism is in crisis today, we will look in vain in the works of Popper, Berlin, or Arendt for a remedy or even a critique. To repeat Jan-Werner Müller's formulation, these founding thinkers of open society are in essence Cold War liberals. They took for granted an international order divided between a liberal capitalist West led by the benign hegemony of the United States and a totalitarian East dominated by Moscow and Beijing. If, therefore, we turn to these original thinkers for guidance in a world where U.S. hegemony is on the wane, North Atlantic unity is fragmenting and the closed societies of the East have opened up to the global capitalist order while retaining single party domination, we will look in vain. They were working with another world in mind.

If next, we consider the economic content of open society, the vision most of them took for granted was Keynesian demand management and the welfare state economics of the late 1940s and 1950s. It is true that one of Popper's closest friends at the London School of Economics, Friedrich von Hayek, launched a devastating critique of the epistemological limitations of central government planning in a free economy in 1944.[7] But by and large, Popper himself, as well as Berlin and Arendt, took for granted a redistributive and welfarist vision of the state's role in regulating a capitalist economy, to the degree that they thought about economic questions at all. At the same time, their change model was cautious: what Popper calls "piecemeal social engineering," as opposed to what Stalin had called the engineering of human souls.

Open society in its origins, therefore, was not neoliberal; it was its opposite.

One critical aspect of open society thinking was the connection that Popper drew between the epistemology of a free society and its morality of

---

[7] Friedrich von Hayek, *The Road to Serfdom* (London: Routledge, 1944).

tolerance. As a philosopher and a historian of science, Popper believed that the key practice that keeps a society free is the scientific method, the constant falsification of theory through systematic reality testing.[8] His attack on totalizing political ideologies derived from this epistemological and also moral conviction that all theory is conditional, provisional, and must give way when falsified by the facts. Few elements of his thinking remain more relevant to a university's mission than this.

From that epistemology Popper developed an ethic of tolerance. If all theory was conditional upon falsification, no one was in sole or exclusive possession of the truth. If we know we can be wrong, it pays to listen to others, to tolerate, even welcome views that diverge from whatever theory or political or moral values we happen to hold. Since our relationship to facts is or ought to be an individual relationship, dependent upon our free minds alone, we have an obligation to get reality, our conception of it, right for us.

Constitutional liberalism entrenches this epistemology within its very institutions. Power checks power, so no single source can impose an ideology from the top or even sometimes a clear political direction. Parliamentary democracy forces executive authority to justify its measures before the adversarial scrutiny of a parliament. Judges bring the critical epistemology of law to the review of administrative and legal decisions. A free media referees the battle over public choice with a complex epistemology of scrutiny, driven by skepticism, scandal mongering, and profit seeking. Universities play their role in subjecting public claims to peer-reviewed research. These institutions— courts, parliaments, media, universities—together, and without concertation or top-down direction, create the epistemological frame in which a free society struggles its way towards the knowledge it needs, or the closure on debate it must accept, in order to chart its collective course into the future. This is how an open society actually operates, and it is a messy, confusing, and often unsatisfying process that produces recurrent nostalgia for rule by experts or charismatic leaders or both.

Open society as a doctrine took on the contours but also the limitations of Cold War liberalism. It shared liberalism's ascendancy between the end of World War II and the economic crisis of the 1970s. It also shared the progress of what should be called the liberal revolution: the decolonization and

---

[8] Karl Popper, *The Open Society and Its Enemies, Vol. II: The High Tide of Prophecy: Hegel, Marx, and the Aftermath* (London: Routledge, 1945), 288.

dismantling of European empires, the triumph of the national independence movements, the victory of the U.S. civil rights revolution, the emergence of feminism and the gay rights movements. We can call this a liberal revolution because it was rights-driven and its objective was freedom, both for nations and for individuals. An open society thus became a society in which everyone—regardless of race, national origin, gender, or sexual orientation—could enjoy the benefits of freedom.

By the early 1970s, however, with the onset of a global economic crisis, the rising cost of the postwar welfare state and a growing backlash from white majority voters against the rights of minorities, a counter-revolution swept Margaret Thatcher and Ronald Reagan to power. From that moment on, the cause of open society began to be associated, ever more closely, with neo-liberalism, with de-regulation, lower taxes, and the scaling back of the liberal state. An open society champion like Hayek influenced Mrs. Thatcher, enabling her to equate the struggle to dismantle a relatively benign welfare state with the battle against socialist and communist tyranny. Not all open society thinkers did align themselves with the conservative, anti-liberal politics of the 1970s and 1980s, but some did, and if open society rhetoric suddenly began to acquire new opponents on the left, it was because of its association with the neo-liberal turn.

While open society increasingly aligned with anti-communist neo-liberalism in Western Europe, it also forged a crucial association with the anti-totalitarian civil society movements of Eastern Europe. Dissidents in Warsaw and Gdansk, in Prague and Budapest launched a challenge to their communist regimes, using the Helsinki Final Act of 1975, to create human rights NGOs at home. They enlisted support overseas from academics, journalists, and philanthropists, and one of these, George Soros, used the concept of open society, which he had learned from his mentor at the London School of Economics, to shape his philanthropic support for the dissidents. In the process, open society advocates developed a change model, in which money and expertise from the outside was to be channeled to inside civil society organizations whose campaigns slowly drained moral legitimacy from communist regimes. This change model, implied in Václav Havel's famous phrase "the power of the powerless,"[9] and then developed by Solidarność and Charter 77,

---

[9] Václav Havel, *The Power of the Powerless: Citizens Against the State in Central-Eastern Europe* (New York: M. E. Sharpe, 1985).

ushered in European civil society's finest hour: the largely peaceful transitions that occurred between 1988 and 1990.

## The Open Society and its New Enemies

It was then, at open society's apparent moment of triumph, that the trouble started. Civil society liberals, who swept all before them in 1989 and 1990, failed to transform loose civil society associations into political parties and trade unions robust enough to survive electoral competition with nationalists, ex-communists, and conservatives in the post-transition era. Václav Havel, for example, refused to create his own political party, trying to remain above the fray as President. Political power began to flow to illiberal challengers. In Hungary in 2002, Viktor Orbán managed to create a major civic movement on the right, while the left failed to institutionalize their own support, as Béla Greskovits explains in his chapter in this volume. The failure of liberals to develop political instruments of power prepared the ground for other political forces with more effective organizations and a shrewder sense of the fears and anxieties unleashed when the certainties of the communist order were swept away. The chaotic character of the sell-off of state property, the privatizations that benefited a new oligarchy while leaving others' lives unchanged, did much to erode the luster of the open society ideal. It seemed to have led not to freedom, but to a nasty new world of inequality.

For a time in the 1990s, the chaotic transition in Eastern Europe was disciplined and incentivized by the European Union accession process. These incentives were all directed towards creating the institutional framework of open society, the separation of powers, free media, a free civil society, the constitutional guarantees of rights, and minority protection. As long as the incentives of the accession process were operating, the countries seeking entry to the European Union followed the path towards open society. Once accession was complete, once they were inside the club, the European Union gradually lost its capacity to entrench open society institutions in enlargement countries. In its place, a new political form, combining single party domination of the political system, media controls, and rent-seeking corruption began to displace open society as the political goal of the ruling elites.

This coincided with the gradual withdrawal of the United States from European integration processes. The Dayton Accord of 1995 was the last moment in which the United States made a concerted political and military commitment to peace and stability in Europe. Since then, both Western European and American incentives towards open society have weakened. When the transitions began to stall in the economic crisis of 2008, new insecurities created a fertile ground that illiberal regimes exploited to consolidate power and move, wherever possible, to permanent single party rule. At the same time, these regimes turned out to be adept at mobilizing their populations against key open society values like multicultural tolerance and openness to migration. After the uncontrolled migration surge of 2015, open society advocates rapidly lost the battle for Eastern European hearts and minds.

Further to the East, Russia lived through the Eastern European experience of transition, but in a still more humiliating and chaotic form. For most Russians, the transition from closed to open society took the form of imperial collapse, economic disintegration, and the weakening of public order and welfare supports. It is no surprise that an alternative to open society began to emerge after a decade of chaotic opening to the global economy. A figure like Vladimir Putin, trained by the one Soviet institution that still worked, the security services, took control of the state apparatus, and used oil revenues to restore state benefits and to rebuild the administrative capacity of the coercive state. He then made a deal with the oligarchs who had benefitted from the privatization of the 1990s. He gave them the stability they needed to make their fortunes, in return for complete political obedience. On this basis, a new form of capitalist autocracy began to take shape in Russia.

Still further to the East, the Chinese went through a similar encounter with openness. Beginning in the mid 1960s, they experienced the chaos and disorder of the cultural revolution. They came out of it, concluding that they must open to the global economy or be left behind. Having opened, the party elite then began to grasp the looming danger in open society's freedoms. Free markets and free ideas would lead to free politics, and once they did, the monopoly of single party rule would come under challenge. The Chinese ruling elite made a clear strategic choice to consolidate single party rule at the expense of open society.

In Western democracies, open society defenders in power often failed the test of continuous crisis ushered in after 9/11. The terrorist attacks sapped faith in the protecting state and undermined confidence in open borders and open institutions. The economic crisis of 2008 weakened confidence in the economic sovereignty of states and their capacity to fairly distribute the benefits of prosperity. These intersecting pressures—terrorism, rising inequality, and job insecurity—created a political opening for populist majoritarianism.

Populist anger has brought about British exit from Europe and the election of an American President committed to a radical nationalist agenda. All in all, these are open society's new enemies: the single party autocracies of Russia and China, the illiberal democracies of Eastern Europe, and the democratic populists in Western Europe and North America.

We are living in what is best described as a counter-revolutionary moment, a concerted attempt to undo the international political order and the open international economy created after 1945. We are moving away from multilateral cooperation and open international markets towards closed borders, the return of the sovereign state, and transactional power politics. This counter-revolution is driven by the polarization of domestic politics, with a politics of enemies supplanting a politics of compromise. The counter-revolution is also targeting the liberal revolution and the gains made by minorities. It remains to be seen how much of the liberal revolution will survive, but it is clear that open society's brief moment of dominance after 1989 has now ended.

## Has Open Society Outlived its Usefulness?

As we take stock of open society's new enemies and their political ascendancy, we need to distinguish them from the totalitarian enemies faced by Cold War liberals. We cannot understand these new regimes according to an open-closed logic. Soviet Russia and Mao's China were closed societies in an ideological sense, committed to a systemic alternative to capitalism—the socialist mode of production—which they tried to export to developing countries in the global south. Today's Russia and China have no alternative economic model to export. They price their goods on the open international market; Chinese companies compete with capitalist multinationals for market share around the world. Capital import and export are fundamental to their economies. Using Albert Hirschman's terminology, the new regimes all allow exit and voice and they do not impose loyalty.[10] Their citizens may not enjoy full speech rights, but they have a right to exit, and this right—together with the right to stash their money overseas—acts as a crucial safety

---

[10] Albert Hirschman, *Exit, Voice and Loyalty: Responses to Decline in Firms, Organizations and States* (Cambridge, MA: Harvard University Press, 1970).

valve stabilizing these regimes against internal discontent. Both the Russian and Chinese regimes allow limited voice rights precisely so that these regimes can listen in, and in doing so, hear rumblings of discontent in time. Finally, unlike Stalin and Mao, neither the Russian nor Chinese regimes demand the intense, all-encompassing regime loyalty of the past. Instead, they channel loyalty to the nation and seek to legitimize their regimes as authentic expressions of nationalist sentiment.

Likewise, if we look at the "illiberal democracies" in Eastern Europe, they are not closed societies in the classic Popperian sense. They are members of NATO, the European Union, the World Trade Organization; they are dependent on free migration of their populations to Western Europe, on inward investment, and on the ability to place their own capital outside. Media pluralism in Eastern Europe is reduced, but opposition voices can still be heard and these new regimes do not need to resort to police terror or overt intimidation. They do not demand public expressions of loyalty to the regime itself, seeking to channel loyalty instead to the nation, and they legitimize themselves through free, if highly manipulated elections. So they are something new under the sun: single party states that allow exit, voice, and canalize loyalty, while maintaining democratic legitimacy. Popper's schema of open and closed societies works neither for the capitalist autocracies, nor for the illiberal democracies. North Korea remains the only society on earth that can still be called closed in a Popperian sense, and even this society may be making a complex opening towards the external world.

The new enemies of open society are integrated into the global economy in ways that render them both more stable, but also more susceptible to external economic pressures. This is the broad context of change that has overtaken the open society paradigm since its first enunciation in 1945. Small wonder that the paradigm is embattled as never before. Open society's Cold War supports—growing liberal democracies with redistributive capacity, American power as defender of open society, and existential confidence that free markets could benefit us all—have all fallen away.

Now, the paradigm faces unprecedented criticism. Let me identify three separate strands of attack. First of all, opponents of open society argue that its change model is antidemocratic. External funding for civil society, for example by Western foundations, amounts to an illicit intervention into the domestic political processes of a society. This argument is frequently made, not just in Hungary, the Czech Republic, or Poland, but also in India. The second criticism is that open society is simply neo-liberalism dressed up and prettified, and as such is a violation of the economic sovereignty of nation states. According to this criticism from the left, open society rhetoric moralizes globalization red in tooth and claw and has nothing to say about the inequalities that open international economies inevitably generate. The third criticism is that open society values are a coercive and intolerant form of political correctness. Open society, in other words, has become a closed ideology instead of a pluralistic and self-critically open set of values.

So, is open society antidemocratic? Only if you equate democracy with simple majority rule. If, on the contrary, you take democracy to mean majority rule balanced by the rule of law and minority rights, then the open society change model may not always work but it is eminently democratic. Civil society NGO's defend vulnerable minorities and enable societies, where constitutionalism is under attack, to hold government to account. Indeed, as János Kis argues in his contribution to this volume, the question should be turned on its head, i.e. not, is open society activism anti-democratic, but is "illiberal democracy," the term used by Viktor Orbán to describe his political vision, a contradiction in terms?

As for the accusation that open society is imprisoned in an ideology of political correctness, if it is politically correct to defend the achievements of the liberal revolution then we ought to plead guilty. The difficulty here, as Jacques Rupnik explains in this volume, is that in Eastern Europe multiculturalism and multi-ethnicity are still foreign concepts for reasons that have to do with the tragic history of the region: the genocide, ethnic cleansing, and enforced partitions between 1918 and 1945 that destroyed the multi-ethnic tolerance of the old imperial states, leaving weakened, resentful mono-ethnic nation states in their wake. And so, even if you defend those values, you still have a battle here, because you are told that open society multiculturalism may apply in Berlin, London, or New York, but not in Budapest, Prague, or Warsaw. As for open society being an apologia for neoliberalism, it is true that some open society advocates aligned themselves with Thatcher and Reagan, but the mainstream defense of open society has always included a vision of a strongly redistributive role for the state.

There are other criticisms of open society, however, that are harder to rebut. Did open society neglect the nation, the deep longing for identity and belonging, the need to live in a country that is sovereign, particularly over its borders? Mark Lilla and Roger Scruton certainly argue so in their contributions. Is there some sense in which open society became the ideology of a liberal cosmopolitan elite who did very well from globalization and who neglected those who did much less well? Ivan Krastev puts forward a number of arguments that suggest so. Did we fail to understand the radically differential impact of globalization and fail to see that openness created losers as well as winners? Dorothee Bohle provides an intriguing account of who won and who lost in the transition in Central and Eastern Europe. Did open society take into account the extent to which it gives voice to some while denying voice to others? Niall Ferguson describes how connections matter in open societies and how not everyone is connected equally. While we were defending the institutions of liberal democracy as the best guarantee of open society, did we think carefully enough about the exclusion reproduced by the institutions themselves? Here Alina Mungiu-Pippidi describes how despite the presence of open society institutions, most transition countries are prone to high levels of corruption and economic and social exclusion.

Going still further, was it not naïve of Popper to believe that the epistemology of a free society could be modelled on the practices of scientific falsification, in which sovereign individuals weigh truth claims against empirical evidence and then make a citizens' judgment? Is there something missing in open society's account of how citizens acquire their view of the public realm and winnow the truth of fact from the chaff of lies? In this regard, Erica Benner explains how citizens in open societies are susceptible to demagoguery, and Jan-Werner Müller demonstrates the role of misinformation in the rise of populism. Did open society put too much faith in civil society, in the idea of self-organizing groups holding governments to account, mobilizing electorates, creating political movements, and bringing about peaceful change? We have seen how easy it is for governments to marginalize, discredit, and silence civil society voices. If that is the case, do open society defenders and advocates need to rethink their change model? Here, Béla Greskovits's piece demonstrates how civil society mobilization can lead to societal closing rather than the opposite.

Despite all these justified criticisms, open society ideals should continue to inspire us, precisely because they are so difficult to live by. To be open to oneself, to hear the inner voices of doubt, to be open to the criticism of friends and enemies alike: these are among the most difficult disciplines of human life, but they are constitutive of the democratic temper, the character we need to have in order to be good citizens. The inner voices of doubt are crucial to good political judgment. To be willing to notice that the truths you take to be self-evident no longer correspond to reality requires openness to oneself, to others, and to doubt. This is a moral attitude to reality and to political life that is of signal importance. When thinking about open society, we should not forget to emphasize the word "society." Conditions of openness are social. No one can be an open person, unless they live in a society that sustains and supports the condition of openness for all. One further insight of the original open society advocates—Popper, Arendt, Berlin, Hayek, and others—is simply that openness and freedom depend on counter-power, majorities balanced by minorities, governments balanced by civil society, a free press, and the rule of law. As a final point, maybe the most difficult one: populist parties in Western and Eastern Europe are reaching down into the deep human longing for belonging, for meaning, for purpose and identity. An open society view of the world has to recognize those fears and anxieties, but has to be very resolute in saying that if you believe in open society, you believe in the adventure of modernity. You believe in living in a world where history has no libretto, a world in which you are not afraid to live with radical uncertainty about the future. Open society makes a very large demand that ordinary citizens can conquer the fears that modernity and change awaken in all of us. That may be its most austere demand, but also the one that calls us to our best.

One final remark may be in order. An open society has the hidden strength, in comparison to its authoritarian competitors, of a democratic epistemology. Its constitutions entrench power, and therefore knowledge, in competing institutions: the courts, the press, parliaments, oversight bodies, regulators, and last but not least, universities. It was Popper's great insight that where knowledge is subjected to competitive evaluation and peer review by autonomous communities of scholars, theories that genuinely advance human progress can be tested and improved. The unseen advantage of open societies over authoritarian ones lies here, in their capacity to innovate, to unleash creative minds, and to turn their knowledge into insights, products, techniques, and systems that reduce human suffering and improve our life together. Single party states have made a very different bet: they are gambling that they can reconcile innovation and progress with political control and single party domination. The key unanswered question about how the twenty-first century turns out is which kind of epistemology, and therefore which kind of institutional form—open societies or single party states—will turn out to be the more successful, which society will best fulfill the needs and aspirations of their people. Put another way, the challenge for single party states is whether the kind of innovation that benefits their people can be sustained in regimes that practice authoritarian political control. In the past at least, regimes that privilege control over innovation have condemned their people to stagnation and entropy. Liberal political orders and the open societies they produce have made a different bet on the future. They have wagered that if power is checked and constrained by law, if it is forced to the test of adversarial justification, the resulting free debate creates the epistemological conditions for creativity and innovation, just as they create the conditions for a certain kind of individual, someone who embraces the discipline, rigor, and emancipatory possibilities of free thought. There is thus a necessary interdependence between liberal constitutionalism, open society, and the epistemology that creates progress in science and the arts. This is the bet that open societies have made about their future. This wager is—or should be— the basis of their confidence in their contest with the single party regimes of the twenty-first century.

# PART ONE

# The Open Society Ideal:
# For and Against

# Open Society as an Oxymoron:
# A Conversation between Mark Lilla
# and Michael Ignatieff

## The Problem with Open Society

*Michael Ignatieff*

I would like to start our conversation by thinking about the open society as a problem. The open society is the product of that unique postwar moment after 1945. You see thinkers like Karl Popper, Isaiah Berlin, J. L. Talmon, Friedrich Hayek, and Hannah Arendt trying to think about the challenges that liberal democracy faces coming out of fascism, as well as the totalitarian challenge posed by the Soviet Union. It is through the ideas and engagement of these thinkers that the open society is born. But if the open society was so specific to this moment, one may ask: Is it done, is it over, has it lost its pertinence?

*Mark Lilla*

Two things should be considered here. First, there is the potentially oxymoronic nature of the phrase "open society." Societies since time immemorial have been closed things. That is what makes them societies. There are borders that are more or less permeable. Unless you believe that there is a world society, the notion of an open society pushes the limits of what a society can or cannot do. Secondly, before we can consider whether its time is over, we need to think a little bit about the way in which it was a product of its time. Those who were proponents of the open society were themselves not brought up in open societies. There are moments in intellectual history when there are leaps and changes by way of important figures that change the way we think. One thing they never do is to think about how they themselves were produced by a society or a way of thinking they are trying to escape. In other words, what made these thinkers who they became were often things they wanted to leave behind. Marx would not have been Marx had he not written his thesis on Democritus and Epicurus. That was not meant to be part of communist education. I believe that the proponents of the open society, given their historical experience of two world wars, the Shoah, the creation of Israel, and the rise and collapse of Fascism, thought too idealistically about freedom and openness. They did not think hard enough about what it would take to reproduce an open society. I do not think that an open society naturally produces people who are devoted to an open society; something else has to provide a sense of belonging, a supplement is necessary. I think we are at a historical moment now, where, on the one hand, we see certain principles of liberty and individualism pushed to their extremes, and, on the other, we end up producing people who themselves are not devoted to an open society.

## Open Society and Political Allegiance

*Michael Ignatieff*

The open society was defined by what it was against, namely, closed and totalitarian societies, but it never had an answer to the questions of political allegiance and attachment within a democratic society once the enemy was gone. The ideal of an open society does not define an idea of citizenship; it does not specify the institutions you need in order to run a society. So, if an open society is an oxymoron, what would it take for the idea of the open society to have enough content to create some form of allegiance?

*Mark Lilla*

Popper's idea of an open society does not tell you much about what institutions should look like. It does not tell you what it is to be a citizen and it does not tell you what an education in citizenship should be. By an education in citizenship I do not only mean something that attaches you to some kind of regime, but also something that teaches you what it is to engage in public debate and discussion. Still, the idea of an open society is precious to me, less as articulated by Popper than by Isaiah Berlin. In order to sustain an open society, we need a deeper anthropological understanding of what we are as political creatures. We need to think about what it is that allows a system to encourage and develop attachment to a political order, to make sure that this political order has enough emotional content. We need to ask what it takes to raise one's children in a way that carries on the values of an open society, what it takes for schools to continue teaching it, so that it seems obvious to people that an open society is the right way. The unexamined idea of an open society does not do that.

Nor did early proponents of the open society idea think about borders, not just in the geographical sense. You cannot have social solidarity without a sense that there is a "we" or an "us." And the concept "us" cannot exist without a "them." I think that those who experienced World War II had a horror towards this distinction, for understandable reasons. But we are facing several challenges now, many of which have to do with immigrants and refugees. Without a sense of what *we* are, what *we* share, and attention to the affective nature of politics, it is easy for people to go off the rails and to feel that they are neither engaged in nor devoted to political life; that their country has been taken from them and they want it back.

## Open Society and Nationalism

### Michael Ignatieff

An open society view of the world simply does not understand nationalism. For an open society credo, nationalism is almost exclusively negative. While proponents of the open society have not thought about borders, they also did not think hard enough about what a nation is, what national attachments are. Nowadays, we see an increasing number of people banging the nationalist drum all over the world, employing an "us" versus "them" narrative. Based on that, how can you salvage a positive vision of nationalism that is not simply another argument for exclusion? How do you chart a course that gives space to the need for sovereign nation states, and that affords citizens a sense of belonging, attachment, commitment, and identity? How do you do that and compete effectively against people who have taken over that language and turned it into a language of exclusion?

### Mark Lilla

There is a key lesson to be learned. If liberals do not present a view of national attachment and affirm it, someone else will. We, liberal democrats, need to be able to articulate why attachment matters, not just abstract attachment in the sense of a Habermasian constitutional patriotism, but real attachment rooted in this earth right here. It is astonishing that as soon as World War II ended, the European project based on Jean Monnet's ideas began. It was not just a flight from nationalism but also from the idea of the nation state alto-gether. So you have to begin by articulating why liberal democracy requires the nation state. In the history of political regimes, at one end you have the tribe and at the other the empire. The nation state is in between. It is small enough for people to have a voice and to govern themselves, but it is not so small that there is no diversity, so that it becomes completely xenophobic. The nation state offers a median between these two political extremes. There-fore, the abandonment of the idea of the nation state in the face of the expe-rience of fascist nationalism was an enormous but understandable mistake. This is also related to the history of Marxism and socialism, which did not see nation states as having any standing. But I think we are now increasingly recognizing the value of the nation state. Because no matter which direction you go into, towards the tribe or towards the empire, you are bound to have problems. The European Union, in its soft bureaucratic and non-militaristic way, is a move towards empire, a system in which people are governed and do not self-govern. Thus, the first step is to resuscitate the notion of the nation state exactly on these grounds. Once you can do that, you can talk about what healthy nationalism is, as opposed to unhealthy nationalism.

The French example shows that it is not only intellectually possible to distinguish between a liberal and an excluding vision of nationalism, but that there can be political movements based on either of the two. There is still a left wing French republican tradition, including figures like Jean-Pierre Chevènement, Régis Debray, and Pascal Bruckner, and you have people on the right who are Republicans too. What they are both passionate about is defending the secular state, so that no public authority is deputized to reli-gious institutions, based on the experience in nineteenth-century France. By leaving particular things like religion aside, you can create a space where you can form citizens and have them become attached to the republican tra-dition that was a result of the French Revolution. The National Front is not about any of this. The National Front is about *la terre*, the soil, it is about Charles Martel and the fight against the Turks. One of the things they do to distinguish themselves is to get together at what are essentially sausage and ham festivals. They do that in order to say that Muslims are not welcome in France, that this is what we eat, this is our tradition. They send all sorts of signals, some subtle, some not so subtle. But this has nothing to do with the republican tradition.

# Open Society and Citizenship Education

## *Michael Ignatieff*

One possible meaning of the open society is as pedagogy: the business of creating and forming citizens. This has an institutional meaning: schools, training and educating people in citizenship, something we are very keen about at Central European University, in Central and Eastern Europe. You have had quite a lot of experience in this region in the past twenty-five years. Has Central and Eastern Europe created citizens?

## *Mark Lilla*

What strikes me is that, simply by an accident of history, after 1989 the cart of state building had to be put before the horse of citizen building. There was an assumption amongst those who were optimistic—and I think it is an optimism that Popper, Berlin, and others shared—that once oppression and tyranny are removed, people naturally gravitate towards liberal citizenship; that we are naturally liberal. This is not true. Liberals are made; they are not born. Creating liberal citizens requires dampening some very natural impulses in the human soul, the concern for one's self, for one's family, and for one's ethnic group. You must dampen those demands to build a different kind of attachment. Instead, what happened is that these states were built in a time of neo-liberalism. What people were educated in and free to do was to become participants in the global market. Some people got wealthy, they opened businesses, their children went to school, they started traveling, and they bought property. But none of this necessarily contributed to creating people who are attached to the nation state and its institutions, who are willing to observe certain norms. It seems to me that the first task would have been to set up civic education programs. Take as an example some people I knew in the Solidarity movement in Poland back in the day. Many of them thought of themselves as liberal democrats, but as soon as they got liberal democracy, they ran towards the Kaczyńskis. Ryszard Legutko, for example. His book about the failures of liberal democracy made the rounds, also in the United States.[1] He was a philosopher interested in Plato who ran a very

---

[1] Ryszard Legutko, *The Demon in Democracy: Totalitarian Temptations in Free Societies* (New York: Encounter Books, 2016).

important magazine in the 1980s. He rejoiced after the revolution, and then he got this bourgeois society without the Platonic grandeur that he wanted. He was not prepared to be a citizen, and now he is a top advisor to Kaczyński.

## Open Society between Liberty and Libertarianism

*Michael Ignatieff*

I think this quotation from your article "The Truth About Our Libertarian Age" fits very well with what we were just talking about: "Since the Cold War ended we have simply found ourselves in a world in which every advance of the principle of freedom in one sphere advances it in the others, whether we wish it to or not. The only freedom we are losing is the freedom to choose our freedoms."[2] What you describe here is the problem of freedom in a post-1989 world, not just in Eastern Europe. There is a deeper problem about market society, about capitalism, and about the very way in which we seem to have lost control over what we think freedom is. Can you explain how you see this problem playing out?

*Mark Lilla*

One of the things I have been arguing is that since the 1970s and 1980s, Western European and North American societies have become libertarian. On the one hand, you saw the rise of a certain view regarding the centrality of the economy, together with the incapacity of governments to control it, the sort of standard neo-liberal views about economic growth. On the other hand, since the cultural revolutions of the 1960s and 1970s in the West, you could observe a similar kind of individualism develop in social terms. The cultural revolution was about freedom from tradition, from family, and from patriarchy, the right to define yourself as your own person and the right to cultural and physiological autonomy. The way in which politics have worked out in Western Europe and the United States is that cultural libertarianism is thought to be on the left and economic libertarianism on the right. But what is striking to me is that these two hands have been washing each other for the past thirty to forty years. Once the idea of the primacy and the full autonomy

---

[2]  Mark Lilla, "The Truth About Our Libertarian Age," *The New Republic* 15, no. 1–2 (2014): 244–67, http://www.newrepublic.com/article/118043/our-libertarian-age-dogma-democracy-dogma-decline.

of the individual—the "elementary particle," to use Houellebecq's term—becomes the foundation of our political thinking, then every advance of the idea of freedom is going to free up things socially and economically. Much of the political debate in the United States has been between two libertarian factions. One faction argues that every time liberty increases in the economy, it also increases in society. The other faction, the conservatives, wants free markets but not complete freedom when it comes to things like abortion or patriarchal authority. On the left, there is a desire for cultural autonomy and individualism, but people are shocked to discover that the same kind of individualism is being given free rein in the economy. Both sides want an impossibility: partial libertarianism. But what our societies have been driven towards is more and more extreme atomization, with various effects on our societies, our families, our psyches, and our politics. I think that starting from this observation, you can begin to understand what the fight between the left and right has been like in the United States, and why we are where we are, also in Western Europe. This fundamental drive towards individualism is shaping everything in such a way that not one political party is able to capture all of it or is willing to bless it. This is our predicament.

Where does a liberal progressive go from here? Frankly, I do not know. First, we need to diagnose the situation and think hard about what sociological and psychological preconditions there are for the functioning of a liberal democracy in an open society, or a constitutional republic in which society is as open as possible while still remaining itself. That takes some very hard thinking. In the short term, it means looking for opportunities to assert the necessity and the attractiveness of a certain sense of citizenship. In the United States we have witnessed the election of Donald Trump, the most overdetermined event in my political lifetime. In this regard I need to point out one thing: Donald Trump defeated two political parties, not one. He got the nomination because he defeated the Democratic Party and Reagan Republicanism, our version of neo-liberalism with a social conservative attachment. That Reagan dispensation is now over and something else will take its place. It could be better or it could be worse. There is a yearning for an explanation for the fact that people find themselves economically worse off, not being able to make a claim on the state or on their fellow citizens for solidarity. Therefore, I think this is such an important moment in American history to speak up for that solidarity, because windows like this do not open that often.

# The Importance of History and the Dangers of Identity Politics to an Open Society

*Michael Ignatieff*

I would like to quote you again: "Our hubris is to think that we no longer have to think hard or pay attention or look for connections, that all we have to do is stick to our democratic values—or our open society values—and economic models and faith in the individual and all will be well."[3] What I think you are trying to convey is that right across the political spectrum there is an enchanted repetition of values that have parted from reality. Take Brexit and the election of Donald Trump. One way to think about this is that we are in a new historical epoch. We have no idea about its shape, we do not know where it came from, we have no idea where it is going, but at least we know we have been thrust back into historical reflection, whether we want to or not. How can we make sense of this moment?

*Mark Lilla*

The quote you mention is very much connected to what we were talking about at the beginning, namely, the founding generation of the postwar open society idea. One of the things that not only Popper but also Hayek and Berlin were reacting against was of course Marxism, as well as historical determinism. They wanted to escape the dead weight of a Marxist version of history that explained everything and that would explain everything in the future. What they themselves did not realize is that their analyses were so acute because they had been brought up thinking about history. But if you are brought up in a libertarian society, where the horizon is always open, you do not have the habit of thinking about your historical situation. You are no longer curious about it. It strikes me how a-historical political theory in our time is, and how uninterested intellectuals have been, except on the post-Marxist left, for example the *New Left Review*. That is not the synagogue I go to, but at least they are still thinking about what our historical moment means, about what this neo-liberal thing is. Liberal democrats or academic liberal political theorists, and even politicians, are not used to thinking and

---

[3]  Ibid.

talking about the deep forces in our historical moment, they are not used to trying to understand them by looking into the past and trying to anticipate how these forces might develop in the very near future, as opposed to a global account of history. I belief this sanctions a kind of lack of curiosity.

What I tried to do in some of the pieces you quoted is to talk about the development of the libertarianism of our time. It has structured the way we think about ourselves, the way we think about our families and society, our economies, our desire to escape from history, and our ignorance about the result of historical developments, on the right as well as the left. One force is neo-liberalism; the other is a certain cultural ideal of individual independence and romantic self-formation. In the 1960s and 1970s, identity politics in the United States meant essentially that African-Americans, women, and, a little later, homosexuals, recognized that they were suffering discrimination, violence, and other problems in society, that they shared a common experience and needed to mobilize around an identity in order to make a political claim. Their aim was to participate collectively as citizens in a political process, to claim equal rights as citizens. People mobilized on the basis of something they shared. Over the past thirty years or so, this notion of identity has shifted in universities from one of collective identity in political action to one of psychological self-definition and self-discovery. The academic discourse is about trying to discover that special mix of identities that "I" in my own very special way "am." The search for self-identity or self-definition in the United States, if you read Tocqueville, Whitman, or Emerson, is an endless psychodrama. Americans are always trying to escape being identified as anything particular, and then they find themselves alone in the desert, as Tocqueville describes it, suddenly longing for human attachment and a sense of meaning. What began as a political assertion of identity has become yet another chapter in the history of American self-definition. At the universities, political energies have shifted from politics in the world towards the exploration of the constitution of the self by power and other post-structural mysticisms. These concerns about identity and pseudo-politics have simply exacerbated fundamental individualism and the anti-political nature of our time. The anti-politics of neo-liberalism has been matched by a pseudo-politics of identity in the university. This is one attempt to historically construct how we got where we are.

In this regard, a key development is that the question of authenticity replaced the question of justice. What is it to be authentically myself, to be authentically gay, authentically a woman? These questions became central concerns of politics. Take the Women's March against Donald Trump in January 2017. Right after Trump's election, women got together, went online and said, "Let's have a million women's march." This phrase, "a million women," is a reference to the million men's march in October 1995, when African-American men came to Washington in order to express their solidarity with each other. The moment the march was announced, black and lesbian women's groups went online to complain that the use of the term "million" was cultural appropriation, that the group of women who had proposed this were not themselves diverse enough to show all the faces you are supposed to show. Immediately, this urge to politics was paralyzed by a factionalism that was essentially about self-definition. As a result, there was a lot of scurrying and liberal scraping to satisfy these factional demands. They created a picture of the group's leadership: a white woman carrying a baby in the center, on the left a woman in a hijab, next to her a Latina woman, and on the right a black woman and an Asian woman. It looks just like an American blockbuster movie, on the starship where everyone has to be of a different group, because that is the way casting is done in Hollywood these days. Every movement, every event has to look like this. It was typical of this way of thinking that it was impossible for these people to put aside these questions and think about the current disaster and the need to mobilize and come together. I felt this was confirmation of what I wrote in my article in *The New York Times*, namely, that the concern with identity has taken the eyes of American liberals off the ball of developing an account of what the idea of America is and what its future should be.[4] There is very little interest among young people to get wrapped up in party politics. Few have wanted to run for office, they are too much in love with the idea of movement politics. (This may change due to Trump.) So they go to the demonstrations, they take a selfie, and send out a message saying: "I spoke truth to power!" Meanwhile, Donald Trump is exercising power.

---

[4] Mark Lilla, "The End of Identity Liberalism," *The New York Times*, November 18, 2016, https://www.nytimes.com/2016/11/20/opinion/sunday/the-end-of-identity-liberalism.html.

# Open Society and Reactionary Politics

*Michael Ignatieff*

You have talked about identity politics, but what about reactionary politics? There is a tremendous surge of nostalgic politics that takes the form of an attack on so-called "political correctness." It often seems like a satire of identity politics, behind which lies a desire to push back women's rights, the rights of gays, or people's access to healthcare across the board. As you noted, Trump defeated two political parties, the Democratic Party as well as Reagan's neo-liberalism of the 1980s, but there is also a tremendous amount of nostalgia in the Trump appeal. This politics of nostalgia is not only relevant for the United States, but for Central and Eastern Europe too. There is a tremendous surge driving politics to claim back a Christian identity, for example. How would you analyze the force and origin of this form of politics? How do you understand its logic, its meaning and implications?

*Mark Lilla*

When we think about reaction or about any related phenomena, we need to take a step back and ask what needs to be explained? If you assume that people are born to be liberal and tolerant citizens, then the thing to explain is how people become reactionaries. If, however, you assume that people are naturally attached to themselves and their own kind, then the thing that has to be explained is how we were able to produce people who did not make that attachment primary but instead were tolerant and good citizens. And if you pose the question this way, then what you are looking for is what has eroded our ability to produce people like that. That becomes the mystery. I am not surprised that people are like this when everything else gets stripped away. I think it is human nature. And it is something quite ugly that the work of political civilization covers up. The term "nostalgia" was in fact coined in the seventeenth century by a Swiss physician named Hofer. It was a neologism, from two Greek terms. Hofer was trying to explain why it was that Swiss soldiers fighting in Europe did not make good mercenaries. They would get depressed, become melancholic, they could not fight, eat, or sleep, and had to be sent home. Hofer developed a psychological notion of what it is like to be home. When you are no longer home, something can develop where you want to go back, and he thought of it in geographical terms. These soldiers would sing a certain song, called the *Ranz des Vaches* in Swiss French, which they would sing at home to call back the cows. They would sing it in a nostalgic way and they would get even more depressed. As a result, the generals banned the song, because soldiers were idealizing it. Hofer's idea was to send people home, geographically. Over time, people started to realize that nostalgia—though generally conceived of as a geographical notion—is actually a temporal notion. We always want to go back to our childhood or to something we had before. People fall into nostalgia when they are *déplacés*—the French word is better than any English equivalent—when they feel displaced, no longer home. There are so many forces at work in the world today that cause people to no longer feel at home: the speed of everything, technological and economic changes. Families have changed; young children are coming out as gay. Church authority has disappeared. People who are older grew up in a very different world than the one we find ourselves in today. This is completely disorienting. When people are disoriented politically, as they are in Eastern Europe and in the United States, it creates an opening for nostalgia and for demagogues to exploit this desire to return somewhere. It comes in many forms, and not just in our societies. Jihadism is a good example of radical nostalgia. The idea that you are going to recreate the golden age of the first four righteously guided Califs and Mohammed and re-apply Sharia law is the most obvious and extreme form of political nostalgia of our time. What it should be telling us is that people are feeling displaced. If there are no political structures, no political education, to give people a sense of voice in the present, those kinds of reactions are bound to happen. In Europe it is even more difficult than in the United States, because Europe has seen both a flight from the nation state and an attempt to create a Europe that is both nowhere and everywhere, that no one can be emotionally attached to. It is not quite possible to be attached to Europe, but it is no longer legitimate to be attached to the nation state. And so you float in the air.

# The Open Society
# from a Conservative Perspective

*Roger Scruton*

The idea of the "open society" was introduced by the French philosopher Henri Bergson in the 1930s, with a view to contrasting two ways of creating social cohesion: the magical and the rational. Magical thinking involves the submission to mystical forces that must be appeased and obeyed, and societies founded on magic are closed to innovation and experiment, since these threaten the dark powers that govern human destiny. Rational thinking, by contrast, involves exploring the world with a view to discovering the real laws of nature, and exerting ourselves to find reasoned solutions to our social and political problems. Rational thinking leads to an open society, in which differences of opinion and lifestyle are accepted as contributions to the collective wellbeing.

The distinction was taken up by Sir Karl Popper, who, writing in the wake of World War II, saw totalitarianism, whether of the fascist or the communist variety, as a return to magical ways of thinking and to a society based on fear and obedience rather than free rational choice. For Popper, magical thinking has persisted in new forms, and the intellectuals—those who live by their reasoning powers—had been in part responsible for this. For Popper, the real enemies of the open society were those thinkers, Plato, Hegel, and Marx in particular, who had advocated submission to the collective, rather than individual freedom, as the goal of politics, and who had failed to see that, without individual freedom, reason has no purchase in human affairs. And the worst of the gods that they had superstitiously imposed on us, in

order to perpetuate our submission, was history itself, whose rule the Hege-
lians and Marxists propose as inexorable, demanding the hecatombs of sacri-
ficial victims offered during the course of World War II.

It is surely clear that the issues to which Popper referred are still very
much alive, even if they have taken on a new form. We are still besieged by
the idea that history is a force to which we must submit, and that attempts to
resist it—whether in the name of freedom, or in the name of tradition—will
always be futile. But the superstitious submission to history is now more commonly associated with those who call themselves liberals than with Marxists
or nationalists. In particular, many who advocate the open society tell us that
globalization is inevitable and that with it come new forms of transnational
government, new attitudes to borders, migration and governance, and new
ideas of civil society and legal order. The message coming down to us from
many of those who propose themselves as our political leaders has been that
"globalization is the future, it is inevitable, and we are in charge of it"—the
same contradiction that was announced by the communists and the Nazis.
(For if it is inevitable, nobody can really be in charge.) But is it inevitable, and
is it, as its advocates claim, really compatible with the open society?

Popper's Open Society conception may derive from Bergson; but it is
also a recent manifestation of a far older idea, namely, that of liberal individualism as it took shape during the Enlightenment. Followers of John Locke saw
legitimacy as arising from the sovereignty of the individual. Free individuals
confer legitimacy on government through their consent to it, and the consent
is registered in a contract, though a contract in which no individual has a veto.
The result is a reasonable and reasoning form of government, since it draws on
individual rational choice for its legitimacy. In such an arrangement individual
freedom is both the foundation and the goal of politics, and the resulting
society is open in the sense that nobody is in a position to impose opinions or
standards of conduct unless the people can be persuaded to accept them. There
will be dissenters, of course, but an open society shows itself by nothing so
much as by its attitude to the dissenter, whose voice is allowed in the political
process, and whose freedom to express dissenting opinions is protected by the
state. This idea underlies Popper's vision, and it is an idea of perennial appeal.
However, it is open to an objection, made vividly by Hegel, whose writings on
political philosophy Popper seems willfully to have misunderstood.

The objection is this: freely choosing individuals, able to sign up to contracts and to accept responsibility for their agreements, do not exist in the state
of nature. Popper himself acknowledges that magical ways of thinking, submis-

sion to dark forces, and the desire to appease them define the original position from which we humans must free ourselves. We become free individuals by a process of emancipation, and this process is a *social* process, dependent on our interactions with others and on the mutual accountability that shapes each of us as a self-choosing "I." The free individual is the product of a specific kind of social order, and the constraints necessary to perpetuate that order are therefore necessary to our freedom. If openness means freedom, then freedom cannot be extended so far as to unsettle the social order that produces it. But then the advocate of freedom must be an advocate of that kind of social order, and this means thinking in terms of something other than openness. We need to know what kind of constraints are required by a free society, and how far we can allow them to be eroded. As I see it, this it what defines the agenda of conservatism, from its foundation in the philosophy of Thomas Hobbes, through Burke, Smith, and Hegel, to its frail and beleaguered advocates today.

## Enlightenment

For some Enlightenment thinkers, individual freedom makes sense only in the context of a universal morality. Individual freedoms and universal values sustain each other, and are two sides of a coin. Such is the position advocated by Kant, in his theory of the categorical imperative. Morality, according to Kant, stems from our shared nature as rational agents, each of whom is governed by the same collection of imperatives. Humanity and free rational agency are ultimately the same idea, and to be human is to live under the sanction of the moral law, which tells us to will the maxim of our actions as universal laws, and to treat humanity always as an end in itself, and never as a means only.

The moral law, in Kant's view, follows immediately from the fact that we are free, in the sense of being guided by our own reason, independently of any threats or rewards that might be waved in front of us. This condition—which he described as the autonomy of the will—can be overridden by tyrants, but never destroyed. Even if we are constrained to do what the moral law forbids, we will inevitably know that we are doing wrong. A regime that maintains itself in being by threats therefore violates what for Kant was the basic condition of legitimate order, which is that rational beings, consulting their reason alone, would consent to it.

There are many complexities and subtleties involved in spelling out that position. But it has lost none of its appeal, and is the best argument ever produced for the human rights idea—the idea that there are universal rights which serve as a shield behind which we can all exercise the sovereignty over our lives that reason itself requires of us, and in doing so express and act out our consent to the political regime under which we live. Rights are equal and universal, and are the way in which the sovereignty of the individual is fitted into the same slot, as it were, as the sovereignty of the state.

Few doubt, therefore, the importance of this idea, and all that it has inspired by way of constitution building. It is the foundation stone of the liberal order. For Popper, as for many others, it is the way to release reason into the community, and to produce a society open to innovation and experiment. But we should not neglect the difficulties associated with the human rights idea, of which two in particular stand out as especially relevant to the times in which we live. First, what exactly *are* our rights, and what prevents people from claiming as a right what they happen to want, regardless of the effect on the common good? Second, what are our duties, and to whom or to what are our duties owed?

The American Declaration of Independence told us that all human beings are endowed by their Creator with certain inalienable rights, including Life, Liberty, and the Pursuit of Happiness. That relatively innocuous summary leaves open as many questions as it answers, and when Eleanor Roosevelt set out to draft the United Nations Declaration of Human Rights, the list began to grow in ways that the American founders might very well have questioned. Human rights, which began life as basic freedoms, soon began to include elaborate claims—to health, work, security, family life, and so on—which are available only if someone is prepared to provide them. That which was conceived as a limitation to the power of the state soon became a way of increasing that power, to the point where the state, as guardian and provider, occupies more and more of the space once allocated to the free acts of individuals. We have seen this process of "rights inflation" everywhere in the postwar world, and much of it issues either from declarations such as that of the UN, or from the courts established to adjudicate our rights under this or that Treaty designed to protect them.

The expansion of rights goes hand in hand with a contraction in duties. The universalist vision of the Enlightenment conceives duties as owed indifferently to all mankind. We have a general duty to do good, the beneficiaries of which are not bound to us by specific obligations but are simply equal petitioners for a benefit that cannot in fact be distributed to them all. No particular person comes before us as the irreplaceable object of our concern: all are equal, and none has an overriding claim. In such circumstances I can be easily forgiven if I neglect them all, being unable to fulfill a duty that will in any case make little difference to the net sum of human suffering.

If you look at recent literature on ethics stemming from such thinkers as Peter Singer and Derek Parfit, you will get a fairly clear idea of what this Enlightenment morality means: futile calculations of cost and benefit, from which all real human feeling and all lively sense of obligation and moral ties have been removed. Unless you have the good fortune to be switching the points in the path of a runaway railway trolley, giving to Oxfam is about all the moral life amounts to.

It should be said that Kant's own position by no means tends in that direction. For Kant, the fundamental moral concept was not right but duty. The free being is bound by the moral law, which imposes the duty to treat humanity always as an end in itself, and never as a means only. If there are universal rights, this is simply a consequence of the fact that there are universal duties, notably the duty to respect each other as sovereign individuals, to tell the truth, to keep our promises. In such a view there is a balance between rights and duties and a clear conception of our specific moral ties—or at least, we can see a path towards those things. But without the underlying metaphysics it is difficult to see how the Enlightenment vision of the moral life will lead to anything other than enhanced claims for me, accompanied by reduced duties to you.

## A Misconception

That imbalance can be observed in a radical misconception that seems to lie at the heart of much liberal politics in our day. The view adopted by many advocates of the open society is that Enlightenment universalism, once adopted, will *replace* all other social ties, providing a sufficient basis on which individuals can live together in mutual respect. Moreover, this replacement *ought* to occur, since universalist values are ultimately incompatible with those historical loyalties and rooted attachments that cause people to discriminate between those who are entitled to the benefits of social inclusion and those who are not. Enlightenment universalism requires us to live in an open and borderless cosmopolis, from which all forms of traditional obedience—whether tribal, national, or religious—are marginalized or banished.

This misconception results from identifying what is in fact a rare achievement, involving extensive trial and sacrifice, as the default position of humanity. Only take away the exclusive loyalties, it is supposed, and people will revert of their own accord to the universal values, having no particularist code to distract them. We saw the effect of this misconception in the so called "Arab Spring," when the Western powers acted on the assumption that we need only to remove the tyrant and democratic politics will emerge from beneath him, as the default position of any modern society. But the default position is neither democracy nor any other system expressive of Enlightenment individualism. The default position is fear, and indeed justified fear, as is proper to creatures living side by side with the most dangerous of all existing animals. Hence people flee towards the next offer of security, usually provided by the army, since that is what armies are for.

## Loyalty and Trust

Human beings have a primary need to trust those among whom they live, and to be settled side by side with them in a shared experience of belonging. Trust grows in small units like the family, in which the members experience each other's wellbeing as their own. But family-based communities are unstable, riven by the all too apparent contrast between the unbreakable trust that unites me to my family and the more feeble obligations that I acknowledge towards families other than mine. Under pressure such communities break down along family lines, with vendettas of the Montague and Capulet kind. In general, kinship loyalties are more likely to sustain closed than open societies, since each family holds its loyalty close to its chest.

Trust in an open society must extend to strangers: only then will it provide the foundation for an outgoing and experimental experience of belonging, one that guarantees free deals and consensual arrangements and that will not be undermined by favoritism and family ties. The question we need to ask ourselves is how trust between strangers arises, and what maintains it in the absence of personal affection or shared commitments? Trust cannot be commanded, any more than affection can be commanded. ("Trust me!" is not a command but an undertaking.) Trust extended to strangers is what enables people in a large modern society, referring to their neighbours, their countrymen, and their fellow citizens, to say "we" and to mean it—to mean it as an expression of obligation and not just of fate.

It is important to recognize that most of us in Western democracies are living under a government of which we do not approve. We accept to be ruled by laws and decisions made by politicians with whom we disagree, and whom we often deeply dislike. How is that possible? Why don't democracies regularly collapse, as people refuse to be governed by those they never voted for?

Clearly, a modern democracy must be held together by something stronger than party politics. There has to be a "first-person plural," a prepolitical loyalty, which causes neighbours who voted in opposing ways to treat each other as fellow citizens, for whom the government is not "mine" or "yours" but "ours," whether or not we approve of it. This first-person plural varies in strength, from fierce attachment in wartime, to casual acceptance on a Monday morning at work. But at some level it must be assumed if we are to accept a shared form of government.

A country's stability is enhanced by economic growth. But it depends far more upon the sense that we belong together, and that we will stand by each other during the real emergencies. Trust of this kind depends on customs and institutions that foster collective decisions in response to the problems of the day. It is the *sine qua non* of enduring peace, and also the greatest asset of any people that possesses it, as the British have possessed it throughout the enormous changes that gave rise to the modern world. Whether the Hungarians possess it, after the disasters of Nazi and Soviet occupation, and all that has flowed from the Treaty of Trianon, is a real question today, and one that I am not competent to answer. But the evidence is that the Hungarian "we" is just as strong, and just as full of conflicts and tensions, as the British.

People acquire trust in different ways. Urban elites build trust through career moves, joint projects, and cooperation across borders. Like the aristocrats of old, they often form networks without reference to national boundaries. They do not, on the whole, depend upon a particular place, a particular faith, or a particular routine for their sense of membership, and in the immediate circumstances of modern life they can adapt to globalization without too much difficulty. The Central European University is itself a clear proof of this. However, even in modern conditions, this urban elite depends upon others who do not belong to it: the farmers, manufacturers, factory workers, builders, clothiers, mechanics, nurses, caregivers, cleaners, cooks, policemen, and soldiers for whom attachment to a place and its customs is implicit in all that they do. In a question that touches on identity, these people will very likely feel differently from the urban elite, on whom they depend in turn for government.

Hence the word "we" in this context does not always embrace the same group of people or the same networks of association. David Goodhart has presented a dichotomy between the "anywheres" and the "somewheres," those who can take their business, their relations, and their networks from place to place without detriment, and those for whom a specific place and its indigenous lifestyle are woven into their social being.[1] These two kinds of people will be pulled in different directions when asked to define the real ground of their political allegiance. This fact is beginning to cause radical problems all across Europe, as the question of identity moves to the center of the political stage.

Liberal individualism grants to each of us a great benefit: sovereignty over our lives, and a shield of rights in the face of all who seek to take that sovereignty away. But it also imposes on us a great burden, which is life among others who enjoy the same benefit, and who may very well use their sovereignty to our disadvantage. And because liberal individualism expands freedom and opportunities, it also amplifies society, bringing in more and more people who do not know each other personally, but who nevertheless want to sign up to the deal. Why and how should we trust them? To that question liberal individualism gives no persuasive answer.

## Forms of Belonging

In a religious community people are bound together by a shared faith, and by traditions and customs that express the faith and are in some way authorized by it. The history of modern Europe is the history of our emancipation from that kind of community. Not that we have turned away from religion (though some people certainly have), but that we have privatized it, removed it from the foundations of our public life and brought it into the house, as Jews have learned to do. In communities founded on religious obedience, such as Calvin's Geneva, the fear and hatred of the heretic will, in any emergency, destabilize loyalties. Like Muhammad's Medina, Calvin's Geneva made no distinction between secular and religious authority, and for both Muslims and Calvinists the move towards purely secular government has been an uphill struggle, and also something that Islam, in some of its versions, actually forbids.

---

[1] David Goodhart, *The Road to Somewhere: The Populist Revolt and the Future of Politics* (London: Hurst, 2017).

Whatever we think about the Enlightenment, a glance at seventeenth-century Europe prior to the Peace of Westphalia, and at the Islamic world today, must surely give credence to the opinion that a modern society needs another kind of first-person plural than that provided by religion. And down the centuries people have always been aware of this. It is why religious communities morph into dynasties or military dictatorships. Those are the real default positions, and vestiges of them remain wherever religion is in retreat from its formerly dominant position.

The religious first-person plural should not be contrasted with those default positions but rather with the first-person plural that we in Western societies enjoy: the "we" of political order. The American constitution was issued in the name of "we the people"—i.e. of people bound together by political obligations in a place that they share. Any advocacy of the open society must begin from this conception, which is the *sine qua non* of open dealings. In summary, the "we" of political order arises in the following conditions:

- There is an inclusive political process, i.e. one in which we all participate in one way or another, and which therefore legislates by consensus building, negotiation, and compromise.
- There are rules determining who is and who is not a member of the first person plural: anyone who seeks the benefit of membership must also assume the cost.
- The cost includes that of belonging to a community of trust, which in turn involves acquiring the attributes that enable trust, such as a willingness to learn the language, to work, to put down roots, and to adopt the surrounding public culture.

Those conditions suggest that political order rests on a pre-political identity, in which neighbourhood rather than religion has become the foundation of belonging. This pre-political identity puts territory, residence, and secular law before religion, family, and tribe. And it is what makes true citizenship possible, as those who assume the burden of a man-made law acknowledge their right to participate in making it.

But who is included in the deal? This is the question of our time, and globalization has made it increasingly urgent. People have wanted the benefit of the open society without the cost of providing a secure answer to that question. But can we have an open society without national sovereignty, and borders secured by a territorial jurisdiction? The European Union says yes; Mr. Orbán says no. And in my own country, it is in part the pressure of migration from the European Union (Hungary included) that led to the Brexit vote, which was, rightly or wrongly, interpreted as an affirmation of national sovereignty and a defense against inward migration.

## What is Openness?

Before returning to that topic, we need to be clear about what openness actually consists in. There are, in fact, two rather different conceptions in the literature as to the nature and value of the open society: one epistemological, the other political.

Popper's conception is epistemological. Only in conditions of open discussion and the free exchange of opinion, he argues, does human enquiry reliably tend towards knowledge. In such conditions, as he puts it, our hypotheses die in our stead. Without the open competition of opinions in the forum of free discussion, beliefs are chosen for their convenience rather than their truth: darkness and superstition reclaim their ancestral territory. The inspiration for Popper's view is the scientific revolution and the benefits that have flown from it, as much as the political philosophy of liberal individualism.

The epistemological benefits of openness have been emphasized by other central European thinkers, notably Michael Polanyi and Friedrich Hayek, for whom free association is the repository of social knowledge—the kind of knowledge that exists only in social networks and never in an isolated head. And we should not overlook the argument, due to Ludwig von Mises and Hayek, that a regime of free exchange is the necessary vehicle of the economic information on which a Great Society depends. But all these epistemological benefits might exist in a society, like modern China, in which personal liberties are seriously curtailed and, in some areas, non-existent.

The political defense of the open society values freedom not as a means to knowledge and information, but as an end in itself. This was the position defended by John Stuart Mill in *On Liberty*, and it raises the question of political order in a radical form. When do we jeopardize the social order by extending freedom, and what kind of order does freedom presuppose? Or does social order arise spontaneously from freedom, when individuals are released from traditional constraints? Those are the questions that underlie conservatism in politics, and I will conclude with a summary of what follows when we take them seriously.

## The Conservative Response

Conservatives have in general been suspicious of the liberal individualist idea, namely, that society is, or can be, founded on a social contract. Deals and contracts *presuppose* trust and do not produce it. Trust is the long-term background condition that makes political order possible.

Such trust comes to us as an objective fact, something that we inherit with our social membership. It is bound up with customs, traditions, and institutions that establish a continuous conversation linking past, present, and future. This conversation exists only where there is a confident sense of who belongs to it and who does not. It requires a conception of membership, and the knowledge that in emergencies each will assume the duties that are needed for our collective survival.

This membership is not simply a matter of acquiring rights that will be protected by the community; it means acquiring duties towards the community, including the duty to inspire the trust on which the community depends. In the case of newcomers, this means displaying a willingness to belong. This willingness to belong has been the norm among immigrants to the United States, but it has not been the norm everywhere in Europe, a fact that has been shockingly brought home to us in the recent terrorist atrocities.

The mobility of populations in the modern world is one reason why conservatives have leaned towards the national idea as their preferred first-person plural: it indicates a way of belonging that is accessible to the newcomer, to the stranger, to the person who has nothing in common with you apart from residing in the place where you are. By contrast, the religious way of belonging presents an existential challenge. To adopt a religious form of membership is to convert, to change your life entirely, to submit to strange gods and alien doctrines. Religious communities present a barrier to the migrant and the refugee, as well as an internal boundary within the nation, a fault line that will open at once in any conflict, as in the former Yugoslavia. As I have argued in recent writings,[2] national identity shapes a pre-political loyalty that is adapted to the most urgent of our political requirements today,

---

[2] See: Roger Scruton, "Speech, Receiving the Medal of Honour from the Jury of the Lech Kaczynski Award," June 11, 2016, https://www.roger-scruton.com/articles/29-sir-rogers-speech-11-june-poland; Roger Scruton, "The Need for Nations," May 26, 2013, https://www.roger-scruton.com/articles/276-the-need-for-nations.

which is that of a single system of law, defined over territory, and resting on a shared attachment to the place where we are, rather than on any religious or family-based imperative. For some reason, liberal individualists are reluctant to concede this, and continue to imagine cosmopolitan ways of belonging that erase all divisions of language, territory, and custom from the map, and attach the legal order to bureaucratic principles that make no reference to the specifics of national history.

Of course, nationality is not enough to establish a viable first-person plural. The nation is a pre-political community that is turned by its nature in a political direction, and may find a political expression in many different ways. There are nations that are bound together under a unified sovereign order, as in Britain, and nations that are scattered across political borders, as in Hungary. Nevertheless, there is a trust between neighbors that comes from a shared attachment to territory and the language and customs that prevail there; and it is this kind of trust rather than shared religious obedience or the fall-out from global markets and cosmopolitan ideals that will sustain the truly open society. It is when people are settled side by side in a condition of neighborliness that they are most disposed to tolerate differences of opinion, freedom of speech, and a variety of lifestyles. It is, in my view, a mere illusion that societies become more open in those respects the more cosmopolitan they are. As we have noticed in Britain in the wake of the Brexit vote, those who voted for national sovereignty against global governance have been the recipients of a wave of spite and condemnation that has at times seemed like a declaration of civil war. Although the nation state is not the only possible form of political order in the world as it is, we have yet to encounter an alternative that really does provide the guarantee of individual sovereignty that defenders of the open society are looking for.

Of course, the idea of nationality has been brought into question by the terrible events of the twentieth century, in which a particular kind of nationalism, spread by the Nazis across Europe, effectively brought all social freedoms to an end. But a comparable tyranny resulted from the internationalist ideology of the communists, and in the wake of those two loathsome experiments it is not surprising that the European Union has tried to look for a completely new conception of political order, which will be immune from the totalitarian disease.

And indeed, the nation state, which seemed to open so tempting a path to democratic government in the nineteenth century, is no longer a clear conception in the minds of the young. At the same time, the question of what to put in its place has received no consensual answer. In one interpretation, the European Union was such an answer; but in all issues in which national sovereignty has been at risk, the EU has slipped away into the realm of wishful thinking, and the nation has stepped forward in its stead. This we have seen in France's response to the regulations that threaten her state monopolies, in the distress inflicted on Italy and Greece by their adoption of the common currency, and at every juncture in the migration crisis, not least here in Hungary. And while the EU has tried by all available means to persuade Europeans to replace their national attachments with a new and cosmopolitan identity, the only effect has been to stir up other, narrower, and more emotional nationalisms, as with the Scots, the Flemings, and the Catalans. The conservative response to all this is to say: stop looking for something that has never previously existed, and think instead of adapting what we have. And what we have is a collection of historic settlements, in which national attachment sustains a liberal rule of law, and in which people can live together without conflict, agreeing about some things and disagreeing about others.

## Liberal Doubts

Liberals and conservatives are united in accepting the epistemological argument for the market economy. And classical liberals will often go further along the road taken by conservatism, and acknowledge that tradition, too, might be an essential part of social knowledge, on which we depend in the unforeseen and unforeseeable circumstances of social change. But liberals, like many social conservatives, argue that markets must be controlled, and that human ingenuity is constantly giving rise to new ways of abusing the trust on which markets depend, as in currency speculation, asset stripping, and similar ways of extracting value from everyone without adding value of one's own. Economic freedoms may impose a huge and unforeseen cost on people who had built their lives around a now defunct economic order. Under capitalism, the *Communist Manifesto* famously said, "all that is solid melts into air." Globalization vastly enhances this effect, as capital roams the world in search of those unexploited margins, detaching one economy after another from its protected enclave. In the face of this, it is normal, now, for governments to offer some protection to their citizens against the global storm. A free economy, it is therefore assumed, must be a regulated economy, if the citizens are to put their trust in it.

But that means that the economy should be regulated in the interests of the given first-person plural, the "we" on which social trust depends. A free economy must be constrained by the national interest. No other policy will gain the acceptance of people who are not, and never will be, part of a "global" workforce, able at any moment to travel to some new place of work.

Liberal doubts about market freedoms are now widespread. More controversial are liberal doubts about religious freedoms. The first amendment to the U.S. Constitution granted freedom of religion, or at least forbade the Federal Government from imposing a religion of its own, and also forbade any interference with free speech and free assembly. But it should be clear to everyone that we have come a long way from those requirements. Does freedom of religion extend to the freedom to teach religion to the young, to wear religious symbols in public, to run an adoption agency that upholds the traditional Christian view of marriage, and which on these grounds accepts no applications from gay couples, to refuse to design a cake celebrating gay marriage, when trading as a provider of wedding cakes? Some of those freedoms are rejected by people who consider themselves to be defenders of the open society idea. Likewise, there is a growing view among people who declare themselves to be liberals that free speech should not extend so far as to protect "hate speech," a term which is itself hostage to the one who chooses to define it.

To put it simply, we have witnessed a closing down of choices in those areas, such as religion and speech, where new interests are competing for space against the old and once settled customs. It is no longer clearly true that self-styled liberals are unqualified in their support for the open society. Yes, they say, an open society—provided it is a society of liberals.

## Conservative Doubts

Conservatives also have doubts about the open society idea, believing that the modern tendency to multiply options might damage the trust on which freedom ultimately depends. The case of marriage has been particularly important, though less so here in Hungary, where the question has been preempted by the preamble to the Constitution, defining marriage as a relation between one man and one woman. Elsewhere, an institution that many believe to be the bedrock of society has been redefined, so as to offer same-sex marriage through the mediation of the state. Is this an addition to our freedoms, or an assault on them?

Many conservatives say that the state, by intruding into a sphere that is, in its true meaning, sacramental, has exercised a power that it cannot legitimately claim. If that is so, the enlargement of choices has been purchased at the cost of the institution that gives sense to them. What is offered to homosexuals by the state, therefore, is not marriage but something else. And by calling it marriage, the state downgrades the life-choice that previously went by this name. Conservatives who mount that argument do not, as a rule, seek to impose their view on those who disagree with it, since they are attached to the liberal conception of law, as the protector of individuals against those who would like to control them. But they also see the enlargement of the concept of marriage as restricting liberties, since it takes away an institution that they would otherwise have wished to commit to. A new option is created, yes; but only by destroying the old option that meant so much more.

Likewise with gender questions. Conservatives balk at the suggestion, seemingly implicit in contemporary theories of gender, that gender belongs in the realm of choice. My being a man is not a condition that I have chosen, they will say, but must be understood as a destiny if it is to be understood for what it truly is. To say that my choices in this matter have been or could be enlarged, once the social pressures for conformity have been lifted, is once again to take away the real choices that confront me, which can be made only against a background that is insulated from choice.

Of course, we can introduce choice, by shifting people's attention from what has hitherto been regarded as given. Maybe we grant a new freedom when we open women's bathrooms to males who "self-identify" as women. But we also lose a freedom that has hitherto been regarded as precious—namely, the freedom of women in moments of intimate significance to lock a door against men. Conservatives are apt to say: allow this kind of thing, and there is no way to distinguish real and responsible choices from attention-seeking fantasies. Is that a real increase in freedom or a step towards anarchy?

I don't say who is right in these discussions. But it is worth drawing attention to them, since the heat they have generated suggests that people who believe in the open society can nevertheless be in violent disagreement as to what it really consists in. Liberals wish always to extend our choices; conservatives wish to preserve the institutions that endow our choices with their sense. Liberals see the open society as a society without conservatives; conservatives would like an open society in which it is still permitted to be a conservative, as it is permitted for me to stand in this lecture hall and say the outrageous things I have just said.

# Conclusion

So how should we summarize the conservative view of the open society idea? Here are a few tentative suggestions:

- Every increase in freedom is likely to have a cost attached to it, and maybe the cost will itself be a loss of freedom, even if only a loss of the freedom to take refuge from the opposite sex in a bathroom or to console oneself with all the stories and conceptions that enable one to think of the other sex as "opposite."
- The liberal enlightenment vision sees individual freedom as a good in itself and requires all attempts to curtail freedom as unjustified until proven otherwise.
- But free individuals arise only in the context of a first-person plural of mutual trust. Otherwise the grant of freedom risks a return to the state of nature.
- This trust must be sufficient to maintain peaceful relations between us and to guarantee the passing on of social capital; otherwise, freedom becomes the freedom to lose our freedom.
- This trust must also be an *open* trust, one that does not depend on surrender to an authority or a custom that closes down those freedoms that are precious to us: freedom of association and opinion. Hence, it must help us to move away from the religious and tribal forms of society towards the condition of citizenship.
- This means replacing faith and kinship by neighborhood and secular law as the primary bonds of civil association.
- This, to many conservatives, was the achievement of Europe: the creation of the nation as an object of loyalty, and the secular state as its expression.
- Conservatism is not against openness and change; it is concerned with the conditions that must be kept in place if those things are to be possible. The danger in liberal individualism is that it sees all constraint as unjustified, until proven to be necessary. It shifts the onus of proof constantly in its own favor, while jeopardizing the trust on which its own policies ultimately depend.

# Educating Skeptical but Passionate Citizens: The Open Society Ideal as a University Mission[1]

*Stefan Roch*

## Introduction

"CEU's mission as a university is to uphold the values of open society—freedom, justice, tolerance, democracy, and respect for knowledge. These values risk becoming empty slogans unless we subject them to continual scrutiny and re-appraisal."[2]

Michael Ignatieff,
*President of Central European University, 2017*

Central European University (CEU) is unique in many ways. It is unique in its history, being a graduate university founded in 1990 to support the newly independent Central and Eastern European countries in their transition. It is unique in its composition, being one of the most diverse universities world-wide. It is also unique in its mission, upholding the ideal of an open society.

---

[1] I use the word *ideal* consciously, as the idea of a mission is to set ideal principles that one should strive for but may not attain in their entirety. Furthermore, as the main text aims to point out, the open society as conceived by Karl Popper is not an end but a continuous process of critical reflection and social engagement.

   I would like to thank Professor Balázs Trencsényi for his invaluable comments to an earlier version of this chapter.

[2] Michael Ignatieff, "Open Society and the Ordinary Virtues," *Rethinking Open Society*, September 18, 2017, https://www.youtube.com/watch?v=7-5zT7_NvDY.

It is unusual for a university to tie its whole raison d'être around a single concept, particularly one that has been so diversely discussed and misunderstood in the recent past.

What does it mean to have an open society mission? What does the open society ideal mean for the functioning of a community, specifically the community of a university? The idea of community is particularly important in this regard. In the past, open society has frequently been understood with a capital *O* and a minor *s*. Openness and individualism were in the forefront, whereas Society, community, and belonging found little attention. As CEU matures and changes, it is important to explore what community it wants to and can be in light of the open society ideal. Therefore, *Rethinking Open Society* is also an introspective endeavor, reflecting on CEU's past, current, and future guiding principles as a community.

In the following, I explore what constitutes the open society ideal according to Karl Popper and how it is reflected in CEU's own history. I argue that CEU's use of the open society ideal, and particularly the values it attaches to it, are closely linked to its own history, the changes in its own understanding as an academic institution, and the political crises it has had to navigate. The final section aims to take the open society ideal further. In light of the contributions to the Rethinking open society process, it asks how a university can exist as a community and create a sense of belonging without becoming closed and narrow-minded, upholding the values of open society.

## The Open Society Ideal:
## Epistemological Foundations and Education

A common misperception is that open society is a political agenda. For example, it tends to be portrayed as an apologia for market-fundamentalism and open borders, partly due to the (mostly false) accusations towards one of its most prominent proponents, George Soros.[3] Despite this, the political aspects of open society, in terms of state and social organization, are much less pronounced by Popper than its epistemological aspects in terms of how knowledge should be sought. Its foundation is the human individual as the

---

[3] Compare e.g.: Gideon Rachman, "Soros Hatred Is a Global Sickness," *Financial Times*, September 18, 2017, https://www.ft.com/content/7f93856e-9c55-11e7-9a86-4d5a475ba4c5.

focal point of all moral and political action, and individual freedom as the utmost value to be preserved. This form of liberal individualism defines Popper's thought and has a considerable impact on his conception of academia.

## EPISTEMOLOGICAL FOUNDATIONS

Open society is fundamentally based on what Popper calls *critical rationalism*. Mark Notturno summarizes it as follows: "Popper believed that all of our knowledge is irreparably fallible, that it grows through criticism and trial and error, and that the claim that a theory is justified not only appeals to authority, but leads unwittingly to skepticism, misologism, and irrationalism when we learn that it is not."[4] Pure knowledge for Popper, particularly in the social realm, is unattainable. All knowledge must be rationally refutable. Broad claims or hypotheses that are hard to test do not constitute true knowledge. Knowledge is rather based on ideas and hypotheses that can be tested with data and refuted. This logic transcends Popper's scientific and political thinking. A closed society, he argues, is based on magical beliefs. This does not only refer to prehistoric tribal worship, but also to pseudo-scientific claims, believed to be irrefutable. Popper was not a skeptic who believes there is no truth. He very much believed in objective truth, but that any argument or judgement, no matter how well reasoned, may be false.

In the Social Sciences and Politics, Popper argues that one of the clearest signs of closed society thinking is *Historicism*, a mechanistic and deterministic understanding of history: "Sweeping historical prophecies are entirely beyond the scope of scientific method. The future depends on ourselves, and we do not depend on any historical necessity."[5] This does not mean that Popper refuted the study and understanding of history. When he says that "History has no meaning," he says that it does not predict one way of action for the future, but rather that "it is up to us to decide [...] our purpose in life."[6] For that the study of history can be of great purpose, for we can: "[...] interpret it, with an eye to those problems of power politics whose solution

---

[4] Mark A. Notturno, *Science and the Open Society: The Future of Karl Popper's Philosophy* (Budapest & New York: Central European University Press, 2000), xix.

[5] Karl Popper, *The Open Society and Its Enemies, Volume I: The Spell of Plato* (London: Routledge, 1945), 3.

[6] Ibid., *Volume II: The High Tide of Prophecy: Hegel, Marx, and the Aftermath* (London: Routledge, 1945), 278.

we choose to attempt in our time. [...] Although history has no ends, we can impose these ends of ours upon it; and although history has no meaning, we can give it a meaning."[7]

This is relevant for the open society mission of a university. The study of history ought not to reproduce accepted truths but empower students, through the critical treatment of past events, to learn from mistakes and develop better, more humane understandings of the societies and communities of concern. A rejection of an essentialist approach to history means for Popper a rejection of an essentialist approach to the present. However, he differentiates between an idealist and a rational approach. The idealist approach is: "utopian social engineering," which aims to "realize an ideal state, using a blueprint of society as a whole, [...] which demands a strong centralized rule of a few."[8] Popper's proposed rational alternative is "piecemeal engineering": "The piecemeal engineer will [...] adopt the method of searching for, and fighting against, the greatest and most urgent evils of society, rather than searching for, and fighting for, its greatest ultimate good."[9]

Political or academic interaction with society must be problem- rather than solution driven. The best we can do is to recognize the injustices in our society, to critically engage with them, and to try to better them incrementally. Any proposed mechanism providing solutions beyond context and concrete problems is utopian social engineering and will do more harm than good. This is at the heart of Popper's humanitarian approach. It calls to the best in every human, to improve one's own and one's compatriots' wellbeing in a small-scale, everyday way, beyond grand political proposals. Ideally, piecemeal engineering provides practical guidance for how to live in and with a community and how to engage with real societal problems, making it particularly relevant for academia.

## THE OPEN SOCIETY AND EDUCATION

To Popper, education is a key part of the open society: "It is the responsibility of the state to see that its citizens are given an education enabling them to participate in the life of the community."[10] And: "All teaching on the University

---

[7] Ibid.
[8] Ibid., *Volume I*, 159.
[9] Ibid., 158.
[10] Ibid., 131.

level [...] should be training and encouragement in critical thinking."[11] The idea that nobody possesses the truth and that the core of scientific inquiry lies in the process of searching rather than finding and possessing truth is closely linked to Popper's core epistemological concept of critical rationalism. Popper even had his own distinction of closed and open society educational systems. Educational systems in closed societies are supposed to resemble the bucket theory of the mind, which assumes that minds are like empty containers that are filled with knowledge and purpose through passing on truth to students. Education in the open society corresponds to the searchlight theory of the mind. The mind should be treated as an active problem-solving device, where learning occurs when we search for solutions to problems and for error in our solutions.[12] As a result, Popper was critical of the existence of core-subjects as a basis of teaching: "What really exists are problems—not subjects [...]. Subjects, such as history or economics, are merely conveniences for university administrators."[13]

Popper's ideal of a university is demanding, and in fact it is difficult to conceive how a university could strictly follow his non-authoritarian, problem-driven approach to education with only a minimal amount of administration. Nevertheless, there are lessons to be learnt from Popper's views on science and education. The idea that rational thought and critique can cross boundaries of subjects and cultural scripts, towards a shared sense of inquiry and problem solving, is something that is highly relevant for a university as diverse as CEU; also as CEU has been based in one country during the recent past yet transcends its educational system. It provides a relevant sense of what learning means in such an institution: not the accumulation of given knowledge, but shared problem definition and solving, where the teacher may learn and develop as much as the student.

## CEU's Mission and its Open Society Foundation

The founding of CEU is closely connected to the transition of Central and Eastern Europe, starting in 1989–1990. In its previous missions, CEU referenced its own history based on "the academic and policy achievements in

---

[11] Ibid., "Normal Science and Its Dangers," in *Criticism and the Growth of Knowledge*, ed. Imre Lakatos and Alan Musgrave (New York: Cambridge University Press, 1970), 53.

[12] Notturno, *Science and the Open Society*, 48.

[13] Ibid., 52.

transforming the closed communist inheritance" as one of its main pillars. As the current mission omits this reference, the purpose of CEU has seemingly changed as its environment evolved.[14] But to what extent has this affected its open society mission?

The creation of CEU can be traced back to the Inter-University Centre in Dubrovnik, a set of workshops hosted from 1976 onwards that brought together scholars from the East and the West to prepare "the ground for a better world, the world of human understanding and peace."[15] One regular participant of those meetings was Miklós Vásárhelyi, since 1984 the representative of George Soros's foundation in Hungary. In April 1989, Soros and Vásárhelyi organized a meeting of scholars to debate the future of Central and Eastern Europe, where Vásárhelyi proposed the idea of founding a university, around the model of the Inter-University Centre. In a concept-note circulated in April 1990, he called for "an educational initiative for Eastern Europe," in which Soros outlined his first ideas for what would later become CEU. He argued that: "The mere fact that a closed system has collapsed does not lead to the establishment of an open society. [...] The creation of a free and open system of social organization will require a tremendous effort, particularly in education. The countries of the region [...] must get to know better each other's cultures and they must digest the experiences of the last half-century. These tasks require greater cooperation among the existing universities of the region as well as the establishment of a new institution."[16]

CEU was at first not conceived as a self-standing entity, but rather as a new kind of institution that would help create a greater web of cooperation among existing universities. Similar to Popper, Soros sought a key role for higher education in the transformation of the newly independent East Central European societies. Yet Soros also differed from Popper's open approach to education as he outlined subject areas, which a "Graduate School for Central Europe" must teach. The political mission of the then post-graduate institution was much more strongly pronounced than nowadays. Soros's

---

[14] Central European University, "CEU Strategic Development Plan 2012–2017," 2012, 8.

[15] Victoria Harms, "Open Society v. Illiberal State: Europe, Hungary, and the 'Lex CEU,'" *Cultures of History Forum*, 2017, http://www.cultures-of-history.uni-jena.de/focus/lex-ceu/open-society-v-illiberal-state-europe-hungary-and-the-lex-ceu/#fn-text4.

[16] George Soros, "An Educational Initiative for Eastern Europe" (Open Society Archives, Budapest, April 2, 1990).

letter does not talk about the furthering of open society values as today's mission, but the establishment of an open society itself. Further, a document entitled "The Mission and Future of the Central European University" of 1993 calls to "strengthen the development of Open Societies as a key aim of the university."[17] CEU's development plan of 1994 sees among the university's purposes: "Supporting the restructuring of higher education within the region and building a group of individuals who have received high quality instruction with which to advise governments, businesses, and educational institutions on the processes related to the democratic transition."[18] Furthermore, in a statement on the eminent establishment of CEU, its first rector, William Newton-Smith, emphasized that one of the overriding purposes of CEU would be in "educating a new political and administrative elite for Eastern Europe."[19] The current mission states none of these aims and rather refers to CEU as being dedicated to "the principles of open society." This arguably represents a considerable shift from a political interpretation of the open society ideal to a more epistemological one.

In his Founder's statement of 1992, George Soros argued that he envisaged CEU: "Not as an institution extolling the virtues of open society, but as a prototype of an open society."[20] It seems that despite the more ambitious political and social engineering aspects of CEU's immediate purpose and mission, its founder was not entirely clear as to the extent to which CEU would fit into the transformation process in Central and Eastern Europe. His vision seemed to oscillate between CEU as an outright transformation instrument and CEU as a laboratory for Open-Society-like interaction, through bringing together scholars and students of different cultural and political backgrounds, to engage in critical interaction and experimental problem solving. In the end, the experimental approach seemed to be favored by Soros as it relates to his approach at the Open Society Foundations. Contrary to other philanthropists, he likes to take pride in the fact that most projects he

---

[17] CEU Board of Trustees, "The Mission and Future of Central European University" (Open Society Archives, Budapest, 1993).

[18] Central European University, "CEU Development Plan" (Open Society Archives, Budapest, 1994).

[19] William Newton-Smith, "Note of the President of Central European University" (Open Society Archives, Budapest, 1993).

[20] George Soros, "CEU Founder's Statement" (Open Society Archives, Budapest, March 24, 1992).

funds fail.[21] Thus, CEU was originally conceived as a five-year project, which, according to Soros, will either "obtain sufficient public support to continue or it will fail."[22]

This is consistent with a Popperian logic of falsification. Yet already in its early years, people at CEU recognized that it might not be adequate to apply the falsification principle to the university itself. Anne-Mary Lonsdale, CEU's secretary general from 1993 to 1996, emphasized this point in 1994: "There is a profound misunderstanding about what establishing a 'University' means between the U.S. and European participants in the Soros networks [...] In Europe, the 'University' is not (yet) a business to be opened and shut. It is a sacred trust. Of some 28 institutions that are over 500 years old, 19 are universities. In creating and chartering a university, Gorge Soros has done something which in Europe is of deep symbolic significance and the perfect embodiment of the open society. Universities have, of course, been closed [...] but this has been seen as a hideous and tragic attack on the open society whenever and wherever it occurs."[23] Lonsdale's argument illustrates the conflicting nature of the early CEU. Having a perceived end as an institution designed for the transition of Central and Eastern Europe is at odds with a continental European university model. Focusing a university mission on the process of transition is not only insufficient because a university is not a political institution, but because continuity is one of its defining features.

In the mid-1990s, CEU started to retreat from its multi-campus approach. Initially based in Prague, Warsaw, and Budapest, it consolidated a unified single campus in Budapest. To an extent this was not planned but triggered by the first political attack on CEU in 1993. The idea of a free university, which functions independently of political developments, was challenged by the Czech government. Among government officials and certain parts of the Czech academia, CEU was regarded as "manifestly leftist," as well as "a haven for Western European liberals longing for socialism with a human face, whose idea of open society" was seen critically by many Czechs.[24] Inter-

---

[21] Stephen Green, "Easten Europe's Ambivalent Benefactor," *The Chronicle of Philanthropy*, December 3, 1991.

[22] Soros, "An Educational Initiative for Eastern Europe."

[23] Anne-Marie Lonsdale, "CEU—The Future" (Open Society Archives, Budapest, 1994).

[24] Barbara Sierszula, "Unwanted University" (Open Society Archives, Budapest, March 21, 1995).

estingly, those claims seem to be mirrored by the Hungarian government in its attack launched against CEU from March 2017 onwards. It is important though to note some key differences. Whereas the Hungarian attack is based on a deeper closing of Hungarian society and the instrumentalization of CEU as a scapegoat, the Czech struggle was based on the clash of political visions between Prime Ministers Václav Klaus and his predecessor Václav Havel. Klaus at the time sought a radical move westward, away from the idea of Central and Eastern Europe as a region. CEU's direction at the time, rooted in the Central and Eastern European region, was something that Klaus regarded as incompatible with his own political vision.[25] This highlighted CEU's conflicting identity: a university that is profoundly international but aims to educate local elites and a university that is on the road to permanence but whose original foundation, the transition from closed communist to liberal open societies, had come under scrutiny.

In the late 1990s, CEU started increasingly to rethink its original mission. Starting to come to grips with the idea of being a "normal university," it changed its own outlook from being "a quick provider of 'supplementary education' to young scholars from the region to [...] the 'first Western-style graduate school of the region.'"[26] The idea of CEU as a regional network university developed. The university recognized the threat of both being regarded as alien to the domestic context as well as being predatory towards domestic universities through "luring away the best scholars from local universities for money."[27] The idea was to become neither an entirely Hungarian university, nor an American one, but a university that stands and works in close connection and cooperation with universities in the region, through for example establishing several "regional joint appointments" at each department. In reality, this plan never took off.

As CEU grew into the 2000s and the Central and Eastern European countries joined the European Union, CEU extended its focus outwards. Its mission statement shifted close to its current state, emphasizing the epistemological foundations of open society that "nobody has a monopoly on truth"

---

[25] Barry Varela, "The Open Society Institute and Central European University: Three Campuses, Three Outcomes," *Duke Center for Strategic Philanthropy and Civil Society*, 2007, http://cspcs.sanford.duke.edu/sites/default/files/OSICEUfinal_0.pdf.

[26] Central European University, "Vision of a Network University: Mission and Practice" (Open Society Archives, Budapest, 1997).

[27] Ibid.

and the "right of people to live together in peace."[28] At the same time, CEU started to expand its outlook towards "other emerging democracies" beyond Central and Eastern Europe.[29]

In 2017, CEU came under attack by the Hungarian government, substantially challenging its existence in Hungary through sudden and targeted legislative action. The criticisms brought forward against CEU included the intentional misinterpretation and distortion of the open society ideal. The historian and close government associate, Mária Schmidt, argued in the Hungarian government's English-speaking news portal that an Open Society would "require Europeans to sacrifice the remnants of their identity at the altar of openness and renounce everything that made them what they are" and that CEU is a place harboring "worn-out American, Canadian, Israeli, and West European Marxists" and training "political activists specializing in political sabotage."[30] As a result, CEU extended its premises, first creating a campus at Bard College in New York State to fulfill the obligations of the Hungarian law.[31] Second, CEU announced in March 2018 that it would open a satellite campus in Vienna, fully functional by 2019, the extent and nature of which would be decided based on whether the Hungarian government signed an agreement with New York State before June 2018 that would assure CEU's continuation in Budapest. Independent of whether an agreement will be reached or not, the open society ideal has become openly stigmatized and discredited, not only but particularly in Hungary, making the idea of CEU remaining a normal and fully integrated part of Hungarian higher education ever harder to conceive.

As CEU moves from a multi-campus entity in the 1990s, to a single campus entity in the early 2000s, back to a multi-campus entity from 2018 onwards, some aims already present in the 1990s and the early 2000s found their way back into its strategic plan from 2017 to 2022, namely, strengthening "CEU's community and academic ties in Central and Eastern Europe" and becoming a network university through creating "the open society university network."[32] This high-

---

[28] 2004 self-study report.

[29] Ibid.

[30] Mária Schmidt, "The Gravedigger of the Left," *About Hungary*, April 25, 2017, http://abouthungary.hu/blog/the-gravedigger-of-the-left/.

[31] Central European University, "New York Registers CEU-Bard Advanced Certificate Program in Inequality Analysis," 2017, https://www.ceu.edu/article/2017-10-19/new-york-registers-ceu-bard-advanced-certificate-program-inequality-analysis.

[32] CEU self-study design, October 2017.

lights again CEU's key challenge over the years in defining where it is from, where it belongs, and for whom it operates; essentially what its constituency is. It is based on the open society ideal, which has a hard time defining just what it means to belong, what a scholarly community, or a constituency effectively is. How can a university community be solely based on rational critique and non-essentialism? How can a university that transcends a given country and culture through its open society outlook exist within a national context? These, I believe, are some of the core challenges that one can draw from both the development of and the attack on the open society ideal and CEU's own mission.

## Rethinking Open Society and the University: Community and Social Inquiry

Popper's insistence on individualism and his outright rejection of communitarianism is problematic when applied to the idea of a university. If we take the open society ideal to be one of an individual being deeply involved in his or her own community, pushing for the betterment of the lives of each person in that community through practical and rational critique, then we cannot get around defining what that community is. Popper did not see that need. Yet, a university must define who its students are, what it demands from them, and what they in return can demand from their university. Defining curricular and academic standards is a form of closing, yet one necessary to uphold the key values surrounding open society, to constitute a university as a free and critical institution.

Wilhelm von Humboldt, the founder of the idea of the modern continental European university, argued that: "Higher institutions of learning [...] treat all knowledge as a not yet wholly solved problem and are therefore never done with investigation and research. In the higher institutions, the teacher no longer exists for the sake of the student; both exist for the sake of learning."[33] To Humboldt, the university ought to be a place of equals, where ideas are rationally explored based on their relevance and merit, not based on hierarchy and preconception. Contrary to his refutation of community and nation, Popper's reluctance towards communitarianism is relevant in relation

---

[33] Arran Gare, "Democracy and Education: Defending the Humboldtian University and the Democratic Nation-State as Institutions of the Radical Enlightenment," *Concrescence: The Australiasian Journal of Process Thought* 6 (2005): 19.

to the dangers inherent to scientific hierarchies and [supposed] expertise. The idea that a scientific theory or explanation is true based on the status it enjoys with a specific academic group, is as much a myth as the status of magical beliefs in closed societies: "An open society (that is, a society based on the idea of not merely tolerating dissenting opinions but respecting them) [...] cannot flourish if science becomes the exclusive possession of a closed set of specialists."[34]

In this light, Humboldt's ideal in relation to Popper's open society encourages the academic community, to allow equal space to all rational ideas, independent of status, historical merit, or the academic or political position of its proponent, as long as they are open to refutation. This does not mean that a university must or even can be a place from which a certain amount of hierarchy is absent. Joan Scott defines a university as "a hierarchically organized cooperative society, perhaps better to say a federation, of experts with different competencies, who share responsibility for its critical social mission."[35] Despite the need for a certain amount of hierarchy and bureaucracy, Scott also acknowledges its dangers, for example through not granting validity to new critical areas of inquiry such as Feminist or Critical-Race Studies. Popper saw a similar danger: "The problem of bureaucracy is the problem of how to organize science and society on a large scale without losing the individual's freedom in a labyrinth of rigid and impersonal rule."[36]

Bureaucracy in a university context is permissible from an open society point of view as long as it does not interfere with the individual researcher's ability to critically study a given problem of his or her choice in the way he or she deems it appropriate. It is permittable as long as it does not restrict the critical interaction of researchers with each other, for example through favoring one form of inquiry over another. To the contrary, university administration should foster and encourage such interaction.

One may argue that freedom of inquiry and expression may mainly concern researchers, but what about the student? Open society learning is not the acquisition of a certain amount of knowledge, but tackling concrete prob-

---

[34] Karl Popper, "Science: Problems, Aims, Responsibilities," in *The Myth of the Framework*, ed. Mark A. Notturno (London: Routledge, 1994), 110.

[35] Joan W. Scott, "Academic Freedom: The Tension Between the University and the State," in *Academic Freedom: The Global Challenge*, ed. Michael Ignatieff and Stefan Roch (Budapest & New York: Central European University Press, 2017), 19.

[36] Ibid., 20.

lems, without reaching a final solution. This idea is problematic in the context of modern higher education in several ways. Even when teachers grant students the right to full critical participation, there is still demand for the acquisition of a certain set of skills in the course of study. Those demands come from the university itself that needs to compete with other universities on the basis of teaching and research outcomes, as well as from students who have a demand to acquire skills that are marketable on the labor market.

How can a critical approach to teaching and learning be maintained? First of all, it is important that knowledge is not treated as an end in itself but merely as a tool for further learning. This entails active classroom participation, limiting lecturing to a minimum, and creating assignments that favor critical engagement over mere reproduction. It is the administration's role to create an environment for teachers and students where students have the time to engage critically with a given subject and where teachers have the capacity to actively engage with their students. The community aspect is of high importance in this regard. Closing can only be avoided if critical engagement within the whole community is actively fostered and treated as the highest value. If not, it leads to inter-university groupism, the creation of critique-free safe spaces, or the active fostering of certain forms of inquiry over others. Thus, it is the role of the open society ideal to help universities in avoiding the creation of narrow-minded experts and groupist ideologists, towards educating open-minded citizens who have a deep concern for their community, empathy for their compatriots, as well as respect for the knowledge and thought of others.

## Conclusions

The open society, as conceived by Karl Popper, does not principle or a blueprint for how a university ought to function, it is an ideal that if aspired to can fundamentally help to nourish key liberal values, such as freedom, understanding, human dignity and as stated in CEU's mission: justice, tolerance, democracy and respect for knowledge. The open society ideal makes considerable demands on social inquiry, which in many situations are difficult to uphold. It asks researchers to work problem- rather than solution-based. It rejects grand societal or scientific claims and rather asks for piecemeal engineering, solving every small problem at a time without developing a grander coherent system. It demands us to learn from history but to never claim we fully understand it or derive laws from it. And in the end, research results ought to be measured by the way they can be criticized and essentially refuted for better solutions.

These may sound like rather disenchanting principles, but they point to the fundamental notion that with the great liberties of free inquiry and individual freedom come great responsibilities; the freedom of one to define a solution may always be to the loss of the other whose concerns was not considered and whose ideas were not heard. It is through this that the liberal foundations of individual freedom and free inquiry can improve and further the collective good, without falling into either collectivism or unrestrained freedom.

The open society ideal of social inquiry as problem solving rather than the establishment of one truth has several core implications for universities. Anything that restricts the open and free inquiry into societal problems should be avoided. Organizational necessities of universities, such as the division of inquiry into subjects, should be treated as means to make research possible, but never as ends. Particularly from Popper's "searchlight theory of the mind," it is clear that problem-based interdisciplinary research should always be favored over dogmatic disciplinary approaches. Rational critique should be possible within and between subjects and approaches, and no group of a certain methodological or theoretical approach should be allowed to isolate itself from the rational critique of anyone else, be it labeled conservative, progressive, or other. The purpose of a university is learning, and to live up to the open society ideal it needs to include everyone, i.e. teachers, students, and administration; everyone should be able to critically engage with anyone else in the community. This not only imposes demands on how to conduct research and work in a university that is open to criticism, but how to communicate it: transparent, understandable, with the least possible amount of technical barriers for anyone to comprehend and critique.

During its 27-year history, CEU has gone through considerable changes, always stating the open society ideal as its foundation, but not always clear on what it entails. One of the key problems that already manifested itself in the beginning is the ambiguous difference between the internal and external aspects of the open society ideal: being something that resembles an open society and building open societies outside. The original aim was to induce the open society ideal into the transition processes of Central and Eastern Europe. This was problematic, as it was soon recognized that transition took a different path than expected, as well as in regards to the expressed aim of building experts and societal elites, which in itself is at odds with the non-essentialist and critical foundations of the open society ideal. Throughout CEU's development, the express political function of building Open Societies vanished, and the idea of upholding the open society ideal and values it presents internally got strengthened. CEU came under considerable political pressure at several moments. During its early years in Prague, it was portrayed as an ideological institution alien to the state it was based in. An even more intense struggle has been taking place with the Hungarian government since early 2017. Both struggles, and the accusations brought against CEU, featured intentional misinterpretations of the open society ideal and some of the influential people and institutions connected to it. Reclaiming authority over the interpretation of the open society ideal will be key in ensuring CEU's future.

We tend to think of open society with a capital O and a minor s. Yet particularly when it comes to the organization of a university, of what it means to be a scholarly community, *Society* is as important as *Open*. As one needs attachment to a nation to engage in its societal discourses, to have a primary drive to work critically towards its betterment, one needs attachment to one's scholarly community to fully engage in critical discourses and actively aid its scientific function. Such a sense of belonging and attachment seems to be precisely the connecting piece in Popper's call to not merely tolerate but respect dissenting opinion. Attachment to the open society ideal itself seems overtly abstract; attachment to a scholarly community, functioning under the open society ideal, can provide a crucial enabling function to its members in becoming critical and informed participants in scholarly debates. It is in this light that the CEU's founder's statement that CEU should be a "prototype of open society" should be interpreted. Through not only encouraging but also rewarding critical engagement within the community, a university can create confidence in its students, faculty, and staff and in their ability to be critical and productive members of their own societies and communities. This is of course only possible if its organizational, institutional, and academic foundations are open to critique and are responsive to such.

Many universities CEU is competing with follow a more Platonian ideal of educating societal elites, political and economic leaders that ought to manage and change society through the knowledge and skills gained during their superior education. CEU started with a similar ideal of educating "political and administrative elites."[37] Partially through the political

---

[37] Newton-Smith, "Note of the President of Central European University."

crises it has faced during its history, leading to a continuous reflection on its original purpose, CEU moved from a Platonic purpose towards a mission that not only has open society in its name, but also resembles its ideas more closely, towards the education of "skeptical but passionate citizens."[38] And it is here that CEU can make its biggest possible contribution to the ideal of open society: that it teaches not to be above, below, or next to anybody or any group of people, but to belong and to be an integral part of one's own community, be it one's university, family, hometown, country, or region.

---

[38] Ignatieff, "Open Society and the Ordinary Virtues."

PART TWO

# Open Society in Practice: Democracy, Rule of Law, Free Speech and Secularism

# Democracy Defended and Challenged

*Thomas Christiano*

## Introduction of the Basic Puzzle

Something not often noted is that democratic societies are societies characterized by a quite complex division of labor. It is a complex division not only in the sense that different people do different jobs; it is a cognitive division of labor, too, such that the formation of policy in a democratic society requires a lot of different people who specialize in a lot of different areas. Scientists, politicians, diplomats, and many others must specialize in the knowledge that they have, which means that a lot of other people do not have that knowledge. The consequence of having such a cognitive division of labor, which particularly makes for difficulty in a democracy, is that each person in that division has only a limited understanding of other parts of that division. We have only a limited understanding at best of the science behind, and the complicated mechanics of, legislation. The problem I would like to discuss is based on two ideas: on the one hand, you have this division of labor, but on the other hand, democracy is characterized by the idea that citizens are the ruling element. In some sense, ordinary citizens are supposed to be driving the whole system. But most ordinary citizens have their own jobs, which are not connected with politics. They have their families, and lead very complex lives, which in some sense make it very difficult for them to know a lot about what is going on in the political system and how it works.

My puzzle is based on this division of labor. You will recognize in this first part Plato's discussion in *The Republic*,[1] where Plato thinks that these facts show that democracy is worthless. The puzzle is that democracies of reasonably high quality have tended to be the most successful societies that we know. There are a lot of different dimensions of this kind of success. For instance, democracies do not go to war with each other. The democratic peace argument is one of the best-established generalizations in international relations theory.[2] A few scholars disagree, but not many. There are a lot of other facts that are quite striking about democracies. Democracies are a lot better than other societies in terms of the production of public goods, the reduction of pollution, or the protection of the environment. They have also had quite high per capita growth rates, protected people and their most basic needs from the most serious economic crises, and protected rights of property and the rights of workers.[3] They are massively better at protecting basic human rights.[4] The economic crisis we had in 2008 was terrible in many ways, but it was nothing compared to what happened in the early twentieth century or the late nineteenth century, and this seems to be due in significant part to the democratic creation of the welfare state.

Democracies have been doing these things despite the fact that the people who are ruling it are not very well informed. The facts mentioned above suggest a broad-based set of advances to human interests. Everyone, not just elites, is being protected, although without a doubt some more than others. So that is the basic puzzle: you have this characterization of ignorance in democracy grounded in the need for a division of labor, which Plato thought would lead to disaster, and you have this other, rather striking fact that democracies are quite successful societies. The question then is how do we explain this? It is hard to fit these two elements together; it is hard to see how a society that seems to be run by people who do not know very much, would not be run into the ground. Plato says that if people who do not know how to pilot a ship were to try to steer the ship in a certain channel, they would run it aground. Why does that not happen

---

[1]  Plato, *The Republic*, trans. Desmond Lee (London: Penguin Classics, 1987).
[2]  Bruce M. Russett and John R. O'Neal, *Triangulating Peace: Democracy, Interdependence, and International Organizations* (New York: Norton, 2001).
[3]  Daron Acemoglu and James A. Robinson, *Economic Origins of Dictatorship and Democracy* (Cambridge: Cambridge University Press, 2006).
[4]  Christian Davenport, *State Repression and the Domestic Democratic Peace* (Cambridge: Cambridge University Press, 2010).

in the case of democracy? This is a puzzle that not enough people have focused on, and which needs to be given a proper and thorough analysis.

## Critics Who are Skeptical of Democracy

I am going to start with a group of critics that have taken one side of the puzzle and pushed it as far as it can go and become extremely skeptical about democracy. Some writers say that democracy has to be a complete failure. The basis of the claim is a certain micro-theory of how democracy works, which is partially supported by evidence. There are two elements to this view: one is what we may broadly call an account of citizenship that implies that citizens are rationally entirely ignorant, and the other is based on a certain amount of survey data and empirical analysis.

The critics' view is that citizens economize on information gathering. How do they do that? The basic economic idea is that citizens collect information in everyday life to the point where the marginal benefit of that information is equal to the marginal costs of collecting it. You stop collecting at a point where there is equality of marginal benefit and marginal costs. The second premise is key here: the value of information in helping achieve good political outcomes, these critics say, is nearly zero, because of the extremely low probability that one's vote makes a difference. If you are voting in a country of twenty million voters, your vote has a very small chance of making a key difference. That is an ineradicable fact about the nature of voting and participation. Since the purpose of information collection is to vote in an informed way and to bring about a more favorable electoral outcome, and the marginal benefit of any piece of information is extremely low, people are not going to be informed at all, or only a very small number will be informed. Those who are informed, who have some knowledge of the political system and of the issues that are in play, are going to use their knowledge irresponsibly, again because participation does not make a key difference. The costs of making a bad decision are very small. The consequence is that democracy is ruled by inattentive and irresponsible know-nothings. That is the way the critique works. The source of this critique comes from Anthony Downs' famous work on the economic theory of democracy.[5] I recommend it to everyone

---

[5]  Anthony Downs, *An Economic Theory of Democracy* (New York: Harper, 1957).

who has not read it; it is one of the best books ever written on democracy. I also recommend to those who have read it only superficially, that they read it again. As we will see, Downs has a much more interesting set of views about democracy than just these simple ideas.

The basic picture the critics offer here—a memorable image from Jason Brennan—is that citizens are generally divided into what he calls hobbits and hooligans.[6] Hobbits do not know anything. Hooligans advance their views intensely and have contempt for all of their opponents under all circumstances, because of intense partisanship and a tribal solidarity with an ideological group. Hobbits are *rationally ignorant*, hooligans are *rationally irrational*, a term coined by Bryan Caplan in this context.[7] The idea is this: because democracies are essentially composed of hobbits and hooligans, it is hard to imagine how it is possible that a society could be well run. There are two basic bodies of evidence that people draw on in support of these claims. The most important body of evidence is composed of national election surveys, going on since the 1950s in the United States, but also in European countries. These surveys ask people basic questions about politics, on issues such as the structure of government, which party controls Congress, or, who is the president? What they find is that a very small proportion of people give the right answers. Oftentimes, a dispiritingly low number, like a third or a quarter, will get the right answer to a question such as, which is the controlling party in Congress? Thus, the first thing to note is that there is a fair amount of ignorance suggested in these surveys (American National Election Studies). The second body of evidence is related to studies of group deliberation, where groups are supposed to deliberate over some issues where people study the processes of deliberation and how it develops. What they have found are mixed results about the quality of deliberation, the extent to which people learn from each other, and how they get things out of these processes. A key process that has been talked about in that regard is the one of group polarization: when you have two different groups deliberating together, they tend to polarize and go into extreme oppositions. They do not learn from each other, but do the reverse.[8] That is

---

[6] Jason Brennan, *Against Democracy* (Princeton, NJ: Princeton University Press, 2017).

[7] Bryan Douglas Caplan, *The Myth of the Rational Voter: Why Democracies Choose Bad Policies* (Princeton, NJ: Princeton University Press, 2008).

[8] Christopher F. Karpowitz and Tali Mendelberg, "An Experimental Approach to Citizen Deliberation," in *Cambridge Handbook of Experimental Political Science*, ed. James N. Druckman et al. (Cambridge: Cambridge University Press, 2011).

what critics are talking about. I think critics overplay this kind of information. The results of studies on group deliberation are pretty mixed; most people say they are sometimes good, sometimes not so good. It is a complicated question of when they work and when they do not work. Nevertheless, this is the kind of evidence that skeptics cite to support the micro-theory. Then skeptics make inferences from this micro-theory and conclude that democracies cannot be successful.

On the basis of micro-theory, skeptics diverge into two different ways. Ilya Somin argues for much smaller government, where more decision-making is left to the market.[9] A second group advocates something Jason Brennan calls *epistocracy*, a rule-by-experts or rule by the educated. Most of these thinkers are skeptical of democracy and believe that the market should replace democratic decision-making. The trouble with the micro-theory is that the argument is deeply problematic because its conclusion is false. If you have an argument that p implies q, but it turns out that q is false, then the first, the second, or both premises are going to be false.

## Why are Democracies Successful and of Reasonably High Quality?

The key problem with the micro-theory is that its conclusion is indefensible. First, many democracies have been of reasonably high quality and quite successful. A lot of people make the argument that the market should in some form regulate our social lives and that the welfare state is a catastrophe. I do not think that is true at all, from an economic standpoint.[10] Second, markets have the same problems as democratic institutions, which is a deficit of information amongst most people who make vital economic decisions for their own lives. This is a very important feature of how markets work. It is hard to say one is better than the other because of the information deficit. Third, contrary to what thinkers like Brennan say, we have had experience with societies ruled by experts. The Soviet Union and its satellite states were claimed to be ruled by experts, the Communist Party was supposed to have superior

---

[9] Ilya Somin, *Democracy and Political Ignorance: Why Smaller Government Is Smarter* (Stanford, CA: Stanford University Press, 2016).

[10] Nicholas Barr, *The Economics of the Welfare State* (Oxford: Oxford University Press, 2012).

knowledge of the interests of the workers. Other societies were not ruled by the experts but by the educated, such as nineteenth-century France or Britain. And we have seen small governments lead societies in the nineteenth and early twentieth centuries. We know how they worked during the nineteenth century, and in general I think contemporary, postwar democracies succeeded much better than those particular societies on all the various dimensions I described above.

The inference is problematic in a fairly straightforward way, but it leaves the question—the puzzle—of how this works, of how we get something that is at least fairly well working? In order to answer this question, we have to go back to the micro-theory and ask what is going on there. I mentioned this already: vital market decisions are made by people who are mostly ignorant of many of the properties of the things they use. I think it is generally accepted that at least in significant areas of life, markets work at least reasonably well, despite the lack of knowledge that people have in those markets. I believe the reason for that is that the lack of knowledge in markets and in democracy does not entail that choices are not made on the basis of good information. This may sound paradoxical, but the key idea here is that people use information shortcuts in their everyday lives and in politics, and these information shortcuts are sustained by networks of varying quality of people. When I want to figure out why I am sick, I do not go get a medical degree, which would take me five to six years, I go to the doctor and it takes me half an hour to get an answer. I will not be able to tell you why I got that answer, but he or she is going to give me the answer and a prescription.

There is another problem with the micro-theory, which is that the extent to which people are ignorant in this model has to depend on the extent to which they care about the common good. Take the case of a person who is purely self-interested. If you vote in an election where there are twenty million or a hundred million other people, the chance of getting the result you want is going to be one out of tens of millions. There may be only two outcomes, but you do not much enhance the probability that your preferred outcome will come about. If you had not voted, the outcome would have been more or less the same. If you are purely self-interested, you are going to think that it is not worth your while to vote. Even if one candidate is a lot better than the other, it is not going to be worth your while to vote. If you are *not* purely self-interested and if you assign great weight to other people's interests, then even if the value of the vote is heavily discounted by the low probability, the value of the outcome is massively increased, so that it might actually be worth your while. My guess is there is no single answer for people generally. Some are very much concerned with the common good, and probably most are concerned to some degree with the common good at least when they vote.[11] And some people are not. How much work they want to put into being informed depends on how much value they ascribe to the outcomes. The problem here is that we have only a very incomplete picture of how people are motivated in politics.

Another big problem with the micro-theory that we described earlier is that it turns out that in all these societies where they do these studies, affluent people, upper-middle class, and wealthy people tend to be fairly well informed. The rest of the population tends to be less well informed. But the theory cannot explain that difference, because each one of them has the same probability of having an effect through voting. Some people tend to be quite well informed, others are not. This is not explained by the theory. Why would some people be better educated about politics? One basic reason: affluent people tend to be better educated in most of the societies under study. In the United States, it is very easy to see that. Either they go to private schools or to public schools in wealthy areas, so they get a better education. Second, the affluent have lower opportunity costs in collecting information. The value of the dollar in collecting information is not as high for them as it is for a poor person. Third, affluent people have a better source of what Downs calls "free information." The whole of Downs' theory is organized around the idea of the free information system, which is absolutely essential for any kind of understanding of the economics of information here. In this context, free information about politics is information that I acquire not because I am interested in politics, but as a by-product of some other activity like my job. A lawyer might know something about the law as part of his job. But that might also be informative to him about politics; in other words, it is free information. Obviously, government officials will have free information of this sort, but generally affluent people will tend to have more of this type of free information than other people because of the kinds of jobs they do, jobs that interact with law and the government. Another main source of free information consists of the people I spend time with at work, at home, and in other contexts. Here, too, the affluent spend time with other affluent people at work and in other

---

[11] Gerry Mackie, "Rational Ignorance and Beyond," in *Collective Wisdom: Principles and Mechanisms*, ed. Hélène Landemore and Jon Elster (Cambridge: Cambridge University Press, 2012), 290–318, doi:10.1017/CBO9780511846427.013.

places. They benefit from each other's superior information and learn from each other.

What we need to do is to think in terms of a better micro-theory. This starts with reconsidering the economics of information. People collect information up to the point where the benefit of the extra increment is equal to the cost of that increment. How do you figure that out, especially if you do not have any information in the first place? This is where free information comes into play, the information we acquire for other reasons. Here are the basics of this economics of information: you have preferences and you have free information, which helps you figure out where to get more information to satisfy these preferences. And you can start to figure out how to invest in information on the basis of that free information. You have information shortcuts, ways to economize on your information collection, so you can satisfy preferences in ways that are not too costly, and you have got networks among people, which is a very important part. The most important thing to notice here is this: how well people are informed depends on the networks of people they find themselves in and the organizations they find themselves in. In short, institutions matter.

The most basic source of free information is just information you get from other people. You get it from your education, from work, from friends. A lawyer or a businessperson will get a lot of information from work, they will get it from their colleagues, who got it from work, too. People talk to each other, have a discussion, and learn things about what they need to know. Friends and family, the most basic starting point of information collection, are part of these relationships among persons. There are other more incidental sources of free information, for example people who watch television. When the news comes on, you learn something, even if you did not seek it out. Affluent people tend to acquire knowledge of government and policy through their jobs. This is true of government officials, and to a great extent of others as well. They have to know these things in order to do their jobs, and of course they are networking with other people that have to have this sort of knowledge in order to do their jobs, too. As a consequence, they are going to have a lot of free information from their jobs and from people who have similar jobs, and so on. There is going to be a big difference between these affluent people and people that work in, say, restaurants or other kinds of jobs like this. It is not part of the job of a restaurant worker to know about policies and government, so they do not get this free information. They are still going to talk to people, but the information transmitted about politics will not be particularly good. That explains some of the difference in information between affluent people and the non-affluent.

An information shortcut is a way of getting information while economizing on the time I spend in collecting information. For example, I might learn something about what the government is doing by reading a set of opinion leaders. In that case, the thought is going to be something like: this person has done a huge amount of research and boiled it all down to a simple and manageable set of ideas, which I then get. That is a shortcut for me; I become informed by somebody else. An information shortcut is a good one to the extent that it helps me satisfy those preferences that I have, without undergoing all the costs of getting information. That is the key criterion for when it is good. A simple case: when I am sick, I go to the doctor. That is an information shortcut to find out why I am sick and what to do about it. If my car is not working, I go to a mechanic. I could spend a long time trying to figure out how cars of this sort work and not use the mechanic, but the trouble is—and here you can see the connection with the division of labor—if I did not use these shortcuts I would not have time for my regular job, my family, and other things that I have to do in life. It would take up all my time. This is a feature of the division of labor, which is an essential feature of modern societies. What you can do, without knowing all these things, is make good choices, and that is really the interesting phenomenon. My choices are based on good information, as long as the shortcuts that I use, the people that I consult, are good sources. That is the key feature. We see this in economic and in political life.

Sometimes shortcuts turn out not to be reliable. Then usually what happens in societies like ours is that some sort of alarm bell goes off. Somebody who knows something about the issues points out the mistake, it gets widely disseminated, and then the shortcut starts to fade; people turn to other shortcuts. There are two different types of shortcuts here: a positive one, i.e. I get information from somebody that something is a good thing; and another one which tells me that this source is a bad or problematic one. We are all depending on networks of people, with experts, networks of friends, colleagues, and so on, as shortcuts to economize on information gathering. That is the essential fact of modern life both economically and politically.

Again, I mention the affluent here, because this is going to come up later in my discussion. The affluent in some sense have some edge here, because they tend to have better free information and better tools with which to evaluate the shortcuts. Notice what is happening here. If you think that good choices are based on good information, and that the good information is in some sense dependent on the networks you have with other people, which help you to economize on information, a lot is going to depend on the quality of the institutions in that society. When you have a society with a lot of corruption, at least in certain areas, the quality of information declines and people become much more self-reliant. That may sound like a good idea, but that is actually a terrible idea, because they end up wasting time getting information, which they could have saved on, had the society been less corrupt. There are many studies about the nature of an economy where there is a low level of usable information, and where there are no reliable shortcuts. The best and seminal study is a famous paper by the economist George Akerlof, called "The Market for 'Lemons,'"[12] relating to the suboptimal market in used cars, because people cannot get the type of information or information shortcuts that they need.

We can see the same kind of phenomena here if we think about political life. People rely on free information from education, work, family, and friends, to start getting some sense of where they are going or what to read. You read the newspapers your parents read; this is the type of shortcut you are taking to figure out where to get more information. People also rely on shortcuts with the help of media, interest groups, political parties, and opinion leaders. One thing that characterizes modern society is the massive amount of investment into the process of information collection and dissemination about politics and arguments. That is going on all the time in newspapers, magazines, or on television. This already suggests that the critical view I introduced earlier is missing something very important, since we already have this huge investment in information people are spreading. But even here, you rely on a report from somebody that makes a very simple claim about what happens, and then you take that to be sufficient knowledge of what actually happens. For example, in the United States, the Democratic Party prefers policy A to policy B, or candidate A to candidate B. This is a good shortcut for me because in general I agree much more with the ideology of the Democrats than the Republicans. I see that they have expertise, so I go along with it. It is a massive shortcut; suddenly very complex decisions can be limited to very small amounts of information.

---

[12] George A. Akerlof, "The Market for 'Lemons': Quality Uncertainty and the Market Mechanism," *The Quarterly Journal of Economics* 84, no. 3 (1970): 488.

Opinion leaders are another source. Of course, it is essential for a democratic society that there is a diversity of groups, political parties, and interest groups. This is because one essential shortcut in the whole system is the kind of system of alarm bells. If suddenly the analysis of some particular opinion leader proves to be particularly weak, and you see lots of people observing this, then you say, maybe I will move away from that and go to somebody else. It is central that you have diversity here, that you have people who are looking at what other people are saying, and that they have some kind of expertise.

Now the thing is that all of this, in order to work well, relies on good institutions. The networks that you get from these information shortcuts have to be reasonably trustworthy. This is a big issue, particularly in the evaluation of these institutions. One thing I do not want to suggest is that people vote their interests. I think we can trust surveys stating that people are concerned about the common good to some degree when they are involved in politics.[13] But it is important that even if people do have a conception of the common good and are thinking in those terms, one fundamental feature of democratic life, and one fundamental element of the justification of democracy, is that we think people are quite biased in their understanding of the common good, i.e. towards their own interest and through their own experiences. Even if they are concerned with the common good, if you leave a particular group out, their interest will not be well served. We have seen this in nineteenth-century France and Britain, in societies that had very limited franchises.

A quick word about the intrinsic and symbolic values of democracy. I spent much of my career trying to argue how democracy might have intrinsic value, and nothing that I am saying here is going to be in opposition to that because the idea that democracy enables people to advance their interests is an essential part of the argument of the intrinsic value of democracy. What democracy is supposed to do is to provide equal instrumentally valuable power. Democracy has symbolic value to the extent that, if people are able to have their interests advanced democratically, they must have political power. When elites deprive certain groups of power, they are showing their lack of interest or concern for the interests of those people.[14]

---

[13] Mackie, "Rational Ignorance and Beyond."

[14] Thomas Christiano, *The Constitution of Equality: Democratic Authority and Its Limits* (Oxford: Oxford University Press, 2008); Thomas Christiano, *The Rule of the Many: Fundamental Issues in Democratic Theory* (Boulder, CO: Westview Press, 1996).

I think what we see in the case of democracy is a political system that is structured in such a way that everybody's interest is advanced to some degree, though certainly not equally by any means. We see that interests are advanced and we see how that is possible, despite extensive ignorance, by understanding the information shortcuts that people can use all the time, namely, what their political party thinks, what an opinion leader thinks, and so on. They can get enough to understand what is going on, at least to some degree, and advance their interests.

Nevertheless, there are two major challenges for democracy, and I am going through these quickly. First, there is a challenge of non-affluent participation. How can that be enhanced? Through better informed citizens? Secondly, there is the challenge of how state- and democratic decision-making can be done, relative to international politics.

As for the first challenge, take the case of working-class politics to see how the non-affluent and the affluent have different sources of information. It is widely observed that representatives and senators in Congress in the United States are much more responsive to the preferences of affluent people than anyone else.[15] And this is partly connected to the level of information of a voter. Why would a representative be responsive to the preferences of people who are not paying attention to the issues or to what the representatives are doing? My hypothesis is that to some degree, the difference between affluent and non-affluent information can be mitigated by the presence of unions. Unions mix economic life and political life in such a way that people, ordinary workers, get some understanding of politics and law just as a by-product of their participation in the union. It is because of this peculiar role of these institutions in economic and political life that they are able to do this. And I think they are uniquely placed to serve this role in a market economy. Perhaps some kind of democratization of the workplace could help in this respect as well. We have reason to think that workers are better informed in unions. Interestingly, we see that where unions are present, representatives tend to be more responsive to the preferences of working class people than where unions are not present.[16]

---

[15] Larry Bartels, *Unequal Democracy: The Political Economy of the New Gilded Age* (Princeton, NJ: Princeton University Press, 2008); Martin Gilens, *Affluence and Influence: Economic Inequality and Political Power in America* (Princeton, NJ: Princeton University Press, 2012).

[16] John S. Ahlquist, "Labor Unions, Political Representation, and Economic Inequality," *Annual Review of Political Science* 20, no. 1 (2017): 409–32.

As for the second challenge, international politics, states have become much more interdependent through trade, as well as the public goods and bads arising in the environment. But the one major challenge in America and most democracies is that the capacity of people to have an understanding of international politics, trade, and the various ways we are interdependent with other countries, is low. Democratic discussion of these things is at a very low level generally in the United States. We had an election where somebody argued against free trade and in favor of protectionism. The contrary argument just was not made. There was little discussion on these matters in the larger society. But without a discussion on the benefits and costs of free trade, you cannot argue how to mitigate the costs of free trade, which is one of the reasons why a protectionist won the election. That is another challenge that is hard to resolve. I think that without the presence of unions, a lot of individuals become prey to demagoguery, increasingly so in the United States, France, or in the United Kingdom, where unions have been weakened dramatically. This is where I think we see part of the rise of nationalism. You have large numbers of people who are not getting enough rational sources of information in their everyday lives.

## Some Conclusions

It is not clear whether unions can be brought back, at least in a society where they are in retreat, like in the United States. The question is: What can replace them to serve the same kind of role of information and free information dissemination shortcuts? In the United States right now, churches are playing some role in that regard. But I am not convinced that evangelical churches do a very good job at disseminating rational information.

There is in fact another puzzle to this. If you think you need to create institutions like unions to make it easier for people to get more access to free information, it means you have to step into the political system in a partisan way. You have to intervene and say: these are the interests we think are being neglected, and we are going to try to enhance information with regards to those. The standard story in democratic theory, however, is that you let the people decide, you do not decide on the institutional framework for them. Yet here you intervene in some sense to do that. I do not think that is an insuperable worry, as you may believe this is better than nothing. But it is still a worry; it is a puzzle about how democracy is supposed to work.

In conclusion, this is a basic puzzle and we have some of the tools to analyze how to resolve it. I cannot say that I have solved it entirely myself, but I think the tools I presented can help us go beyond what the skeptics have been saying. The economics of information and the institutional background necessary to the wide dissemination of good information are essential here. These tools may help us understand how democracy can work well and maybe can help us understand how democracy can be made better.

# Free Speech and the Defense of an Open Society

*Timothy Garton Ash*

## Introduction

The Hungarian chocolate is a little bittersweet for me, because the great privilege of my life was to be allowed to chronicle the emancipation and then liberation of Central and Eastern Europe, the transition from a post-totalitarian dictatorship to what we hoped would be a durable liberal democracy, from a closed society to an open society. Now we are witnessing something of a—I hope temporary—transition in the opposite direction from what we hoped would be a stable, liberal democracy to something which might most kindly be called an illiberal democracy, and perhaps more accurately in the language of political science, electoral authoritarianism, from an open society to a more closed society. The defense of an open society and free speech is therefore more important than ever.

In February 2017, I was speaking on free speech at the Bosphorus University in Istanbul, in a country where free speech is under furious attack, where thousands of academics have been dismissed, a country that has more journalists in prison than any other. I was very moved to see a banner at the Bosphorus University that said: "Truth cannot be expelled." I think that is a great motto for any university. We have challenges to free speech even in universities in America and Britain. Students suggest that we should ban speakers like Germaine Greer in the name of so called "safe spaces." I would insist that a university should need a safe space, a safe space for free speech.

I want to do three things: First of all, I am going to lay out very briefly the Oxford project http://freespeechdebate.com, the basic framing of the issue in my book *Free Speech: Ten Principles for a Connected World.*[1] Then I want to look more closely at the particular issue of the media and journalism we need for democracy and whether we are losing them. Finally, I want to take up Michael Ignatieff's challenge, which is a really interesting one, and think about these issues in the context of rethinking open society.

## Free Speech in a Connected World

The subject of my book and of this project is, in essence, John Stuart Mill meets the smartphone. It is a world in which the basic arguments for free speech are very old and time-honored, but the conditions for free speech in a connected world have been totally transformed. Though we all agree that freedom of speech is a good thing, maybe we would not all be absolutely clear why it is so. Let me quickly remind you of the classic arguments for free speech, which I summarize in the acronym, STGD—Self, Truth, Government, Diversity. Without free speech, we cannot express ourselves. The thought is in the mouth, said the Dadaist Tristan Tzara. You may have freedom of thought in prison, but even that is barely possible without the freedom to communicate. T for truth recalls the classic argument from John Milton to John Stuart Mill, central for a university, that we need free speech to seek, and, insofar as we have found it, to speak the truth. G is for good government: we need the twin sisters of freedom of expression and freedom of information to govern ourselves well, ideally through democratic self-government. The most recent argument, and a very important one, is D for diversity. In increasingly diverse and multicultural societies we need free speech in order to understand the Other. How can I know what it is like to be a Muslim, a Roma, a Kurd, a Lesbian, or a conservative Catholic, if we have not been able to explain it to each other? I quote at the beginning of the book a wonderful song by Nina Simone, called "I wish I knew how it would feel to be free." A key line in this song is "I wish you could know what it means to be me," which captures the essence of my point. It refers to both speaker and listener. I tell you and you understand what it means to be me.

---

[1] Timothy Garton Ash, *Free Speech: Ten Principles for a Connected World* (New Haven, CT: Yale University Press, 2016).

The conditions of free speech have been utterly transformed by two things: mass migration and the Internet, in particular the smartphone, this magic box in your pocket. You can theoretically communicate instantaneously with nearly half of humankind, three billion people roughly. There has never been such a chance for free speech in human history, but of course with it come great dangers. Because now we all tend to become neighbors with each other, either physically, virtually, or both. The chances are obvious, but so are the dangers. A fatwa is spoken in Teheran or Raqqa, someone dies in London or Paris. A stupid little video called "Innocence of Muslims" is posted by a convicted Egyptian fraudster in Southern California and more than fifty people die in riots in Pakistan and Afghanistan. The connected world is a place of huge opportunity, but also a place of huge risks. The question of my work is how we maximize the opportunities and minimize the risks.

What this connected world does is to destroy the old framework in which we used to think about free speech, and the image in which most of the literature in the libraries about free speech is framed. Roughly speaking the rule was: when in Rome, do as the Romans do. If you are in the United States, you have the First Amendment, in Germany, you have German law, in India, Indian ways, in China, Chinese laws and customs. This is blown apart in a world where there are people from everywhere in Rome and what anyone says in Rome can be heard by much of human kind. So the national framing of the debate is far too narrow.

I further argue that your effective freedom of speech is a product of the interaction of four different forces. Firstly, and quite important still, are international treaties, organizations, and networks. A judgment of the Strasbourg Court has influence almost everywhere in the Council of Europe. ICANN, the organization assigning IP names and numbers, has a big influence on what you see and what you do not see. Then there are three others, I call them the big dogs, the big cats, and the mice. The big dogs are states and their governments. The big cats are what I call the private superpowers: Facebook, Google, Twitter, Amazon, Apple, what the French call "Les GAFA." And we are the mice.

What are we going to do about it? We, the mice, faced with these big dogs and big cats and these great brand superpowers. We had the illusion of the optimistic 1990s that the Internet in itself sets you free. But no technology sets you free; people set people free. At that high point of liberal optimism, Bill Clinton famously said that for China to try to control the Internet would be like trying to nail Jell-O to the wall. The Chinese communist party turned around and said: "Bill, just watch us." And over the last fifteen years, the Communist party made a pretty good attempt at nailing Jell-O to the wall, at controlling the liberating potential of the Internet, by what a Harvard study argues to be the largest operation of censorship in human history.[2] This is not just because it is a big country, but simply because there is so much more speech made possible by the Internet, you need more censors to control it.

To the big cats: through network effects there is an extraordinary concentration of power in Facebook, Google, Twitter, and a few others. In 2009, the use of social networks was still quite heterogeneous in the world, and different social networks were used in different countries. Fast forward to 2014, the empire in which the sun never set used to be the British Empire, now it is the empire of Facebook. Facebook is the leading social network almost everywhere, except Russia, China, and a couple of other places. It has 1.9 billion regular, monthly users. If Facebook were a country, it would be the largest country on Earth. What we have in effect is a privately owned global public sphere. Every day, every second, Facebook is deciding what you can see, and what you cannot see, by algorithms and automated decisions. Unlike the decisions of a public power in a democracy, these decisions are not transparent, non-accountable, and non-appealable.

Despite that, networked mice do have extraordinary possibilities of collective action. It is interesting that the Harvard study of Chinese censorship shows what the censors take down within twenty-four hours is not necessarily criticism.[3] They allow very extensive criticism particularly of provincial and local officials, because the problem of all dictatorships is how you find out what is going wrong apart from by the secret police. They do not allow criticism of Xi Jinping and they do not allow criticism of the censors, but they allow criticism of lower officials. What they take down almost instantaneously is anything that could lead to collective action. Even if that collective action is not oppositional but actually sympathetic to the goals of the State, they will still take it down because what they fear is collective action.

If your effective freedom of speech is actually determined by these four forces, then what we need to do is to go down to the level not of specific national laws or constitutional traditions, but of first principles, or norms.

---

[2]  Gary King, Jennifer Pan, and Margaret E. Roberts, "How Censorship in China Allows Government Criticism but Silences Collective Expression," *American Political Science Review* 107, no. 2 (2013): 326, doi:10.1017/S0003055413000014.
[3]  Ibid., 328.

Only when we have worked out, in the simplest possible terms, what it is that we want to achieve in an Open Society, can we go back and say: How can we achieve that? What are the key actors for this particular area? If it is privacy, the key actor may well be Facebook and Google rather than a particular government.

In January 2017, I was speaking about free speech in India and I had a chance to visit the place where Mahatma Gandhi was assassinated. It was extremely moving. On the wall of Gandhi's bedroom you can read one of his sayings: "Simplicity is the essence of universality." A very simple statement, but a very profound one. If you are attempting to have a trans-cultural, not an inter-cultural, conversation in a connected world, you need to strip things down to the simplest possible level. If you are going about it using the terms of common law or European legal tradition or the First Amendment, then there will be an immediate barrier of understanding.

What me and my team did in a project based at Oxford University, freespeechdebate.com, is to set out a first set of ten draft principles, stripped to essential rules of the game, as propositions in thirteen languages. We then travelled around the world both virtually and physically debating these principles in all these languages, online and in person, in India, China, Turkey, Egypt, Germany, and in the United States. We then put up revised versions of the ten principles for further discussion. This is of course a very risky undertaking, because if you try to strip things down to the simplest essentials, you are going to be accused of being naïve and idealistic. I keep being accused of being optimistic and panglossian, but such simplicity is essential to the enterprise of trying to work towards a more universal universalism.

Then what you do is to try to translate them into all the other twelve languages, and in the very act of translation you discover some deep, not merely linguistic but foundational, differences. Here is a simple example: our very carefully formulated principle on religion is, we respect the believer but not necessarily the content of the belief. However, if you are trying to translate that into Urdu or Farsi or Turkish, you immediately come up against a difficulty. There is no commonly used familiar word for the generic believer in all faith or belief systems or none. There is either a version of Mu'minuun, which means the believer of the one true faith of Islam, or some very academic word, only found in the academic literature. So already in the act of translation you discover the difficulty of the trans-cultural conversation.

I would also just draw your attention to our second principle, on violence: we neither make threats of violence nor accept violent intimidation.

What is novel about it is that it does not just take the ban on incitement on violence, which exists in all liberal jurisdictions; it puts on the same plane not accepting violent intimidation. Because one of my key arguments is that one of the greatest threats to free speech in free societies at the moment is what I call the "assassin's veto." This says: "If you say or publish that, we will kill you." It makes that threat credible by, for example, murdering the journalists of Charlie Hebdo in Paris. This has a major chilling effect, producing self-censorship out of fear, a fear that often does not dare to speak its name. Incidentally, one of our Indian students developed this way of thinking and wrote a really interesting piece about the "rapist veto" and the fact that women cannot dress as they please, because of the widespread threat of rape.

## Media and Journalism for Democracy

"We require uncensored, diverse, and trustworthy media, so we can make well-informed decisions and participate fully in political life." That may seem to many rather banal and obvious, but actually the three words—uncensored, diverse, and trustworthy—are very carefully chosen. I start a chapter in my book *Free Speech* on this very subject with the question: What happens in ancient Athens? If there is a big decision to be made, all adult citizens walk for many hours to gather on the Pnyx at the foot of the Acropolis. When they gather, the herald says from the bema, the speaker's platform: "Who will address the assembly?" Any citizen has an equal right to speak for the public good. You hear all the arguments on the particular issue at hand, for example, how shall we fight the invading Persians, you are given all the evidence that is available, and then having before you all the arguments and the evidence, you come to a democratic decision. First voice, then vote. It is no accident that in many languages there is the same word for voice and vote: "Stimme" in German, "głos" in Polish, "sawt" in Arabic. Thus is, as it were, the epitome of free speech for democracy. By this deliberative democracy, the ancient Athenians decided to fight the Persians on sea rather than on land. This is how they got to win the Battle of Salamis and to save the world's first democracy. This is the ideal of media for democracy. It is obviously difficult to get sixty million people to gather in one place. That is why we have media, because we have mediated democracy. In order to have the media you need for democracy, you need to have evidence, you need to hear all arguments, and you need to be able to make up your mind. Thus we require a media that is uncensored, diverse, and trustworthy.

Uncensored: one could probably say that the media are uncensored in Hungary. In Article 9 of its Constitution, it has a rather well developed formulation of free speech: "Hungary shall recognize and protect the freedom of pluralism of the press and ensure the conditions for freedom of information necessary for the formation of democratic public opinion." However, when you come down to the level of law and further down to the level of media regulation, it is a different story.

Diverse: this is an interesting one. What is the ideal of diversity? Diverse in the sense that all major political viewpoints are represented? Diverse in the sense that all significant groups and identities in a society are represented? The key is not direct state control, but control through ownership. This is the way in which things are more often done these days. A telling case is how the Turkish media covered, or rather, did not cover the Gezi Park protests a few years ago. Most of the main TV-channels in Turkey, although privately owned, were famously showing a documentary about penguins when these great protests were going on in the middle of Istanbul. Kerem Öktem showed how that control was exercised mainly through ownership by conglomerates, which had many other business interests, which Erdoğan and the government could significantly influence by giving contracts or withholding contracts. A. J. Liebling famously said: "Freedom of the press is enjoyed only by those who own one." But the other kind of diversity is significant: important groups in a society should be represented in and by the media. It is a double representation. On the one hand, if your society has a significant number of Muslims or Kurds or Roma or LGBTQ2 people or any other, you should see those faces on Television. On the other hand, there should be representation by the media. The affairs of those communities should be reported in the media adequately, accurately, fairly, and with imaginative sympathy. That is a big demand on most of us including the American, British, and German media.

Trustworthy: we are living—so we are told—in a world of alternative facts, post-fact and post-truth. We need media in which we have the facts, in which when there is a quotation mark around a statement, somebody actually said it. When a journalist says, "I saw it," he or she actually saw it. This requires an ethos, an ethics of journalism. It requires a journalist to understand their profession as a noble and honorable one and to have a contract with the reader. The contract does not have to be "I'm impartial," let alone,

"I'm objective." No one is objective. But it has to be some relationship of trust with the reader, which is sustained over time and understood by both sides.

Now, here is the problem. The Internet, which in principle offers all these great possibilities for the enhancement of free speech, is also a threat to the media we need for democracy. It is this in two distinct ways. Firstly, the very fact that now there is an almost infinity of platforms online. As a result, you have a fragmentation of the media. Rather than all meeting on the same physical or virtual Pnyx, there is a fragmentation which makes it much easier for people to retreat into their own echo-chambers: Trump voters here, Clinton voters here; Brexit supporters here, Remainers there; Kaczyński voters here, Civic Platform there. This of course makes it easier for fake news, and for true news distributed with malicious intent. The DNC emails that were hacked by Russian sources and then spread via that conduit called Julian Assange were not fake news; they were true news maliciously distributed. Secondly, what the Internet does is to blow out of the water the business model of most newspapers. Most papers in the world are struggling to find a new business model, with a few exceptions. Established media are shouting for their survival. If it bleeds it leads, if it roars it scores. In this desperate competition for the click-stream, they are shouting. Fox News is shouting from the right and MSNBC is shouting from the left. That too diminishes the quality of the debate we need for democracy.

## The Defense of an Open Society

Let me now turn to Michael Ignatieff's challenge, which is the defense of an open society. The way I have been thinking about free speech has not been precisely in those terms. It has rather been about the defense of liberal democracy, and the defense of a civil society, that is to say, a society that exercises a robust civility in talking about human difference. So I went back to look at what Popper says, and it is very interesting.

Let me summarize some of the key points Karl Popper makes. First of all, going from a closed society to an open society is a historical process. He dates it back to ancient Greece and he attributes it partly—this is very interesting—to the development of sea-communications and commerce, technological and economic developments. Now, on one reading of Popper's logic, it seems to follow that if our equivalent of sea-communications and commerce are the Internet and globalized free markets, then we should have had an extraordinary powerful push towards more open societies. Well, arguably we have, and arguably there is a reaction against that.

Secondly, he identifies what I would call an epistemology of democracy, which is very similar to a classic western liberal argument for free speech. But it is also problematic, because it sees politics as a kind of truth seeking. That is to say, it is a world of rational, autonomous agents seeking truth through deliberative democracy, as in an idealized ancient Greece. That is the ideal of free speech for democracy, for good government. But is it what real people are like? Is that our societies? What about emotions, what about feelings and about passions?

Thirdly, Popper acknowledges that there is a problem with Open Society. It risks becoming, he says, *abstract society*: cold, atomized, tending towards anomie. He talks about the strain of civilization, the unhappiness and uneasiness that comes from precisely the open society that he is advocating, and then he does something quite remarkable, which most people have not noticed and I had forgotten. He talks about a closed society at its best as a semi-organic unity, held together by ties of kinship—I quote—"living together, sharing common efforts, common joys, and common distress." This is almost a lyric tribute to a closed society.

To what extent is the reactionary transition we are now seeing from open to more closed, towards populism, a reaction against the extreme, radical, and rapid spread of open societies itself, in the form of globalization, immigration, and social and cultural liberalization? To some degree I think very much so. The classic populist line you hear in Turkey, in England, in India, or in Poland, is: "I don't recognize my country anymore." These are precisely the feelings that Popper was talking about almost lyrically, coming out in significant parts of the population, by no means all of whom are racist or xenophobic. I find that important to stress. These are people who are just utterly shaken and bemused by the rapidity of change. I have mentioned Hungary a few times; so let me take you to Poland for a moment, where Jarosław Kaczyński, the effective leader of the Law and Justice party said the following: "Poland today is the subject of pressure regarding the shape of our life, the situation of an average Pole; the shape of our society. We are being offered to radically change, to create a multicultural society, to create a new identity. [...] It is a matter of sovereignty. If we maintain it, we will defend ourselves. [...] The concepts of Mr. Soros, the concepts of societies that have no identity, these concepts are convenient for those who have billions because such a society is extremely easy to manipulate. If there is no strong identity, the society can do everything."[4] This is a passionate plea for the closed society against the open society.

What we are seeing is not just illiberalism, but anti-liberalism. The distinction is important. There is a conscious reaction against the spread of liberalism in the context of globalization over the last twenty-five to thirty years, and frankly I think in different forms from Xi Jinping, Vladimir Putin, Recep Tayyip Erdoğan, from Viktor Orbán through Jarosław Kaczyński to Donald Trump. They represent in significant degree anti-liberalism, a conscious reaction against liberalism. And here comes the problem: the developments I am describing in the media under the impact of the Internet actually facilitate the return to a closed society. If we have these echo chamber effects as a result of the Internet, if we have this shouting, this sensationalism, as a result of the destroyed business model of conventional media, it is an open invitation for populists and authoritarians to get into those echo chambers and be heard and supported. Donald Trump is a classic example of this. The challenge here is not just ideological, it is not just cultural; it is epistemological. It goes to the very epistemological foundation of democracy. It challenges the assumption that we have a shared basis of evidence, fact, and reason on which we build a democratic project.

Some of you will know that Donald Trump insisted that Barack Obama was not born in the United States, whereupon Obama published his birth certificate. You might think that is a fairly adequate refutation of that claim. Not a bit of it. You know how Trump likes to say: "Many people think." Well, in this case he said something even more interesting. He said: "Many people feel that this was not a proper certificate." Think about that. It is a really interesting statement. I may think this jacket is dark blue, but you feel that it is pink, and your feeling trumps over the evidence. I think more than fake news, it is a phenomenon of these simple, brightly colored, emotionally appealing narratives of populism that prevail over reality-based discourse. A friend of mine was trying to describe, very calmly and fairly, the pros and cons of Britain leaving the European Union and he talked about what would happen to GDP. He was in an old, impoverished area of England with a lot of unemployment. And a working-class woman got up and said "Professor

---

[4]  Adam Balcer, "Beneath the Surface of Illiberalism: The Recurring Temptation of 'National Democracy' in Poland and Hungary—with Lessons for Europe," *Wise Europa Institute*, 2017, 58, https://pl.boell.org/sites/default/files/beneath_the_surface_illiberalism_national_democracy_poland_hungary.pdf.

Menon, you are talking about your GDP, that is not our GDP." That may be worth thinking about.

Michael Ignatieff also posed the question in his remarks to what extent open society gives voice to some while denying it to others? I do not actually think that it is a failing of open society as such, but what I do think is that liberal media neglected some important parts of our society. How many articles did you read in *The Guardian* about poor post-industrial towns in the north of England? How many articles were there in *The New York Times* written with sympathy and understanding about the sufferings of the Rust Belt, how many articles in the *Gazeta Wyborcza* about the poor parts of South-Eastern Poland? I think that was a real failing of liberal journalism, liberal academics, liberal writers. This enables the populist to advance into the vacuum and say, as Donald Trump does: I am your voice. I speak for you. You had no voice, no representation, either in or by the media. I am the voice of the voiceless, the heart of the heartless world. On the night of the victory of Brexit, Nigel Farage said: "This is a victory for ordinary people, decent people, real people," thus clearly implying that people like me, and the forty-eight percent who voted against Brexit, were neither ordinary, nor decent, not even real. There is a real challenge here in the relationship between free speech and the defense of an open society; it is not simply the challenge to reassert the facts, the evidence, the reality-based discourse. It is to get that reality-based discourse into the echo chambers where the populists are prevailing, to get it across to people who do not necessarily want to hear it in a language to which they can respond.

# Conclusion

A wonderful First Amendment judge, Justice Learned Hand, said in a speech in 1944: "The spirit of liberty is a spirit which is not too sure that it is right." It is a self-doubting, self-questioning spirit. Now, the challenge is to us, as academics, writers, journalists, students who are in the broadest sense (small-L) liberal, who believe in the values of liberal democracy, pluralism, and open society, whether on the right, the center, or the left. The challenge is this: We must be self-critical, and question and interrogate and doubt the project on which we have been engaged, many of us for thirty or forty years. The spirit of liberty is a spirit that is not so sure if it is right, is self-questioning, self-doubting, as is the spirit of Karl Popper. But at the same time, we must fight.

We must fight to defend these values, to defend the open society against those in all our societies who are trying to take us back towards a closed society. Now this is not something that soldiers normally do. I have to tell you, I have met many self-critical soldiers. But liberal intellectuals have to be self-critical soldiers. We have to do self-criticism and at the same time keep fighting for the defense of free speech and an open society.

# Religion in the Open Society

*Tim Crane*

## Introduction

My aim in this essay is to make some remarks about a tradition that lies at the heart of the idea of an open society: the tradition of religious tolerance. The idea of religious tolerance that open or liberal societies have endorsed is a massively important part of the history of liberalism, and it was arguably one of the things that gave rise to the modern liberal state. But the question of religious tolerance is also very important for us today. To what extent should secular, liberal societies tolerate those who do not share all of their secular liberal assumptions? To answer this question requires us to say something about what tolerance is, what it means to be tolerant, and about what we should tolerate and why.

In the first part of this essay I look at religious tolerance, and how tolerance in general should be understood. In the second part I look at the object of tolerance: in other words, what is it that should or should not be tolerated (in this context religious belief and believers). Then I will widen the angle of the lens, so to speak, and say something more general and speculative about the nature of religious belief. Many of the things I argue here are summaries of arguments from my book, *The Meaning of Belief: Religion from an Atheist's Point of View*.[1]

---

[1] Tim Crane, *The Meaning of Belief: Religion from an Atheist's Point of View* (Cambridge, MA: Harvard University Press, 2017).

# Religious Tolerance

There is a widely agreed narrative about the emergence in the West of religious tolerance as an ideal, and the correlative idea of religious freedom as a human right. This story has it that these things emerged in Europe (and later in America) as a result of the failure to impose religious conformity after the "wars of religion" of the sixteenth and seventeenth centuries. That failure evolved into a success: the development of the liberal doctrines of religious tolerance as a positive value, and of religious freedom as a human right.

In the first edition of the dictionary of the Académie française, tolerance is defined as "sufferance, forbearance that one has for what one cannot prevent." Tolerance in this sense is a way to come to terms with the admission of defeat. Why is such a defeat inevitable in the case of religious belief? Part of the answer was given by John Locke in his *Letter Concerning Toleration*, published in 1689.[2] Locke argued that the state must tolerate different religious faiths because the state is unable itself to constrain or compel belief. The state can constrain your action, it can control your behavior, but the state cannot control what you believe. This is taken to be a psychological or social fact about human beings and their societies—but it is not difficult to see how this fact fits into a conception of individual freedom and its value, something that came to lie at the heart of the liberal political tradition, of which Locke of course is one of the founding fathers.

So it was that a hundred years after Locke's letter, Article 10 of the *Declaration of the Rights of Man and of the Citizen* of the French Revolution read: "No one shall be disturbed on account of his opinions, including his religious views, provided their manifestation does not disturb the public order established by law." So what had originally been an admission of defeat— the acknowledgement that you could not get everyone to believe the same thing—is now elevated into one of the rights of man. In the very same year the Bill of Rights of the United States contains the claim that Congress "shall make no law respecting the establishment of religion or prohibiting the free exercise thereof." This became incorporated into the First Amendment of the U.S. Constitution. The historical situation is summed up nicely by Lynn

---

[2] John Locke, "Letter Concerning Toleration," in *Locke on Toleration*, ed. Richard Vernon (Cambridge: Cambridge University Press, 2010).

Hunt when she says that the Enlightenment of the eighteenth century played a major role in "turning religious toleration, a grudging government policy, into freedom of religion, a human right."[3]

The question for liberal societies today is this: given that religious freedom is perceived to be a value of open or liberal societies, to what extent should religions be tolerated? It is one thing to say that freedom of religion is a value; but in saying that, you do not impose exact limits on what behavior and what practices should be tolerated. (There is also a question for religious societies, which I cannot address here, about the extent to which these societies themselves can tolerate secular views and other religions.)

We need to start thinking about this question with the right conception of tolerance in mind. Tolerance is something that is frequently misunderstood in some public debates—in particular in those debates about whether to allow a variety of different kinds of speech in public. I think this misunderstanding of tolerance is very easy to correct, but nonetheless very important. The misunderstanding is that tolerance has something to do with respect for all opinions: tolerating an opinion is *ipso facto* respecting it, or giving it some credibility. So, on this understanding, to defend a doctrine of religious tolerance is to regard all religious views as worthy of respect or invulnerable to a certain kind of criticism. This view is related to clichés like "everyone is entitled to their opinion," and to a crude form of moral relativism which holds that you are not entitled to criticize someone else because their values come from one (psychological, cultural, historical) source and your values come from another source; no one can occupy a neutral standpoint without any particular source, but this would be needed for criticism. Another part of this collection of ideas is that it is in some way arrogant or conceited (or perhaps even "imperialist") to criticize other views and other cultures, and that therefore a true doctrine of tolerance ought to be opposed to the critique of religion. This comes out most strongly in contemporary discussions of the phenomenon of Islamophobia and the place of Islam in predominantly non-Islamic societies. Often these discussions include the view that a truly tolerant society would welcome all views and should not judge among views. That is what tolerance is sometimes said to be.

---

[3] Lynn Hunt, *The Enlightenment and the Origins of Religious Toleration* (Amsterdam: Felix Meritis, 2011), 10.

I think this involves a mistake about the very idea of tolerance. Tolerance does not imply respect for all views. Consider a view that you hold and think is very important: for example, you are in favor of gay marriage or you support the abolition of torture. These are not views that you tolerate: if you are in favor of gay marriage you do not tolerate gay marriage. On the contrary, toleration of something presupposes that you disapprove of it. The very act of tolerating something, as the definition from the Académie française implies, presupposes that you object to it in some way. I might tolerate my neighbors' loud music on New Year's Eve because I like my neighbors, I want to get on with them, even though I really object to this music, and maybe I think this music should never have been created. But I tolerate it until five o'clock in the morning because I want to live in peace with my neighbors. I might tolerate the smelly food that they cook, because they are my neighbors, they tolerate me, and maybe they tolerate my music and my smelly food, too.

The point that toleration implies disapproval was made many years ago by Bernard Williams.[4] Though simple and obvious once recognized, it is an important point, and a profound one in its application to religious tolerance. One reason for its importance is because it implies that a sensible doctrine of religious tolerance does not exclude critique. It does not exclude disapproval, objection, or some other kind of negative attitude to aspects of the religions that you are tolerating. Another reason for the importance of this idea is that it shows explicitly why the attitude of toleration is not based on any kind of relativism about values; it is consistent with a wide variety of views about the nature of value. It does not imply relativism; it implies only that some views or practices are objectionable.

At a deeper level, tolerance is less an attitude towards the truth of opinions, but an attitude towards the people who hold those opinions. In other words, it is a *practical* rather than a *theoretical* attitude. Tolerance is not aiming to arrive at a true overall conception of all the things that you tolerate, as if you could incorporate all views in one happy synthesis. Rather, the aim of tolerance is to live in peace with the people whom you tolerate. There is a connection here with the concept of respect. It is not true that toleration implies respect for all other views, or even that you must respect any other

---

[4] Bernard Williams, "Toleration: An Impossible Virtue?" in *Toleration: An Elusive Virtue*, ed. David Heyd (Princeton, NJ: Princeton University Press, 1998), 18–27.

views. Some views are not worthy of respect. There are some opinions people are not entitled to. The idea that you must respect all opinions is not something that follows from any sensible principle of tolerance.

But again, what we should respect are not views, but the people who hold them. I mean this, though, in a rather abstract sense. Why should you respect someone who holds a view that is objectionable, a view no one should hold? If you are not obliged to take their view seriously, why are you obliged to take them seriously? The answer—the sense in which you must respect those who have such views—is that you acknowledge their autonomy as a human being; you treat them as a person like yourself, someone to whom a certain kind of attention is due. If you respect them in this sense, you do not have to like them, or acknowledge that their views have any merit. But you must acknowledge that they are human beings with the capacity for freedom of thought.

So, in so far as tolerance involves respect, it is only respect for people and not respect for opinions, and it is respect for people in this very abstract sense. It is the same idea, I believe, that underlies the conviction that everyone, even those who have committed the most vile crimes, are entitled to a fair trial, or that everyone is equal before the law. It is that kind of abstract sense of "respect" for someone.

These claims about toleration raise the question of what exactly we should tolerate. If tolerating something implies that we object to it, then it does not follow that we should tolerate everything we object to. All I am saying here is that the things we should tolerate are, as a matter of fact, things that we object to. I am not saying that everything that is objectionable should be tolerated. Obviously not. In this essay I will avoid the substantive and difficult question of what should be tolerated and why, by appealing first to the rule of law. If a state has a rule of law that has its own integrity, then all toleration must be constrained by that. So we do not have to tolerate people who break the law, who do things that are against a proper legal code or system.

When I say toleration is constrained by the rule of law, this is not meant to be a surprising fact, or something that somehow deflates the idea of toleration. The subjection of tolerance to the rule of law is no more a deflation than is the idea that free speech should be subject to the rule of law. A sensible doctrine of freedom of speech should not allow people to broadcast obscenities in public, or—extending the meaning of "speech" a little—to put up obscene pictures in public. These things should not necessarily be permitted by a belief in freedom of speech. If somebody thinks that freedom of speech should ideally imply the right to say anything, anywhere, at any time, then this would not be a workable, plausible, or even desirable doctrine of freedom of speech. Whether free speech should extend as far as these things is not a real, practical question. Of course it should not. Actually, the same is true of democracy in a broad sense: we should not think that a sensible doctrine of democracy entails that every decision of a democratically elected government should be validated by a vote of its citizens. (The United Kingdom has been suffering from an overenthusiastic application of that idea in the last few years.)

Tolerance implies objecting to something. But it does not imply that everything that you object to is something you should tolerate. What and which things you should tolerate, how toleration should be constrained, are matters for serious philosophical, political, and legal debate. But future debate must begin with the correct understanding of the concept of toleration and its purpose.

## Religious Tolerance and the New Atheists

What is the role of the intellectual in discussing these matters, in an open society? Just because toleration should allow critique of religion, and because it should be possible within a liberal, tolerant open society to criticize religion without this being in some way inappropriate or offensive, that does not mean that any critique of religion is acceptable within an open society. From the point of view of an open society there can be no objection to an atheist critique of religion—that is a fairly obvious point. And critique as such is not incompatible with tolerance—this may be slightly less obvious. In the rest of this essay I would like to make some remarks about some recent critiques of religion by intellectuals in public life in Britain and the United States (and I know that these views have spread elsewhere, too).

I said above that what we really tolerate are people, but let me abbreviate that to saying that we are tolerating religion. So what is it that we are tolerating when we tolerate religion? One popular image of religion has been offered by the so called New Atheists; those like the biologist Richard Dawkins, the philosophers Daniel Dennett and A. C. Grayling, and the journalists Christopher Hitchens and Sam Harris, who have written a number of polemical works attacking religion from a moral and intellectual point of view.

Their general outlook can be summed up in terms of two ideas. The first is about the content of religion: a religion is a combination of cosmology and morality. By cosmology, I mean a theory of the universe, and by morality I mean a code of how to behave towards others. The second idea is about the value of religion: religion is in general a bad thing that should be eliminated by rational argument and scientific evidence.

It is not difficult to find examples of the first idea—about the content of religion—among New Atheist writers. In his book *Breaking the Spell*, Daniel Dennett writes that "religions are social systems whose participants avow belief in a supernatural agent or agents whose approval is to be sought."[5] Seeking approval is the role of morality in this picture: participants seek approval from the supernatural agent by how they behave towards others (amongst other things). But we also find this view expressed by some who do not belong to the New Atheist grouping. The late Ronald Dworkin, for example, was a philosopher quite sympathetic to religious belief. In his book *Religion Without God*, he describes the essence of religious belief as follows: "The conventional theistic religions with which most of us are most familiar, Judaism, Christianity, and Islam, have two parts: a science part and a value part. The science part is a theory of the explanation of the world, the value part is the theory of how to live."[6]

The second main component of the New Atheist view is that religion is a bad thing. Here is the characteristically splenetic Christopher Hitchens: "Religion poisons everything. As well as being a menace to civilization, it has become a threat to human survival. It is violent, irrational, intolerant, allied to racism, tribalism and bigotry, invested in ignorance and hostile to free inquiry, contemptuous of women and coercive towards children. It ought to have a great deal on its conscience."[7] And you can find similar tirades in the writings of Dawkins, Grayling, and Harris.

One very striking fact about this recent public discussion is that neither side recognizes itself in the other's description of them. The New Atheists accuse believers of mindless irrationality and their religious critics say that the New Atheists just miss the point. Why is this?

While many religious participants in these debates are perfectly capable of missing the point, here I want to concentrate on what seems to be lacking

---

[5] Daniel C. Dennett, *Breaking the Spell* (London: Allen Lane, 2006), 9.

[6] Ronald Dworkin, *Religion Without God* (Cambridge, MA: Harvard University Press, 2013), 23.

[7] Christopher Hitchens, *God Is Not Great: How Religion Poisons Everything* (New York: Twelve, 2007), 25.

from the New Atheist picture of religious belief. The first thing that is so obviously inadequate is what Dworkin calls the "science plus value" picture. The picture does not give a satisfactory answer to the question of why people go church, mosque, temple, or synagogue. What is this all about? The short answer to this question was nicely expressed by Durkheim over a hundred years ago in his *Elementary Forms of Religious Life*, when he pointed out that a religion is not something you believe, it is also something you belong to. That is what is left out of the cosmology plus morality (or "science plus value") picture. Cosmology is a theoretical explanation of how the world came into existence, and morality tells you how to behave towards others. But religion also involves belonging to a group, going to church, going to the synagogue, going to the mosque. That these things are at the heart of religion is revealed in typical capsule summaries of religion—for example, the five pillars of Islam. Of the five pillars—the declaration that there is no god but Allah and that Mohammed is his prophet, the injunctions to fast, to make the pilgrimage, to pray, and to give alms—only one of them is a cosmological claim. The others are claims about what you should do. And although giving alms is a moral matter, as usually understood, prayer, fasting, and pilgrimage are neither morality nor cosmology.

In *The Meaning of Belief*, I draw a different, rather abstract picture of the essence of religion. My claim is that religion involves two elements: what I call the religious impulse and identification. What I call the religious impulse is captured in William James's remark (in *The Varieties of Religious Experience*) that the heart of religion is the belief that "there is an unseen order and that our supreme good lies in harmoniously adjusting ourselves thereto."[8] The unseen order he speaks of is not the invisible order or structure discovered by science. It is rather the supposed reality that transcends the world of experience. This commitment to the transcendent—to something that transcends everything we see around us and everything science finds out—is what is expressed in the very familiar assertions that there "must be more to it than all this" or "surely, this cannot be all there is!" This is what people attempt to articulate in great detail and sophistication in the doctrines of religious belief. It is a good question, which has no single general answer, how these more sophisticated doctrines relate to the convictions of ordinary

---

[8]  William James, *The Varieties of Religious Experience* (London: Longmans, Green & Co., 1902), 53.

believers. But the belief in the transcendent—no matter how precisely or imprecisely you think of it, or how metaphorically you think of it, or how literally you think of it—is an essential component to the vast majority of the things that have deserved the name of religion.

I am not attempting to define religion, in any strict sense of the word "definition." I agree with Nietzsche when he said that nothing that has a history can ever be defined.[9] Sometimes philosophers who spend their time thinking about the subject matter of logic and mathematics—subject matters which themselves have no history—have that paradigm of definition in mind. But that paradigm is very hard to apply to reality. What I am trying to characterize are general features of most of those things that have counted as religion in human society, even if there are also things that people call religion that do not have those features.

The religious impulse is not anything like a scientific hypothesis. It is a claim about the world; but it is not a scientific theory. Not all claims about the world, about reality, are scientific hypotheses. Recognizing that this is not a scientific hypothesis and it is not strictly speaking incompatible with any scientific theory—no scientific theory says that what it describes is all that there is to reality—then we can begin to see how there ought to be potential for much apparent conflict to disappear from the debate. Whether this potential can be realised depends on all sorts of contingent conditions, including the psychological traits of the influential personalities involved, and on all participants' interest in genuinely trying to understand one another rather than in winning the argument or showing how clever they are. I am not saying that it will be easy to create such conditions.

Identification is the second element of my characterization of religion; it is what is captured by the slogan that religion is not just something that you believe but also something you belong to. Durkheim writes that "religious beliefs proper are always held by a defined collectivity that professes them and practices the rites that go with them."[10] Identification necessarily involves rites and rituals. To identify with others in a religious group makes you part of a tradition that in many cases goes back hundreds or even thousands of years. Being a member of that tradition can involve saying words that people

---

[9] Friedrich Nietzsche, *On the Genealogy of Morality* (1887), ed. Keith Ansell-Pearson, trans. Carol Diethe (Cambridge: Cambridge University Press, 2007), 53.

[10] Émile Durkheim, *The Elementary Forms of Religious Life* (1912), ed. Mark S. Cladis, trans. by Carol Cosman (Oxford: Oxford University Press, 2001), 42.

have uttered for centuries—words that perhaps they do not fully understand or that they do not conceive of as making "literal" claims about reality. But this lack of understanding—and this figurative component in religious language—are not supposed to be shortcomings of religious practice, but are rather a part its essence. This is because at the heart of religion is the commitment to the mystery of the world.

Identification also means that for most religious believers, the world divides into two: there are people of your kind, and there are people who are not of your kind. This can be one of the most difficult aspects of religion to incorporate within an open society. The division can give rise to hostility, intolerance, discrimination, and violence. How then can an open society—which in its very nature aims to eliminate such things—allow religious divisions to flourish? I will not say anything further about this difficult question here. At the moment, I am simply claiming identification to be a part of the essence of religion.

I am saying all this as an atheist. I was brought up a Catholic, but now retain nothing of my youthful belief. I myself do not have a religious impulse, but what I am trying to describe—from the outside, as it were—is something that is, in one way or another, the commitment of about eighty per cent of the human race. You might say, "How can you generalize about eighty per cent of the human race, about six billion people?" I agree—it can seem like an absurd thing to attempt. But what I say in my defense is that when anyone starts talking about "religion" in these general terms, then they cannot escape doing just this. The only way to escape it is to not talk about religion *as such* at all and just say something much more specific and much more detailed. But then it will not be possible to engage effectively with others who talk about religion as such. That is my excuse for operating at this stratospheric level of generality.

So this is my claim: religion involves two elements. One is the religious impulse; the other is identification. Of course, it is possible that these can come apart, and they do actually come apart in some things that are called religions. Maybe there are religions that are not committed (or are less committed) to the transcendent, and it is entirely conceivable, I think, that you could have someone who is some kind of a solitary mystic who had a religious impulse but participated in no identification with others whatsoever. So, of course these things can come apart factually, empirically, and conceptually. But the question I want to ask is: when there are these two things, is the connection between them purely accidental or contingent? Or, is there any explanation that we can give of the connection between these things, at this level of abstraction? I think there is, and this will be my final point.

## The Religious Impulse and Identification

The explanation of how the religious impulse is connected with identification is based around the idea of the sacred. Here I again appeal to Durkheim, who defined religion as a "unified system of beliefs and practices relative to sacred things."[11] The idea of the sacred was central to Durkheim's conception of religion. The sacred is not the magical: although some religious traditions hold that miracles—supernatural interventions in the course of nature—can be performed with the help of sacred things, it is not essential to sacred things in general that they have such supernatural or magical powers. Believers who think that the Bible is a sacred text do not normally think that the Bible has to the power to (for example) turn lead into gold or water into wine. It is in terms of the idea of the sacred that we should understand religion, and not the idea of the supernatural—that idea which features prominently in the writings of Dawkins and Dennett and others.

The division of the world into sacred things and profane things marks a distinction in what sorts of things can be done to these objects. An object of any sort can be a sacred thing: a text, a book, words, the actual words spoken that can be repeated again and again; an animal can be a sacred being, a place can be a sacred place. What is important is that when something is sacred, then it is not profane, and something profane is not sacred. The distinction is exclusive and exhaustive. Sacred things carry with them prohibitions about how they can be treated and respected. When a sacred thing is treated without the required respect or reverence, this is what is known as profanation or desecration. Certain objects have to be treated with this kind of reverence by believers because of what they mean to them. This is not a difficult idea to understand in general—even an atheist can appreciate the meaning of a grave or burial place, and the significance of violating it or defiling it.

Now I want to link the element of identification with the religious impulse through the idea of the sacred. (This is the central claim of my book.) These two things are linked because sacred things—the objects and

---

[11] Durkheim, *The Elementary Forms of Religious Life*, 46.

the books and the texts—the buildings, the places, have two important features for believers. One is that they point outwards towards the transcendent: they indicate something other than this world; they are a sign or a symbol of something beyond. The second is that these sacred objects bind people together in and across time with others who have shared their history. For example, it is because a group of people has been saying the same words together in church, synagogue, mosque, or temple—the same words that people have been saying together for hundreds or thousands of years in one form or another—that they belong to that group rather than another group. Groups are bound together by the things that they regard as sacred. This unites the two elements of anything that counts as religious belief. The sacred is both a manifestation of the transcendent in our world and the unifying factor in religious identification. In that sense, Durkheim was right.

It is not that Dennett and others are completely wrong in what they say about the content of religious belief. It is rather that to understand a worldview, a vision of the world, or a philosophy, it is not enough just to list some of the propositions that the worldview contains. You also have to understand what is central and what is peripheral to it, what is at the core of the worldview—what are its moving parts, so to speak—and what is just extra material around the periphery. What I tried to do in my book is to describe what I think of as the core of religious belief. I appeal to the idea of the sacred to show how believers are unified around the same objects that are involved in their rituals and their practices, and how objects themselves "point" beyond the empirical world towards a transcendent reality. That is a very different picture from the one you get in Dawkins and Dennett, and I hope that it is a picture that might be recognizable to religious believers.

## Conclusion

A secular, liberal, open society should tolerate religion; but this is not because all views have equal value. On the contrary, toleration itself presupposes that some views are objectionable. It follows that, as a corollary of tolerance, an open society should also permit the critique of religion—religion in all its forms. Such a critique is consistent with the doctrine of respect for those people with whom you disagree, respect in the abstract sense I described above.

These rather theoretical points are compatible with a wide range of practical proposals about which practices should be tolerated, and to what extent. And these practical—mostly legal and political—questions are where things become very difficult. I have offered no suggestions here about how to go about answering these questions. Rather, I have described some elements of a big picture of the phenomenon of religion. The next stage would be to enter the practical, political, and legal debates. But it is crucial, when we begin to properly address these questions, to start in the right place. Any critique of religion should be based on an adequate conception of it, and this is one reason why the critique contained in some recent New Atheist writings are so inadequate. By failing to make sense of religious belief itself, they also fail to make sense of the failure of their own debate with the religious.

# Constitutionalism in Closing Societies

*András Sajó*

## Introduction

In the following I will show how internal weaknesses in constitutional structures and the abuse of democratic constitutionalism have contributed to the contemporary threat of perpetuation of governmental power. I argue that this is related to unfinished and imperfect elements in the constitutional project. Constitutions are full of theoretically unjustified compromises, resulting in shortcomings and gaps. While the internal shortcomings of constitutionalism are important in its current demise, these developments originate in a broader social-cultural development. Under the pressure of our stressful age, vulnerabilities in the social psyche and social culture become visible and are targeted and abused.

No surprise here. Present day societies were half-ready in their heart for not having certain liberties, and to welcome illiberalism. And in societies where a narcissistic culture prevails, resistance is inevitably limited. Being disillusioned and alienated from politics and public responsibility, many citizens chose leaders of their own stripe. There is nothing new under the sun when it comes to the abuse of the rule of law. Abuse is an inherent part of the history of constitutional law. Politics regularly relies on legal means, which makes constitutionalists desperate even today. Technically speaking, even Hitler, in his coming to power through the democratic electoral process, relied on the relentless abuse of the gaps of the Weimar constitution. But the instrument, the imperfect law was not the cause. The cause was the successful closing of the mind of Germans, left and right, by hate and fear, as well as German resent-

ment. The mindset that accepted and welcomed its own closing had its potentials for such closing even without the brown shirts marching on the streets.

It is in the context of closing minds that I would like to discuss the
demise of constitutionalism. By constitutionalism I mean a set of liberty-
enhancing ideas and corresponding institutions, protective of liberty. From
this perspective, not all constitutions and documents of similar names are
constitutional. The contemporary legal phenomena that undermine constitutionalism, the cobblestones of the road to a new serfdom, are increasingly
known, although well-paid legal minds serving aspiring despots continue to
innovate abuse. By the way, it would be interesting to know the terms of reference of the public call to produce these cobblestones.

## Constitutionalism

The list of the acts of disregard of the rule of law serving the undoing of constitutional democracy becomes longer by the day, but its fundamentals are
pretty clear already. Let me mention a few of these anti-constitutionalist
tricks. The current inventory includes the refurbishing of the judiciary, and
the politicization of the civil service. Where this does not help, access to
justice, especially recourse against administrative decisions, is restricted. Retrospective rules become widespread. Biased preferences are written into the
law, as if they were neutral rules. More generally, legal logic is twisted, in disregard of the logic of the rule of law.

I think I can illustrate this constitutional chicanery by a joke: Three
patrons go to the bar and ask for three cocktails and a clean glass. The waiter
comes back, with the three cocktails, and asks, who ordered the drink with
the clean glass?

As to substantive law, the rule of law is subject to regular tinkering. Definitions in criminal law become non-specific, as is the case with the definition
of extremism and terrorism, for example in the United Kingdom. Such broad
definitions enable, of course, mass surveillance. Terrorists are suspect, they
have to be surveilled. If everyone is a terrorist, everyone has to be surveilled.
Emergency exceptions become part of the ordinary legal system, as in the
fresh French piece of legislation that is charmingly called "Act on Reinforcing
Internal Security."

The economic sphere is not exempt either. Private property is taken
without compensation. State broadcast monopolies emerge under the veil

of private ownership. As to public law, plebiscite without proper procedures and substantive limits becomes the accepted norm of authentic popular will-formation. Brexit and other one-sided declarations of the genuine will of the people are accepted as normal. Emotions replace argument. Welcome to global Venezuela.

Elections remain free, not necessarily fair: gerrymandering and electoral threshold rules as well as rules on access to the media and campaign finance are all tailor-made to perpetuate the power of the incumbent. To give you an idea what is at stake, the Supreme Court of the United States just had a hearing in a case, *Gill v. Whitford*, where the issue is whether Wisconsin's redistricting plan is an impermissible partisan gerrymander that is a manipulation of electoral boundaries to favor a specific party. Today, in the United States, any given majority in a state is capable of determining the outcome of the U.S. congressional election in the respective district perpetuating the power of one or another party. That is the issue in so many countries.

To take another example, sorry to report that for the European Court of Human Rights, a ten percent electoral threshold, that is to say, an electoral system that allows the total non-presentation of ten percent of the electorate was found legitimate. The concerned electoral system was that of Turkey. No more on this.

Let me continue the litany with other tricks. The level of human rights protection declines. This is so not necessarily because human rights are declared to be irrelevant or imperialistic, although you hear this very often, but just because people's right to security is played against traditional liberties, or, another example, victims' rights prevail against traditional due process considerations. Special interests are elevated into human rights, even Berlusconi's self-amnesty by legislation was carried out in the name of human rights. After all, that was the justification, the European Court held, in respect to Italy, that lengthy proceedings violate the right to fair trial. Therefore, there shall be no trial.

Once all these practices become a system, law will generate and sustain personal dependence. Dependence quickly breaks the spin and opens the mind for closing. Fundamental institutions of the constitutional state are also losing their autonomy. Churches depend on state subsidy, business hangs upon state aid and public contract, the communication of ideas, science and the generation of ideas in universities, supplicate state benevolence. The legally protected sources of autonomy disappear. Moreover, law itself becomes the source and instrument of dependency.

Now add to this the stirring of hatred and fear. Where fear mongering becomes part of daily democratic politics, the cocktail looks lethal. An example: televisions spots begin by asking viewers, "Who will keep your family safe"? And the political opponents, turned into enemies, are presented as indifferent to the threat of gang violence from illegal immigrants. Ed Gillespie, candidate for governor of Virginia, sponsored this advertisement. To avoid misunderstanding, he was the *more* moderate republican candidate.

The current state of affairs is partly due to the prevailing understanding of democracy as the ultimate and supreme expression of popular will. For generations, democracy was the natural darling in politics and electoral democracy remains an uncontested source of legitimacy around the world. Democracy is the only game in town. But the celebratory mood, the adulation of electoral majoritarianism, is turning into a serious hangover, not the first in the history of democracy. (Except for those who master it.) What we see in the demise and backlash of *constitutional* democracy, just to use two euphemisms in one single sentence, is the exposition of the internal weaknesses and contradictions of an electoral democracy that relies upon the unmediated wish of a poorly structured constituency. It is at this moment of the unfolding drama that constitutionalism should enter the stage. It does not.

In an apotheosis of electoral democracy, constitutionalism was exiled to the basement of irrelevancy. It remains largely absent, although the role written for constitutional law would be to structure and inhibit people. But instead of disciplining democracy, it is constitutionalism itself that is constrained and paralyzed. The constitutional containment of majoritarianism has been delegitimized by democracy itself, by democracy unbound. Unruly electoral democracy has little understanding of and respect towards its keeper, constitutionalism. But wild horses, fast as they are, hardly win the derby. You may have noticed by now that although this lecture series is about open society, and even more about rethinking open society, I dared to entertain you with a little inventory of the demise of constitutionalism, without uttering the word "open." I understand open society to be the opposite of what Karl Popper detested in Plato, whom he famously accused of defending lying, political miracles, tabooistic superstition, the suppression of truth, and ultimately brutal violence.

Societal openness presupposes mental openness, and constitutionalism could be an institutional mechanism to enable society to be and to remain open. Open to ideas, and action. It is not by accident that the freedom of speech was the first liberty for the founders of the American republic. Of course, law is not alone in the protection of mental openness. Other institutions, like education, or inclusive and open religious practices can be mentioned here. Openness requires freedom even beyond thinking. It is enough to refer to the freedom of exit, a fundamental concern for Albert Hirschman. This fundamental right was vehemently denied in closed societies, like communism.

Be as it may, the relation between some kind of open society and liberty-enhancing constitutionalism is more or less generic, and natural. Unfortunately, there is no openness by social design only. Minds can be manipulated for the purpose of manufacturing a closed mindset. But this does not work the other way around. This is the handicap of open society, and this is why the law of freedom overprotects speech.

Now, what about the third element of the title—rethinking—in "Rethinking Open Society"? Rethinking makes sense if it means the critical review of those theoretical assumptions that underline and mobilize for openness. Given the poor performance of constitutionalism, there can be a problem with it. Rethinking consists in the identification and overcoming of the sloppiness of the design that facilitates the populist closing of open societies.

Let me emphasize, institutional shortcomings are the common heritage of the constitutional structure in all concerned democracies, and an Eastern or post-communist peculiarity. The East-West division that attributes backwardness to the "East" is created by a defensive need of Western supremacy, which recognizes with astonishment and even horror its own traits in the mirror of the East. It is true that most contemporary illiberal techniques were invented far away from the shores of the Atlantic Ocean. But it is enough to look at the ghostly tricks of De Gaulle to see how creative the West can be in matters of constitutional disrespect. Eastern and Western democracies sail the same boat, although perhaps on different decks.

The real difference is that happier societies are more resilient, thanks to the value-preferences in those societies. See for example the strong commitment to fairness in the United Kingdom, and French economic and intellectual autonomy, a matter sustained by the rule of law. These are the sources of resistance to governmental efforts to close the social mind. Social institutions, including constitutional institutions, which regulate and constrain power, are intended to prevent the effects of emotions that would close the mind, in particular emotions such as fear and envy and hatred and resulting tribalism.

Unfortunately, emotionalism became part of electoral democracy even in so called mature democracies. To again quote Popper, the great secret of the revolt against freedom is to take advantage of sentiments, not wasting one's energies in futile efforts to destroy them. This is perfectly understood by those who colonize emotions under the guise of electoral democracy.

It is not surprising that constitutional institutions cannot resist for long the revolt of these emotions. Contemporary democracies were hardly ever immune to populist emotionalism; electoral politics was for a long time based on toying with and manipulating emotions. The emotionalism of democratic politics has led to what Plato has already found inevitable for the success of the *tyrannos*. Tyrants must stir up war, one war after another, in order to make the people feel that they need a general.

How sad for these poor adult children, the electorate, they were manipulated! But no need to cry at this point. That the good people were manipulated may very well be true, but the manipulators cynically say that manipulation is but another name for politics. We are also told that people have the right to determine their values, which cannot be imposed on them by past generations. Human rights activists who live in a cloud cuckoo land and/or serve who must not be named would claim the opposite. They do not matter: If the citizens prefer security to free speech, it is up to people to decide so.

The Rousseauist argument prevails in its totalitarian version. People cannot be wrong, and people's will is the one that is expressed within the existing formal structures, whatever the said structures happen to be. Hence the legitimacy of populism.

Let us be honest. People are not innocent and passive recipients of manipulation in emotional politics. They are often reasonable and brave in adversity, but they are also the ones who find liberation in hatred that serves the blogosphere. Hatred was fomenting on the black burners already waiting for liberation. This is the social-cultural aspect of the demise of constitutionalism.

Nevertheless, there is a certain form of republicanism that is afraid to see the shortcomings in the empirical reality of people. Before the ail and fury of the self-appointed friends of the people will excise me to a Schmittian inferno, for the present alleged people-bashing and democracy snubbing, let me quickly mention that the political participation of citizens can be reasonable and true to the spirit of the constitution—just you cannot take that for granted. De Gaulle, who relied on plebiscite with gusto, called one after the 1968 upheaval. This 1969 referendum intended to curtail the powers of the Senate, which, disrespectfully, even if occasionally, resisted certain initiatives of the General. At the referendum there was a high turnout, and around 53 percent rejected the detailed and more or less sensible reform proposals, which today are part of the French constitution—ninety per cent of it. The day after the referendum, De Gaulle, who always claimed to rely on the trust of the French, resigned. In this story, for whatever reason, people resisted a further concentration of power. Most likely, the majority was simply fed up with the General, but not necessarily with his anti-constitutionalism. Was this event an expression of people's wisdom, or populist whim? We will never know for sure. Fact is that the President, who scorned the rule of law, respected the popular spirit of his own constitution.

The problem begins where the players are not possessed by the constitutional spirit.

How can constitutional design mitigate the destructive potential of majoritarian electoral democracy that threatens the openness of society? Classical constitutionalists offered an institutional solution that is animated by distrust towards people's decision. But at the same time, the same classics of constitutionalism were very much aware of the foundational role of equal respect of all individuals. Observing the inclinations of public opinion, constitutional thinkers, beginning with Tocqueville, recognized that democracy has to be accommodated. It is irresistible, but it has to be tamed. Constitutionalism became an old friend of democracy, trying to preclude democratic self-destruction, a fall into the abyss of majoritarian oppression. Democracy and its institutions and principles, such as free and fair elections, public opinion and equality, became a healthy addition to the instruments of limiting government. People as electorate became a branch of power, checking on the traditional branches of power, and democracy became institutionally structured.

There is no free lunch. This came at a price.

A distance had to be and was created between government and society, which was then used to mobilize against constitutionalism as well as against democracy. For many reasons, constitutionalism could not live up to this task of moderation. It did not always protect substantive democracy against itself, among others because Rousseauism forced upon the popular imagination an exaggerated respect of people, the ultimate source of sovereignty.

## The People

Now let me name one of the reasons for this shortcoming. There is a problem with *people*, at least with the concept of people in constitutional theory. *People* is over-respected, even if understandably so. Otherwise it would be difficult, if not impossible, to legitimize and sustain people's sovereign supremacy. This supremacy is vital, when you would like to renounce more dangerous supremacy aspirants—kings, oligarchs, despots. The elimination of royal power has created a power vacuum. Such a vacuum is unsustainable for a state as it risks anarchy. But constitutionalism was intended not only to replace, but also to curtail sovereign power. After all, it was created to preclude all unlimited power, including that of people, hence the need for representative government, separation of powers, fundamental rights, and their protection, and protection of minorities, and all the institutional arrangements serving it, laws and habit, which sustain the edifice.

Because of the foundational belief in people as a source of power, which is an absolutely correct assumption against the usurpation of power by anyone, majoritarianism prevails. In republican theory of Rousseauist pedigree, and also in theories of *Volksgemeinschaft*, people's community or nation, *people* is postulated as being beyond criticism, hence it becomes problematic to criticize people even when it behaves in an unreflective, collectively suicidal and oppressive manner. If one of us disparages people, that is understood as disrespect and offence to one's neighbor. Now, what to do with this? Contrary to the unhappy secretary of the Writers' Union of the German Democratic Republic, in Brecht's poem "The Solution," we cannot propose for government to dissolve people and elect another. There is no alternative people, even if the existing people are sometimes unwilling to be recruited for the cause of tolerance.

So what is the problem with *people*? The difference between We, the people, as a normative concept, and what is often called the multitude, or the community of citizens, is forgotten. Let me explain this by a reference to ancient republican Rome, wherefrom the term and usage of people, the *populus*, originates. There was a fundamental social and legal class division between plebs and patrician aristocracy in republican Rome. Secession, as a form of resistance, of the plebs resulted in a law called the Lex Hortensia in 267 BCE, and that law made plebiscites, decisions of the plebeian council, binding on all. Arguably, a sovereign Roman people was born. Decisions by all members of the citizens were binding on people. What matters for us is that the term *populus*, the people, refers to a concept of political inclusion of all citizens. The *populus* were not sovereign: sovereignty was exercised jointly with the Senate. However, the orators, in search of popular support, spoke of the *dignity, majesty, authority, freedom of the Roman people, populus liber, a free people*. So the habit of thinking of themselves as free and sovereign was quite ingrained in people. This, by the way, was in itself a major liberating moment. Moreover, reference to *populus romanus* was reference to an alleged common interest, the best interest of the entire populus. As Henrik Mouritsen has masterfully put it, in assemblies the people were present as a political concept, and it was this concept, rather than a random gathering of individuals, which was addressed by the orators who spoke of free people.

What matters for the present purposes is that *people* is a normative concept that refers to a source of sovereign power. Constitutional democracy needs that concept. The fact that the members of society do not have all the properties attributed to them in the normative concept does not necessarily undermine the legitimacy of the sovereignty claim. National communities and individuals can be much worse intellectually and morally than what is attributed to people in the normative concept. Kant, once again, was right. We must assume equal cognitive capacities to all, as there cannot be human development and self-realization without assuming full capacity of all people. But so far, humans have only partly come out of their self-imposed tutelage. Moreover, people in morally bankrupt societies can have traits that shall force the power holders to deny the attribution of sovereignty to such people. That was the case, for example, after World War II in respect with Germany. Even today, Germans, perhaps not only the political and legal elite, go very far in constraining people when it comes to respect of human dignity, and for this very same reason.

Because of the shortcomings in actual human and collective behavior and reasoning, the institutional design of constitutionalism sets all sorts of procedures for a structured and reflexive expression of the will of human collectives. But the actual behavior and beliefs of the masses continue to pose a genuine problem for constitutional practices. Unfortunately, the constitutional mechanism of structuring popular will through representative government often undermined the legitimacy of government in the public eye, partly because of the poor performance of politicians and bureaucrats.

# Remedies

What are the remedies? One of the most common remedies proposed is referendum. This is the prescribed medicine. I will not argue against referendum. It is an important corrective of political mismanagement, especially if it originates from popular initiative. But even such processes need proper structuring in view of human cognitive bias and prevailing legalized mass manipulation. I do not want to mention at the end of every paragraph the word Brexit to illustrate the problems of ill-designed referendum. But I am rather unenthusiastic about plebiscites that are initiated by power holders on an agenda of their liking, be it even a matter of constitution making.

Beyond the insufficient restraint upon people's will, many other intellectual developments in constitutional law have contributed to the demise of constitutionalism. The loss of interest in liberty among our fellow citizens in constitutional law and in human rights in general, is particularly troubling.

Is there an institutional answer to the demise of constitutionalism? Let me repeat, the constitutional project was unfinished and unaccomplished from day one. Midnight judges were not invented by the previous outgoing democratic government of Poland in 2015, but by the Adams administration in the United States in 1801. Chief Justice Marshall, credited with the establishment of modern judicial review, a great institution, was one of such midnight judges, elected after his party lost the elections. By the way, until his appointment he served as Secretary of State in the Adams administration, providing a wonderful example of picking your most trusted political ally to become a judge and chief justice. The successor to the Adams administration, no less a constitutionalist than President Jefferson, threatened that same Supreme Court under Marshall. His Congress simply ordered a recess for one year, so that the Supreme Court will not render judgments or decisions unpleasant to the Congress in power. And all this was made possible by gaps in the U.S. Constitution, the most respected constitution that we know. And it was made possible by the evaporation of the constitutional spirit, the same spirit that animated the same people, the Jeffersons, the Adamses, the Marshalls, and the American public only a decade earlier.

Constitutional solutions can be made more robust and have to be made more robust. I promised you not to mention Brexit, but it is inevitable.

In some constitutions, certain topics, including the revocation of international treaty obligations and the diminution of fundamental rights, are off limits to referendum. There was no written constitution in the United Kingdom and the tradition and habit that was the spirit of the British constitution did not make itself present anymore. Other constitutions, like the American or the German, simply do not allow for national referendum at all, admitting more or less that this is too risky a tool. Now, such restrictions on referendum, like limiting the scope, could have been more easily digested elsewhere, had the popular vote not been treated as the ultimate form of people's sovereignty. So there is an intellectual obstacle to introduce those perfectly reasonable and necessary constrains.

Let us consider constitutional amendment, allegedly the ultimate domain of people's exclusive power. Even the most incomprehensible amendment can be accepted via referendum. Therefore, for the protection of the constitution, its amendment has to be made particularly demanding, at least on non-technical matters. A constitutional change should be turned into political risk for the powers-to-be, as is the case in the so called Dutch-Norwegian constitution-amending system. There, the legislative that accepts an amendment has to be immediately dissolved, and it is for the next elected parliament to finalize the amendment. This is a real risk to politicians. It is also important to have judicial review, to check legislation, the will of the people, to the extent necessary for upholding the constitution, and, "deblocking stoppages in the democratic process," to quote Professor Ely's famous definition.

Consider elections—the kitchen that manufactures representatives. As the saying goes, you should not enter the kitchen if you wish to enjoy the food of the restaurant. Electoral democracy was left to a great extant to the political process, although electoral litigation became pretty standard. Here, too, constitutional control is appropriate and necessary, and can be successful, as the recent Kenyan example indicates, even if on the long run it may not change the nature of the rule by Kenyatta. But people became aware of a certain possibility because of a judicial decision. Such decisions clearly indicate that there are limits.

Beyond referenda, electoral design too shall be seen as a fundamentally constitutional issue. There is a lot of resistance and reluctance to accept this view. To quote an opinion of the conservative wing of the U.S. Supreme Court, in a case decided about 13 years ago, an excessive injection of politics in redistricting is unlawful, but the Federal Court should stay out of this political thicket because there is no principled way to determine how much partisan favoritism is too much. The result of such deferentialism is that for many decades, electoral systems all over the world were and are designed in such a way that the actual representation to a considerable number of people is denied. A small minority may run a country, legitimately being elected under prevailing rules. And this is justified in the name of governability.

Of course, you may say that refurbishing constitutional institutions seems belated for many democracies. A perhaps fatal shift has already occurred. Even where constitutional democracy is still in place, it is likely that little time is left to carry out these preventive changes. Politicians, even if well intentioned, are not statesmen. They resemble Minerva's owls; the owl prefers night flights.

The story of the lack of amendment to the Constitutional Tribunal Act in Poland, under the previous government, is exemplary in this respect. There, notwithstanding continued reminders coming from experts, the government did not push for a change in the Constitutional Tribunal Act, although it was crystal clear that the mandate of too many justices on the Tribunal will expire at the same time. Last minute, the outgoing Sejm started to elect new judges, and, I must say, they started to elect judges in abundance. In some instances, there was no vacancy and there were no applicable rules. The rest is history, and the history is the following: anything can happen and even more.

So far, multilayered constitutionalism, the exercise of constitutional control by international actors also failed to deliver. And it did not correct the shortcomings of national rights protection. It failed because of its own imperfections. National democratic deficits were countered only by an international deficit. But perhaps people in Europe, and even their political leaders, even if they are captives of each other, will understand that Western life forms, democracy, and even tribal values, cannot be sustained in the global competition where China may become the world's taskmaster.

Still, institutions matter. In my profession, constitutional law, unfortunately, an intellectually attractive and perhaps even legitimate deconstruction has contributed to the loss of self-confidence in constitutional law. That is a fact. But it is time for democracy fans to end their little games, high citation generating as it may be, and stop attacks on their ally, constitutionalism.

I spoke about the imperfections of democracy, which are not corrected by constitutional arrangements due to constitutional imperfections abused by populists. And here comes the good news. Trust me. Illiberal democracy is imperfect too, and it is an easy prey to contingency. Thanks to the commitment of the world to democracy, elections remain the Achilles' heel of illiberal regimes. Vice renders its ordinary service to virtue. In most part of the world, the political regimes still have to remain committed to democracy and they do remain committed to democracy, at least to a sort of electoral democracy. President Maduro wants to assert himself as a democrat and not as an autocrat. He did allow state gubernatorial elections to take place in December 2017. The elections were not fair and the results were disappointing. But principles are confirmed in their disregard. And principles are confirmed by the importance of the violation. It is not taken for granted that people lose elections even among adverse circumstances. Even military coup coups are carried out in the name of restoring democracy. Autocrats in the making look at ratings all the time. There is something left of the respect of democracy. Autocrats cannot get rid of it as long as people consider election their right. Populists remain democrats, at least in the sense that they cannot but play by the formal rules of democracy, even if they tend to recalibrate democracy at their liking. These autocrats are far from cherishing Stalin's truth, who said that it does not matter how people vote, what matters is who counts the votes. The supremacy of national unity, which is the real alternative to democracy, as in Hun Sen's Cambodia, remains a non-appealing outlier. Democracy as a recognition of personal equality is hard-wired even in closed minds. At least for a while.

Moreover, constitutional institutions are resilient, even if vulnerable by design. Neither the Jefferson administration nor De Gaulle meant the end of democratic constitutionalism. On the contrary, constitutionalists came out enriched from those conflicts with autocracies. Today, constitutionally inspired judicial decisions are still executed in many countries, at least formally. And we should look beyond the law. Evolution theory may be left out of the curriculum, but continues to be accessible, and educators continue to whisper Darwin's truth into the ears of Turkish students. Many of the churches in the world remain open to openness. For good or bad reasons, people continue to vote for non-autocratic solutions, even at plebiscites. The freedom in the private sphere cannot be totally abandoned. That would be cause for revolution.

At the moment, populists do not dispose of totalitarian possibilities for that closing of autonomous spheres. And there are good reasons to assume that populists like Wilders will never stand for that kind of totalitarianism that is needed for an imposed single mindset. It is still not too late to take precautionary measures at the institutional level, to make constitutionalism more resistant. There are elements in the surviving democratic constitutional structure, and in the leftover of the open mind, that can be used to reverse the current drift towards less and less mild despotism.

Good luck and good night. Good luck, or a not so good night!

# PART THREE

# Open Society in 21st Century Geopolitics

# War and Open Society in the Twentieth Century

*Margaret MacMillan*

## Introduction

In the following, I will discuss the relationship between war and society, and in particular between war and the open society. Karl Popper saw his work on the open society and its enemies as his "war effort." It was published in 1945, at a time when democracy was apparently triumphant over Fascism, but democracies themselves were under siege in the heart of Europe. Like many others, he was deeply concerned about the futures of those democracies and the need to defend their values, to defend the use of reason, to try to understand what was going on, and to defend the very tolerance that makes democracies open against those who are intolerant. I think at least some of the things he was worried about are still relevant today.

There are many descriptions of what an open society is, but I would like to start with one given by Michael Ignatieff in 1995: "In civil society, however, division and diversity, checks and balances, are of the essence. Political power is fenced on cultural authority, and social position does not entail cultural or political influence. A free society, acting through the press and its elected representatives, restrains the state, and the law restrains both."[1] I think this is about as good a summary of what an open society should be as you can get. It might seem strange that I want to talk about war and open society, because

---

[1] Michael Ignatieff, "On Civil Society: Why Eastern Europe's Revolutions Could Succeed," *Foreign Affairs* 72, no. 2 (1995): 128–29.

war brings with it connotations of discipline, repression, and mobilization for an end. But I think we need to look at war for two reasons. One is that war is deeply embedded in and intertwined with human history. We tend to look at wars in aberration, as something that happens as an unfortunate breakdown of peace or the normal state of affairs; and once the war is over, we go back to that normal state of affairs. I would argue that the relationship is much more complex than that. Certain types of societies, certain failures and actions in societies, can produce wars, and the type of war is often affected by the type of societies fighting it. At the same time, as it is fought, war will often bring great changes to a society, particularly when we reach the century of total war, the twentieth century. A war that is all consuming is inevitably going to affect everything in a society.

The second reason I want to look at war in the open society is an uncomfortable paradox: Wars bring enormous destruction, horror, and death, something we should all want to avoid at all costs; but it can also bring progress and peace. Historians and anthropologists have long argued about the utility of war and the effect of war on human organization. There is an argument I myself find persuasive, namely, that war has often produced larger political units, though not in a pleasant way. The Roman Empire was not produced because the Romans were being nice; it came into existence because the Romans were better and tougher and nastier than anyone else they fought against. But what their wars resulted in was a very large Roman Empire, where a great many people lived peacefully, enjoying prosperity and the security of their property and lives. Thus, sometimes war has the unintended effect of producing larger political groupings that aid human progress.

The second thing war can do is affect society in beneficial ways. At the end of great struggles, governments will often be required to reward or to somehow compensate people for what they have been through, particularly in the twentieth century. There are many types of war, and there is a very long history of war, but the trends in the late nineteenth and the entire twentieth century have been towards total war. What total war means is that the entire effort of what are increasingly complex and prosperous societies is bent towards the war itself. You have to think of this in the context of the changes that were occurring in the world, starting in nineteenth-century Europe: massive industrialization and urbanization, when more and more people chose to live in cities and make their livings in ways that were unforeseen a hundred years before. Whereas at the beginning of the nineteenth century, nine out of ten Europeans lived off agriculture in some form or other, by the end of the century, nine out of ten Europeans lived in cities and worked in factories, offices, or shops. They worked, in other words, in ways that would not have been possible at the beginning of the century. Such changes made it possible to sustain war for longer and on a much larger scale.

## The Domestic Effects of War

In many ways, Europe had a very good century. In 1900, Europeans could look back at what they considered was almost unbroken progress. There had been the occasional revolution and the occasional war, but those wars tended to be short and decisive; they tended to settle something. As Europeans looked back at what they felt was a century of progress, prosperity, and peace, they credited themselves for this, rather than their good luck at simply being alive at a time when social changes were taking place. And Europeans talked confidently of how their institutions, their values, and their civilization were better than other kinds of institutions, values, and civilizations. They believed in progress, they saw their societies change and new forms of government take root with the spread of the law and the growth and power of representative institutions. They admired this progress, and they had faith it was going to continue. If you asked most people in 1914, "Do you think it is all going to come to an end?" they would have answered, "No." They would have said that there are wars in other places; we do not do that here anymore.

The Carnegie Institute commissioned a report on two wars that occurred in the Balkans in 1912 and 1913, and it said that atrocities had been committed in these wars. Civilians had been targeted, but this would not happen elsewhere in civilized Europe. The report came out in August 1914, as Europe was going into World War I and indeed such atrocities were about to happen. Even before World War I, when there was faith in progress, there were other strands in Europe that threatened its stability both domestically and internationally. There were illiberal forces in European society, as much as there were liberal forces. I tend to think of Europe before 1914 as a continent in play: it had a number of pathways before it, and war was going to close off some of them. On the other side of the balance—as opposed to the institutions and values contributing towards a more open society—you had the growth of chauvinism, a growth of the fear of the Other, resistance to the impact of globalization; not unlike what we are seeing in our world today. It was a fear of things moving too fast. There was a disease that most of you will probably never have heard of, called *Neurasthenia*. The idea was that modern life was so fast that your nerves got jumbled, and this was very bad for you. When the Paris Metro opened in 1900 during the World Fair, French newspapers warned about how travelling too fast was going to leave your nerves irremediably broken.

So, there were other, less liberal tendencies running through European societies, but those seemed to be temporary. However, if you look back, you can see them more clearly than people could see them at the time. This was a period of intense nationalist feelings. Many people at great European universities were writing about other nations, such as a German professor who said that the problem with the French was that they have always been deeply immoral and very frivolous. There was one passage I read with pleasure, which claimed that the French were depraved, and advised its readers exactly where to go in Paris if they wanted to see this in action for themselves. There were also French professors saying equally silly things, such as, that the trouble with the Germans, particularly the Prussians from the North, was that they had no moral sense, because they lived in a very flat landscape and so they did not see hills and they did not see valleys. There was a strong irrational, foolish element to such writings that motivated people to despise and fear their neighbors. When educated people say such things, there is a tendency to believe them.

There was a sense of progress in Europe, but there was also this other, more illiberal side. There were those, often in positions of authority, who thought that things had gone too far, that unions and left-wing parties had too much power or that the press was too free. When World War I broke out, the German Chancellor had to fight to prevent the Kaiser, his advisers, and the German military from abolishing all the unions, suspending all freedom of speech, and dissolving the Reichstag, because he said this would be counterproductive. Thus, there were illiberal tendencies as much as there were liberal ones. Nevertheless, you could see a real movement of progress in Europe, and real hope. If you asked people in 1914 how society was going to change, the answer would be that freedom and prosperity were going to increase, rather than diminish. There were also very significant changes in international law, for example, and Europeans looked at this with a certain amount of pride. There had been occasions in the European press of sustained thinking about how the international order should function.

Sadly, sometimes it takes a great catastrophe to make us think seriously about what sort of world we would like and how to make it better. After the

Thirty Years' War, in the seventeenth century, Europeans came to the conclusion that they needed a different type of international order. So, they came to a series of agreements, known as the Westphalian Peace, in which they agreed to respect the sovereignty of each other's states. This actually made a difference: it helped to bring an end to a series of ghastly and destructive wars in Europe. After the Napoleonic Wars, a similar thing happened: the recognition that international relations was not a zero sum game, as it had been seen in the eighteenth century, and that, in fact, most European nations had something to gain from living in a stable international society in which they could deal with problems collectively. After 1815, the Concert of Europe emerged, a conservative force in many ways, which brought order and stability to Europe, at least during the first half of the century. And then, of course, after the two world wars, we began to think again about an open international order that could move all societies along towards a fairer and more just future.

Even before World War I, there was a great deal of thinking in Europe about how to change international relations. There was great interest in new institutions and new ways of thinking. The same things happened after World War I and World War II. So, if we look back throughout history, we see that it does not move in a straight line. We see a movement towards a more open society, both domestically and internationally, but we can also see the very real challenges it faced. As I said before, war has a paradoxical effect. As it becomes more total, it becomes important for governments to explain to their own people what it is they are doing and what they are fighting for. One of the things they found is that people want to hear that they will have a better society when the war is over, a more equal, more tolerant, more open society, where people will be looked after better. In a number of European countries after World War I, women got to vote. It was not granted all that willingly, but there was a feeling that could not be denied, based on the evidence that women had played a very important role in the war. Before the war, one argument for women not to have the vote was that they spent most of their time in the household. They did not understand the great issues; they would simply get confused if they were asked to vote. In any case, they would simply vote the way their husbands or their fathers told them to. So why increase the number of voters if nothing would change in the way votes were allocated? This argument simply fell to the ground during World War I because women did things like driving tractors, running offices, working in factories, and managing things that until then they had not been thought capable of. At the end of the war, most European countries moved to give women the vote, sometimes piecemeal, as they did in Britain. In 1918–1919, only women of age thirty or older got to vote, because they were thought to be more mature and sensible, but by 1928 all British women had the vote at the same age as men, 21, and this made a difference. What also happened after World War I was that greater social benefits were brought in, again with the recognition that ordinary soldiers and their families had contributed and suffered enormously in the prosecution of the war.

Importantly, too, governments had to articulate what they were fighting for. Quite often, it was portrayed in defensive terms, i.e., we are fighting against the menace from our neighbors or others. The German military and the German political leadership portrayed Russia's attack in World War I as Slavic hordes overrunning Germany; in other words, as a civilizational struggle. The French did much the same thing with the Germans, and the British with the Germans. But the war effort needed more than that. What governments increasingly did was to portray a better future, the struggle for a better world. The Allies in particular—with the exception of Russia, but certainly Britain, France, the United States, the British Commonwealth, and smaller powers such as Belgium and Portugal—talked of a better society and of fighting for greater democracy and freedom. This was a very important part of their war propaganda, and they found themselves actually having to account for this after the war, although not necessarily during it. What usually happens during a war is that there is a push towards more centralized control over society, as governments have to allocate resources. That push often involves managing societal opinion. In World War I, governments used press censorship and propaganda, but they began to realize that if they were going to talk about fighting for democracy, they had to show it at home. A very important shift in this regard is the way that the British began treating conscientious objectors, people who refused to be conscripted on the grounds of opposing the war. This often included Quakers, people of religious conviction, but sometimes also people who simply thought that war was wrong. The initial response of the British authorities was to treat these people badly, to beat them up and put them in prison camps or on the front lines, hoping they would be killed. It is not an edifying story, but gradually, as the war went on, it became evident to the British that this was undercutting the very argument they were making about fighting for greater freedom and democracy. By the end of the war, they had recognized the status of conscientious objectors. It was to be recognized as well in the much darker days of World War II, when Britain came a lot closer to defeat than in World War I.

Democracies became better at articulating what they were fighting for—and again I am going to use the British example, this time from World War II. The BBC fought the government and said in effect: "We are not going to tell lies, we are going to tell the truth: we will talk about it when we are defeated; we will be as straightforward as we can; we will not betray British military secrets but we must be honest as much as possible." The result was that all over Europe, people listened to the BBC—when they dared—because they trusted it, and because, unlike the Vichy radio or the Nazi Germany radio, it was telling the truth. I think this was a very important signal the British were sending out. In their propaganda, particularly in World War II, they stressed that they had not wanted this war. There is a wonderful movie, *Britain at Bay*, which shows the British countryside, where people say: We have lived here, we did not want to fight anyone, but we are fighting now to defend what we see as an impregnable citadel of free people. Often, wars force people to artic-ulate what it is they consider important and what values they hold dear.

Wars also have added to the sense of social cohesion. Émile Durkheim wrote a famous article years ago (which has since been challenged), arguing that suicides happen during wars, particularly during the type of war where everyone is being drawn into the war effort.[2] People who otherwise would not feel part of their societies suddenly play a role, and they feel needed. It has also been argued, with evidence provided by Walter Scheidel and Thomas Piketty, that wars can bring about greater equality, and that they narrow the gap between rich and poor, partly because the rich have to be taxed to pay for the war, and partly because governments need the poor as contrib-uting members of society and therefore have to look after them. Statistically, inequality went down markedly during and after the two world wars.

The wars of the twentieth century have also discredited authoritarian and totalitarian regimes, because in the end they lost, and they lost badly. During World War I, Germany moved toward become a military dictator-ship, which was not very efficient and not very good at mobilizing Ger-many's resources. Britain, a democracy, was much better at mobilizing the resources it needed in both world wars. If you look at the Nazi war effort, it was perhaps efficient in the opening stages of the war, but in terms of mobi-

---

[2] Emile Durkheim, *Suicide: A Study in Sociology* (The Free Press, 1897).

lizing resources for society and equality for its members, it was terrible. Germany really showed the effects of an inefficient totalitarian regime. The same is true for the Japanese militarists. The danger in any authoritarian or totalitarian society is that those running the society live in echo chambers. They only hear what they want to hear, i.e. the praise from those below them. If you were a German general, you would not go to Hitler's bunker and say, "Dear Führer, I think you are making a total mistake in staying at Stalingrad, you must back off." In democracies, in more open societies, people can speak truthfully to their leaders, even in war, and I think this is a great strength of democracies.

## The International Effects of War

War has made a difference domestically, but it has also had a significant impact on international relations. In a number of democratic societies, there has been increased acceptance of the idea that foreign policy is about protecting the interests of your own nation, but also about something more. Let me give you an example from a speech that the Canadian Minister of External affairs, Louis St. Laurent, gave in 1947, when he said that Canada's foreign policy must promote Canadian unity and its beliefs and values, but also political liberty and the rule of law. Since these were the early days of the Cold War, he was explicit about where he saw danger: "A threat to the liberty of Western Europe, where our political ideas were nurtured, was a threat to our way of life." That meant that Canada had to be prepared to assume external responsibilities.

You could argue that these were simply self-serving words, but I think it has become increasingly understood that foreign policy should be about more than only furthering the material interests of your country. Before World War I, there was an increased recognition that international society and shared values and norms were important. It went, step by step, along with war, because war had become much deadlier. Europe's very successes in industrialization, production, and technology, its advances in the sciences and in organization, made Europe and Europeans better at killing each other. It was now possible to kill people on an industrial scale. At the beginning of the nineteenth century, the average weapon that a soldier had was accurate at about fifty meters. By 1900, the average weapon that a soldier had was often accurate at 500 meters. It was also possible to fire more rapidly because of machine guns, and artillery was much stronger. Napoleon's army was still using heavy cannons, made of bronze or iron; by the end of the nineteenth century they were using steel cannons that could be moved into the battle-field by trucks and trains. It is not that wars have ever been about *not* causing death, but the capacity to inflict massive death has become much greater. In World War I, thirty thousand men could be killed in a single action on a single day; over nine million died in total. These numbers are so large that it is difficult for us to comprehend them.

There is evidence that this was also happening before World War I. The American Civil War saw killing on an industrial scale. The Franco-Prussian War of 1870–1871, the Russo-Japanese war of 1901–1905, and the Balkan wars also saw casualties that numbered thousands. This helped stir and promote the arguments that many were making in favor of a greater and more open international order. Citizens' groups, but also governments, began to think of ways in which disputes could be dealt with and armed conflict be averted. There was, for example, a great deal of interest in arbitration. If two countries were having a dispute over territory or an event, they could submit it to an arbiter and agree to be bound by the result. There were around 300 arbitrations held between 1794 and 1914, and well over half of those were held after 1890. You can really see a trend here, namely, that people were prepared to think of imaginative ways in which societies could work inter-nationally as well as domestically. More international organizations were founded. The International Red Cross (IRC) was founded in 1866, after the war between Prussia and Austria-Hungary, when a young Swiss doctor was appalled by the fate of those left behind on the battlefield. Many of these international organizations were created based on the belief that with the spread of democracy, they would be able to help spread peace, through the gradual emergence of international norms, international values, and other ways of thinking about how to avert war.

By 1914, there was a powerful peace movement in Europe. An interna-tional Peace Bureau was set up, which organized peace crusades, parades and, of course, a famous peace prize. The Nobel Prize was created shortly after the turn of the century by a very successful manufacturer, Alfred Nobel, who carried a certain amount of guilt about the increasingly powerful forms of explosives he had unleashed in the world. People could see the beginnings of a new world order and a new way of thinking about the world. Tied in with this was the increasingly influential belief that the more nations were trading with each other, the less likely they were to fight. The more open the international economy, the more open it was to trade and to the movement of investments and people, and the less likely nations would be to fight each other. This seemed to make sense before 1914, which was a great age of globalization, as great as the age in which we are living in now.

Then World War I came, and suddenly these hopes looked foolish. An International Peace conference was scheduled for August 1914, and some of the delegates had already arrived. The organizers decided to postpone the conference to 1915, when they expected the war to be over. Of course, the war was not over in 1915, and its length and the damage it did shook European self-confidence to its core. Europe, the most civilized part of the world, had descended into barbarism for four long years, it had destroyed many of its own people, it had wasted its own resources, and at the end it saw its political, social, and economic structures crumbling. Russia went into revolution and parts of the old Russian Empire collapsed. Austria-Hungary, too, collapsed in the aftermath of World War I, and the Ottoman Empire shortly thereafter. There was concern that revolution, i.e. the Bolshevik type from Russia, was going to spread through Europe. Quarreling ethnic nationalisms continued to fight and there were a number of smaller wars after 1918. As Winston Churchill said, "The wars of the giants have ended. The wars of the pygmies have started."

In this atmosphere of disillusionment, fear, and worry, the world's powers came together in Paris and talked about how to build a new international order. Their leaders came to believe that they had to do something; the evidence of what would happen if this international order was not created was all around them. They feared that Europe would never recover fully from the war, and that another, equally destructive war might follow. They were both apprehensive and hopeful. The man whose ideas have been identified most with the emergence of a new and open international order is the American president Woodrow Wilson. There is a myth, promoted by Wilson's supporters, that Wilson arrived with noble ideals and Europeans greeted him with derision and scorn. This is not the case. Europeans had been talking about these ideas—open democracy, open trade, disarmament, a better world for everyone—for a long time during the nineteenth century. The very shape of the League of Nations that Wilson promoted as the institution to help build a better world was derived from British and European thinking; its very structure was based on a Committee Report that had been issued by the British Government during World War I and elaborated by Jan Smuts, the great South African general who was in the British War Cabinet. There was a feeling on both sides of the Atlantic and around the world, in countries such as Japan and China, that this was the moment to create a different sort of international order, and that the main fundament of that order was going to be the League of Nations. Wilson envisioned it as something like the British Parliament, not in legalistic terms, but as something that would grow organically and work out its own procedures and goals and become a place where nations would meet and learn to agree.

This, as we know, did not happen. But I think what is important about the League of Nations is that it introduced new methods and ideas to international relations. At the time, there was tremendous public support for the League. People formed societies to support it. In Britain, for example, a League of Nations Union had 400 thousand members in the late 1920s. Between 1934 and 1935, it ran a Peace Ballot, and half a million volunteers went out to encourage people to vote. 38 per cent of the total population of Britain voted. They were given very simple questions. I will just mention two: Should Great Britain remain a member of the League of Nations? Yes: 11 million, No: 350 thousand. Are you in favor of an all-round reduction of armaments by international agreement? Yes: 10.5 million, No: 800 thousand. It appears there really was a deep desire in many countries for a different world order.

Other new bodies were organized, too, such as the World Health Organization and the International Labor Organization, which the League of Nations incorporated. Those laid the groundwork for many of the institutions we have today. New think tanks were created in the aftermath of the Paris Peace Conference, such as the Council on Foreign Relations in the United States, the Royal Institute of international Affairs in Britain, and the Canadian Council on Foreign Affairs. Universities around the world established chairs and institutes of international relations and foreign relations. There was a real willingness on the part of the world and the public to contemplate a type of international order that would be open and that they could support. The new order would help to create peace, not just for its own sake, but so that the world could progress in harmony and the many issues and problems facing it could be dealt with. A very important part of the League's work— something that has not often been recognized sufficiently—was to deal with things like the opium trade, slavery, international health, or the exploitation of labor around the world. Behind this was the desire for a better form of society that would bring more benefits, not just to the people at the top, but to everyone.

War came again in 1939, and it looked like the League of Nations had failed. But this did not end the hope for a better world. If you look back at World War II, perhaps one of the key lessons is that aggression does not pay. Germany and Japan, which started the war, were occupied, and their societies were profoundly transformed as a result. The victorious Allies believed it to be more important than ever that nations work together for the benefit of humanity. Allied leaders, with the exception of Joseph Stalin, agreed that war would only be worthwhile if afterwards the world was a better place. (Stalin paid lip service to the idea of a better world but of course did not understand it.) Again, the spokesperson for a new order was an American president, Franklin Delano Roosevelt. In his State of the Union Address to Congress in 1941 (often called the Four Freedoms Speech), even before the United States entered the war, he said:

> In the future days, which we seek to make secure, we look forward to a world founded upon four essential human freedoms. The first is freedom of speech and expression—everywhere in the world. The second is freedom of every person to worship God in his own way—everywhere in the world. The third is freedom from want—[...] everywhere in the world. The fourth is freedom from fear—[...] anywhere in the world. That is no vision of a distant millennium. It is a definite basis for a kind of world attainable in our own time and generation. That kind of world is the very antithesis of the so called new order of tyranny which the dictators seek to create [...].[3]

Roosevelt reiterated this in the Atlantic Charter of 1941, which in many ways is much like Woodrow Wilson's Fourteen Points, talking of a new international order and making the world safe for democracy and independent nations. Roosevelt, Churchill, and Maxim Litvinov, on behalf of the Soviet Union, signed the Declaration by United Nations, which said: "Being convinced that complete victory over their enemies is essential to defend life, liberty, independence, and religious freedom, and to preserve human rights and justice in their own lands as well as in other lands [...]."[4] In the war years, there was a strong feeling, especially in democracies, that they were going to

---

[3] Franklin D. Roosevelt, "The 'Four Freedoms,' Franklin D. Roosevelt's Address to Congress," *Congressional Record* 87, no. I (1941).

[4] United Nations, "Declaration by United Nations," 1942.

build a better world and to improve their own societies, but what they really wanted to build was a better and more open world order.

We have been trying to do this since 1945, with many new institutions. None of these are perfect, and the values that underpin them are not universally accepted, but they are there and they have become part of what we expect in our discourse; we have accepted the fact that these institutions exist. When the United Nations was founded at the San Francisco Conference in 1945, its Charter stated its purpose as: "To maintain international peace and security, [...] To develop friendly relations among nations based on respect for the principle of equal rights and self-determination of peoples [...] To achieve international cooperation in solving international problems [...]."[5]

This, I think, reflects a genuine wish. If the United Nations has not lived up to all the hopes that were placed in it, it is because international politics, in particular the Cold War, made it difficult. But we must look at what advances have been made. It has now become possible to talk of a better world; we now have institutions that, imperfect as they are, appear as though they can do something to achieve that; and we have new international norms, including the outlawing of genocide, which became a crime in the aftermath of World War II, as well as the Right to Protect.

If we made a score sheet of building better societies and a better and more open international order since 1945, what would it look like? Of course, the results are mixed; this is true for all human history. For a long time during the Cold War, there were societies in which values were espoused that were the very antithesis of an open society. But those ideals remained. Even in societies behind the Iron Curtain, there was a longing and willingness for a different kind of society, and sometimes people dared to express it. In the end, as we know, the Communist regimes failed in part because their record on human rights was so dismal. Perhaps internationally we have also seen some successes. We have not had a major conflict between nations since 1945, although of course this may have as much to do with nuclear weapons as it has to do with new international institutions and norms. But it seems to me, even when nations have intervened in other nations, that they have tended to explain what they are doing in terms of maintaining peace, punishing aggression, and supporting legitimate governments. This may be hypocritical, but there is something at least in the recognition of these values.

---

[5] United Nations, "Charter of the United Nations" (1945), Article 1.

# Conclusions

Where do we stand today? I would like to conclude with a few thoughts on this question. There have always been threats to democratic values, both internally and from outside. George Kennan, the American who first came up with the idea of containment, warned about the damage the long struggle to contain the Soviet Union and its allies might do to the United States. He said there was a danger that American society would take on some of the features of its enemy, becoming less liberal and less willing to tolerate dissent. This has always been a danger, and I think we saw it again in 2001. When the Twin Towers were attacked, the reaction in many parts of Congress and the United States was, "We need more powers of government, more censorship, more repression to deal with the war on terror," and I think this has been a dangerous result. Today, we see the same kind of fears about Islamic terrorism in the United States and in many other countries, including in Europe, as well as the willingness of people to give up certain freedoms in order to combat what they consider a deadly and difficult enemy. I find the idea of the war on terror improbable, and it should probably never have been conceived like that.

The open society is also under threat from other forces. Our world is in some respects similar to 1914; we, too, are seeing a backlash of globalization, a fear of the impact of the movement of capital, trade, and people around the world, and the rise of illiberal populist movements on both the right and the left. The results of the elections in many democracies, for example the Italian election of March 2018, are disconcerting. We still have an international order, which has managed to struggle along since 1945, but I worry that an international order can only take in so many countries that refuse to buy into it, and it seems to me that Russia under President Putin is now beginning to ignore the norms of that international order. Will Putin encourage others to behave in similar ways, and will this finally destroy what remains of the international order? We still have people who think that the use of force can be a positive thing, something they can use to achieve their ends and settle their disputes. This is very dangerous indeed, because if the weapons of World War II were terrible, the weapons of the present day are much worse.

Finally, it is dangerous that we tend to forget. The people who made the new institutions and talked about new ways of doing things had seen for themselves during the two world wars what they wanted to avoid. With the passage of time, we forgot why we wanted the European Union in the first place, or the United Nations, which we increasingly see as that silly organization by the East River. I think this is very dangerous, because the impetus behind such organizations, and the impetus behind trying to build a better society, is very important. If we forget it, we will find that we have let the door open to things that in the end will damage us.

# Open Societies at Home and Abroad

*Stephen M. Walt*

## Introduction: Liberalism Gone Wrong

I am known as a "realist" in academic circles, and realists are often accused of being hostile to, or at least skeptical of, the ideals of liberalism. Yet I am going to approach those notions from a sympathetic perspective in this essay, and try to separate out the positive elements of the liberal vision from some of its unintended negative consequences. To do that, I will start by comparing the liberal optimism of the 1990s with the more worrisome developments we observe today. I will then define liberalism's core principles and explain why it is such an attractive model for organizing a society. Then I will consider how that model has gone wrong in recent years, focusing primarily—but not entirely—on the consequences of trying to spread this model abroad. I will close with a few suggestions on how we ought to proceed in the future.

The 1990s were the high point of liberal optimism. The collapse of communism in the USSR and the velvet revolutions in Eastern Europe convinced lots of smart people that liberal democratic orders were the only viable model for a modern society, especially in an era of globalization. In his book *The End of History and the Last Man*, political scientist Francis Fukuyama famously argued that the grand ideological struggles of the past were now behind us, liberal democracy had won, and humankind had reached the "end of history." There would be little need for generals, heroes, or visionary leaders, and all that was left to us was mere "economic activity."[1] Not to be outdone, Thomas Friedman of *The New York Times* spent the 1990s arguing that globalization was forcing all countries to don the "golden straightjacket" and embrace the liberal model: democracy, market economics, the rule of law, and active participation in global institutions. All of this, he said, would lead to unprecedented prosperity.[2]

In Europe, the European Union was expanding and deepening and creating a common currency. Some observers even saw it as an alternative to the American model, one based on civilian power and law rather than military dominance. In the United States, the Clinton administration committed itself to "enlarging the sphere of democratic rule," and this broad objective did not change significantly under Presidents George W. Bush and Barack Obama. U.S. leaders and policy experts thought the tides of history were running their way and that liberal principles would be easy to spread (peacefully if possible but if necessary by force). A few pesky dictators might hold out for a while, but eventually all the other major powers, including Russia and China, would embrace the liberal model. Or so these liberal leaders thought.

Liberals also believed it was time for global institutions to play a bigger role, especially in defending human rights. This impulse produced well-intentioned proposals like the *Responsibility to Protect* doctrine, which suggested that the international community had a responsibility to protect foreign populations whose own governments were unwilling or unable to do so themselves.[3] In the 1990s, in short, many thoughtful people believed an expanding liberal world order would produce an unprecedented era of peace, progress, and prosperity, under the benevolent leadership of the United States.

What has happened since then? Russia has reverted back toward autocracy, and NATO's eastward expansion has poisoned relations with Moscow and helped trigger the crisis in Ukraine. Efforts to build workable democracies in Iraq and Afghanistan failed and the "Arab Spring" quickly turned into an "Arab Winter." The EU has been in a prolonged economic and political crisis since 2008, culminating in Britain's decision to leave the Union in 2016.

---

[1] See Francis Fukuyama, *The End of History and the Last Man* (New York: Free Press, 1992).

[2] See Thomas Friedman, *The Lexus and the Olive Tree: Understanding Globalization* (New York: Farrar, Straus & Giroux, 1999).

[3] See "About R2P," Global Centre for the Responsibility to Protect (2018), http://www.globalr2p.org/about_r2p.

Turkey, Israel, Poland, and Hungary have all moved in illiberal directions in recent years, and according to democracy expert Larry Diamond of Stanford University, "between 2000 and 2015, democracy broke down in 27 countries, while existing authoritarian regimes became less open, transparent, and responsive to their citizens."[4] More recent assessments from Freedom House and *The Economist* magazine's Democracy Index are equally gloomy. My own country has seen the election of Donald Trump, a man whose commitment to liberal principles is paper-thin and whose actions may yet trigger a constitutional crisis. Globalization may have helped lift a billion people out of abject poverty, but it has also had disruptive economic and social effects in many countries. Meanwhile, China's market-oriented one-party state has proven to be surprisingly resilient, and Beijing shows no signs of converging toward more liberal political forms. The past 25 years, in short, have not been kind to the liberal project. I may be a realist, but I take no pleasure in this development. Why? Because the liberal vision has much to commend it.

## Liberalism's Origins and Virtues

Liberalism was a revolutionary development in political philosophy, and we often forget how original it was when it first emerged. Liberalism arose in response to the prevailing political forms in seventeenth-century Europe, during a period of recurring religious and civil wars. Those conflicts raised fundamental questions about the relationship between religion and government, and about the legitimacy of absolutist or authoritarian rule, and liberalism's creators sought a new foundation on which to establish a just and effective political order.

Liberalism begins with the claim that all humans have certain natural rights, rights that should not be infringed. It stresses the role of human reason, which liberals see as the main engine of human progress. In particular, liberals believe that political arrangements can be created and refined by reasoned debate, which means politics can become more and more effective, equitable, and progressive over time. Because all humans have rights, liberals believe men and women should be free to pursue their individual

---

[4] Larry Diamond, "Democracy in Decline," *Foreign Affairs*, June 13, 2016, https://www.foreignaffairs.com/articles/world/2016-06-13/democracy-decline.

desires, provided that their actions do not harm others. Accordingly, liberals emphasize the need for tolerance and strive to keep personal choices, such as religious belief, outside the sphere of political contestation. Finally, liberalism maintains that the legitimacy of any government depends on the consent of the governed. In practice, this principle requires not just the holding of elections (or some other means of expressing or withholding consent), but also rests on free speech and a legal order that is administered in a politically neutral fashion. For liberals, leaders can only be held truly accountable when citizens have access to accurate information and are able to express their views openly.

These ideas are undeniably appealing. The liberal vision says individual humans have rights that should be protected. It says leaders should not have unchecked power, and insists that torture, the slaughter of innocents, slavery, unlawful detention, and other abuses are morally wrong and should not be tolerated under any circumstances. This vision also implies that the world would be better off if law and moral norms helped regulate the conduct of war and other relations between countries. At first glance, this is a much more appealing vision than the realist view of politics, which emphasizes conflicts of interest and recurring rivalries and maintains that law and norms have only limited effects on what states actually do.

Not only is the liberal vision intrinsically attractive, societies based on its principles have a pretty good track record at home. On average, the economic performance of liberal states is much better than most authoritarian states.[5] Liberal societies are less likely to commit mass killings or other human rights violations, and when liberal states make mistakes, as all countries do, they are usually quicker to figure it out and take corrective action. Liberal states have longer life expectancies, higher rates of education, and they do not engage in intense fratricidal quarrels or ideological schisms with each other. After all, it would be inconsistent for one open society to tell another open society how to run its own internal affairs. The Soviet Union and communist China nearly went to war over the proper way to interpret Marx and Lenin, but liberal states do not threaten each other over the right way to interpret Locke or Madison or Montesquieu.

---

[5] See Morton Halperin, *The Democracy Advantage: How Democracies Promote Prosperity and Peace* (New York: Routledge, 2004).

Most importantly, liberalism prizes the free flow of information, of ideas, of culture, and of commerce. Open societies do not just tolerate differences within their own borders; they tend to be more open to the world. Over the past 250 years, in fact, no country has ever improved its position by shutting itself off from others, stifling the free expression of ideas, and censoring its academic, scientific, and intellectual communities. The Soviet Union did modernize under a Leninist dictatorship, but the price its citizens paid was enormous and it would have done far better with a more open economy and society. China under Mao Zedong suffered man-made famine and repeated internal convulsions, and had a pro-capita income of less than 300 dollars when he died. China is not a liberal society today, but it is much more open to outside influences and much more successful than it was under Mao. It is also worth noting that some of the more obvious authoritarian success stories, such as Singapore or South Korea, have either relaxed their once rigid orders or become fully democratic in recent years.

As a blueprint for running a country, in short, the liberal vision has a lot going for it. Or, as Churchill famously said, democracy is the "worst form of government except all the others." But if that is true, then how do we explain the setbacks of the past 25 years and especially the last two?

## Liberalism's Five Blunders

Liberalism's present difficulties can be traced to five distinct but related errors. The first error was the familiar sin of hubris, and it manifested itself in several ways. In Europe, the most obvious mistake was the creation of the Euro, an ill-considered political act undertaken despite economists' warnings that the EU lacked the political institutions (such as a common fiscal policy) necessary to make it work. European leaders and publics also failed to realize that continued EU expansion would make it too heterogeneous to function well and inhibit prompt and effective decisions, which began to undermine the legitimacy of the entire project.

In the United States, hubris took the form of an aggressive effort to re-make the world in America's image through a strategy of "liberal hegemony." It was *liberal* because it sought to spread democracy and other liberal principles; it was *hegemonic* because it saw the United States as the "indispensable nation" that had the right, responsibility, and wisdom to lead an ever-expanding liberal order. As John Mearsheimer explains in *The Great Delu-*

*sion*, powerful liberal states have a tendency to become crusaders, seeking to export their principles wherever and whenever they can.[6] That tendency flows directly from liberalism's universalist premises: if all human beings have the same basic rights, then logically those rights apply everywhere there are humans, and powerful liberal states should do what they can to see that no humans are denied them. It is that impulse that led to the expansion of NATO, the invasion of Iraq, U.S. support for regime change elsewhere in the Middle East, and the endless war in Afghanistan, and it has contributed to the tragic conflict in Syria and thus the refugee crisis that engulfed Europe and boosted the fortunes of rightwing, xenophobic nationalists.

With the benefit of hindsight, U.S. efforts to spread democracy were an error of vast proportions. For starters, trying to spread liberalism abroad requires regime change, and threatening non-liberal states with regime change encourages them to do whatever they can to prevent it. Fear of Western-sponsored regime change goes a long way toward explaining Russia's policy in Georgia, Ukraine, and Syria, and also explains why countries like Iran and North Korea are interested in acquiring nuclear weapons. Moreover, it is now clear that liberal states do not know how to create new liberal orders once they have ousted the old regime. Their inability to do so is not surprising: it took liberalism several centuries to achieve firm roots in the West, and its eventual triumph was the result of a bloody and contentious process. For Americans to assume they could instantly create stable liberal orders in places that had never been democratic before was frankly delusional, yet this belief commanded a powerful consensus among America's foreign policy elite.[7] Unfortunately, instead of producing flourishing open societies, the latest liberal crusade created failed states, costly occupations, and a heightened risk of global terrorism. Even worse, fear of the latter eventually led the United States and other liberal states to respond with targeted killings, drone strikes, and intrusive government surveillance, actions largely inconsistent with liberal values. Ironically, trying to spread liberalism abroad ended up endangering it at home.

---

[6] John J. Mearsheimer, *The Great Delusion: Liberal Dreams and International Realities* (New Haven: Yale University Press, 2018).

[7] On this point, see Stephen M. Walt, *The Hell of Good Intentions: America's Foreign Policy Elite and the Decline of U.S. Primacy* (New York: Farrar, Straus & Giroux, 2018).

The second major error was assuming that economic globalization will be uniformly beneficial and would not produce a powerful political backlash. Globalization had many positive effects: it made goods cheaper and helped lift perhaps a billion people out of the direst poverty. But Wall Street did better than Main Street did, economic inequality rose dramatically, and people who lost their jobs as a result of increased foreign competition were hardly enthusiastic about globalization's broader benefits. Globalization also made the international financial system more fragile, as we learned when the collapse of the U.S. mortgage market in 2008 triggered a global recession.

The third error was a growing tendency for elites throughout the liberal order to insulate themselves from accountability. No matter how badly they led or corrupt they became, leaders and officials throughout the West seemed to get away scot-free while others suffered. In the United States, none of the bankers who created the 2008 financial crisis were ever prosecuted or even properly investigated. Similarly, the architects of the disastrous war in Iraq moved on to new positions or landed in safe sinecures and most of them never acknowledged their mistakes. In Europe, elites like Tony Blair, David Cameron, and François Fillon all seemed increasingly out of touch and unconnected from ordinary people and more interested in hobnobbing with the One Percent. The loudest defenders of the liberal order were doing just fine, but other members of their societies were not.

Fourth, the liberal order is in trouble because its proponents forgot about nationalism. Writing in 1999, for example, liberal scholars John Ikenberry and Daniel Deudney claimed that a broad transnational "civic identity" was emerging in the West and supplanting traditional national loyalties. In their words, "As civic and capitalist identities have strengthened, ethnic and national identity has declined, although it is still customary to speak of the West as being constituted by nation states, *the political identity of Westerns is no longer exclusively centered on nationalism.*"[8]

Transcending nationalism was one of the long-term goals of European integration, but the events of the past decade have shown that it was premature at best. In every corner of the world, in fact, nationalism and other forms of local identity are proven to be remarkably durable. We see this stubborn

---

[8] Daniel Deudney and John Ikenberry, "Realism, Structural Liberalism, and the Western Order," in *Unipolar Politics: Realism and State Strategies after the Cold War*, ed. Ethan B. Kapstein and Michael Mastanduno (New York: Columbia University Press, 1999), emphasis added.

force in the Brexit vote, the broad hostility to immigrants, the Catalans' continued striving for independence, and the often fierce resistance to foreign interference in Afghanistan or in the Middle East. Contrary to the cosmopolitan image of a borderless world, most people are still wary of those who are different—even in broadly liberal societies—and worried about changes that threaten familiar ways of life. Muslims in the Middle East are angry when they have to take orders from an occupying army and Europeans complain about obeying rules set by anonymous bureaucrats in Brussels. These reactions do not mean the liberal vision is wrong, but they remind us that nationalism is alive and well and cannot be ignored.

The final error was the assumption that history ran in only one direction. Liberals assumed that once a liberal order was firmly established, it would never break down. In particular, they assumed elected officials would never use the tools of the open society to subvert its core principles. We should have known better. In fact, political leaders in a liberal order can be just as venal and just as fond of power as any dictator. Liberal societies depend not just on formal constitutional rules, but also on the informal norms and restraints that Steven Levitsky and Daniel Ziblatt have called the "guardrails of democracy."[9] These norms have eroded dramatically in recent years, especially in the United States, as politicians take maximum advantage when they happen to be in power and refuse to cooperate or compromise when they are in the minority. Even in a liberal society, unscrupulous leaders can harass the press, exaggerate foreign dangers, keep secrets from the public, pander to the wealthy and powerful, prosecute dissidents, pressure universities, think-tanks, and other independent sources of expertise, suppress the vote, and rig the political system in their favor, thereby guaranteeing electoral successes and allowing them to claim (falsely) that they represent "the peoples' will." We have seen these tactics used in Turkey, in Israel, in Hungary, in Poland, in Russia, and even in the United States. When an American President under investigation fires the head of the agency doing the investigating, both the rule of law and the basic idea of accountability are in jeopardy.

As a result of these five errors, the forward-looking optimism of the 1990s has been replaced by today's dark politics of pessimism and nostalgia. Instead of pointing to a new and brighter future, political leaders today seek

---

[9] Steven Levitsky and Daniel Ziblatt, *How Democracies Die* (New York: Crown, 2018), esp. chapter 5.

to build support by heightening fears about the future and by invoking a rosy, mythical past. It is Donald Trump saying he will make America great *again*, by taking the country back to a bygone era. It is Brexit voters yearning for an England that is independent and sovereign and homogeneous and free to chart its own course. It is Poland's Law and Justice Party rewriting history to cater to Polish national pride, or Vladimir Putin invoking Russian history, the Orthodox Church, and the global status Moscow once enjoyed to sustain public support and keep himself and his cronies in power. And as one would expect, it is older and less-educated people who are most strongly attracted to these backward-looking visions. If one is searching for a bit of optimism in today's politics, consider that if people over 65 were not allowed to vote, there would have been no Brexit and no President Trump. Yet it is the younger generations who have the most to lose from all of these worrisome trends.

## Conclusion: What Is To Be Done?

With the liberal vision under siege, how should liberals (and sympathetic realists) respond?

First, we should resist any temptation to abandon or dilute the core principles of an open society. As I suggested, the liberal vision has many positive features and its underlying norms are both admirable and have many beneficial effects. Human beings do have rights. Leaders should be accountable and not have absolute power. Societies work better when ideas can be debated openly and when tolerance is promoted and protected. Education, knowledge, intelligence, and skeptical but honest inquiry all work better than passionate certainty and centralized control. To repeat a point made earlier: no society ever improved its situation by encouraging greater ignorance or insisting on blind obedience. For that reason alone, efforts to pressure and possibly destroy a wonderful institution like the Central European University are 'worse than a crime, they are a blunder.'

Yet those who seek to defend liberalism at home must be wary of overzealous efforts to spread it abroad. We have to be honest with ourselves: we simply do not know how to do this quickly, and even well-intentioned attempts often trigger hostile backlash. Changing a social and political order in fundamental ways inevitably creates both winners and losers, and the latter are often all too willing to take up arms to regain power and restore their fortunes. Foreign-imposed regime change also produces many unintended consequences, especially when it is done by outsiders with little understanding of the society they are trying to shape. With hindsight, the attempt to expand the liberal world order after 1989 was too much, too soon, and too fast, and we are now dealing with a backlash that might have been avoided had we proceeded with greater humility.

At the same time, we also need to reaffirm our own faith in the virtues of an open society. If we genuinely believe that open societies are best, then we should be more confident that this vision will ultimately triumph. If that is the case, then we can afford to be a bit more patient, and we do not have to try and create a liberal world order overnight. As I have said, liberal states have been the world's most successful over the past century or more, and if we believe their open character has been a key ingredient in that success, we can view the future with greater confidence.

Lastly, the best way to encourage the gradual and enduring spread of liberal values is to set a good example. If people around the world see how open societies live and like what they see, over time they will want something similar for themselves. Instead of being imposed from without, open societies will take root on their own, appropriately adapted to particular historical and cultural traditions.

In other words, the future of open societies is in our hands. It will not be determined by events in Afghanistan, in Moscow, in Syria, in the South China Sea, or in Eastern Ukraine. First and foremost, its fate will be determined by what politicians and citizens do in the countries that are liberal and open today. Paradoxically, defending and strengthening liberalism at home remains the best way to promote it abroad.

# Eurasia, Europe, and the Question of U.S. Leadership

*Robert D. Kaplan*

## Introduction: From Geopolitics to Shakespeare

What I would like to do in my contribution is to share what I have learned in thirty years as a foreign correspondent. The thing that I have learned the most is that it all starts with geography and geopolitics, but it ends with Shakespeare. By that I mean: you can talk as much as you want about geography, geopolitics, ports, landscapes, but at the end of the day so much of human history is driven by crucial decisions made by individuals in a fever of passion, with all kinds of pressures upon them. That is the Shakespearean element that we can never lose. Here, I emphasize the geographical and geopolitical half of that argument. If I had looked at the globe today, what I would say is that technology has not defeated geography, but it has shrunken geography. It has made the world more anxious, more claustrophobic, more interrelated than it ever has been before. Think of the taut string of a web work, you plug one part and the whole system vibrates. Crisis zones, like the South and East China Seas, the Baltic Sea Basin, and the Black Sea Basin are more and more interrelated in a way that they have never been before because of communications, transportation infrastructure, and the cyber world. Crises are migrating, in a way that they never did. That is why we have to be very careful, when we listen to defense advocates say things like, "A war in the South China Sea would be a short, sharp war that would be over in a few days." I am very skeptical of that because of the way that the system can vibrate and crises can migrate. I think that after Iraq, after Afghanistan, we should not talk flippantly about prognoses in terms of war.

I believe that Eurasia is coherent. That is not to say that Eurasia is understandable as a system to the degree that Europe still is. It only means that we can talk about Eurasia and use the word in a way we could not ten years ago. That is what I mean by the shrinkage of geography due to technology. Take India and China. For most of history, outside of the exceptions of Buddhism spreading from India to China in Middle Antiquity, or the Opium Wars in the nineteenth century, India and China were generally two separate great world civilizations that had relatively little to do with each other, separated as they were by the high wall of the Himalayas. Because of the way that military technology has defeated distance, we now have a whole Indian intercontinental ballistic missile system that can hit Chinese cities.[1] We have Chinese fighter jets in Tibet that can include the Indian subcontinent in their rocket operations.[2] We have Indian warships occasionally in the South China Sea,[3] and we have Chinese warships increasingly in the Indian Ocean and China building or helping develop ports, state of the art commercial and even military facilities surrounding India in the Indian Ocean.[4] Because of technology, we have had a whole new geography of rivalry developing, not of war, between India and China that never existed before.

Technology does not defeat geography, but geography is mutable. Take Croatia: Yugoslavia, when it existed, had the ability to centralize things in the interior so that Zagreb became important, Belgrade was important. But after the end of the Yugoslav war, in the previous decade and early in the present one, the Croatians built a series of massive superhighways, connecting Zagreb with all major points along the Adriatic Sea. What used to be a difficult six-hour journey is now done easily in ninety minutes and that has totally changed the Croatian character. It is an increasingly Mediterranean, cosmo-

---

[1] Kai Schultz and Hari Kumar, "India Tests Ballistic Missile, Posing a New Threat to China," *The New York Times*, January 19, 2018, https://www.nytimes.com/2018/01/18/world/asia/india-ballistic-missile-icbm.html.

[2] "China Operationalizes its Stealth Fight, Tested in Tibet," *The Times of India*, March 10, 2017, https://timesofindia.indiatimes.com/world/china/china-operationalises-its-stealth-fighter-tested-in-tibet/articleshow/57578934.cms.

[3] Franz Stefan Grady, "India Sends Stealth Warships to the South China Sea," *The Diplomat*, May 19, 2016, https://thediplomat.com/2016/05/india-sends-stealth-warships-to-south-china-sea/.

[4] James Kynge et al., "How China Rules the Waves," *Financial Times*, January 12, 2017, https:/ig.ft.com/sites/china-ports.

politan country in a way that it did not use to be. Geography itself is overcome because of these buildings, of these massive superhighways.

## "Breaking down Eurasia": The Middle East and U.S. Influence

When I talk about Eurasia, what I want to do is break it down like a watch. The world may have shrunk, and the watch may be small, but in order to understand how it works you have to take it apart and look at all the gears and mechanisms inside of it. In this sense, I want to explore what has been happening in the Middle East, Europe, and East Asia.

Why is all this violence, fighting, and state breakdown occurring in the Middle East? Why now? I would say that for the first time in living history, the Middle East is in a post-imperial phase. Remember that there was a book published in 2008, by Oxford historian John Darwin, called *After Tamerlane*.[5] What the book is about is that most of humanity, most of history took place during some imperial system or other. He said that it was not just the British and the French and the European Empires, it was the Indian Empires, the Chinese Empires, the Iranian Empires, the African Empires. And, he goes on to say that even the United States and the Soviet Union were empires in all but name during the Cold War in terms of their influence or the way they could project power.

The Middle East is, and I use the term advisedly, in a post-imperial phase. That means that the Ottoman-Turkish Empire is gone; that ended in 1918. While it existed, despite all of its problems, despite all of its weaknesses, despite all of the communal tensions, everyone, whether Sunni or Shi'ite, or Arab or Jew, owed sovereignty to the same Sultan. Divisions over territory were somewhat muted. That is gone. The British and French mandate systems, another aspect of imperialism, are gone too. That left in the late 1940s, in the years after World War II. We had what I call "post-imperial strongmen"—people like Gaddafi in Libya, a series of Iraqi dictators that culminated in Saddam Hussein, but included quite a few before him, and the Assad family in Syria. All these places were ruled under borders that were

---

[5] John Darwin, *After Tamerlane: The Rise and Fall of Global Empires, 1400–2000* (New York: Bloomsbury Press, 2008), 22–23, 469–70, 479, 491.

drawn up by European colonialists, that were often averse to ethnic and sectarian divisions and therefore secular identities had to be created. Because some of these places were quite artificial, they required a particularly suffocating form of authoritarianism to govern. These people were generally awful, but they governed and they ruled, and there was stability.

Then you have what I call "the questionability of the United States in the Middle East." It is a bit ironic. It was a liberal democratic country during the Cold War, but it was able to govern and exert incredible influence through dealing with dictators. And, it was able to do that because with dictators there was one phone number, one fax machine, the dictator himself, a few advisors—that was all you needed when there was a crisis. There is a crisis in Jordan, call King Hussein; there is a crisis in Egypt, call Sadat or Nasser. It both made it easy, and allowed for a very efficient form of power projection from Washington throughout the region. Much of that is gone now.

I divide the Middle East into two kinds of places. First, age-old clusters of civilization—that means places that have a deeply embedded state mentality, even without Arabism or Islam. If you travel around the northern third of Tunisia, most likely you will be driving on the road that was originally laid by the Byzantines or the Romans. Morocco has more Roman sites than almost the rest of North Africa combined. Egypt has the gift of the Nile Valley civilizations. When the Arab Spring happened, and there was turmoil in these countries, demonstrations, chaos, and misrule for a time, the state itself was never in question. There was an identity of the state that held, so that discussions were about what kind of political form the country should have, not whether there is a state in the first place. Then you have another group of countries I call "vague geographical expressions." Places like Libya, Syria, Iraq, and to a certain extent Yemen. Places whose borders did not as easily cohere with an old state mentality as in the case of Tunisia and Egypt. In those places, because the state was more artificial, dictatorship had to be much more suffocating and intense.

As a journalist, I always get angry when people divide the world between democracies and dictatorships because I experience so many grey shades in between. Going from Iraq under Saddam Hussein in the eighties even to Syria under Hafez al-Assad was like coming up for some liberal humanist air, because the Ba'athist dictatorship in Iraq was so much more intense than in Syria. Governments in Tunisia and Egypt were so much more moderate, even though they were technically dictatorships. And then you had Oman, another age-old cluster of Indian Ocean civilization, where you had an absolute dictatorship, governed according to liberal humanist principles, with clinics for women, environmental programs, debates, open society, all very informal. This is where the Middle East is now, where you have age-old clusters of civilization holding together with difficulty, and these vague geographical expressions, that are still at war.

The United States was a very uplifting dynamic democracy in the print and typewriter age. I am unconvinced that it will be the same in the digital and video era. The digital and video era has been with us, depending upon how you date it, since the 1970s or 1980s. But we only saw a big dramatic effect in the U.S. election of 2016. Without going into personalities, I am very skeptical not only about America's ability, but also its willingness and self-awareness to lead, which has a lot to do with the age of technology that we are going into.

A final word about Iran. I talked about all those artificial states in the Middle East. Iran is not artificial. Iranians have a civilizational sense of themselves that only the Indians and the Chinese and some others have. It is a real state, going back to antiquity. There have been Iranian states and empires on the Iranian Plateau going back twenty-five hundred years. Iran will always be there as a consequential power. I am not convinced that Saudi Arabia will always be there. Compared to Iran it is artificial; it is involved in a debilitating Vietnam-style conflict in Yemen. It has real problems with the new generation of leadership, which is divided among many grandchildren, as opposed to the unique, narrow pyramid in previous decades. It has thirty per cent male youth unemployment[6] and a diminishing underground water table.[7] Iran can have its political crises and regime crises, but the state, I would argue, is much firmer than in Saudi Arabia.

## "Breaking down Eurasia": Europe and the European Union

For Europe, I have several questions. Is the EU like the weakening Holy Roman Empire? Of course this is a very rough and imperfect analogy. In the sense of a shared space, I do not believe that the EU will collapse. I think it is too important for that to happen and I think it is too well integrated for that to happen. In places like Romania and elsewhere, the EU is not looked upon

---

[6] Figures from the World Bank.
[7] Hazel Sheffield, "Saudi Arabia is Running out of Water," *The Independent*, February 19, 2016, https://www.independent.co.uk/news/business/news/saudi-arabia-is-running-out-of-water-a6883706.html.

as cynically, as it is by many in Western Europe. It is seen as the legal state over ethnic nations, of the rule of law over arbitrary fiat. And it is seen as a set of impersonal institutions, where connections do not matter as much for how you deal with the bureaucracy. I think the EU has a lot of good to give and will survive. But it may increasingly share space with strong states like Germany, emerging region states.

I think globalization has not only torn open divisions in European societies, but in the United States as well. What I saw driving across the United States two years ago was that the middle class has visually disappeared. You would have a whisky- or chardonnay-sipping upper middle class, even in western Nebraska or eastern Wyoming, where there was always one restaurant catering to the elite and then a much larger lower-middle, poverty, semi-poverty stricken restaurant that was one or two misfortunes away from outright poverty.

There is an analogy here with Brexit and with what has been happening in Hungary and in other places. Globalization, by creating a global upper-middle class, has taken parts of society with it into the cosmopolitan borderless realm, but the other parts of society, for one reason or another, cannot compete, or do not want to compete, as they are left behind.

There is the question of Russia. During the Cold War, when the Soviets had several hundred thousand troops in the heart of Germany, Russia was an unambiguous threat. And there you had a division throughout the Cold War. Russia today is a much more ambiguous threat than it was. Instead of hundreds of thousands of Soviet troops in the heart of Germany, you have maybe a hundred thousand troops east of the Baltic states, in the Kola peninsula and North of Ukraine.[8] This is a different order of threat. Yet although the threat is ambiguous, it is real. Vladimir Putin has realized he cannot recreate the Warsaw pact. But what he wants is a soft zone of traditional imperial influence, stretching from the Baltics in the north, to Bulgaria in the south. I would even say over to the Caucasus, over to the east, which would be influenced by the many forms of subversion. Buying media through third parties, influencing corrupt politicians, running organized crime networks, intelligence operations, disinformation, or cyber activities, many of these activities are infinitely deniable and that is their beauty from the Russian point of view. And because this

---

[8] Michael R. Gordon and Eric Schmitt, "Russia's Military Drills Near NATO Border Raise Fears of Aggression," *The New York Times*, July 31, 2017, https://www.nytimes.com/2017/07/31/world/europe/russia-military-exercise-zapad-west.html.

is an ambiguous threat, you can have more divisions over it than you could over the Soviet threat. You can have people in France, in the United States, and certain elements of some political parties actually sympathizing with Putin.

I think one of the ways you judge where Europe is going is through its weakest link. And that would still be the Balkans. I would say that Romania, Croatia, and Slovenia, which is really sandwiched between Central Europe and the Balkans, have all done well. They have had their crises, Slovenia has had its banking crisis,[9] Croatia has its problems with corruption and so has Romania. But if you look at their growth rates, and at measures of political stability, they have essentially been success stories. The rest of the Balkans is different. The rest of former Yugoslavia, Bulgaria, and of course Greece, because it suffered essentially what in U.S. terms would be a "great depression," those places have not done well. They are either semi-failed states or states that are going nowhere, that have not really built robust economies and civil societies. I believe that the Balkans can be stable and prosperous, but it requires a rejuvenated European Union because only the European Union can essentially solve and smother out the continuing ethnic rivalries between Albanians and Serbs and the others.

Then we have the whole question of Germany. Konrad Adenauer, who was the chancellor of Germany in the late forties and who, throughout the fifties, set the mold. It was German leadership that would have a moral and historical obligation and memory to the legacy of World War II and to membership in the West during the Cold War. Every German chancellor since him, with varying degrees and in different ways, has essentially adhered to the Adenauer mold. The question is whether future German chancellors will adhere to the Adenauer mold. Remember, it has already been 73 years since the end of World War II, three quarters of a century. How long can this go on, before Germany becomes a normal nationalistic nation in some way or another? I think this is the real question of Europe going forward.

In the mid-nineties, when nobody saw a problem in the European Union, Tony Judt of New York University published a small book[10] in which he made the point that what gave birth to a successful, united Europe had

---

[9] "Euro Zone Leaders to Discuss Bank Problems in Slovenia," *Spiegel Online*, September 12, 2013, http://www.spiegel.de/international/europe/euro-zone-leaders-to-discuss-bank-problems-in-slovenia-a-921815.html.

[10] Tony Judt, *A Grand Illusion? An Essay on Europe* (New York: New York University Press, 2011), 17, 26–29, 41.

to do with a confluence of factors, none of which can repeat themselves in history. The sense of general defeat throughout the continent, a total American security umbrella, the need to be united to confront the Communist threat—none of those things will repeat themselves. Using history, he forecast trouble ahead for the European Union. And I think that essay proved to be very clairvoyant. When we are 75 years out, will Germany change? I consciously use Germany, because it is the most important state in Europe.

Will the United States continue to provide the engine of liberal order building and leadership in Europe, the way it has for the past 75 years? We all take stability for granted, because our lifetimes just happened by accident to coexist with the 75 years after World War II, but that may turn out to be an aberration in history. We do not know. And I say that I am not sure about U.S. leadership, not because of America's lack of economic or military capacity, but because of the capacity of the American system itself, which was built on a prosperous middle class, which no longer exists in a way that it did. And that has political consequences in the new age of technology.

## "Breaking down Eurasia": Asia

Asia's tensions, its anxiety, its geographic claustrophobia, are the opposite of the Middle East. In the Middle East, it is about weakening states. In Asia, it is about strengthening states. Why is there so much military build-up and tension in the South and East China Seas? After all, these disputes go back decades and centuries. Throughout the Cold War, China was internally focused. First it was internally focused on Mao Zedong's upheavals. Then it was internally focused on Deng Xiaoping's new economic mechanism, building pseudo-capitalism. Japan was somewhat internally focused or neutered, because it adopted quasi-pacifism as a response to its bad experience with militarism in World War II. Vietnam and what used to be called the Malay Peninsula were involved in their own bloody insurgencies, communist wars throughout much of the Cold War. Singapore was only just getting started in the 1960s and really did not emerge as a great success story until the end of the 1970s. Three decades of capitalist, or in the Chinese case, pseudo-capitalist, development leads not only to prosperity, but also to military acquisition. In the last three decades China has gone through the same crises and the same development pattern as the United States between the end of the Civil War and the outbreak of the Spanish-American War. What did America do in those quiet decades in the late nineteenth century, when its economy was growing by seven to eight percent a year? It built a great military. It built the General Staff College at Fort Leavenworth in North Kansas to professionalize the army; Teddy Roosevelt built the great navy. China has been doing the same. It has built a great navy, air force, and ballistic missile systems, because it is richer, it has more trade throughout the world, and it has security issues it never had before. The question of status enters into it ultimately, in all of these cases. Because China built a great military, Japan, which sees China as an existential threat, has to respond in kind. They discover nationalism as a default option. Vietnam and Malaysia have not been at war for decades, they built strong states with infrastructures and bureaucracy.

Whenever I go to Asia, I say this area is all about two things: shopping malls and submarines. Shopping malls are booming, but all these states have also been acquiring submarines in large quantities, which is really the coming weapon of naval warfare. China sees the South China Sea much like the United States saw the Greater Caribbean. Domination of the Greater Caribbean gave the United States domination essentially of the Western Hemisphere so it could affect the balance of power in the Eastern Hemisphere during the twentieth century. Domination or parity with the U.S. Navy in the South China Sea gives China access to the Indian Ocean.

China and Russia could be tactical allies. I do not think, though, they could be strategic allies. They have a long, troubled border, thousands of miles in Central and East Asia. They are competing in the former Soviet Central Asian republics. Russia could probably never enter into a strategic partnership with China because Putin would be the junior partner, and I am not sure that is something he could stomach well.

## Conclusions

When I look at Russia, China, and the United States, I think that in different degrees, and for different reasons, all these states' absolute power is declining. China's last thirty years have been very successful and boring. It was the same group of enlightened technocratic collegial autocrats averse to risk, who governed and weaned the country away from ideology. The next thirty years in Chinese history are going to be far more tumultuous internally. The richer and more complex Chinese society becomes, the more unsatisfied, counterintuitively, people become. You make people wealthier and wealthier, and sooner or later they do not care about wealth, they want freedom. And that is where China has its problems.

Russia is even weaker internally, with a declining economy and a badly institutionalized network of authority, in a sense that there is one man on top with a politburo-style regime. Russia could conceivably, in a worst-case scenario, be like a low-calorie version of Yugoslavia in future decades.

The United States is structurally stronger than Russia or China, but has real political problems. The United States used to consider itself "the city upon the hill" where you had an enlightened form of democratic mass-governance that was an example to the rest of the world. I think that is less and less so. The American system is less and less an inspiration than it is a spectacle. I totally disagree with comparisons between President Trump and President Nixon or President Clinton. They do not hold, as they are very forced. This is the first president in modern times who is post-literate in a sense. He has made an end run around literacy. He lives in a digital universe, where facts are wrong, made up, and most importantly there is no context to things. President Nixon and President Clinton may have had their faults, especially President Nixon, but they were serious people. They thought seriously, they had well-disciplined staffs, composed of the most brilliant people Washington could find. That is not the case now. This is the real crisis of the American system. Remember, the American system has been the most important factor among many that has created these seventy-five years of liberal world order. We are in what I call a geo-political recession, where global public goods, like fighting climate change or free trade pacts, are harder to achieve, because of the lack or the weakening of this U.S. engine.

I want to conclude by saying that the biggest question, which in and of itself will not determine the future of the world, but will determine more things than any other question, is: What is the future of China? What will happen to China in the 2020s? America could run out of gas in terms of leadership, but China could have an internal crisis, precisely because of its success. If you would have a room of X amount of people, all brilliant economists, I would wager that they all disagree about where the Chinese economy is going, because it is so hard to fathom. We have never had a system of 1,3 billion people that is pseudo-capitalist, run by authoritarians. State companies owe money to state banks in an authoritarian system and people argue about what all of that means. What are the consequences of all that? I think the real question in our world, especially in Asia, is the future of China in the 2020s. And in Europe of course it is the future of Merkel, the future of Germany I would say, in the era beyond Merkel.

# The Open Society in a Networked World

*Niall Ferguson*

## Introduction

How can an open society maintain itself in a world that has turned out to be much less benign than many of us expected just a few years ago? Central European University is a rather appropriate place to discuss this question and to reflect on some of its implications. Evan Williams may not be a household name in Budapest, but as one of the founders of Twitter he is a household name where I hang my hat, which is at Stanford, not far from Silicon Valley. These were Williams's words in *The New York Times* on May 20, 2017: "I thought once everybody could speak freely and exchanges information and ideas, the world is automatically going to be a better place. I was wrong about that."[1]

As I read those words, I thought to myself: Why is this so surprising? Yes, the world is indeed networked as never before, and Evan Williams did his share to network it. The data in Figure 1 show the extent to which the world has become networked, by comparing social network usage, cell phone ownership, and so forth for the United States, China, and Egypt in 2010. The most striking thing about this chart is how similar these three very different countries are in terms of cell phone ownership, the use of cell phones for the Internet, especially amongst young people, and the use of phones for social

---

[1] David Streitfeld, "'The Internet Is Broken': @ev Is Trying to Salvage It," *The New York Times*, May 20, 2017, https://www.nytimes.com/2017/05/20/technology/evan-williams-medium-twitter-internet.html.

networking. Notice that in 2010, Egypt actually led China and the United States by that last measure.

**Figure 1: The world is networked as never before**

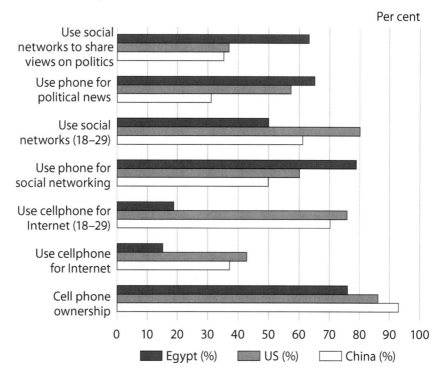

Source: Pew Research Center 2012.[2]

When I go to work and listen to the National Public Radio, there is always a little advertisement for the *Eric and Wendy Schmidt Foundation*, which includes the catch line, "In a world where everything is connected." That has become on of the great clichés of our time. The question is not, "Is the world more connected than ever before?" Of course, it is. The question is, "Why did it not turn out to be that great?"

---

[2] Pew Research Center, "Social Networking Popular Across Globe: Arab Publics Most Likely to Express Political Views Online," December 12, 2012, http://www.pew-global.org/2012/12/12/social-networking-popular-across-globe/.

John Perry Barlow

Source: Wikimedia.

Some of the most famous things about the Internet were said by John Perry Barlow back in the glory days of open source software. Barlow offered a "Declaration of the Independence of Cyberspace." "We are creating a world," he declared, "where anyone, anywhere may express his or her beliefs, no matter how singular, without fear of being coerced into silence or conformity." To go back to Silicon Valley in the 1990s or even the early 2000s is to go back to a time of almost teenage utopianism. And you can still encounter that utopianism. Just read Mark Zuckerberg's blog post, which he published in February 2017, implicitly challenging Trump's administration with a vision of a global community with universal norms.

I was always deeply sceptical about this vision of "a world of connected netizens," all equal, all with the same rights. One reason for my scepticism has to do with my education. I grew up in central Scotland, which is the most Western part of Eastern Europe that you will ever visit. Anybody who has spent their childhood in Glasgow in the 1970s found nothing in Eastern Europe to surprise him or her when they went there for the first time. The alcohol abuse, the deep bleak cynicism, the assumption that all people in authority are corrupt—all of that I grew up with. It was the way the Labour party ran the Strathclyde regional council. When I first travelled to what was then called Eastern Europe—before Mitteleuropa's revival after 1989—I had many of my deepest held assumptions validated.

If Dostoevsky had been around Silicon Valley in the 1990s and had met Barlow, or if he met Zuckerberg today, and he listened to the cyber babble of the global utopia, he would say something like the following: "You seem certain that Man himself will give up erring of his own free will"—as he wrote in *Notes from Underground*, published in 1864. "That there are natural laws in the Universe, and whatever happens to him happens outside his will. All human acts will be listed in something like logarithm tables, say, up to the number of 108,000, and transferred to a timetable."[3]

---

[3] Fyodor Dostoevsky, *Notes from Underground* (1864).

There are people at Google working on this right now; none of them have read Dostoevsky. "They will carry detailed calculations and exact forecasts of everything to count [...] But then, one might do anything out of boredom, because man prefers to act in a way he feels like acting, not in a way his reason and interests tell him. One's own free, unrestrained choice, one's own whim, be it the wildest, one's own fancy, sometimes worked up to a frenzy—that is the most advantageous advantage that cannot be fitted into any table [...] A man can wish upon himself in full awareness something harmful, stupid, and even completely idiotic in order to establish his right to wish for the most idiotic things." Dostoevsky actually said the above in response to an earlier utopian generation, the Utilitarians, who began to hypothesize in the mid-nineteenth century that social science would make it possible for human actions to become predictable. This is in some ways an explanation of last year's election in the United States. John Kerry once unwittingly made the mistake of telling a joke in Berlin when he was Secretary of States. In America, he said, "You have a right to be stupid if you want to be."

The right to be stupid is really what Dostoevsky was talking about. And the designers of the Internet forgot about that right.

## The Importance of Network Theory

The answer I give to the question "Why did it turn out to be so awful?"—"Why is Cyberspace not paradise, but a kind of Inferno?"—is different from Dostoevsky's answer, however. It has to do with networks and their peculiar properties. I am very struck by the fact that many people talk about networks casually; they use the term on an almost daily basis. If you search *The New York Times* on any given day, you will find the word *network* in multiple contexts. It is perhaps the most overused word of our time. But the proportion of people using the word who understand even the most fundamental basic elements of network science is tiny. What I want to argue is that if you do not understand the properties of networks, you are doomed not to understand the consequences of creating the world's biggest social network, which is, roughly speaking, what we have done.

In Figure 2, I have tried to sketch the key concepts of network theory. Think of yourself as a node, with edges that are your relationships. When you look at network structures, a thing to look for is which node or nodes have hub-like properties, which nodes have the highest *betweenness centrality*. The

**Figure 2**

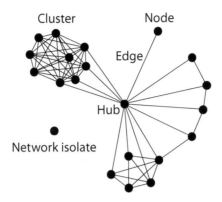

hub marked here is the node through which most nodes have to go to reach all the other nodes in the graph. Having betweenness centrality makes you a kind of junction. It may help you to think of busy junctions you reach when you are driving to work. Most people are part of several clusters, groups of nodes who all know one another better and more closely than the average node. And some are *network isolates*. That is the lonely node with no edges: it does not know anybody and is not known by anybody. These are some of the key concepts of network science.

What is remarkable about networks is that they were not invented by Mark Zuckerberg. No, they have always existed, they are all around us. Your brain, for example, is a neural network. Social networks were not invented by Mark Zuckerberg either. In every human setting, from the very beginnings of our existence as a species, we have been in social networks. So all we are really contending with in 2018 is that we—or rather, the people in Silicon Valley—have built the biggest and fastest ever social networks. When we say to one another that the world has never been so connected, we are right, but we do not understand what that implies because we do not understand network theory. But you have to understand network theory to begin to make sense of a hyper-connected world. You need to understand network structures to understand the properties of the network that you are in. And we are only just beginning to grasp the implications of this simple insight.

There are six key things pertaining to network structure I want to tell you:

One: No man is an island.

That is an old insight. Not all nodes are equal. We are all interconnected, but some people are more connected than others. Some nodes have centrality. They have a high degree, and others do not.

Two: Birds of a feather flock together.

There is something called *homophily*. We hang out with people like us. In a mixed-race high school in the United States, the white kids tend to hang out with the white kids, and the African-American kids hang out with the African American kids. There are an enormous number of studies that show this.

Three: Weak ties are strong.

Mark Granovetter, a Stanford sociologist, made the observation that if we are all just in clusters of people we really like, the world would be completely disintegrated. What connects these clusters are acquaintances, the people we know slightly, who are often quite different from us. It turns out that those slight acquaintances are bridges. They are the edges that connect different clusters, tying the world together. The weakness is the fact that you do not know the person intimately; the strength is the fact that this one relationship, this single edge, connects extraordinarily diverse, geographically distant, and culturally distant communities. This is why the world is small. The notion of six degrees of separation originated in a Hungarian short story long before anybody fully understood that it was true.[4] But when Stanley Milgram actually ran the experiment to see how many steps it would take for a letter to get from the Midwest to a Boston stockbroker, it turned out that it was roughly six. He would send out a letter to random people in the Midwest and say: you have to get this to somebody you do not know—a stockbroker in Boston—so you need to figure out who is likely to know them of the people that you do know and send it to them, and they need to do the same.

Four: Things go viral.

Whenever you hear somebody say that something went viral, it is not necessarily because it is a really great idea, which we tend to assume is the case. Things go viral as much because of the structure of the network they enter as because of their inherent infectiousness. This is also true of diseases; and it turns out that ideas behave a lot, though not exactly, like infectious diseases. It is the structure of the network that determines the speed of contagion.

---

[4] Frigyes Karinthy, "Chains," in *Everything Is Different* (Budapest: Atheneum Press, 1929).

Five: Networks never sleep.

Networks are not static. They are always evolving, they are complex adaptive systems with emergent properties, and they are subject to phase transitions, something that has best been described by CEU's László Barabási.

Six: Networks network.

A lot of what we call change in history turns out to be interaction between networks. And sometimes this is benign. John Padget argues that lots of what we call innovation and invention happens when networks interact. Network interactions are not always benign, however. Sometimes a network can attack a network; then you can have network outage, and networks can collapse when attacked.

Let me give you an example. Economists do not generally think of the economy as a network; that is simply not how standard macroeconomics works. That is a bit weird though, because the economy is a network, a super-network in fact. If you as an economist do not understand networks, you can get into some very serious trouble.

They told you: You are all going to be netizens, and everybody was going to be equal in cyber-utopia. They lied. In fact, the network promotes massive inequality. There are two kinds of people in this world: the people who own a network and the people who use it. The users are the people who make the owners billionaires. It is no accident that five of the eight richest men in the world are men who in different ways own networks.

So maybe the most important idea I can convey here is that networks, particularly the kind of scale-free networks that Barabási talks about, are profoundly inegalitarian. Superstar economists argue that massive returns go to the guy who owns the platform that permits massive online social networking. Thomas Piketty's book missed this point. The story of wealth inequality in our time is partly just a story of network structure. It has nothing to do with the rate of profit being higher than the rate of growth.

**Figure 3:**
**Network Analysis and the**
**Study of History**

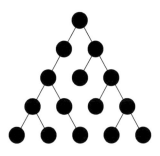

Notice that hierarchy is just a special kind of network. Look at the diagram in Figure 3: the key to a hierarchy is that it is a kind of network that enforces the centrality of one node, the ruler. You see in this diagram that most of the other nodes can only communicate with the rest of the nodes through the top node. This is a very important concept in a number of ways: one, it helps us understand how authoritarian regimes are structured and why they are so hostile to what I casually call "horizontal communication" that does not go through the top node; two, it does not take many new edges to destroy the hierarchy. To drastically reduce the betweenness centrality of the top node, you just draw a few horizontal lines between the other nodes. This explains why hierarchical structures are insecure, and often paranoid. They are right to be.

We focus on the tower and not enough on the square

Piazza del Campo, Siena.

My book *The Square and the Tower* is a history book that takes the concepts I have discussed above and applies them to the past.[5] I would like to tell you a story about the past that essentially exploits the insights of network science, which I do not think anybody has done before. The key concept, symbolized by the picture of the Piazza del Campo in Siena, is that most of history is characterized by hierarchies dominating informal social networks. There is a special network—the pyramidal structure in Figure 3—that has been the dominant network in the realm of government and economics throughout most of history. But in two eras that was not true. In two eras, partly (though not solely) because of technology, hierarchies were challenged by new dynamic networks that were characterized by high levels of contagion. Phase one starts in the late fifteenth century. Phase two starts in the 1970s. We are in the second great era of connectedness, of network revolution. It is the printing press on one side and the personal computer or smartphone on the other.

What can we learn from studying the first era? Gutenberg's printing press and Luther's printed theses seemed at first like a terrific way to achieve reform of the indeed very corrupt Roman Catholic hierarchy. What happened, however, was that a Pandora's box had been opened, and Europe was plunged into more than a hundred years of religious conflict, some of it staggeringly violent. All attempts to stamp out the Reformation by violence failed, because Protestantism, in all its varying brands, was a very resilient network.

---

[5]  Neil Ferguson, *The Square and the Tower* (New York: Penguin Press, 2018).

**Figure 4: The English Protestant network before (left) and after (right)
John Bradford's execution on July 1, 1555.[6]**

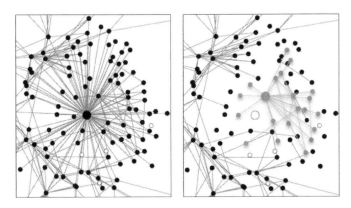

In Figure 4, you can see an example of what I am referring to here. The English Protestant network came under ferocious attack in the 1550s. Many leading Protestants were executed, usually burnt at the stake. But even when you took out a crucial node like John Bradford and disrupted the Protestant network, you could not destroy it. After his execution, all the white-coloured nodes were disconnected and had no other way of connecting to the black-coloured nodes. You could really attack these networks and take out the key nodes, but it did not suffice. You could not kill it. And the Reformation was only the first of a succession of network-propelled revolutions. They followed hard on each other's heels.

**Figure 5**

The story of the Enlightenment, as some excellent research at Stanford shows, is a story of correspondence networks. In Figure 5, you can see the Scottish Enlightenment correspondence network based on the Stanford *Mapping the Republic of Letters* database.[7] The "Republic of Letters" existed, and although it was quite nationally segmented—people

---

[6] Ruth Ahnert and Sebastian E. Ahnert, "Protestant Letter Networks in the Reign of Mary I: A Quantitative Approach," *Elh* 82, no. 1 (2015): 27, doi:10.1353/elh.2015.0000.

[7] Stanford University, "Mapping the Republic of Letters," 2013, http://republicofletters.stanford.edu/.

mostly wrote to relatively nearby philosophers—it nevertheless became a transatlantic network.

The American Revolution was a networked revolution. When you do a careful network analysis of the people who led the Revolution in Boston in the 1770s, it turns out that there were two crucial people or network hubs: Paul Revere and Joseph Warren. Paul Revere is famous for his midnight ride, but a wonderful paper published by Shin-Kap Han in 2009 shows that the reason his ride was significant was because he was a believable person.[8] There was another rider who went the same route, but nobody really knew who he was, so they did not really believe him. But when Paul Revere told people that the redcoats were coming, he had credibility—because Paul Revere knew everybody.

When you start studying networks historically, it turns out that there is a surprising side to the story. The networks of the Enlightenment were not quite networks of theorists exchanging philosophical ideas; they were also networks of Freemasons. Freemasonry was actually one of the most important institutions of the eighteenth-century Enlightenment, and a surprisingly large number of Founding Fathers, including George Washington, were masons.

It was very difficult to restore hierarchical order after networks had brought the massive disruption of the French Revolution, but ultimately, the nineteenth century achieved a restoration of hierarchical order. It began at the Congress of Vienna. Why was it possible to re-order the world on the basis of royal and imperial hierarchy after 1815? It was partly because the technology that developed in the nineteenth century favored centralized control. The great thing about the telegraph, the railways, the steamship lines, and later the telephone, was the capacity they created, with their hub-and-spoke structures, for central control. Nobody planned it that way; it was just a quirk of the technology of the industrial revolution. The technology that developed in the nineteenth century was so conducive to central control, that the ultimate hierarchical regimes eventually appeared. I think Stalin's Soviet Union was the supreme example of a hierarchy that tolerates no network that is not centrally controlled. It executes people on the mere suspicion that they may belong to such a network. This was the high tide of hierarchy. And it was not just in the communist world. Everything was hierarchical in the mid–twentieth century. Every corporation wanted an "org-chart" like Alfred

---

[8]  Shin-Kap Han, "The Other Ride of Paul Revere: The Brokerage Role in the Making of the American Revolution," *Mobilization: An International Quarterly* 14, no. 2 (2009): 143–62, doi:10.17813/maiq.14.2.g360870167085210.

Sloan's for General Motors. This era of restored hierarchy that began in 1815 lasts right down until the 1970s.

**Figure 6**

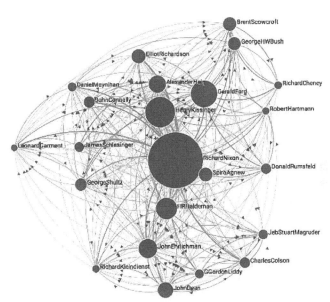

One of the most interesting questions for me is why networks made a comeback in the 1970s and why hierarchies began to lose the influence they had enjoyed in the mid-twentieth century. I have a hypothesis about this, which I cannot go into very deeply here, but I would like to illustrate it with the case of Henry Kissinger. The hypothesis in relation to Kissinger is the following: He was powerful precisely because he was networked. Kissinger intuitively understood that the world was becoming more connected, so that power derived not from the hierarchy of the Federal Government (for which he always had the highest contempt), but from social networks. Figure 6 shows that Kissinger was a supreme networker, within and also outside the Federal Government. In terms of betweenness centrality, he was the most important figure after Nixon in the Nixon-Ford governments.

That leads me to my hypothesis that Silicon Valley happened not because the technology happened, but the technology happened because the hierarchy was weak. Beginning with ARPANET, everything in Silicon Valley happened because the Department of Defense could not and did not really want to control the innovation that was happening in California. Causation here is not what you expect; it was not the microchip that led to the network age. It was a crisis of the hierarchical state. There was—let it not be forgotten— a Soviet Internet, an institution in Kiev that was supposed to build a Soviet network of computers. It failed, almost pathetically, because the Soviet Union was still too hierarchical; it could not let go. In the United States, they just let it happen. They essentially delegated innovation to people like Steve Jobs and Bill Gates.

**Figure 7**[9]

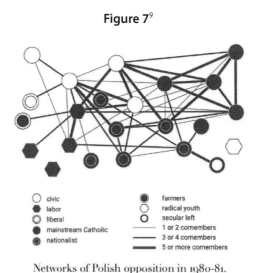

Networks of Polish opposition in 1980-81.

One reason I do not think technology is the key to this story is that the networks that overthrew the Soviet order were not technologically sophisticated. You did not need complex technology to run Solidarity. Maryjane Osa's work on what happened in Poland is fascinating because Osa shows that Solidarity was just one of a whole range of different social networks in civil society in Poland.[10] It became the hub within the network of associations hostile to the regime. It is the black hexagon in the diagram in Figure 7, and you can see that it is embedded in an entire complex of different institutions.

---

[9]  Maryjane Osa, *Solidarity and Contention: Networks of Polish Opposition* (Minneapolis, MN: University of Minnesota Press, 2003).

[10]  Ibid.

### Figure 8[11]

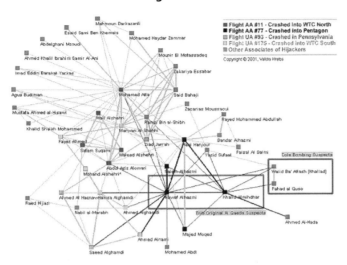

Likewise, you did not need complex technology to carry out the 9/11 attacks. Fantastic research by a man named Valdis Krebs analyses the network of the 2001 plotters.[12] Figure 8 is the original diagram Krebs drew that identified, among others, Mohamed Atta as the key hub of the 9/11 network. There was nothing sophisticated about 9/11. It did not use complex technology; box cutters were the weapon of choice. But the network had the distinguishing feature that this group of people with Mohamed Atta at its center was almost completely cut off from any surrounding network that might have detected what they were doing. I call this the anti-social network.

You may remember my remark that the economy is a network. Well, the problem is that if you do not understand that, and you think that Lehman Brothers should fail because Dick Fuld is not worth bailing out—which is basically the policy that was adopted in 2008—you fail to see that Lehman Brothers is a hugely important node in an increasingly complex financial network. Andy Haldane, the chief economist of the Bank of England, was about the only person in a major central bank that really grasped this. Everybody else was working with macro-models that did not take network effects into account. The financial system was an international network that was not robust; it was

---

[11] Valdis Krebs, "Connecting the Dots: Tracking Two Identified Terrorists," 2002, http://www.orgnet.com/prevent.html.

[12] Ibid.

fragile. And the removal of Lehman Brothers caused a far greater cascade than anybody in the Federal Reserve or the U.S. Treasury imagined.

# Conclusions

Ten years ago, the financial world was where we all are now. It got connected first, because it could afford to do so when it was still expensive. In the intervening ten years we all have become as interconnected as the banks were ten years ago—thanks, in large measure but not exclusively, to Facebook. We were all supposed to be netizens, and we were all going to support free expression and vote for the "Netizen of the Year."

What we had forgotten was that it is all about network structure. Anything can go viral, including videos of beheadings or videos of pilots being burnt to death. One cannot understand phenomena such as the Islamic State until one understands its network architecture, because it is the network architecture that allows its videos to go viral.

And then, along came another network: the Trump network. And the Trump network, which everybody who was a professional politician underestimated, brilliantly understood how to exploit the Facebook network. If Mark Zuckerberg had known, as he sat in his dorm room in Harvard, that Facebook would ultimately become Donald Trump's vehicle to the Presidency, he would have changed from Computer Science to History and Literature and never founded Facebook.

Finally, let us not forget the other network I call Cyberia: the network that was being operated from the Kremlin to subvert the U.S. election and also, of course, to penetrate, in ways yet to be fully disclosed, Trump's campaign.

So we return to the question: Why did it turn out to be so upsetting? Why has the networked world proved to be such a disappointment—a paradise for both populists and authoritarians? If you actually think about it for a matter of seconds, it is obvious: The creation of massive interconnectedness was never likely to result in "I would like to teach the world to sing in perfect harmony" or "Imagine all the people," any more than the printing press did so in sixteenth- and seventeenth-century Europe.

It all comes down to squares and towers, to the relationship between networks and hierarchies. Just how badly our networked age will turn out, I cannot begin to predict. But that the outcome will ultimately be decided by a contest between Facebook and the Trump Tower, of that I have very little doubt indeed.

# Germany and the Fate of Open Society

*Daniela Schwarzer*

When thinking about Germany and the fate of open society in Europe, we have to consider three moving pieces. The first is Germany itself; the second, which is interrelated, is the future of the European Union; and the third is a discussion of what can be done, from the point of view of Berlin, to engage more actively in open society building in Europe. Before the German parliamentary elections in September 2017, we could not have imagined that German politics could become this interesting, and that the country many regarded as the leader of the European Union—or perhaps even of the west, since Donald Trump became president of the United States—would be in a prolonged situation of governmental insecurity. Eventually, in early March 2018, the Social Democrats approved the coalition treaty in an inner party referendum. Thus, after half a year of political uncertainty, a grand coalition government with the Conservatives, CDU/CSU, could finally be formed.

The formation of the German government received a lot of attention in Europe and around the world. Questions were raised with regards to Germany's foreign policy orientation, while Germany's policies towards the European Union are likely to remain in line with the policies of the previous grand coalition. It is in Germany's profound interest that the European Union remains a stable foundation for German policymaking, both in political and economic terms. Germany's economic model depends to a large extent on the functioning of the single market and the euro area. Indeed, Germany had strong political and economic interests to push for the creation of the single market, and later, in the late 1980s and early 1990s, for the European Monetary Union. Brexit is happening much to the regret of the German government and many Germans. The United Kingdom was an important partner to Germany in various initiatives to shape the single market and accompanying policies.

Moreover, Germany looks to the European Union as the prism through which it defines its foreign policy, in the same way it looks to NATO for defense. The foreign policy review conducted by then foreign minister Frank-Walter Steinmeier underscores this point. Experts and policymakers were invited to share their thoughts on fundamental questions about Germany's interest, Germany's strategy, and the implementation thereof. It emerged that Germany continues to think of foreign policy as conducted in close partnership with its most important partners, in particular within the European Union and the United States.

In terms of its geographical outlook, it seems that the more unstable Germany's surroundings are, both to Europe's east and to its south, the more Berlin recognizes the need to work together with other countries to stabilize it. This is due to the increasing external influences that have an effect on the European Union, partially aiming to destabilize liberal democracy. This interest is growing even further nowadays. Secondly, there is a stable interest related to Germany's economic situation. Germany is a country that greatly benefits both from the single market and from a single European currency. Germany undoubtedly benefited from the fact that the European Union enlarged towards East Central Europe. Economic success plays an important role for Germany. Thus, German policymakers are quite concerned about the splits that are now projected as being challenges to the European Union, both the north-south and the east-west divide.

Despite clear continuities in its foreign policy thinking, Germany has also gone through various learning processes. The first of these was triggered by the Eurozone crisis, in particular the sovereign debt and banking crisis, and the way these challenges were handled. When the sovereign debt crisis hit the Eurozone in 2010, Germans saw how polarizing their country's approach was and how much political pressure Germany was exerting on others. But pressures were reciprocal, as tensions were emerging between Germany and Greece, for instance, not only on the political level but also in the broader public sphere. The extent of public naming and shaming and the harsh words in the press towards each other were a shock to many people at the time. It showed that the political culture of the European Union was not as stable as we thought and that mutual polarization and blaming could be unleashed rather quickly. The second learning process concerned the real-ization that not all the policies that Germany firmly believed were right for sovereign countries in the European Union turned out to be as successful as expected. Since 2010, certain positions on crisis management in the euro area have been revised.

The third learning process is closely connected to the first two. Over time, an understanding developed in Berlin that what had to be achieved was not only financial crisis management, but also stability, both in political and social terms, in European Union member states. Two years ago, I had a conversation with a German Secretary of State, who, at the time, said that he understood that with regards to Germany's approach to Southern Europe, something had to give. While the reflection process in Berlin has moved on, there is not yet an answer to the question of what Germany should and would be able to give up in order to rebuild consensus and keep the Eurozone together in a more sustainable way. In that regard it is notable that the current coalition treaty does not contain any red lines on the European Union and in particular on euro area matters, but only states that Germany is ready to pay more into the European Union's budget. There is a growing understanding that the Eurozone needs particular tools in order to maintain the functioning of the euro, but it also needs economic and social stability within the currency union. Nevertheless, the German government, or more precisely, Chancellor Merkel, has not yet responded to Emmanuel Macron's proposals. France's President has put his cards on the table and made important proposals that until now have remained unanswered from Berlin.

The second divide Berlin is increasingly worried about is the so called east-west divide. Obviously, it is problematic to use classifications as "the east" and "the west," but what I see emerging in the political exchange in Berlin is a growing concern that some countries in East Central Europe are backsliding on democracy, questioning western liberal norms, and implementing reforms that undermine open society. The law tabled by Viktor Orbán on Central European University was a wakeup call, and as such it was much debated in Berlin. I think a consensus emerged over time, namely, that this is not about Hungary or a particular Hungarian problem, but that to some extent this is about the credibility of Europe, precisely about the question whether we can watch a university that subscribes to the norms of open society and western liberalism such as Central European University being forced to close its doors. This was certainly an important moment that changed the political discourse in Germany. For political, economic, and geostrategic reasons, it remains in the German government's firm interest to bridge both of these divides, north-south and east-west. But the situation in the European Union is more complicated than this. A different way of thinking exists in Germany and in some other countries, particularly in France. Germany thinks of the future of the European Union predominantly as the EU 27, meaning all members of the single market. Other governments are more willing to move forward in smaller groups. Recently, several policymakers suggested that if countries like Poland or Hungary do not wish to any longer subscribe to the values and norms of democratic governance the European Union is built on, they should just leave the Union. From a German perspective, this is a worrisome development, and in general, additional polarization is not helpful towards making progress in the European Union.

Germany's new government is facing high expectations with regard to its leadership role. This is partly due to what we have seen happening in Europe over the past years. I mentioned the Eurozone crisis, at the moment when Germany was able to define the terms of crisis management in partnership with others, as being the largest financial contributor to the European Union. Germany was viewed as the country that took the lead in handling the migration crisis in a way that led to a lot of criticism and polarization. It was also seen as the country that together with France took a leadership role in Europe and faced one of the major foreign policy challenges during the past few years, namely, the confrontation with Russia over Ukraine, in particular the annexation of Crimea.

There are as many expectations as there is criticism of the potential role of Germany in Europe. I spoke about the learning processes I observed in Berlin, the acute awareness that part of Germany's task is to balance the various interests within the European Union and then try to incrementally build a consensus and move ahead. But the picture is more complex. The different national interests that are emerging, and in particular the new and stronger discourse on national sovereignty and on reclaiming certain competences back to member states, is something Berlin policymakers are aware of and worried about. While I see high expectations wherever I go in regards to Germany's leadership, the debate in Berlin is still very much on the level of "what can we actually do and what is our responsibility?" At this point, the notion of responsibility is most debated in the areas of security and defense. There is a persistent criticism towards Germany for not doing enough in terms of defense, investment, procurement, and its engagement in NATO and the recently created European Structured Defense Cooperation PESCO.

There is a strong desire to engage, and Germany has committed to increasing its defense expenditure. We will have to wait and see how the new government handles the balance it is trying to maintain in the coalition treaty, if it gives as much to defense as to development policy. So far, there is no strategy on how Germany intends to achieve the increasingly complex task of holding the European Union together.

An area in which Germany has been strongly engaged is normative leadership. If you look at how chancellor Merkel reacted to Donald Trump on various occasions, reminding the President of the United States about the fundamental values that transatlantic relations and partnership are built upon, Germany was quickly positioned as the leader of the west. But, much in the tradition of Germany's postwar approach to foreign policymaking, it rather wants to co-lead the west together with other partners.

In terms of European policy, the new government will hopefully pay closer attention than its predecessor to the challenges democracy and open society are facing in some countries of the European Union. This is something that needs the highest degree of political attention, simply because the European Union at this point does not have tools that work to prevent the backsliding of democracy. One debate that is ongoing in Brussels, Berlin, and elsewhere, is how incentives can be provided to countries that moved away from democratic norms, implemented when they joined the European Union. In this regard, the discussion on the future of the European Union's budget is interesting. Changes are hard to implement because you need unanimity to amend the multi-annual financial report of the Union. But the question is indeed whether certain expenditures can be linked to the respect of the rule of law, such as, for instance, the fight against corruption. This is an important issue for the European Union, and I hope that the German government uses its leverage as the largest contributor to the Union's budget when negotiations come to full speed.

The second task from a German perspective is to keep up and maybe even increase the engagement with other societies and member states. Germany runs a powerful and impactful network of political foundations present in many European Union member states and abroad, and they are a good platform to engage in broader dialogue. The exchanges brought about by these political foundations, but also by other actors of civil society, in particular the younger generations, encouraging mobility and encounters across European borders, are something not only a country like Germany but the European Union as a whole should invest more in.

Germany's third task is to engage even more in parliamentary exchange. Take the example of Hungary, with the current governing party belonging to the European People's Party in the European Parliament. A stronger exchange between parliamentarians, including the German side, to discuss issues of open society and backsliding democracy, could possibly be a powerful way forward towards deepening the discussions we need to have in Europe.

# PART FOUR

# Open Society's New Enemies: The Authoritarian Competitors

# The Puzzle of "Illiberal Democracy"

*János Kis*

## I.

Liberal democracy is in trouble. Anti-system parties are on the rise. In some European countries, from Finland to Austria, they have entered government as minor coalition partners. In Italy, a populist party and an extreme right party agreed to create a government coalition. In Hungary and Poland, leaders openly committed to replacing liberal democracy with an illiberal regime gained comfortable majorities, enabling them to govern without cooperating with parties of the democratic center. In mid-2018 illiberal state building entered its third parliamentary cycle in Hungary.

Some of the anti-system leaders, once brought to government by an electoral landslide, take recourse to juridical and extra-juridical violence to consolidate their regime. Chávez and Erdoğan are good examples. The regimes they built are nothing but new versions of a familiar type of authoritarianism. Other cases are less familiar. These are cases in which political violence is sporadic, if it occurs at all; opposition politicians are not killed or incarcerated; opposition parties are not prohibited, demonstrations are not disbanded by brutal police force, and critics of the government rarely, if ever, face criminal prosecution. And yet, the grip of a hegemonic party and its leader on state and society is progressively tightening. A major example of this is Viktor Orbán's regime in Hungary.

How can we characterize such a regime? The term most often used by political observers is "illiberal democracy." Yet there is something odd about this term. On the one hand, "illiberal democracy" successfully crowds out alternatives. On the other hand, even for the ones who use it, it carries a certain discomfort. "Illiberal democracy," the historian and journalist Anne Applebaum writes, "is an unfortunate term that exists because it is hard to think of a better one."[1] What is so unfortunate about it? How has an unfortunate term come to more or less dominate the language of political analysis? This is an interesting puzzle. More precisely, it is only the introduction to an even more complicated puzzle. For, when trying to solve it, what we find is not a solution but a difficulty. First, we discover that illiberal leaders are happy to embrace the term and use it in their attack against liberal democracy. The arguments they make are demagogic, but they find genuine support in the way partisans of liberal democracy tend to think about democracy in general and about liberal democracy in particular. This is the more complicated puzzle I am after. In what follows, I attempt to show that solving this puzzle demands a revision of mainstream thinking about what democracy is and what reasons we have to cherish it.

I begin with a brief outline of the idea of "illiberal democracy." Then, I address the question why the term is regarded as "unfortunate" even by the ones who apply it. As a third step, I reconstruct what I call the mainstream conception of democracy, aiming to uncover the puzzle that it implies. I will argue that the mainstream conception is flawed, and discuss how it should be revised. I conduct my argument in terms of normative democratic theory. Comparative political scientists might wonder whether the normative argument I am proposing has any relevance for empirical research. In my conclusions, I offer the glimpse of an argument of how I believe it does.

## II

What is said about a political regime when it is classified as an illiberal democracy? First, that the regime in question is democratic but not liberal. The claim that such an animal can exist was first made by Daniel A. Bell and his co-authors in a book published in the early 1990s.[2] The book was meant

---

[1] Anne Applebaum, "Illiberal Democracy Comes to Poland," *Washington Post*, December 16, 2016.

[2] Daniel A. Bell, David Brown, Kanishka Jayasuriya, and David M. Jones, eds., *Towards Illiberal Democracy in Pacific Asia* (London: Palgrave MacMillan, 1993).

as a criticism of modernization theory, aiming to debunk the claim that socio-economic modernization invariably leads to liberal democracy. The authors argued, through the case of Pacific Asia, that although modernization comes with a transition to democracy, beyond the boundaries of Western civilization it leads not to liberal, but to illiberal democracy.

It is this claim that Fareed Zakaria extended, in a celebrated paper from 1997, to the new democracies from Peru to Pakistan, from Sierra Leone to the Philippines. He described illiberal democracies as "[d]emocratically elected regimes, often ones that have been reelected [...] through referenda, [that at the same time] are routinely ignoring constitutional limits on their power and depriving their citizens of their basic rights and freedoms."[3]

So, a regime that counts as illiberal democracy is a democracy in the sense that the government is elected and reelected. And it counts as illiberal in that the constitutional checks and balances are too weak to enforce their constraints on the government, allowing for a practice of depriving citizens of their liberal rights.

In an illiberal democracy, genuine opposition parties exist. They set up their candidates independently, rather than just nominating potential candidates for the slot assigned to them on a unique electoral list.[4] The electoral system is far from being perfectly competitive, but there is some degree of competition: the victory of the ruling party is not secured independently of the vote.[5] The system is democratic, since the rulers are authorized to govern by regular elections. But it is illiberal, because the government fails to respect the liberal rights of the authorizers.

Such an animal was unknown until the last decades of the twentieth century. Regimes without constitutional protection of rights lacked multi-party elections, and regimes without multi-party elections were reckless towards individual rights. But if the set of illiberal democracies was empty, it was not due to conceptual impossibility. "Illiberal democracy" is not an

---

[3] Fareed Zakaria, "The Rise of Illiberal Democracy," *Foreign Affairs* 77 (November–December 1997): 22–43. See also his book *The Future of Liberty: Illiberal Democracy at Home and Abroad* (New York: W.W. Norton, 2003).

[4] As was the case in some of the "people's democracies" such as Czechoslovakia, Poland, and the GDR.

[5] By reducing the proportion of contested seats below fifty percent or less, for example.

oxymoron. There is nothing in the concept of democracy that would make it necessarily liberal.[6] Then what is there to worry about "illiberal democracy"?

# III

"Illiberal democracy" does not lack critical potential. It condemns government not reined in by constitutional checks for its arbitrariness and its tendency to violate individual rights. But, as Jan-Werner Müller points out, the kind of critique implicit in the idea of "illiberal democracy" does not go far enough. It objects to the illiberalism of the regimes to which it is applied but it fails to contest their democratic credentials.[7] This is a weakness in the struggle for the language of politics. Ironically, leaders such as Orbán and Kaczyński are happy to embrace the term. "A democracy is not necessarily liberal," Orbán likes to argue.[8] And this is precisely the message conveyed by "illiberal democracy." So the concept, proposed with the aim of delegitimizing would-be autocrats, is easily appropriated by these same would-be autocrats for self-legitimation. It allows Orbán and his likes to claim the mantle of democracy while attacking liberalism—an idea now under fire from many sides. It also allows them to blur the distinction between liberalism as a political worldview in an ongoing debate with conservatism and socialism, and liberal constitutionalism, which has its historical origins in the liberal tradition but is now understood to belong to the foundations of democracy, not just by liberals but by most conservatives and socialists as well. This is why Müller finds the choice of the term inauspicious. I think he is right, but I also think that the problem is more profound: it poses a challenge to the very theoretical core of the mainstream conception of democracy.

Self-proclaimed "illiberal democrats" attack constitutional constraints on government, such as judicial review in the name of the will of the people,

---

[6]  See Jeffrey C. Isaacs, "Is There Illiberal Democracy? A Problem With No Semantic Solution," *Public Seminar*, Special Publication, July 12, 2017, http://www.publicseminar.org/wp-content/uploads/2017/07/Isaac-Jeffrey-Is-There-Illiberal-Democracy-Public-Seminar.pdf.

[7]  Jan-Werner Müller, "The Problem with 'Illiberal Democracy,'" *Project Syndicate*, January 21, 2016.

[8]  See Viktor Orbán's speech at Băile Tuşnad (Tusnádfürdő) on July 26, 2014, available at https://budapestbeacon.com/full-text-of-viktor-orbans-speech-at-baile-tusnad-tusnadfurdo-of-26-july-2014/?_sf_s=Viktor+Orb%C3%A1n+speech+at+Baile+Tusnad+&sf_paged=4.

which, they argue, is represented by the holders of elected office, i.e., by them. Democracy, they insist, is compromised when unelected judges are allowed to overrule the decisions of the representatives of the people. What is commonly called liberal democracy is, according to them, a system where power is kidnapped by "liberal elites." Illiberal democracy restores full power to the people. It is not just *a* legitimate version of democracy on a par with illiberal democracy—it stands for what democracy really is.[9]

Demagogic as such a discourse is, it turns the mainstream conception of democracy in general and liberal democracy in particular against itself. This may sound like a radical claim in need of clarification and defense. The following sections address this task.

## IV

When asked to define "democracy," something like "the rule of the people" comes to mind. There is considerable consensus about such a definition. No matter what a theorist, a researcher, or an ordinary citizen understands by "the rule of the people," they tend to agree that if there is such a thing as democracy, it must consist in "the rule of the people." This is the concept of democracy as it is commonly understood.[10]

Although "democracy" is a highly abstract concept, it is not empty. There are things that it evidently excludes from its scope. Government by experts is clearly not democracy. Its advocates propose it as an alternative to democracy.[11] Its opponents reject it precisely because it is not democracy.[12] There

---

[9] "The Curia [Hungary's supreme court] has clearly and grossly interfered with the elections as it has taken a mandate away from the electors of the governing parties," announced Orbán after the April 2018 elections through his press secretary, attacking a decision that invalidated about four thousand votes on procedural grounds. See http://www.kormany.hu/en/the-prime-minister/news/curia-has-grossly-interfered-in-elections.

[10] See Michael Coppedge et al., "Conceptualizing and Measuring Democracy: A New Approach," *Perspectives on Politics* 9 (2011): 241–67.

[11] See Jason Brennan, *Against Democracy* (Princeton: Princeton University Press, 2016).

[12] See Thomas Christiano, "Jason Brennan: Against Democracy. A Review Article," *Notre Dame Philosophical Reviews*, May 19, 2017, http://ndpr.nd.edu/news/against-democracy/.

are further things the concept explicitly excludes, but it does not exclude everything that we would not accept to be instances of "democracy." For example, Carl Schmitt notoriously argued that the rule of a leader authorized by general acclamation is democratic.[13] Few people nowadays would deny that Schmitt's claim is blatantly false. But the concept "rule of the people" does not make it false *by definition*.

Other times, we disagree on how to classify a regime. Take for example the present Hungarian regime. In May 2018, a group of Western academics and intellectuals published an open letter to Angela Merkel, saying: "Leading political scientists are convinced that the survival of Hungarian democracy is now acutely imperiled; some even believe that it has already been effectively dismantled."[14] The majority believes that the regime is an endangered democracy; a minority believes it is not a democracy at all. Their disagreement may express differences of judgment about the particular case. But it may also hinge on a disagreement about the normative standards that the judgment is supposed to apply. Again, the concept of "democracy" does not in itself decide which of the conflicting views on the relevant standards are true.

So, the concept of democracy is in need of interpretation. The interpretation must fit the cases about which there is general agreement, and it must provide guidance for deciding about the controversial cases. Since democracy is a value-laden concept, the interpretation must be based on an account of what makes it valuable. Following John Rawls, I call the interpretations of the concept of democracy its *conceptions*.[15]

While the concept of democracy is more or less consensual, its conceptions are contested. Different conceptions offer different and competing interpretations of what democracy really is. Consequently, their judgment on whether a particular regime is or is not democratic may not be the same. What conception *A* identifies as an instance of democracy, conception *B* may characterize as an autocracy.

However, one of the rival conceptions rose to dominance in the twentieth century. This is what I call the mainstream conception. The mainstream

---

[13]  See Carl Schmitt, *Constitutional Theory* (Durham: Duke University Press, 2007), 131, 272–75.
[14]  "Merkel's Shameful Silence," Politico.eu, April 17, 2018, https://www.politico.eu/article/angela-merkel-viktor-orban-shameful-silence-viktor-orban-hungarian-election-fidesz/.
[15]  See John Rawls, *A Theory of Justice*. 2nd edition (Cambridge, MA: Belknap, 1999), 5.

conception is widely accepted, and it is accepted rather uncritically. Only a small minority of political theorists stands up to it.[16] Let us now have a closer look at the mainstream conception.

V

States claim a right to make and enforce binding rules for all within their jurisdiction. When that claim is true, we say that a state has legitimate authority over its subjects. According to the mainstream conception, this is true when the rules are made by the very people to whom they are applied. This is because the people has a right to give laws to itself, and not to be subjected to any law of which it is not the author. In modern societies, the people directly makes laws only on rare occasions, in referenda or during popular initiatives. More often, it legislates indirectly, through representatives authorized in popular elections.

Thus, in a democracy, whatever the people decides should be law, either in a referendum or by way of elected representatives, is law, and there is no law other than what is authored by the people. It is a necessary and sufficient condition for a regime to be an instance of democracy that the legislator is either the people or a body of the people's elected representatives.[17]

Unlike authorization by acclamation, referenda and elections are based on well-defined decision procedures. According to the mainstream conception, not all kinds of voting procedures count as legislative acts of the people. The relevant procedure must satisfy a number of normative criteria. Popular decisions must be taken on the basis of universal and equal adult ballot; citizens must be in a position of taking informed decisions; they must be free to

---

[16] See, in particular, Ronald Dworkin, "The Partnership Conception of Democracy," *California Law Review* 86 (1998): 453–58. Cf. Dworkin, "Equality, Democracy, and Constitution: We The People in Court," *Alberta Law Review* 28 (1990): 324–46.

[17] For an interpretation of democracy as an electoral system where legislators are elected by the people, the head of the executive is elected either by the people or by the elected legislature, and the incumbent can be removed at another election held under the same rules, see Mike Alvarez, José Antonio Cheibub, Fernando Limongi, and Adam Przeworski, "Classifying Political Regimes," *Studies in Comparative International Development* 31 (1996): 3–36, and José Antonio Cheibub, Jennifer Gandhi, and James Raymond Freeland, "Democracy and Dictatorship Revisited," *Public Choice* 143 (2010): 67–101.

participate in public deliberation; when the people elects representatives, the election must be competitive and it must be held with periodic regularity; the election must be free and fair, and so on.

What a complete list of the relevant criteria consists of, and how the norms included in it are related to each other, has momentous implications for democratic theory. For now, however, this question can be set aside. It is sufficient to establish that if the procedure satisfies the relevant criteria, then the outcome commands democratic authority. Whatever the content of the law, it deserves the obedience and support of each individual and the state has the right to enforce it against the disobedient, just because it has been adopted democratically.

# VI

It is a virtue in a legal system that its laws are binding and can be rightfully enforced independently of their content. In modern, large-scale societies, divided along cultural, sociological, and economic lines, people disagree on nearly everything, including the law. But they need shared laws in order to be able to coexist peacefully and to cooperate for mutual benefits, including the benefit of justice.[18] If the law had no legitimate authority independent of its content, then those who disagree with it would be entitled to disobey and would have a justified objection to being coerced into obedience. The government would be despotic, or there would be no government at all.

Thus, the democratically made law has legitimate authority regardless of its content. The content-independence of its authority is not a problem in itself. It becomes a problem, however, if the legislative procedure systematically yields grossly unacceptable outcomes. The mainstream conception insists that this is precisely the case with the "rule of the people."

It is at this point that the adjective "liberal" comes into play. It is a core claim of liberalism that individuals have rights and that those rights impose normative constraints on morally permissible decisions, whether taken by an individual, a group of private individuals, or by the public authorities of a state. The mainstream conception takes this liberal claim for granted, and it concludes that a decision system that allows for violating the rights of the indi-

---

[18]  See Jeremy Waldron, *Law and Disagreement* (Oxford: Clarendon, 1999), 1–17.

vidual is morally defective. Decisions adopted in a process of impeccable democratic credentials are not an exception. As Tocqueville and John Stuart Mill
have put it so eloquently, the tyranny of the majority is still intolerable tyranny.

Democracy understood as legislation by the people or by the elected representatives of the people may yield decision outcomes that violate rights. No
matter how democratic the legislative procedure, its internal character leaves
the outcome of the decisions underdetermined. Ultimately, it is the beliefs
and preferences, intentions and aims, hopes and fears, sympathies and antipa-
thies of the voters that will carry the day. Whether these factors add up to
yield decisions that respect the rights of individuals or violate them is a contingent matter. Not even the best democratic procedure can guarantee that
the rights of individuals will not be violated or curbed, especially if the individuals in question are members of marginalized minorities. Democratic and
liberal values are likely to clash.[19]

Rights are not self-enforcing: they need institutional powers to identify and
enforce them. Individual rights call for liberal constitutionalism. They demand
institutions such as the rule of law, the separation of powers, and checks on the
government by independent public authorities, especially the judiciary.

Let me take stock: the mainstream conception insists that democratic
government on its own is not enough. Liberal constitutionalism is also
needed. Democracy is a regime type, while liberal democracy is one of its
subtypes. There are two distinct sets of political institutions: democratic and
liberal. Liberal democracy unites them in a single regime, it is both democratic and liberal. Illiberal democracy separates them; it is democratic but not
liberal. At face value, this view seems appealing. But it has a number of rather
awkward implications.

## VII

In this conception, liberal democracy appears to be a hybrid, a regime under
the joint supervision of two separate and mutually independent principles:
the democratic principle and the liberal principle. The democratic principle

---

[19] This is what Isaiah Berlin has identified as the conflict between negative liberty as
freedom of the individual from undue interference and positive liberty as collective
self-government. See Isaiah Berlin, "Two Concepts of Liberty," in *Four Essays on
Liberty* (Oxford and New York: Oxford University Press, 1969), 161, 165, 169.

regulates the *procedures* of succession in office and of legislation, and argues that the people has the right to enact—directly or indirectly—whatever law it wants to give to itself. The liberal principle imposes normative constraints on the legislative *outcomes*. From the point of view of the liberal principle, violating the rights of some or all members of a political community is a moral loss. From the point of view of the democratic principle, it is the fact of imposing constraints on popular decisions that counts as a moral loss. It follows that liberal democracy, while morally superior to illiberal democracy from the point of view of the *liberal* principle, at the same time compromises the *democratic* principle.[20]

And this is precisely the claim of the self-proclaimed "illiberal democrats." Only illiberal democracy is fully democratic, they argue.

To be sure, the mainstream conception has a response to the illiberal challenge. When values conflict, compromise is unavoidable. "Illiberal democrats" advocate majority rule without any concessions, but an unrestrained pursuit of majority rule comes with a heavy moral cost, the cost of leaving liberal rights unprotected. Liberal democracy, on the other hand, achieves a compromise. It accommodates both liberal rights and majority rule to some degree.[21]

Unfortunately, the mainstream response raises more difficulties than it solves. First, it fails to appeal to anyone not already convinced about the superiority of liberal democracy over democracy without constitutional constraints. Second, it delivers the defenders of liberal democracy to the charge of "liberal elitism." For it argues that when it comes to the protection of individual rights, democratic decisions of the many can be overridden by the decisions of a few men and women without any popular mandate. Finally, it fails to secure enough room for protecting liberal rights against democratic decisions. Individual rights calling for protection are not equally stringent. Some are clearly robust enough to outweigh the value of democratic decision-making. Others are less robust; they may lose out if balanced against the value of collective self-government. The idea of a right, however, amounts

---

[20] This is what the American legal scholar, Alexander Bickel, famously called "the counter-majoritarian difficulty." See Alexander M. Bickel, *The Least Dangerous Branch: The Supreme Court at the Bar of Politics*. 2nd edition (New Haven, CT: Yale University Press, 1986), 16ff.

[21] A forceful expression to the compromise answer was given by Isaiah Berlin in "Two Concepts of Liberty," 169 ff.

precisely to the claim that the interest protected by it should not be sacrificed even for the sake of the greater collective good.

To conclude: the illiberal challenge exposes the weaknesses of the mainstream conception. It provides reasons to revise it.

# VIII

For the mainstream conception, "liberal democracy" and "illiberal democracy" are subtypes of a generic type "democracy." I argue, rather, that they are rival conceptions of what the generic type "democracy" really is. If one of these is true, the other cannot be.

When discussing the term "rule of the people," I set aside the question what "the people" is. I have done so because this question is at the core of the conflict between the liberal and illiberal conceptions of democracy. Now it is time to confront it.

The people is a collective agency. Its members own their state together, as a people. As owners of the state, they have the right to decide together, as a people, how their state should make and enforce the law and what laws it should make and enforce. Up to this point, the liberal and the illiberal conceptions share a common ground. But their understanding of what this common ground is points in opposite directions.

In the illiberal reading, the people, as a collective entity, is an ultimate bearer of political value. It has its own good, independent of and superior to the good of its members. It has rights of its own that protect its interests even against the individual interests its members might have. This is what qualifies it to be the owner of the state, and to make decisions regarding the law.

This characterization of the people divides its members into two categories. There are those whose personal views and lifestyles conform to the cultural identity of the people, and there are those with unconventional views and projects. The first have a privileged status with respect to the state and the law. It is appropriate that their beliefs and ways of life are given special support by the public authorities, and that the authorities discourage those with unconventional beliefs from advocating their ideas and pursuing their unconventional projects.

In the liberal reading, the people is a collective owner of the state and a collective lawmaker not because it is an entity of superior political value and a possessor of supra-individual good, but because its individual members are each other's equals. They have equal moral status as human beings, and their moral equality demands that they have an equal civic status as members of their political community. No citizen can be legitimately denied equal part-ownership in the state, having jurisdiction over the territory they inhabit. Citizens can only own their state together, as a people. Equal part-ownership in the common state entails that no one can be legitimately denied an equal say in the decision about what the law should be or who should have the mandate to make the law. This is why citizens can only make decisions regarding their state together, as a people. But equal part-ownership entails more. It entails that the state and the law must treat each individual with equal respect and concern. They must pay equal respect to the rights citizens have to conduct their lives in accordance with their own ideals, rather than being forced to live as others think they should. And they must advance the interests of each citizen with equal concern.[22]

According to the liberal interpretation, the people is a political community of equals, and the rule of the people is self-government by that community. Yes, the people has the right to give law to itself. And, yes, this claim is generally taken to mean that the right of self-legislation is held by the majority. But the majority has no such right. Democratic decision rules are majoritarian because consensus is rarely if ever available. The majority does not make law in its own name. It makes law in the name of the people as a whole, and the law cannot be attributed to the people as a whole if the minority has sufficient reason for disowning the decision outcome. It clearly has such a reason if its members are denied an equal part in the decision-

---

[22] See Ronald Dworkin, "Constitutionalism and Democracy," *European Journal of Philosophy* 3 (1995): 2–11. Liberal political philosophers tend to agree with Dworkin that the value and identity of democracy are determined by a principle of equal civic status. See Allen Buchanan, "Political Legitimacy and Democracy," *Ethics* 112 (2002): 689–719; Thomas Christiano, *The Constitution of Democracy* (Oxford: Oxford University Press, 2008); Elisabeth Anderson, "Democracy: Instrumental versus Non-Instrumental Value," in Thomas Christiano and John Christman, eds., *Contemporary Debates in Political Philosophy* (Malden, MA: Wiley-Blackwell, 2009), 213–225; and Niko Kolodny, "Rule over None II: Social Equality and the Value of Democracy," *Philosophy and Public Affairs* 42 (2014): 284–336. But they accept the restriction of the concept of democracy to the collective decision procedure and, thus, insist that democratic equality is obtained once citizens are treated as equals, as participants in the decision-making procedure. See, for example, Kolodny's argument that persistent minorities do not raise a special problem for democratic theory. Kolodny, art. cit., 326–329.

making process. But even if they are treated as equals in their capacity as participants in the procedure, they still have a reason for disowning the decision if their good is not given equal consideration by the outcome, or if their rights are sacrificed for the sake of the common benefit.

It is a *democratic* deficit in a regime if its laws systematically disadvantage a minority group or if particular pieces of legislation involve setbacks to significant personal interests; interests whose importance calls for the protection by rights.

If this is correct, liberals are in a position to resist the claim that democracy and liberal rights are in conflict. It is possible for procedurally democratic political decisions to violate justified individual claims against interference or discrimination. But such decisions have no *democratic* legitimacy: they cannot be attributed to the people as a whole. Collective decisions commanding democratic legitimacy do not conflict with liberal rights: their legitimacy presupposes that the rights of the individual are respected by the decision outcome. Overruling collective decisions that violate liberal rights does not compromise democracy. It provides for more democracy, not less.

This is the first conclusion of my argument. The second conclusion is: If the liberal interpretation of democracy as I reconstructed it is correct, then the species called "illiberal democracy" does not exist. This "unfortunate term" must go.

# IX

You may suspect that even if the first conclusion is correct, the second is premature. After all, the concept "democracy" stands for a political ideal. Its liberal conception provides an interpretation of that ideal. When it argues that an illiberal regime is not a democracy, what it points to is only that the regime in question does not qualify as a full realization of the democratic ideal. But no existing democracy qualifies as a full realization of the democratic ideal. Existing democracies approximate that ideal to different degrees, and even the best ones far from satisfy it fully. Take the example of the United States: even before the presidency of Trump, when its democratic credentials were not seriously contested, its electoral system was heavily distorted by practices of gerrymandering, voters' exclusion, and campaign spending getting out of control. Thus, either there are no democracies in the real world, or the full satisfaction of the democratic ideal cannot be a condition for a regime to count as an instance of the regime-type "democracy."

In sum, a regime does not need to be *fully* democratic in order to count as a democracy. It needs to be only *sufficiently* democratic. But, then, it is conceivable for a regime to be sufficiently democratic overall, but not uniformly across all its subsystems. It is a plain fact of comparative politics that regimes of roughly equal overall democratic quality tend to perform fairly unequally in their different subsystems.

Consider a regime that is sufficiently democratic overall. Suppose its overall democratic performance is a combined outcome of, on the one hand, an electoral and a legislative subsystem that satisfies the requirements of participatory equality to a high degree, and, on the other hand, a subsystem for the protection of individual rights that does a very poor job. This would be a democracy tainted by a tyranny of the majority. It would count as a subtype of democracy with illiberal features.

If this is so, then it is conceivable for an existing regime to be democratic and illiberal at the same time. Interpreting the democratic ideal is not a way to decide whether illiberal democracies are possible in the real world.

In conclusion, I would like briefly to address this objection. I agree that a regime-type that is sufficiently democratic overall and counts as illiberal at the same time is conceivable. Is there any interesting empirical instance of such a type? I have my doubts about this. What I have no doubts about is that the regimes that the term was coined for are not among its possible instances. These regimes are illiberal in a way that excludes them from the class of low-quality democracies. And although confronting them with the democratic ideal is not sufficient to reach this judgment, it has its role among the reasons that together give firm support to this judgment.

The liberal ideal of democracy points to a set of institutions and procedures that together provide solid protection to democratic equality. Here is a list of the main institutions and procedures that keep democracy in reasonably good egalitarian shape:

– A high court with the mandate to exercise constitutional supervision of legislative and executive acts, deciding each case in accordance with its best judgment on what the constitution requires in that case.
– Ordinary courts that decide legal disputes impartially, obeying only the law that applies to the case, between public authorities and citizens, and between two public authorities.

- A prosecutor's office that effectively resists pressures from the executive to indict political opponents of the ruling party and to shield its leading members from criminal charges.
- A civil service doing its job in the spirit of objectivity and professionalism, and within the strict limits of the rule of law.

In the real world, all these institutional checks discharge their role more or less imperfectly. But in order to live up to the norms applying to them at least sufficiently well, they must enjoy a high degree of independence from the government. That independence is secured to different degrees in different democratic countries, in different times. It is a complicated task to judge whether the reduction of the independence of one institution or the other still leaves the regime within the family of liberal democracies or deprives it of its liberal character. But suppose that the independence *of all of them* comes under simultaneous assault by a government in possession of a strong enough legislative majority. In this case, the regime ends up being neither liberal nor democratic, for such an assault undermines not only the rights of the individual but also the integrity of the political process.

It does so indirectly, as some of the endangered rights are distinctly political. Abridging freedom of expression, for example, does not only harm the personal interest of citizens in being able to give public expression to their views and in having access to the views of others, but also the fairness of the voting process. Not surprisingly, the assault on the institutional checks on government comes with transforming the public media into a means of propaganda, hate mongering, and spreading fake news, and with attempts of silencing or coopting the commercial media.

Furthermore, the dismantling of the institutional checks and balances directly undermines the integrity of the political process. So far, we have scrutinized these checks and balances exclusively in the context of protecting rights. But they also play a key role in keeping a level playing field, securing the transparency of the government, enabling the public to hold the government accountable between two elections, and reining in political corruption. Once they are put under effective governmental control, curbing political rights and the distortion of the political process can advance without encountering any institutional resistance. Democracy comes to an end together with liberal con-stitutionalism. Liberal democracy is replaced by some version of autocratic rule.

Is the state Orbán and Kaczyński are building illiberal? It surely is. Is it an illiberal version of democracy? It surely is not.

# How Can Populism Be Defeated?

*Jan-Werner Müller*[1]

## Introduction

We read and hear every day that, across the globe, "the people" are rising up against "the elite." Supposedly everywhere we find what is sometimes quite unashamedly called a "revolt of the masses" against the establishment. One metaphor in particular has gripped the imagination: allegedly, a populist "wave" is rolling across the globe, washing away establishments everywhere. I think this is a profoundly misleading picture of our political reality today. There is nothing inevitable about what is happening. To make that thought plausible, I want to propose as a first step an understanding of what populism actually is, especially in light of the inflationary use of that word in political commentary today. In a second step, I would like to say a few words about what populism in power can mean. And then, thirdly, I want to move to a somewhat more constructive set of observations about what can be done about or—to put it bluntly—against populists.

[1] I am grateful to Michael Ignatieff for the invitation to speak in the lecture series on reconsidering the open society and to Stefan Roch for preparing the transcript (this chapter preserves the nature of the talk as a talk as much as possible). I am also indebted to many interlocutors in Austria, and to the Institute for Human Sciences, Vienna, as well as the Institute of Advanced Study at Central European University, both of which enabled me to spend an eventful, highly educational year in *Mitteleuropa*. Most of this lecture was inspired by my book *What is Populism?* (Philadelphia, PA: University of Pennsylvania Press, 2016). The paragraphs about culture wars and polarization have been adapted from "The People vs. Democracy?" *Project Syndicate*, March 2018.

In the process I also hope to show that a chastened liberalism has to hold on to the diagnosis that populism is dangerous for democracy—while at the same time understanding that populism is not a sure sign of how irrational or ill-informed the great unwashed really are. Seeing the perils of populism clearly does not mean that one has to dismiss some of its underlying structural causes, or that one gets a license to indulge in the clichés of nineteenth-century mass psychology—often the default option for liberals who were distrusting the people all along. If the phrase had not become so toxic, or at least clichéd, one might be tempted to say: tough on populists, tough on the causes of populism.

## What Is Populism?

Contrary to conventional wisdom, not everybody who criticizes "the elites" or "the establishment" is automatically a populist. In fact, you might well wonder: How can it be that for decades any old civics textbook would have told us that democracy is, among other things, a matter of keeping a close eye on the powerful— and all of a sudden, at the beginning of the twenty-first century, anybody who seems to be doing this is automatically deemed a dangerous populist. The seemingly obvious starting point of so much political commentary today—criticism of elites equals populism—cannot be quite right. Of course, when they are in opposition, populists criticize the government, or, if you prefer, "the elites." But the crucial feature of populists is something else. It is that they always claim that they—and only they—represent what populists tend to call the "real people," or, sometimes also, "the silent majority." Just one brief example to give you a sense of what I am after: then Prime Minister Erdoğan, a couple of years ago at a congress of his party, gave a speech where he simply said, "We are the people." And then turning to his critics inside Turkey, he asked the question: "Who are you?"

Now, you may say that this does not sound immediately dangerous for democracy. It is not immediately the same as racism or, let's say, a fanatical hatred of the European Union. But what follows from this claim to a monopoly of representing the "real people" are two stances that are always dangerous or at least detrimental to democracy. First, populists will always say that all other contenders for power are fundamentally illegitimate. And this is never just a matter of disagreeing about policy or even values, which is of course completely normal and ideally even productive in a democracy.

Populists make everything immediately a moral question—and they make it very, very personal; it's always about character, which is to say, the supposed fact that their opponents are corrupt characters. I do not want to repeat any of the things Donald Trump said about his opponent in the 2015–2016 election. What I want to underline is that, as far as populism goes, Trump was an extreme, but he was not really an exception. All populists deny the legitimacy of their opponents in one way or another.

The second consequence of populists' claim to a moral monopoly of representing the real people is perhaps less obvious. Populists will say that all those among the people themselves, all citizens who do not share their ultimately symbolic construction of "the real people," can have their status as properly belonging to the people put into doubt. Again, a few brief examples might be helpful. Think back to Nigel Farage giving a speech during the night of Brexit and saying that this had been, as he put it, "a victory for real people." By implication, the forty–eight percent who wanted to stay inside the European Union are not quite real, are not truly members of the British people. Or consider a statement from Donald Trump. He gave a speech on the campaign trail in May 2016, where he said: "The only important thing is the unification of the people—because the other people do not mean anything."

It is a cliché that every winner in an American election says something along the lines of "Now it is time to heal divisions." But when Trump tweeted, "We will unite, and we will win, win, win!" it meant something rather different. It was not a liberal democratic promise to accept difference and diversity. It was a threat of sorts. Populists talk about unification of the people all the time, but it is always unification on exactly their terms and according to who they think properly belongs to the real people and who does not.

Long story short: the decisive thing to grasp about populism is not some vague "anti-elitism." Anybody can criticize the powerful. That does not mean that anyone who does so is automatically right, or an exemplar of engaged citizenship. What matters about populism is anti-pluralism—the fact that populists exclude others morally and, if possible, politically, both at the level of party politics and, less obviously, at the level of the people themselves, where some citizens are said not to be part of "the real people" at all.

Now, some of you might be tempted to reply: "But wait a minute, can it not still be the case that, at least in some contexts, populism might have a positive effect?" Is it not possible that sometimes populism acts as what in the social scientific literature is often called a corrective for the faults of established liberal democracies? Or could it not be that populists mobilize people and bring them closer to the political system?

Undoubtedly, there is plenty to criticize about our political systems today. But I reject the idea of populism as a proper "corrective." For notice how populists effectively operate. The first step for them is always a symbolic construction of who the "real people" are. In a second step, they deduce from that construction a supposedly singular authentic will of the people. And then, in a third step, they claim, like Trump during the Republican convention in July 2016: "I am your voice." Notice that in this entire process nobody else has really spoken. It has been a more or less theoretical exercise. Populists are not interested in an open-ended process of deliberation among citizens who exchange views and where the outcome of such deliberation generally cannot be known in advance. Populists always already know the right answer, because they deduce it from their conception of who the real people supposedly are. That also means that, in a referendum, the only real task of the people is to tick what, according to the populists, is the right box. Populists are not per se interested in more popular participation.

If you find my suggestion about how to understand populism at all plausible, it should be clear that populists who do not win electoral contests have a quasi-logical problem at their hands. For how can it be that, on the one hand, they are the only authentic moral representatives of the real people, and yet at the same time, they did not win the election? That cannot really be the case at all. One obvious way out of this contradiction is to resort to some version of conspiracy theory. For the populists, if the silent majority had not been silent, the populists would always already be in power. The fact that they are not in power shows that the majority is still silent, which, so the reasoning goes, must mean that somebody has kept it silent—in short, the elites must have been doing something behind the scenes to prevent the true majority from expressing itself. I am not saying this happens all the time, but if you think back over recent history, it is not an accident that populists so frequently contest election outcomes. Just think how Trump, before November 8, was in effect conveying the message that he might not accept what he took to be an illegitimate outcome; or, to put it more bluntly, how he was pre-emptively articulating the view that if Clinton won, the election must have been rigged.

Allow me to give you another example, somewhat closer to your academic home, of the mechanism I am flagging. Think back to the referendum that took place in Hungary in October 2016. The government obtained the result it had wished for—98 per cent in effect voted against "Brussels settling migrants in Hungary." But an insufficient number of citizens participated; legally, the referendum had to be declared invalid. Clearly, the government at that point could not possibly explain that the process had been rigged—for, if anything, Viktor Orbán himself has been busy rigging things in Hungary since 2010 (and, in this case, spending an extraordinary amount of money on a campaign to get the "correct" outcome). Did it matter that the result was legally invalid? Absolutely not—the Hungarian government now simply subsumed those who had not participated under a fictitious silent majority, which was said to support the government's line. So Orbán could still claim that, at last, the people themselves had spoken on the refugee issue, and had clearly come out against the policies proposed by what he has frequently called the "liberal nihilists" who are in charge of the EU.

My point is this: even in cases where populists themselves have created or even control political and legal procedures, they might violate these procedures if they fail to produce the "populistically correct" outcome. If in doubt, populists play off "the real people"—an almost mystical entity "out there" somehow—against the existing democratic institutions. It is a pattern that was already identified (and advocated) by Carl Schmitt in the 1920s, when he opposed real democracy, which could be based on an existential choice through acclamation by the people, to the merely statistical apparatus of liberalism, where, in banal fashion, secret ballots are added up, and one gets a numerical, empirical outcome. But the fact is that in democracies we ultimately only have numbers, as opposed some mystical substance of the people.

Now, please don't get me wrong: I am not saying that anyone who criticizes election systems, or even the institutions of contemporary representative democracies more broadly, is automatically a danger. Far from it. Again, it can be a sign of good civic engagement that one criticizes a lack of chances to participate, or the fact that many citizens are not properly represented, or—not to put too fine a point on it—that some election systems have become deeply corrupted (just think of the situation in the United States). But it is one thing to criticize a system; it is another thing categorically, under all circumstances, to assert: "Because we (populists) did not win, it must have been rigged," or something like, "Ours is not a real democracy because we did not gain a majority at the ballot box." These are simply not democratic arguments.

# Populism in Power

There is widespread view that populists, almost by definition, cannot govern or maintain themselves in power. It is frequently asserted that populists have such horrendously simplistic ideas about policy that, on day two of their time in office, everyone will see clearly that none of their ideas work in practice. Another variation of this view is that all populist parties are essentially protest movements—and that, logically, they cannot govern qua as populists, since, once you are in government, you cannot keep protesting against yourself. One way or another, then, the problem is going to solve itself: populists fail outright, or they are bound to become more "moderate" and "reasonable," as the constraints of the office civilizes them (as a patronizing language among liberals often has it).

These assumptions—very popular among many liberals, I fear—are highly naïve. We have plenty of examples in our age of how populists in power have been able to govern—and able to govern specifically as populists, which is to say: as actors who on a basic level do not truly recognize the legitimacy of an opposition. Hence the typical reaction of populists in the face of criticism from other parties, courts, or independent media: these other actors are not elected, or, in the case of parties, have failed to gain majorities, hence have no right to thwart the implementation of the will of the people who are exclusively represented by the populists.

I would go further and say that we have seen the emergence of a distinct "populist art of governance," with at least three distinct elements. First, if we look at examples such as Hungary, Turkey, Poland, Venezuela, but also a significant number of other countries, what we can discern is a decided attempt by populist parties in power to appropriate the state itself in one way or another, which is to say more concretely: abolish a more or less neutral civil service and place their own partisan actors in important positions. You can of course reply that many non-populist parties also try to do that. Fair enough. But the difference is that populists engage in these practices very openly, and they do it while advancing what they think is a genuinely moral claim: in one way or another, they end up asserting that the state is there for the people—and that the people, of whom the populists are of course the only legitimate representatives, should appropriate the state for their own proper purposes. Whoever stands in the way of that appropriation is then accused of obstructing the people's authentic will.

Secondly, what we have also witnessed in many of these cases is what political scientists tend to call "mass clientelism"—the notion according to which parties in power reward their supporters with material benefits or also bureaucratic favors. Again, you can tell me that many decidedly non-populist parties also try to do that. True, but the difference is once again that populists can engage in mass clientelism in the open, advancing what from their point of view is a moral claim. For remember that, from the get-go, not all the people are "the real people"; the empirical entirety of citizens is not automatically the same as "the people" which populists claim only they represent. Only some people are the real people. And if only the real people receive benefits, then, from the point of view of the populists, that is actually exactly how things should be.

This pattern can perhaps explain what otherwise would be very peculiar outcomes in a number of countries. In so many contexts populists first came to power with the claim that the old elites are corrupt, and that their most urgent task is to "clean up" (or "drain the swamp"). And then, it turns out that a lot of these populist actors are substantially more corrupt than their predecessors. And yet often they do not seem to be paying a price for this—when one would have thought that breaking their most important moral promise must spell political death. One explanation might be that in the eyes of their supporters, what they do is not really corruption at all. Figures like Erdoğan and Orbán are not creating clientelistic mafia-states; they are just doing the right thing for us, the real people.

Lastly, I think it has not been an accident that in virtually all populist regimes, whenever there is protest from within civil society, it is symbolically extremely important for these governments to delegitimize it entirely, even under circumstances where these protest movements are probably not much of a real threat at all. By definition, from the point of view of the populists, it simply cannot be that parts of the people themselves are rising up against their only morally legitimate representatives. As a result, time and time again, we have witnessed a strategy that in certain ways was pioneered by Vladimir Putin in Russia. Namely, the strategy of in effect claiming: "What you think is authentic civil society is all steered—and paid for—from the outside." What matters for populist regimes is to communicate that citizens demonstrating on the streets and squares are not "real people." They are, according to the Putinist template that has been copied by so many populists-in-power, "foreign agents." In this manner, the populists' claim to exclusive moral representation of the "real people" also remains intact.

In short, what I have tried to present to you are a number of patterns or characteristics that form part of that peculiar populist art of governance. Identifying this art is not the same as saying that these regimes are invulnerable or that nobody can do anything when it comes to organizing effective opposition against them. But we should give up the naïve view that once they come to power, they will automatically moderate or they will very obviously fail, especially in the eyes of their own supporters. For that view is simply incorrect. They really can govern. And they can govern specifically as populists. And, furthermore, they can easily sustain an "anti-elite" discourse, even if naïve liberals think that once you are in power you are by definition the elite and hence cannot keep blaming "the establishment" for whatever goes wrong. Well, no populist has ever run out of scapegoats to explain why the real people's singular authentic will is being thwarted. It's the elitist courts; it's the "opposition media," the supposed enemy of the people, according to Stephen K. Bannon; it's a shadowy network of "globalists," and on and on. There is always someone to blame, always yet another conspiracy to be uncovered.

## What Can Be Done Against Populism?

Let me put the question bluntly: What can we do against populism? I would like to suggest some tentative answers for politicians on the one hand, and for citizens on the other. But before doing that, I want to underline that one should resist the temptation of treating populism as ultimately just a kind of PR problem. One gives in to that temptation if one thinks that we just have to have better "narratives" for liberalism, or the EU, or globalization, or what have you. One also gives in to that temptation if one says that citizens' "anger" has to be taken seriously—but then adopts a quasi-therapeutic, patronizing approach, where citizens' actual claims are never listened to, because one is always already so sure that one can explain that anger with economic factors or with psychological patters (as in: they must all have authoritarian personalities...). Dealing with populism is not just a PR challenge; it is above all a question of policy content and a question about the adequacy of some of our political institutions.

Related to this fixation on PR is a tendency to treat some of the enabling conditions of populism—polarization, cultural divisions, *Kulturkampf*—as simply given. Take seemingly neutral statements such as "The country is so divided." But divisions are not a problem as such for a democracy; after all, democracy is supposed to help us deal with divisions and conflicts. The problem starts when citizens view every issue purely as a matter of partisan identity—think of a stance that comes down to saying, "Because I am a Republican, I cannot possibly find climate science findings credible." It gets worse when partisan identity becomes so strong that no argument from or about the legitimacy of the other side ever gets through. After all, Trump was not elected as the candidate of a grassroots movement of angry white losers of globalization, but as the leader of a very "normal" establishment party. But that party—and its cheerleaders in the right wing media—had, long before Trump, started to demonize those on the other side of the political divide and effectively told its followers that they could never opt for "European-style socialists" and other un-American abominations under any circumstances. Hence the curious outcome of the November 2016 election that a number of Republicans went on record with the view that Trump was not qualified to be president—and yet they voted for him.

In the United States, then, polarization is not an objective reflection of given cultural differences; it has at least partly been a conscious elite project to divide the country for political advantage and sometimes even personal profit. After all, polarization is also big business, as a quick look at the earnings of major figures on Fox "News" and talk radio can confirm. Populism thrives in conditions of culture war, but culture wars never just happen spontaneously. They have to do with larger structural issues, especially the media, schooling, but even infrastructure: whether people who live close to each other will never meet because, so to speak, they do live on different planets is not so much about "culture" in general, but specific socio-economic circumstances. I only need to think of the place where I happen to live: Princeton is about a fifteen-minute drive away from Trenton, one of the poorest, most problematic places in New Jersey. And yet I can probably count on two hands the people I know who have been to both places in a meaningful way.

Now, allow me return to actors, as opposed to structures. What can and should professional politicians do in the face of populism? To stick with the theme of self-critical liberalism, let me first of all say that one very typical mistake has been to retreat to a de-facto technocratic position, to end up saying that we can always be absolutely sure that all populists necessarily have simplistic, unworkable policy proposals, or even that they are necessarily lying in whatever they say, because all populists are by definition demagogues and purveyors of "alternative facts." We, on the other hand, the liberals, we do competence, we do reason, and, of course, we do the truth.

It is very easy, after the fact, to have a list of the mistakes made by the Clinton campaign ready. But I do think that it is worth pointing out that it was fateful to end up in a position where the political contest appeared to be one between competence and incompetence. I am not saying that the incompetence charge against Trump was wrong—far from it—but it was still a mistake no longer to make substantial arguments in a contest of distinct visions for the country. One ends up basically telling people that if they are attracted by the other candidate, they are irrational, they are incompetent, there is something wrong with them. Talk about "deplorables" was a large gift to the Trump campaign.

Whoever retreats to a purely technocratic position claims in the end that for every policy challenge, there is only one rational answer. All that citizens can do is to consent to that one rational answer; debates are unnecessary, even parliaments are really just there to nod through the one rational policy proposal. This is a caricature, to be sure, but something clearly resembling this stance has been particularly prominent in the EU context over the last decade or so—especially during the Eurocrisis.

It is important to recognize that this kind of rhetoric provides an excellent opening for populists. For they are then right to ask: Where are the people in all this? How can there be a democracy without choices? I am not suggesting that populists genuinely want to bring the people back in; as hopefully has become clear enough, I do not regard populism as a "useful corrective" or a principled stance in favor of more citizen participation. But technocracy makes the game so much easier for populists, especially if many other parties converge on the single rational policy with technocratic arguments (think of social democratic parties during the Eurocrisis).

More important still, technocracy on the one hand, and populism on the other, can start to reinforce each other in a particularly fateful manner. Even if they seem so different, technocracy and populism actually have one important thing in common: they are both forms of anti-pluralism. The technocrat says in effect: there is only one rational solution, no need for debate, if you disagree you reveal yourself as irrational. The populist says: there is only one authentic will of the people (and only we know it), there is no need for debate, if you disagree you reveal yourself as a traitor to the people. Everything that we might think of as central to democracy—exchange of arguments, debates, competition between different options, in other words a sense that citizens have real choices—ends up being eliminated. Politics becomes a contest between two options only, whose proponents keep saying that there is no alternative.

It is probably often more convenient, even more comforting, for liberals to retreat to technocracy. It can feel good to think that only "we" have the truth. It can also be a way to allow oneself to indulge in all the prejudices about "the masses," which liberals long cultivated from the nineteenth century onwards: if in doubt, assume that "the people" are irrational, or at least very ill-informed, and hence capable of anything, when it comes to political choices. I hope I have made it clear why I think this kind of liberal approach is deeply mistaken.

At the risk of seeming overly negative, allow me to continue a bit with what I take to be serious mistakes for politicians. Often, it has seemed both the morally and practically right thing to try to exclude populist actors altogether. Politicians might then refuse to appear on the same platform with them. When deputies of a populist party ask questions in parliament, there will not be an answer, or there will be an ostentatious walkout. I think by now we can say with a great deal of confidence that this kind of *cordon sanitaire* is a mistake. It is actually a mistake both on a strategic level, and, less obviously, also on a normative level. As to the strategic level: total exclusion is bound to confirm the very narrative populists tell their supporters: the elites never listen, there are all these taboo subjects that nobody is allowed to address, the elites are so afraid of us they do not even dare to talk to us. Etc. But there is also a problem here, if you like, at the level of the demands democratic theory makes on us. When populist parties are already in legislative assemblies, excluding their representatives effectively means disenfranchising their voters. And not all those who cast their ballot for populist parties can be assumed to be committed anti-pluralists with anti-democratic tendencies.

Hence there is no other option than engaging with populists. But that does not mean that one has to start running after them. Talking with populists is not the same as talking like populists. We have seen a number of very instructive recent examples for how the "running after strategy" is bound to fail—and, again, the failure happens both on a strategic and a more normative level. As to the strategic, or, if you prefer, instrumental level: just think back to the autumn of 2016, when Nicolas Sarkozy was effectively running after and trying to overtake Marine Le Pen, when it came to immigration, integration demands for Muslims, etc. No matter how fast one runs, one is unlikely to catch up with populists on questions like immigration. Moreover, this strategy leaves populists with the common sense response: why vote for the copy if the uncorrupted original is still on offer? And on a more normative level, the peril is clearly that this kind of opportunism of supposedly mainstream parties can shift an entire political spectrum to the right—without that shift ever having been authorized by majorities in a comprehensive manner (we have seen such fateful shifts for instance in the Netherlands and Denmark).

As I said, I believe there is no alternative to engagement, to debate and deliberation. Clearly, it is not easy to do this well. But a good politician will be able to sustain a real debate with populists and face them on the substance of a whole range of issue that can be freely debated in a democracy. The hope here—and this can sound like a pious hope, of course—is that the unforced force of the better argument will prevail. So far, so relatively banal. But here is the less banal part: on certain occasions, when populists reveal themselves specifically as populists, other politicians should immediately draw red lines as clearly as possible. Think of a situation in which a populist politician switches from a debate about immigration or refugee policy, which in a democracy is entirely legitimate, to the claim that Angela Merkel has a secret plan to replace the German *Volk* with Syrians. This is a real world example. Now, that is the kind of moment where I think a politician has to say, wait a minute, of course we can debate immigration or refugee policy, but this you cannot say. You either give us the evidence for this theory now or you stop doing this. Now, the populist is unlikely to recoil and apologize for having spouted conspiracy theories. But the hope—and I concede again that it might sound like the pious hope of a democratic theorist—is that the audience, democratic citizens, will say, "I even agree on some of these points about immigration that they are putting forward, but ultimately I do not want to be in the same boat with people who keep repeating conspiracy theories. I do not want to be in the same boat with people who tell us [again a real world example] that we already live in a dictatorship that is run by Angela Merkel." This requires a particular set of skills, and also a particular capacity for judgment, a sense of timing and tone that cannot be learnt from bullet points in a manual for professional politicians. But it is something that we should legitimately expect from the people who engage with populists—and if they do it well, we should honor that achievement.

Let me also address what I think, normatively, is a challenging issue, especially when one is serious about liberals taking a hard look at their own ideas (and previous conduct). Earlier, I argued that populists are anti-pluralists. One might be tempted under the circumstances to think that all we have to do then is reassert pluralism. On a very general level that is not wrong. But what does pluralism really mean here? After all, pluralism is not a first order political value such as liberty and equality. And the point of democracy as such is surely not to maximize pluralism in and of itself. Now, for some people, pluralism is just a fact. For others, pluralism is a very important value—diversity is a good thing in and of itself (John Stuart Mill, and, to some degree, Isaiah Berlin came close this view). I think the most plausible way of presenting the case is to say that in a political space with diverse identities and interests, we have to find fair terms of sharing that space (as some of you will recognize, this thought is partly inspired by John Rawls). This is rather different from saying "the more diversity, the better." But it is also different from simply saying that we just have to put up with the fact that there are so many different people and that a kind of modus vivendi solution is the best we can achieve under the circumstances.

Let's put the point a bit more sharply, or, put differently, let's make life a little more uncomfortable for those holding liberal views: if we are serious about pluralism, it is going to mean the inclusion of political positions that a lot of us do not agree with. Pluralism cannot mean just stuff liberals like anyway. For instance, there is space in a democracy for politicians who advocate a very restrictive immigration policy. There is a space in democracy for proponents of very conservative views on family policies. I do not like these positions, but it would be a mistake automatically to condemn them as per se undemocratic. If liberals are serious of pluralism, they have to accept the legitimacy of those holding those positions—and then fight the latter with everything they got by way of arguments, moral claims, empirical evidence, etc.

Why does this matter in the present context? It matters because one thing that liberal democratic politicians can plausibly do is to say: We are willing to accept that a populist party mobilizes citizens for its positions. We do not advocate prohibiting such a party (in countries where parties can be banned) or de facto excluding them completely from democratic debate. But at the same time, we do not say that populist parties are just like all others, with perhaps just a bit of uncouth rhetoric or bad manners. We want these parties to move away from their anti-pluralism. And one concrete idea to make that happen is developing what has sometimes been called a "catalogue of criteria." This has been tried—largely unsuccessfully, to be sure—in Austria, where the Social Democrats announced that they were open to coalitions with all kinds of parties, as long as they fulfilled specific criteria. If populists continue, let's say, to incite hatred against minorities, or advocate an exit from the European Union—then no coalition. At least in the abstract, that is a very promising idea because it takes away the argument from populists that they are eternal victims of mainstream parties who keep them from power no matter what. Such criteria also make the process more transparent for citizens because it becomes predictable what certain parties may or may not do (which also can be a check on the opportunism of the mainstream, which I touched on earlier).

This brings me back to the metaphors I mentioned at the very beginning: the wave, the tsunami (according to Nigel Farage, for whom the wave was apparently an insufficiently grandiose and world-historical image), the dominos (according to Marine Le Pen's theory), the tide of history (according to Stephen K. Bannon). Why are all these images misleading? They are misleading because the narrative of Brexit, Trump, etc. suggests that these populist triumphs were entirely brought about by populists—and that the latter are now an irresistible historical force. But, with all due respect, Nigel Farage did not cause Brexit singlehandedly. He needed his Boris Johnson. Maybe even more, he needed his Michael Gove, because Johnson was seen as a bit of an eccentric character as well, to put it mildly. Gove, after all, is a real intellectual among Tories. When someone like that says, "People in this country have had enough of experts," it really means something because, after all, he himself is an expert. So it was not just anybody from the street who told the British people that expertise was overrated—it took an expert on expertise to make that claim plausible.

And at the risk of reminding us of the obvious: Donald Trump did not become president as the leader of a populist, grassroots movement of angry white workers (as the cliché has it). As said earlier, he was the candidate of a very established party. It is worth remembering that the single most important factor that explains the outcome of November 8 is simply partisanship. More than ninety percent of self-identified Republicans voted for Donald Trump. If he had not received the blessings of the likes of Chris Christie, Rudy Giuliani, and Newt Gingrich (another intellectual among conservatives, by the way), he would not be in the White House. What I am trying to remind you of is simply that this supposedly inevitable string of populist victories would not have happened without the collaboration of established conservative elites. It is a mistake to remain fixated on populists in isolation. They are always part of a larger party-political dynamic. The real question is how do other actors respond to populists?

Here, Austrian political experience might hold another lesson. That is the place where, contrary to many predictions, the domino did not fall during the presidential elections in 2016. That story is complex, but surely one important factor was that a lot of conservatives, members of the Austrian People's Party—actually not so much the very top, but lots of local mayors— explicitly came out against the populist candidate. These were people who had a lot of credibility with conservative voters, especially in rural Austria (if the Greens from Vienna had shown up, they would hardly been seen as the best figures to make the case against Norbert Hofer, the self-declared man of the people).

It is also worth remembering that many of us might in the end not have terribly much direct influence with populist politicians and parties. But at least some of us might have influence when we interact with conservative politicians and parties. Just think of the European People's Party, the mainstream of the EU mainstream if ever there was one. You might put the question to them: Why are they still treating Fidesz like a normal Christian Democratic party, when Fidesz in many ways is closer to the far right? Will that have an effect? I cannot guarantee it, of course, but it makes a difference whether potential mainstream opportunists feel they are being closely watched—and possibly be punished for their unprincipled conduct.

So we should not buy into the narrative of inevitability. In a perverse way, this narrative can provide certainty—even if the trend is disconcerting, there is comfort in knowing where the trend is going (irresistibly, or so it seems). Such certainty then also relieves us of responsibility—after all, there is nothing that can be done. In fact, there is plenty that can be done.

This brings me to my last point, about citizens (or, as patronizing language has it, "ordinary people"). Again, there are interesting lessons from the Austrian presidential election here. Many volunteers came out for the campaign of Alexander Van der Bellen. The campaign leaders made it clear that one would not have to be completely in synch with Green party programs to support their candidate; all that mattered was that one agreed as to Hofer posing a danger to Austrian democracy. Volunteers were then encouraged to go to places they would not normally go, and to talk to men and women with whom they would not usually talk. They were also encouraged not to let these conversations end with accusations of "You're a fascist! You're a racist!"

Talking to strangers matters. Connecting with people outside a media where profits are made by maximizing polarization matters. If nothing else, it concretely pierces the populist fantasy of a fully homogeneous "real people." Remember also Obama's moving farewell address. He encouraged citizens to stop arguing with strangers on the Internet and talk to them offline instead. In memorable prose that I cannot improve on: "If you're tired of arguing with

strangers on the Internet, try talking with one of them in real life. If something needs fixing, then lace up your shoes and do some organizing. If you're
disappointed by your elected officials, grab a clipboard, get some signatures,
and run for office yourself. Show up, dive in, stay at it." Yes, this all can sound
like a pep talk from an elite whose members know that in real life things do
not work quite so easily. But it is still the best hope we have.

# Beyond Demagoguery?
# The Contemporary Crisis of Political
# Communication

*Erica Benner*

## Introduction

I would like to begin with this wonderful quote from Thomas Hobbes: "The most noble and profitable invention was that of Speech [...] whereby men register their Thoughts [...] and declare them to one another for mutual utility and conversation; without which, there had been amongst men, neither Common-wealth, nor Society, nor Contract, nor Peace, no more than amongst Lions, Bears, and Wolves."[1]

Hobbes is writing near the end of the English Civil War in 1651. For several decades leading up to the war, he had witnessed the breakdown of political language in England. He blamed firebrand orators, who used their eloquence to whip up patriots among otherwise peace-loving people. These orators, he said, used the art of words to represent good in the likeness of evil and evil in the likeness of good, thus discontenting men and troubling their peace. Behind the orators, Hobbes identified even worse troublemakers: schoolmen in the universities. In his words, universities were what the wooden horse was to the Trojans: a poisoned gift of counterfeit wisdom that wreaks havoc in civil societies. Academics, he said, worked as propagandists for rival fractions and they taught future clergymen and politicians how to appear wise and morally superior to less educated people.

I doubt that many of us here would go as far as Hobbes did in blaming academics for present pathologies of political communication. Some people

---

[1] Thomas Hobbes, *Leviathan*, 1651, Chapter IV: Of Speech.

argue that universities nurture excessive liberalism or excessive political correctness, which tends to broader the divide between us and other people; I do
not endorse this view. I start with Hobbes because what he says in this quote
underlines a basic truth that sounds rather banal until we realize the consequences of not taking it seriously. This banal but essential truth is that political communications—healthy political communications—are very important. It might be true that language does not always seem like one of the
bedrocks of civil society. If you want to keep societies together and avoid civil
wars, you might think that your main priority is to keep social and political
institutions strong and satisfy people's material needs. I agree with this, but
it would be wrong to think that most of the time speech is merely an instrument we use to achieve these things. Hobbes' point is that there is nothing
mere about political communication. Language is what makes society possible. It is what allows people to communicate their opinions, give reasons
for their actions, and make laws and compacts that prevent war. If you want
to keep our human species from going the way of the wolves, there can be
no more important task than that of clarifying and defending the shared
meanings of words, and getting a clearer understanding about the norms that
ought to regulate political speech. Then, there is the question of what counts
as reasonably well ordered political speech. Philosophers have answered this
question in all sorts of ways; some of them set the bar very high, and many
of them presented ideal standards of deliberative reason or communicative
rationality.

Healthy practices of public communication are not always obvious.
You can disagree passionately, you can hurl verbal abuse at your interlocutors and still have order, as long as people observe certain limits most of
the time. Some of these limits are defined by laws and as such enforced, but
many of them are tacit, and different limits are expected in different contexts.
Shouting and heckling is a venerable tradition in the British Parliament, but
if it happened in Japan, it would look like the end of civilization. When in
democracies politicians communicate with citizens, we expect them to use a
certain amount of spin as part of the competitive game they have to play, and
it would be naïve to demand from them perfect transparency. We complain
when we catch politicians trying to mislead voters in obvious ways, but we
do not usually think that the free world is about to turn on its head because a
leader bends the truth or whitewashes an indiscretion.

In robust open societies, even healthy political communications can look
deceptively unstable. One of the marks of open society is that it welcomes

different opinions and values, and encourages hard-hitting debates between them. Defenders of open society tend to agree that when political systems allow vigorous arguments among citizens, they become stronger and more stable than systems that repress debates. Pluralism and freedom are not just nice liberal words; they are powerful things, social powers in their own right. They create strong political associations because they do a better job than closed societies in getting citizens from all walks of life firmly behind them, giving people a stake in their country's political fate because they play a part, however small, in deciding what that fate should be.

But if freedom of speech makes politics look somewhat noisy and turbulent, how do we know when we are facing a genuine crisis of political communication? This is a big question today. We have information wars, we are in the age of post-truth politics, fake news, and attacks on experts, and many people are shouting crisis and going into panic mode.

## A Crisis of Political Communication

My first question is: How do we know what happens when things start to go bad? As a preliminary answer, let me just give a description of how things look when norms of speech start to go downhill:

> All Greece was in commotion, and quarrels arose everywhere between the leaders of the demos, who wanted to side with the Athenians, and the oligarchs, who wanted to bring in the Spartans. And many terrible things happened, that had been seen before, and shall be seen again as long as human nature is the same. The accepted value of words was changed to people's pleasure. Reckless audacity was counted as brave loyalty to party, prudent deliberation was called cowardice, reasonable moderation was called a covert for weakness, frantic impulsiveness was praised as manly. The hotheaded man was always trusted, his opponents suspected. Men of the same party were bound not by divine law, but by common transgression of the laws.[2]

---

[2] Thucydides, *History of the Peloponnesian War*, trans. Charles Forster Smith and Loeb Class (Cambridge, MA: Harvard University Press, 1921), with translations by the author.

This is the Greek historian Thucydides writing in the fifth century BC about the long war between Athens and Sparta. I will briefly give you some of the results he mentions. It was the "less high-minded people," he says, who won the day. Because they were afraid of their own defects and of their opponents' cleverness, so that they might not be defeated with words, they resorted to audacious deeds. Their opponents, on the other hand, i.e. the opponents of the less high-minded people, contentiously assuming that there was no need to secure with deeds what they could have secured by wit, were caught off guard, and perished in greater numbers.

The collapse of political speech norms throughout ancient Greece happened after a long process of corruption. It did not happen overnight, Thucydides says, as soon as the war broke out. Corruption had been happening for a long time, driven as much by malpractices of speech as by deeds. Thucydides gives a detailed account of the various speeches that first led the Greeks towards war, and then keeps pressing this question further and further. He shows his readers how speakers changed the meaning of words, often subtly, so nobody noticed until it was too late. This change of meaning was what pushed things to worse and worse violence, starting with a word like justice. At the beginning of the war, all Greeks understood the word "justice" to mean, "What is fair to all from a general perspective." It means a lot of other things, too, but this is the most common meaning. It is a word that helps you adjudicate conflicts between different groups of people. As the war proceeded, people began to use the word in their speeches, and tried to rally groups of people and their populations around the idea that justice had to be justice for "us." It became a self-centered concept of justice, and at the later stage of the war, justice deteriorated to meaning "the advantage of the strongest," by which point people were no longer speaking the same political language.

I would like to believe that we are not at a similar stage of crisis in our present-day democracies. Nonetheless, there are good reasons to worry that we might be heading towards a more critical stage. Also, there are good reasons to try to think calmly about how political language could contribute to human crises, as well as ways of trying to solve them.

## Demagoguery and Political Communication

I am now turning to one kind of political language game, demagoguery. I will ask what it is, how it works, what harm it does, and how it commits this harm. Then I will turn to the second part of the question, the contemporary part: Is it still the same kind of language game as it was in the past, or are new technologies and social media changing its character, giving demagoguery a larger or smaller, a more or less dangerous role in politics?

In Greek, demagogue comes from the words "demos" and "agein," "the people" and "to lead." Thus, a demagogue was traditionally a leader of the people, but quite early on the term acquired a rather pejorative connotation, which it still has today, with synonyms like rabble-rouser or agitator. Nowadays, we think of a demagogue as a political leader who seeks support by appealing to popular desires and prejudices. I am talking about demagoguery as a style of political mobilization that relies heavily on distinctive methods of manipulative speech and on supplementary images, performances, and theatrics. Here, I will talk about speech, and not so much about the performative aspects, important as they are, particularly in today's television-, video-, and media-driven world.

In my definition, manipulation is the key word. To be clear about what a manipulator is: it is someone who seeks to control or change thoughts and behavior, without the subject's full understanding or participation. Manipulation is not forced; i.e., you know when somebody is forcing you, but you do not always know when someone is manipulating you. As Kant put it: "The art of persuasion [seeks to] to win minds over to the advantage of the speaker before they can judge and to rob them of their freedom."[3]

Manipulation involves the subject, somehow without their knowledge, but nonetheless robs them of their freedom. Of course, other kinds of political discourse are manipulative, too, but in different ways. Something that distinguishes demagoguery is that it aims to elicit strong public support in a short time. It tends to use distinctive shortcut methods of persuasion. This makes it different from complex systems of ideas, or ideologies, which tend

---

[3] Immanuel Kant, *Critique of the Power of Judgment*, trans. Paul Guyer (Cambridge: Cambridge University Press, 2000), 5327, http://www.cambridge.org/hu/academic/subjects/philosophy/philosophy-texts/critique-power-judgment?format=PB&isbn=9780521348928#XI2lUESApdw0xeRu.97.

to dominate minds over longer stretches of time. It also distinguishes demagoguery from systematic strategies of manipulation backed by the resources
or the machinery of the state, which I think is one common understanding of
the word propaganda.

I want to suggest that we might be wrong to neglect demagoguery. It is
true that demagoguery is a normal and often relatively harmless part of democratic politics: It is there all the time, it is everywhere, and it does not just
crop up in times of crisis. This is something Thucydides makes very clear, as
does Plato. Nonetheless, demagoguery has the potential to do a lot of damage
to both our societies and our psyches, in the short as well as in the long term.
Part of what makes it so dangerous is just that it is so commonplace. It is a
constant factor in our lives, and often we do not notice what it is doing to us,
until it goes too far and extensive damage is done.

So how does demagoguery work? I think it has two main signature
methods, quick and easy ways to mobilize support. One method is flattery.
This is what ancient writers, from Thucydides, Plato, and Aristotle to the
early modern thinkers, singled out: flattery is one of the key elements of
demagoguery. Aristotle has a famous quote that says that all men are willing
to listen to speeches that are in agreement with their own character, opinions, and values, and to speakers who resemble them, or appear to resemble
them. Demagogues are of course not the only speakers who take this to heart;
anyone who is speaking to someone else tries to adjust a little to them. But
demagogues push their resemblance with their listeners to extremes. How do
they do this? Several ways. First, they try to confirm their listeners' perspectives and feelings as true and just. However unrealistic, narrow-minded, or
self-regarding these opinions and desires might be, the demagogue tells you,
"You know best" and "The customer is always right." Another thing they do
is to indulge, or try to expiate, weaknesses, insecurities, and private shames.
Finally, the demagogue cares about and identifies strongly with you and your
in-group.

The second signature method of demagogues is quackery. This is a funny
word that first appears in seventeenth-century England. It comes from the
Dutch, from a word that means, "boasting the ability to cure." Quack doctors
are charlatans, fakes; they make big promises to solve illnesses without the
knowledge to diagnose or cure them. In politics, quackery is basically a spurious epistemic authority on the part of a leader, a party, or a speaker, and
it has a couple of signature techniques: scapegoating, i.e., claiming that
the cause of your problem is external, i.e. some person, group, country, or

phenomenon "X," rather than having a more complex view of it; and constructing a highly misleading view of the world wherein the patients, i.e., citizens, are far more powerful, wise, persecuted, or preyed upon than the evidence suggests.

Do not all political speakers resort to quackery and flattery to some extent? Surely even the most honest politicians try to persuade people by appealing to their emotions, their tastes, and their temperaments? Well, my answer is yes, but there are different ways to do this. Today, for example, most politicians have to address voters' feelings of insecurity in the face of economic globalization. If they want to win campaigns, they need to show sympathy with their voters' concerns. Let us say voters keep telling them: "We have too many foreigners, this is what worries us. All these immigrants keep coming here, they keep setting up shops and bringing in their plumbers and they are taking away our business." Politician from media outlet A responds: "I don't blame you for being unhappy, I don't blame you for being uncomfortable with this situation. We have had immigration before, and there is always friction, there are always adjustments. But the real problem lies somewhere else, and it has to do with economic pressures and policies; it has nothing to do with these people. Here is how I am going to try to deal with those pressures and create policies that make your life better." Politician in newspaper B takes the same anxieties and says: "You are absolutely right, immigration is the problem." They go further than what many voters are actually telling them. They say: "And if you think it is bad now, just wait, it is getting worse and worse. If you are worried about the Poles and the Romanians in Britain, just wait for all the Turks who are about to come in." This is one of the things that the Brexit campaign told British voters before the campaign: "They are not just trying to steal your jobs, they also have links to Islamic terrorists." The lines between demagogues and non-demagogues are blurry; there is no scientific line you can draw between them. But I do not think it is all that hard to separate demagoguery from other forms of rhetoric and everyday political spin.

Another point I am trying to make is that political speech is not just a reflection of pre-existing needs, desires, or opinions. What political speakers say mediates, articulates, and reshapes the opinions, desires, and needs people have. It re-describes them, and in re-describing them it shapes people's choices and actions much more than we tend to realize. Especially when we think that the main problem we have is political crisis, or that it has to do with social and political discontents. Yes, this is true, but do not ignore speech and what is happening to it—this is equally important.

Of course, some demagogues publicly deny that they shape opinions at all. After the Brexit referendum, the editor of the tabloid *The Sun* said it was true that they fed people's enthusiasm for leaving the European Union, but it is delusional, he said, that they, a mere newspaper, could "somehow drag otherwise unwilling readers to a point of view they don't already have."[4] Here, we should remember that demagoguery is a species of manipulation; it is not a species of outright domination or force, so manipulated people are not dragged in against their will. Manipulation is a subtler process that involves people's beliefs, but not always in ways that can be reflected upon or grasped. This means that demagoguery is always a two-way street, not a relationship between a puppet master and a marionette, pulled by strings. The result is the emergence of opinions that are not necessarily entirely false or unreasonable. Opinions that result from demagoguery—partly the listener's and partly the speaker's—are often a hybrid of facts based on evidence, distortions, and inventions. They blend concerns that are not entirely unreasonable with other worries that are exaggerated, half true, or downright irrational. It is not unreasonable to worry about how newcomers will fit into a society, or how immigration might affect your economic well-being. It is unreasonable to scapegoat them. This mix can make it very hard to challenge the opinions that arise from the interactions of demagogues and citizens.

## How Demagoguery Harms Societies

How does demagoguery harm open societies? In many ways, according to some of the best sources on this, such as Thucydides, Plato, Hobbes, and Machiavelli. First, it misrepresents reality, which means that it fails to tackle real problems effectively. Second, intensive manipulation turns citizens from active participants in debates into increasingly passive spectators. They are not puppets, but they do become easier to control the more demagoguery takes over. Third, quackery disparages intellectual, legal, and political expertise, the kinds of expertise that might be useful in adjudicating differences in opinion and informing people about the facts. Fourth, scapegoating inflames citizens against each other, or against others, making discussions harder than they

---

[4]  Katrin Bennhold, "To Understand 'Brexit,' Look to Britain's Tabloids," *The New York Times*, May 2, 2017, https://www.nytimes.com/2017/05/02/world/europe/london-tabloids-brexit.html.

would be otherwise. Fifth, flattery tells the flattered what they want to hear instead of trying to come to terms with fellow citizens and make civil peace. Sixth, and last, demagoguery breeds contempt among fellow citizens. For interesting examples of contempt, you just need to look on the Internet today.

Here is what American writer Henry Louis Mencken said in 1926, defining demagoguery, demagogues, and their supporters: "The demagogue is one who preaches doctrines he knows to be untrue, to men he knows to be idiots. The demaslave is one who listens to what these idiots [the dema-gogues] have to say and pretends to believe it himself."[5] When you read the first part, you think Mencken is saying that these people are idiots, stupid, uneducated, and not as bright as Mencken himself or the demagogues who are manipulating them. But in the second part, where he talks about "demaslaves" as pretending to believe what the demagogue says, you realize that it is not that they are stupid, and that they have a reason for choosing not to believe. This kind of naïve complicity arouses Mencken's contempt. I am pointing this out not because I share this contempt, but because it is a real problem. I think we have to be very honest with ourselves and ask: Are we feeling this contempt, too, and how does it affect the way we try to overcome divisions in our societies?

## What Is New About Demagoguery?

Have the Internet and social media changed how demagoguery works? And do these changes make it less important as a form of political communication and manipulation? First, politicians are using social media to communicate directly with voters. If you did not realize it before, the current U.S. president has made us all painfully aware of the potential for campaigners and leaders to spread their message through Twitter and other social media. This has the effect of creating an illusion of intimacy, chumminess with leaders. It inten-sifies the easy and generally misplaced trust that flattery seeks to foster. All these down to earth words and my personal iPhone are creating the impres-sion of transparency, which makes me want to trust this person more than perhaps in the days when you just saw them from a distance, giving a speech on television.

---

[5]  H. L. Mencken, *Notes on Democracy* (New York: Knopf, 1926), 103.

Second, there is what I call horizontal demagoguery, a form of citizen-to-citizen demagoguery. With the help of Facebook and Twitter, every citizen can become a persuader, not just taking the lead from politicians and parties, but contributing persuasions of their own. We have more people than ever daily engaging in acts of horizontal demagoguery, without being on anyone's political payroll. They spend hours trolling opponents online, posting comments on behalf of their cause or their candidate, and creating political websites. Some of this might give them a little sense of the power that demagogue leaders have. I am not saying that this is my view necessarily, but people are concerned about it. As a result, citizens become more directly invested in the opinions, policies, and candidates they are advocating, because they are no longer just passive spectators and consumers of the messages of demagogues.

Third—something that might look like it is new—is the international scope of persuasions, i.e. the way persuasions no longer take place within national borders due to Internet technology. This issue has two dimensions. One is the ability of outside parties to influence foreign elections with fake news, or other means, manufactured anywhere in the world; the other is foreign or partly foreign ownership of national and global media. This creates international conflict over illicit interference and gives nationalists pretext to thump down on news outlets that publish contrary views, claiming that they are foreign-owned or foreign-influenced. I am not convinced that any of these issues takes us far beyond old-style demagoguery, towards different kinds of manipulation or even different degrees of manipulation. Yes, Twitter and Facebook allow leaders to engage in more intensive and direct flattery with millions, or billions, of people, but it is not yet clear that tweeting politicians win more hearts and minds than leaders who talk to you on television or on the radio in your living room. The jury is out.

The second dimension concerns the millions of new Internet citizen-demagogues. They are an interesting phenomenon, worth keeping an eye on, but demagogues have always sought to light fires among their supporters and encourage them to spread the good word in their own, often hard-to-control ways. The global scope of possibilities for manipulating information and voting behavior has become wider and much more porous with the Internet, but fake news, spreading from abroad, is as old as Thucydides, and indeed much older. Yet I do think that the developments I outlined here create new and serious challenges to democracy and open society.

There are two other, connected features of communications today that might have more far-reaching and problematic effects, or even change the game of demagoguery itself. First, Internet-based social media gives rise to new tools of psychological data collection that allow for targeted, personalized manipulation. In mid-2017, *The Guardian* and *The New York Review of Books* featured long stories of how a data science firm called Cambridge Analytica collected personal data on U.S. and UK voters from Facebook, developed political messages tailored to appeal to them, and sold this to the Trump and Brexit campaigns, among others.[6] Obama's re-election campaign, these articles pointed out, also used strategies of this kind, to target and design personalized messages aimed at persuadable voters. So it is not an entirely new thing used only by the right, rather than the non-right.

Second, journalists attribute both the Brexit vote and Trump's election to these kinds of operations. Some people call Trump "the first Facebook president" and say he won because of this. The article in *The Guardian* said that the Brexit vote was basically determined by those votes, which pushed it over the edge during the very last weeks of campaigning, and by the people who are buying and using this sort of data on voters. In some way, this gives a few billionaires who own data collection firms or who buy their data unprecedented scope to influence campaigns. There are two things that seem to go beyond what we have seen with political communications in the past: It allows for more intensive manipulation if you collect these personal data from people, and it creates potential for a few people with funds to dominate the game of persuasion in a way that small numbers of people have never been able to do. These two things combined, I think, make demagoguery look more obviously worrying than it did so far. There is the risk that the powers of quackery and flattery end up in a few hands, depending on massive wealth and on audiences that might find it harder to recognize that they are being played, because the targeting is so sophisticated and so personalized that you do not realize it is happening to you. If you add to this the globalized nature of ownership, it is easy to imagine the sort of dystopian, not too distant future where a handful of individuals and companies control information flows and shape opinions.

---

[6] Tamsin Shaw, "Invisible Manipulators of Your Mind," *The New York Review of Books*, April 20, 2017, http://www.nybooks.com/articles/2017/04/20/kahneman-tversky-invisible-mind-manipulators/; Jamie Doward and Alice Gibbs, "Did Cambridge Analytica Influence the Brexit Vote and the US Election?" *The Guradian*, March 4, 2017, https://www.theguardian.com/politics/2017/mar/04/nigel-oakes-cambridge-analytica-what-role-brexit-trump.

The other potentially game-changing development is the privatization and segmentation of information and opinion through Internet-based sources. As Cass Sunstein and many others have pointed out for years, the Internet lets people choose what news they want to read or hear, far more than people were able to in the past, and discuss it on Facebook or Twitter with self-selected friends or followers who share their views.[7] The effect of this—and we all know it—is epistemic self-deprivation, i.e., you are being deprived of knowledge by your own choices as much as by what others are imposing on you or allowing you to know by repressing certain information outlets. The effect is a disengagement from any wider society, other worldviews, and legitimate differences; the formation of bubbles where individuals and groups of like-minded people are seldom exposed to other views. Why does this seem to so many people potentially lethal for democracies and open societies? In the short term, it risks making people more susceptible to quack solutions and spurious knowledge claims and sources of information, including fake news. In the longer term, these highly privatized new forms of political discussion separate citizens from each other, and break up the public realm in very passionate terms. The public realm is the key to holding together any political society. When you fracture it, it does not take long before things go to the dogs.

This is really happening. In other words, citizens nowadays seldom have encounters with others who challenge their views, and they lose the habits of listening, reasoning, and compromise that are so essential to democratic life. Views tend to become more extreme and more dogmatic: people who think differently are presented in a caricatured way, our party versus theirs, people versus elites, our nation versus foreigners or cosmopolitan fellow citizens. And the leitmotivs of these self-centered discussions screen out facts that do not fit in, and end up defining how participants see the social and political realities around them. In this way, we see the birth of what we now call alternate facts, or alternate realities.

The phenomenon of alternate realities is not new in itself: ideologies and religious worldviews have features similar to what I have just sketched. But the concern is that new technologies and information markets sharpen their ideological divisions and deepen their psychological intensity, which makes

---

[7] Compare: Cass R. Sunstein, *Republic.com* (Princeton, NJ: Princeton University Press, 2001).

it a lot easier for demagogues to work with them than when they just go and speak on public television or on the radio, or through the printed media. As such, with demagogues who have at their disposal these already formed groups, politics can turn much more quickly into a gladiator sport, with fanatical teams arranged on different sides, no clear rules in the arena, and no generally agreed upon restraints.

## Reasons for Being Optimistic

So is it all terrible? Should we start panicking? I would say not yet—I am a cautious optimist. Some reasons for being optimistic, or not too pessimistic, however, are a lot better than others. One reason not to panic is the Janus-faced nature of so much of human technology throughout the ages, including the ones we have now. The same Internet technologies that generate the world of self-revolving people in bubbles and fewer social polarization can also be used to overcome isolation and revitalize political life; both online and by getting bodies of people onto the streets or into meetings, by organizing different forms of politics, and by galvanizing people to form new movements when they feel the need for change.

Another kind of upbeat view comes from people who think of themselves as realists about the activity of politics. Manipulation, they point out, is the normal state of politics. It is not a pathology we should denounce from the moral high ground at every small whiff. Politics is a rough game; leaders need to spin at all times, occasionally even to lie. As long as they are talking about countries like the United Kingdom or the United States, which still have basic freedoms of expression, and as long as democratic institutions and the rule of law provide checks, there is no need to worry.

Now, I think the first part of this is true. As I said in the beginning, it is not helpful to see Fascism looming behind every over-the-top utterance of political leaders if you are in a place where institutions and laws are strong. If you go into panic mode too early, you risk speeding up the polarizing process and you might lose the chance of trying to find creative ways to bridge the gap between citizens who are not on what you regard as your side. But I do not agree with the realist view that believes that laws and institutions can be relied upon to ward off threats all by themselves; I think there is often a bit of complacency in this. As we have seen in the United States and the United Kingdom, the line between people trying to keep the laws strong and demagogues trying to erode them can easily be crossed. The main thing you need is a critical mass of citizens who know their own value and the value of their laws and institutions and who work hard to defend them.

This means that we are right to worry if things get bad, even if they are not yet critical. Even in this age of high-speed communication, the norms of public speech do not go away overnight, as Thucydides reminded us. Change as it happens in public discussions can be subtle, and until an event shocks us into self-awareness—such as the Brexit referendum or an election result—most of us barely notice that we have lost the ability to talk politics with some of our fellow citizens, or in some cases even our friends and family. When it comes to demagoguery, we need constant vigilance to stop the run. We need to understand how it works and how quickly and deeply it can make bad situations worse, and we need to try to check its harmful effects at all times, not just when democracy has come under direct attack.

A final argument that things are not so bad springs from a deeper kind of realism. Michael Ignatieff suggested that when dealing with fake news or attacks on the epistemic authority of academics and other experts, "Reality always strikes back." This got me thinking: What are the realities that always bite in the end? Partly they may be the hard, material realities, the things you can see and measure and calculate. Money dries up, arms races flag, bombs drop—those are realities. There is another kind of "biting" reality, namely, human realities. Most people do not like to be played for too long. They do not like it when governments make it harder for them to travel, to seek out the education and the work they want, and to say openly what they believe. When governments go too far in a certain direction, people have a way of getting fed up, deciding that their leaders have overstepped their limit and voting them out or taking to the streets. Flattery can start to grate on people if it shows them an image of themselves they are ashamed to own; if it highlights their narrowness or their inhumanity a bit too much. Commentators say about Macron's victory in France that French voters might have been worried that Le Pen was too much like Trump. Having seen the kind of embarrassment on the U.S. stage, they wanted somebody who seemed more respectable. These are what I call the psychological or moral realities that bite back against the alternate realities that demagogues try to create. Another kind of human reality that tends to shatter virtual realities is the social one, the simple fact that human beings have to share limited social space and resources with other people. Different people have different views about how to deal with this fact. As Thucydides told us, if you refuse to share this space with other people, or if you insist on sharing it only on your own terms, it is natural and reasonable for others to revolt.

And here is one of demagoguery's inherent weaknesses: it has to do more with flattery than quackery. Flattery is a risky tactic. It is a failure of realism, because it encourages citizens to be even more obsessively self-centered than they, or we, already are. And politics is never only about oneself, even our collective self. Politics involves managing conflicts with others. Without a realistic picture of the other people you interact with, the strength of their desires, and their capacities to make life hard for you, you cannot design realistic policies to overcome your problems or promote your own interest. So those who hope to counter the demagogues' alternate realities still have some grounds for hope. There is *that realism*, but there is still another level of realism we need to keep in mind, which is how demagoguery can be surprisingly resistant even to these deep kinds of reality bites. If demagoguery were just a matter of countering exaggeration and outright lies with facts and genuine expertise, or showing people that they are being pushed too far into appearing inhumane and unkind, then it would be pretty easy to cut through the fog. But reality resistance comes more from flattery than from quackery. Flattery creates moral confusion in the flattered. It starts with people's own opinions and beliefs about what is right and what is wrong, and sticks with the familiar language we use to express our beliefs. But flattery uses sophistry, subtle shifts in meaning or tone or import, to advance opinions and defend actions that the audience might not accept at first or at least not knowingly. The label sticks with them and they have to go along with their choice because they voted for that policy. This process becomes reality resistant because it is hard to detect when it is happening, and it makes people complicit; in other words, it makes people the co-authors and co-owners of the actions and opinions their demagogues stir up. It is harder to disown policies that you helped author. So instead of buyer's regret, we tend to end up with denial and self-deception.

## Conclusion

I conclude with a couple of brief thoughts. One, it is a mistake to think that communications do not matter that much. It is usually true that behind every crisis of political speech there are deeper and more concrete problems: the broken or discredited political system, the inequalities and insecurities that cause people to support quick-fix solutions. We need to understand better how these material conditions feed into and poison public discourse, and what makes different people rally around populists or right-wing extremists. But even if crises of communications arise from social and political crises, they are not just epiphenomenal. For one thing, speech matters in its own right, as it mediates and re-describes needs, desires, and realities. People buy into these re-descriptions, not always realizing it. These re-descriptions distort reality.

The other point is that friends of the open society, however they want to tackle the socio-political problems that fuel the demagogues' success, also need to win people over by persuasions, as well as by policies. Despite some glimmers of hope from France and elsewhere, we have been doing badly at the game of persuading people away from demagoguery. We, as academics and journalists, need to get out of our enclaves and spend a lot more time trying to understand what demagogues and their supporters are saying. And this means trying to understand the reasons they actually give for why they are voting a certain way. We should not just be second-guessing the true reasons or true economic and political concerns that lurk behind their rhetoric; we need to listen and engage directly with their reasons.

My closing point is the following: It is not just the lesser educated who vote unwisely or get played by demagogues. We, educated people, also get manipulated in various ways. I think we should ask to what extent demagogues flatter and manipulate us—ruthless cosmopolitans, educated elites, experts—even as they make us into the enemy. Demagoguery, especially its populist variety, strives on inequality and flatters the special status and moral high ground claimed by elites, as much as it needs the discontents of the rest of the population. Are we willing to recognize this and see ourselves as equals among the citizens in democracies, and talk to fellow citizens accordingly?

# Populism and Democracy in the Twenty-First Century

*Pierre Rosanvallon*

Contemporary democratic disenchantment clearly belongs to a history of unkept promises and betrayed ideals. Part of the problem has to do with the mistakes and shortcomings of politicians, who are often out of touch with society, concerned primarily with their own careers, and, in some instances, corrupt. Another issue is the parochialism of political parties. But these charges against the political world, from which populist parties have benefited considerably, do not explain everything. Disillusionment also arises from more structural causes, which characterize the contemporary phenomenon of democratic disaffection. I would like, in the first place, to emphasize one of these causes: the declining democratic performance of elections.

## The Declining Democratic Performance of Elections

To measure the nature and scope of this phenomenon properly, one must begin by recalling the classic theory of democratic elections—a theory that I will reconstruct, as its status is implicit and fragmentary. If one considers all the justifications of election by universal suffrage, one sees that it was expected to fulfill three essential democratic functions:

- *Representation*: to select elected officials who express the interests and problems of various social groups.

- *Legitimation*: to give legitimacy to political institutions and leaders.
- *Monitoring elected officials*: upcoming elections put pressure on representatives to keep their promises and fulfill their platforms, thus giving full validity to the idea of popular sovereignty (the concepts of *retrospective voting* and reelection have always been central to determining an election's democratic character).

By giving power to the general will, universal suffrage was expected to produce not only a democratic *government*, but also a democratic *society* (a society of similar people in which inequalities were reduced). The father of universal suffrage in France, Alexandre Auguste Ledru-Rollin, famously declared on the day in 1848 when it became official: "Starting today, there are no more proletarians in France!" Like the English Chartists, he assumed that giving the masses the ability to express themselves would automatically lead political power to concern itself exclusively with the general interest.

If they fulfilled these functions, elections could, in practice, be considered the *democratic tool par excellence*. But it quickly became apparent, once universal suffrage was established, that by no means were these three functions automatically fulfilled. Hence the long story, beginning in the early nineteenth century, of projects seeking reform and institutional change by improving elections' democratic performance. They include, for example, the introduction of proportional representation, the formation of class-based parties (replacing gatherings of dignitaries), and, more recently, the adoption of the principle of male-female parity as a way of making elected officials more representative; the creation of electoral committees and primaries to limit the influence of political machines and involve citizens in the selection of candidates; the adoption of rules making it impossible to hold several positions simultaneously, or imposing term-limits that restrict the professionalization of politics; recall and impeachment mechanisms for monitoring elected officials, interrupting their terms, and triggering new elections; the creation of independent commissions ensuring that electoral processes are proper and elections are honest; finally, the placing of caps on electoral expenses in order to reduce the role money plays in politics and the organization of official campaigns that place all candidates on the same footing. Projects of this kind are still numerous, and there remains much to be done, along these lines, to improve the quality of electoral processes. But such a vision of democratic progress is inadequate if one's goal is to achieve it.

## THE AGE OF BAD REPRESENTATION

In the first place, elections today are, for sociological and institutional reasons, less able to fulfill their representative function. From an institutional perspective, the increasing importance of executive power has altered the concept of representations. The project of representing society was conceived, of course, as consisting in the creation of parliamentary assemblies. They were imagined, as Mirabeau famously put it in 1789, as a picture of society on a smaller scale. The concept of representation was, in this sense, inseparable from the expression of diversity. But today, the election of executive power has become the heart of democratic life (whether such elections be direct, as in France, or emerge from a parliamentary majority, as in Germany, Japan, or Great Britain). This has been dubbed the "presidentialization of democracy." Henceforth, the problem is that a single individual—the chief executive—cannot, strictly speaking, be representative, as representation implies, by definition, the expression of a plurality (except if one claims to embody the people in a populist sense—a point to which I will return).

From a sociological perspective, the concept of representation was implicitly underwritten by the notion that society was comprised of orders, corporate bodies, classes, and populations with well-defined characteristics (which led Rousseau to observe that there was something medieval about the idea of representation). The concept is still meaningful, but society can no longer be understood in these terms. We do indeed find ourselves in a new era of social identity, tied to the development of an *individualism of singularity*. The latter alters perceptions of society and the expectations of citizens. Its advent is the result of the growing complexity and heterogeneity of the social world, including changes in the nature of capitalism. But at an even deeper level, it arises from the fact that individuals are henceforth determined as much by their own life stories as by their social condition. Some psychological studies have, for instance, emphasized the fact that individuals are now less concerned with what they own at a particular moment than what they fear they could lose or hope to gain. They increasingly see their lives in dynamic terms. The "individual as history" has thus superimposed itself on the "individual as condition," identified with the characteristics of a specific group. It thus becomes necessary to represent "life histories," with all the breaks and opportunities that punctuate them, whereas previously all that needed representing was social *conditions*. In these circumstances, selecting a representative is less important than publicly recognizing individuals' difficulties and life experiences. Indeed, the latter entail a new way of producing a common world. "Communities of difficulties" have thus replaced traditional class identities.

## A DECLINING CAPACITY FOR LEGITIMATION

Elections have, on the one hand, become less efficient at legitimating power, even if the primary and most basic characteristic of a democratic regime clearly remains the choice of the government by the governed. Yet from the outset, this foundational assertion harbored a major ambiguity: the general will was, practically speaking, equated with the majority. That a majority of votes established power's legitimacy was universally accepted as the very essence of democratic life, though the substance of this claim was never considered. In this way, a *justifying principle* and a *selection technique* became intertwined in democratic elections. The problem is that these features are different in nature. One can understand why, as a selecting process, the concept of majority became compelling, given the self-evident arithmetic on which it is based. But this is not the case if it is considered sociologically. For "majority" always refers to what remains a fraction of the people. The real justification of the power of the ballot box has, however, always been the idea of the *general* will, and thus of the people insofar as it represents society as whole. We have, in this way, pretended *as if* the majority were identical to the totality. This ambiguity allowed us to forget that electoral democracy is based on a *fiction*, in the juridical sense of the term (which can be defined as a way of thinking the real that renders it governable). This fiction has become increasingly problematic for one major reason: the term "majority" itself has lost the symbolic and practical value it once possessed. If it has remained perfectly defined arithmetically and, consequently, juridically, its sociological meaning is far less clear. The interests of the largest number of citizens can no longer be associated as directly with those of the majority as was the case in the past. The "people" no longer conceives of itself as a homogenous mass; it presents itself as a series of personal stories, an accumulation of specific situations. This is why contemporary society increasingly makes sense of itself through the concept of minority. A minority is no longer just "a little piece" (which must yield to the "bigger piece"): it has become one of the social totality's multiple, refracted expressions. Society now appears to us as a vast series of variations on the minority theme. "People" has become the plural form of "minority."

In purely quantitative terms, majorities, in divided societies, become very narrow, with victories hinging on a few percentage points. This reality is reinforced by vote counts, whether due to low turnout or blank ballots (hence the bitterness of contemporary discussions on this topic), which end up making some electoral victories appear very fragile when compared to the total number of registered voters.

## NEW POLITICAL TEMPORALITIES

The temporalities of political life have, for their part, been transformed in various ways. First, the concept of platform (*programme*) has, in an uncertain world, lost its coherence. Platforms, which used to be centerpiece of election campaigns, revealing the major dividing lines between parties, were expected to be put into practice after the election. They established, in this way, a relatively strong connection between the moment when elections occurred and the moment when governments acted. A new relationship to the future and the increasingly personal nature of political conflict altered the ability of elections to project their democratic effects into the future (a concept that, in French, I have called "*projection démocratique*"). Elections have, by the same token, been reduced to little more than nominating processes. In this way, the gap has increased between electoral moments and governing moments. I should add that, in this context, "retrospective voting" functions only as a system of democratic rejection, as negative democracy. In a context of growing executive power, the *parliamentary functions* of oversight are, moreover, atrophied, as the parliament's essential role becomes of supporting or criticizing governments.

The different forms of elections' declining democratic performance have, in this way, considerably exacerbated the original tensions inherent in democratic representation, which were tied to various modes of indeterminacy (*who* is the people? what is sovereignty? should democracy be direct or indirect?).

## AN INCREASINGLY REMOTE PROJECT: THE SOCIETY OF EQUALS

Finally, the project of building a society of equals lay at the heart of the foundational revolution of the eighteenth century, in America as much as in France. The right to vote was considered one of its most obvious symbols. Elections had a deliberative and communal character, which brought to life an "electoral body." But this dimension has disappeared, as seen in decreasing voter turnout, on the one hand, and the reduction of substantive debate to simplistic slogans, on the other. Elections have, by the same token, become privileged moments for expressing democratic emotions rather than instantiating the political community. The dramatic rise in inequality has, moreover, undermined the earlier ideal of a society of equals.

For these various reasons, elections have lost much of their democratic performance. Elections, of course, still have an essential role to play. They have an inescapable regulatory and necessary function, and have the power of the "final word." The virtue of this minimal definition, as Joseph Schumpeter put it, is that they bring conflict to an end in a peaceful way, since everyone can at least agree on the mathematical fact that 51 is greater than 49. Yet this is not enough to satisfy expectations. This is why, at present, we find ourselves on a quest for a "*post-electoral* democracy" (a more suitable term, I think, than "post-democracy"). In what follows, I would like to suggest some of its characteristics while emphasizing from the outset that it must be conceived as a complication of democracy's forms and mechanisms. This requires that one first consider the populist ideology that now presents itself throughout the world as a response to many democracy frustrations, while attracting great audiences we know exist on every continent.

## The Populist Project

Populism presents itself as a project for regenerating democracies that have withered and lost their way. Contrary to the totalitarian regimes of the twentieth century, which sought a substantive break with democratic forms deemed "bourgeois" (such as parliamentarism and pluralism), populism claims to restore an "original democracy." To assess this project and the dangers it entails, I propose constructing it as an *ideal type*, that is, to consider it as a *political form* with its own consistency and coherence. This means abandoning elastic uses of the term, which refer vaguely to a political style considered "demagogic" and which have stigmatizing connotations that are ambiguous due to their frequently contemptuous implications, with the "people" of populism often being conflated with the problematic "populace" of Antiquity. Populism, in the serious sense in which I understand the term, refers to a specific conception of political representation, the exercise of sovereignty, and the reign of the general will.

## REPRESENTATION AS INCARNATION

Populism bases itself on a conception of incarnation as the best form of representation. The leader is supposed to be the embodiment of the people; he is "the people as a man" (a phrase, it is worth noting, that was invented in the early nineteenth century to apply to Napoleon). The specter of bad representation characteristic of ordinary parliamentarism can, in this way, be dismissed, at the same time as power's legitimacy is strengthened. It was in Latin America that this conception was theorized as early as the mid-nineteenth century. "I am not a man, I am the people": these words, instantly repeated by Colombia's leader in the 1930s and 1940s, Jorge Eliécer Gaitan, set the tone for later populisms across the continent. He was admired by Fidel Castro, as well as by Peron.

Recently, in the twenty-first century, during the 2012 presidential campaign in Venezuela, Hugo Chavez, while also explicitly referring to Gaitan, would repeat the magic words. "When I see you," he would typically tell the crowds at his rallies, "when you see me, something tells me: 'Chavez, you are the people … I am embodied in you. We are millions of Chavezes; Chavez is no longer just me, Chavez is the entire people!'" In his first inaugural address as president of the republic in 1999, he went so far as to tell his audience: "I hardly exist. Get ready to govern!" There could be no clearer way for legitimating a presidential regime that clings to the illusion that it is democratic.

## DIRECT SOVEREIGNTY

This conception of "representation as incarnation" is logically connected to a conception of direct sovereignty in the form of election-by-acclamation (which Carl Schmitt theorized and championed in the thirties). The "people" was supposed to exercise power directly through the mediation of its double (a concept that, in its own way, drew on the political theology of the king's two bodies)! This theory was defended by Ernesto Laclau, the thinker behind Kitchnerism in Argentina in the 2010s.

Referenda are also, from this perspective, seen as an ultimate means of democratic expression. They are sanctified as the most indisputable form of popular sovereignty. The same can be said of the idea of a "constituent assembly."

## THE MAJORITARIAN GENERAL WILL

While a political culture of unanimity underpins these conceptions of representation and sovereignty, it is nonetheless majorities that, at the same time, are seen, in the populist vision, as the way to express the general will. Populism is, on this point, very traditional. But this conception is tied—and here is the rub—to the claim of populist movements to bring together the "real people," whereas their opponents are accused of only representing minority groups and (foreign) imperialistic or oligarchical interests. A simple majority can, in this sense, express the entire people. Even as minorities, populist movements can make the same claim, on the grounds that the "real" people has been blinded and fooled by a news media in the pocket of foreign interests.

Populist movements reject, consequently—and this is a crucial point—other forms that express the general will, notably constitutional courts and independent authorities. This is a constant that admits no exceptions (witness the current situation, in Europe, with the Hungarian and Polish governments).

## AN IMPLICIT SOCIOLOGY: THE PEOPLE UNITED

In the populist conception of the world, the people's unity is experienced at a practical level as a community based on rejection and separation, consistent with substantive conception of national identity. Maurice Barrès, one of the first theorists of this negative conception of identity, remarked very tellingly: "The idea of the fatherland implies inequality, yet at the foreigner's expense." Through the divide resulting from an unequal relationship, he sought to bring the people closer together. This negative equality was directed externally as well as internally: it united the "throng of little people"—a blend of petty capitalists and laborers—against the "great barons" and "great feudal lords." It is clear, from this standpoint, that identity can even become tied up with a racist and differentiating approach (this point, it must be stressed, is what distinguishes right wing from left wing populism, as the latter is characterized by a socio-economic approach to identity that emphasizes redistribution).

## A PHILOSOPHY AND ECONOMY OF JUSTICE:
## NATIONAL PROTECTIONISM

Economic protectionism can, consequently, be logically understood as an appropriate tool of identity-based equality. This is why populist movements in Europe have determinedly aligned themselves with the critics of the Euro and, more broadly still, of the European Union.

## MOVEMENTS AND REGIMES

Such are the main intellectual bases of populist *movements*, that is, of populist *rhetoric*. The slide towards authoritarianism on the part of regimes that arise from these movements is justified by the radicalization of the difference between the "real people" and an opposition that is reduced to being nothing more than oligarchies or American imperialism in disguise. These associations justify bringing these groups into line, as well as quashing of the media, which stands accused of being merely the voice of minority interests and subversive projects. This slide towards authoritarianism can also be achieved by submitting to *majority* approval constitutions that, in practice, creates regimes based on personal authority (in the form, for instance, of unlimited reelection).

## THINKING POPULISM

The fact that populist movements frequently shift to authoritarianism means that they have naturally been accused of being illiberal. But this charge is not enough. Worse, it is powerless if it is not accompanied by a *genuinely democratic critique* of populism. What remains to be accomplished on this front is considerable. Even if one takes the sole example of the referendum and its uses, it is clear that, at present, there exists no critical analysis of it that is genuinely democratic.

One finds, in populism, an "obviously democratic" aura that must be systematically deconstructed. Elaborating a critique of this assumption is one of the decisive intellectual and political tasks of the moment. The first step in the right direction is to show that it is not by simplifying democracy, but, on the contrary, by complicating and multiplying its modalities that one can overcome its incompleteness and move it forward.

# Complicating Democracy in Order to Fulfill It

Describing the advent of the democratic world that he witnessed first-hand, Alexis de Tocqueville observed: "The idea of government is becoming simpler: number alone is right and lawful. All of politics is reduced to a question of arithmetic." Today, one must say the exact opposite: democratic progress means preserving democracy's complexity, by multiplying the means through which the general will expresses itself, by broadening the modalities of representation, and by establishing pluralistic forms of sovereignty.

## TOWARDS BROADER FORMS OF REPRESENTATION

In 1789, the French *Declaration of the Rights of Man and of the Citizen* vigorously noted that "ignorance, neglect, or contempt of the rights of man are the sole cause of public calamities and of the corruption of governments." This point is crucial: the quality of democracy depends precisely on the permanent *presence* in political life of the lived experience of citizens and the recollection of their rights. "Representation" means *making* the social world *present* in public life. Democracy does not only mean popular sovereignty, public deliberation, and the selection of representatives; it also means *consideration for everyone*—taking every condition explicitly into account. Consequently, this implies developing *narrative representation* alongside the more traditional idea of *delegation-representation* (which, incidentally, works very poorly, as the representative function of political parties has eroded as they have ingratiated themselves in the world of government). Indeed, not being represented means being invisible in the public sphere, not having one's problems considered and discussed. Representation has, in this instance, a cognitive and expressive dimension. The latter goes beyond *representation as the imparting of form*, which is traditionally opposed to procedural notions. There is indeed an active and polymorphous character in narrative representation, whereas representation as the imparting of form presupposes giving particular consideration to social conditions conceived very generally.

The project of a narrative democracy is, moreover, a way of building a society of individuals, completely equal in dignity, recognition, and consideration, who form a common society. Greater visibility and legibility, moreover, make society more governable and reformable. A society that falls short in representing itself oscillates between passivity and fear. It tends to be ruled by resentment, in which anger merges with powerlessness. Thus it is unable to imagine in concrete terms ways of acting upon itself. Indeed, it must constantly caricature reality in the hope of making it malleable. In this way, society ends up being shaped by a phantasmagoric image of itself, designating scapegoats as the source of all evil. Democracy, however, can survive only if women and men recognize each other as they are, in order to build a shared world. This means that it is necessary that some degree of mutual understanding exist between its members. For this reason, the price we pay for bad representation is as much social and moral as it is individual. "We are terribly ignorant of one another," the historian Jules Michelet when explaining the difficulty that individuals faced in forming a fraternal people with the onset of the new democratic republic in 1848. When reality is masked and when people's lives remain hidden, the imagination is governed by the effects of prejudice and fantasy. It also fuels mistrust and fear: when people are unknown to one another and are unknown to political authorities, mechanisms encouraging retreat into the private realm and ghettoization proliferate. A society cannot develop mechanisms of solidarity and reciprocity without some degree of trust. Yet the "invisible institution" of trust is, in some respects, purely cognitive.

The implementation of a narrative democracy depends less on institutional mechanisms than on the polymorphous development of academic and activist endeavors seeking to "tell society's story." Social sciences play a role in these efforts, but so do literature, photography, and film. In the United States during the Great Depression of the 1930s, an effort along these lines was made with the launching of the Federal Writers' Project. In France, I have, for my part, recently taken a step to create a "Parliament of the Invisible," with similar intentions.[1] Such efforts are essential democratic undertakings.

## NEW FORMS OF DEMOCRATIC LEGITIMACY AND OF THE EXPRESSION OF THE GENERAL WILL

The new forms refer to approaches to democratic generality that mitigate the achievements of its traditional electoral and majoritarian expression by seeking to reconnect with an idea of the general will understood as society's unanimous expression. Two concepts can be used along these lines to formulate from a different perspective the power of all that is the foundation of the democratic ideal: the "power of nobody" and the "power of anybody." The power of nobody emphasizes the principle of impartiality. It harks back to a negative definition of the general will. An impartial institution is an institution that *nobody* (no interest group, no political party, no specific individual)

---

[1] I have done this by creating a small research center associated with the book series and the website *Raconter la vie* ("Telling Life's Stories").

can claim to appropriate. The democratic power of everyone appears, in this way, as the *power of nobody*. Independent monitoring and regulatory authorities are based on this principle. Some were created by parliamentary assemblies to control and balance executive branches that are suspected of being partisan; others were launched by the executive branches themselves, in order to restore credibility or to hand over some of their power in areas in which they did not feel technically competent. Their number, at present, is constantly on the rise, due to pressure from citizens who fear that authorities will abuse their power simply because they are majoritarian.

The power of anyone refers to the fact that "the people" is not simply a population: it also consists of individuals, each of whom has rights that must be defended. It is in this sense that it is historical—when it understands itself dynamically as a community founded on shared values. And how is this collective dimension to be described if not in terms of the principles upon which it is based? To give the "people as principle" its proper political place means representing a people that can also be called "legal" in the term's constitutional sense. This justifies the normative superiority of the constitutional order. The function of constitutional courts is to represent this "permanent people" where every individual counts, because their rights are guaranteed, whereas the majoritarian order often makes decisions under the sway of events or in order to emphasize specific interests. The power of all is thus defined, in this context, as the *power of anyone* (that is, the power of every individual who has the right to have its rights protected and the means to make good on them).

The growing influence of these two types of institutions has gradually changed the character and scope of legislative and executive powers as they were conceived in classical liberal and democratic theory. As their role has grown, independent monitoring and regulatory authorities, as well as constitutional courts, have changed the terms in which democracy can be understood. But these changes have only been empirical; these institutions have yet to be conceptualized as new political forms, which have a specific role to play in democracy. By the same token, they are just as likely to bring about an unprecedented enrichment of democracy as to bolster a timid form of liberalism or a government of experts or judges. The question of the appropriateness of limiting majoritarian power implicitly belongs, in these instances, to the longstanding liberal view that denounces the risk of a "tyranny of the majority," which was leveled during the nineteenth century by those who feared they would be overwhelmed by the advent of universal suffrage. But the development of such institutions can also be seen as a tool for limiting a government's leeway—and thus as a means of increasing social control over elected representatives. A constitution, as a nineteenth-century thinker along these lines explained, can be understood as a "guarantee that the people creates against those who do its business, so that they do not abuse the mandate with which they have been entrusted (Édouard René de Laboulaye). Because the "power of the people" is only expressed in a conventional and limited way through majority voting, a richer definition is needed if one is to arrive at a more accurate understanding. This enrichment should go hand in hand with the possibility of broadening the concept of majority itself, with "super majorities" (*majorités qualifiées*) (for instance, a two-thirds majority) being required for constitutional referenda.

## A PERMANENT DEMOCRACY THAT GOES BEYOND ELECTORAL DEMOCRACY

Our regimes may call themselves democratic, but we are not governed democratically. This is the greatest split feeding contemporary disenchantment and disarray. Let me explain. Our regimes are considered democratic in the sense that power arises from the ballot box after open competitions and that we live in states based on the rule of law, which recognizes and protects individual freedom. These democracies are, of course, to a significant degree incomplete. The represented often feel abandoned by their legal representatives, and the people, once elections are over, rarely feel sovereign. But this reality must not hide another fact, which has yet to be clearly identified in all its specificity: the bad government (*mal-gouvernement*) that afflicts our society at its core. While political life may be organized around institutions that constitute a particular type of regime, it also consists in government action, that is, the daily management of public affairs, a body that makes decisions and issues orders. It is the locus for the exercise of power, which, in constitutional terms, is known as executive power. It is the latter that citizens deal with directly and on a daily basis. The center of gravity of the democratic imperative has, in this way, quietly shifted. Whereas the latter was, for a long time, primarily tied to establishing a positive connection between the represented and their representatives, it is henceforth the relationship between the governed and those who govern that must be considered.

For citizens, insufficient democracy means not being heard, decisions being made without consultation, ministers who fail to fulfill their responsibilities, leaders who lie with impunity, the corruption of cocooned and unaccountable political caste, and an opaque bureaucracy. The problem is that this aspect of democracy has never been considered as such. Democracy is always conceived as a regime; it has rarely been viewed as a form of government. This is evident in the face that the words "regime" and "government" have, historically, often been conflated. The question may seem secondary from the standpoint of democracy's first historical form, that is, the *parliamentary-representative* model in which legislative power prevailed over all others. But executive power has now become pivotal, leading democracies to shift towards a *presidential-governance* model. Whereas previously the feeling of bad representation was the focus of all criticism, it is that of bad government that must henceforth be addressed. The relationship between the governed and the "governors" has become the major issue.

In an age when executive power dominates, the key to democracy lies in the mechanisms whereby society can control this power. The problem is that the only answer currently offered to this imperative is the election of the chief executive. But only an *electoral democracy* (*démocratie d'autorisation*) has, in this sense, been established; a "governing permit" has been granted. Nothing more, nothing less. This is hardly sufficient, given how many elected officials we see behaving in ways that are far from democratic.

Hence the pressing need to enhance electoral democracy through *permanent democracy* (*démocratie d'exercice*). The purpose of the latter is to determine the qualities expected of governors and the positive rules organizing their relationship with the governed. Henceforth, what matters is establishing such a democracy. It is because we lack such a democracy that the election of a chief executive can pave the way to an illiberal and even a dictatorial regime. The modern world is full of examples of this kind, of which French Caesarism in the nineteenth century was the first instance. The new democratic pathologies of the twenty-first century result from the restriction of democracy's governing dimension to nothing more than an authorizing process or to referenda that are, typically, an impoverished expression of the general will. Insofar as there is such a thing as a "disease of presidentialism," it is to be found in this atrophy.

It is worth noting that the concept of *permanent democracy* is more robust and expansive than the idea put forth by political scientists of considering *democratic quality*. We do not include the latter, which has a managerial tone, in our comprehensive redefinition of the very concept of democracy. Permanent democracy can be considered from two standpoints. First, that of the principles governing the relationship between the governed and the "governors." Three principles strike me as essential: *legibility* (a broader and more active concept than transparency); *responsibility* (with its implication of a rendering of accounts and policy evaluation that goes beyond the simple act of resigning); and *responsiveness*. These principles trace the contours of a *democracy of appropriation*. Their implementation would allow citizens to exercise more directly the democratic functions that were long monopolized by parliamentary power alone.[2] They also give all its meaning to the notion that power is not a thing, but a relationship, and that it is thus characteristics of this relationship that make all the difference between a situation of domination and a simple functional distinction, within which a form of citizens' appropriation of power can develop. Second, permanent democracy can be considered from the perspective of determining the personal qualities required to be a "good governor." These qualities are necessary for establishing a bond of trust between the governed and governors—to found, that is, a *democracy of trust*. Trust is defined as one of the "invisible institutions" whose vitality has become decisive in an age when democracies are so personalized. Two qualities are particularly important: *integrity* and *truth telling* (or *parrhesia*, which, as Michel Foucault reminds us, played a central role in ancient Greece).

Building a democracy of trust and a democracy of appropriation are the two keys to democratic progress in an age of presidential government. These principles of good government must not simply be applied to executive power's various forms. They must be summoned to rule all non-elected institutions that have a regulating function (such as independent agencies), magistracies of various kinds, and the entire realm of public service. These are all people and institutions that, in one way or another, have the right to command others and participate, in this way, in governing bodies.

Nothing less than a second democratic revolution—following that of universal suffrage—must occur along these lines. Such a revolution will usher us into an era of post-electoral democracy. I described its broad directions and the ways it can be implemented in my last book, *Good Government* (*Le bon gouvernement*).[3] I will simply refer you to it. Rather than the intermittent democracy of elections, the principles we have been describing seek to establish a permanent form of democracy.

---

[2] These are functions that parliaments exercise less and less at present, due to the fact that they are structured around the majority/opposition principle. In practice, their primary function is to either support or criticize executive power.

[3] Pierre Rosanvallon, *Le bon gouvernement* (Paris: Seuil, 2015).

## FROM THE PEOPLE'S VOICE TO THE PEOPLE'S EYE

At first, democracy was understood as the voice of the people. Traditionally, this meant the ballot box. It also used other forms of expression, such as petitions or street demonstrations, for example. But in an age of permanent democracy, the *people's eye* must also play major role. Alongside the citizen-as-voter, the citizen-as-monitor must become increasingly important. The surveilling eye became one of the major themes of revolutionary imagery in France in 1789. It was a way of transforming a form of distrust into an active democratic virtue. It also proved instrumental in consecrating public opinion as one of the people's most tangible and quotidian forms. Because it was associated with the Terror's excesses, the term "surveillance" was abandoned. The duality between electoral trust and citizens' distrust on which it was based gave way to the far less rich distinction between direct democracy and representative democracy. This partook in an impoverished conception of democratic life, as the latter implies, above all, the deliberate construction over time of a shared history. It cannot be reduced to a disorderly succession of nominations and decisions. The notion of a democracy of monitoring or surveillance, with the quality of permanence that it implies, deserves, for this reason, to be revived today. I tried to describe its various forms in my book *Counter-Democracy*.[4] I emphasized the distinction between *positive distrust*, a civic form of surveillance and a sign of high democratic expectations, and a *purely negative distrust*, a systematic critique of authority and rejection of government. It is all the more essential as this second type is, at present, prospering in the form of populist rhetoric.

Complication as opposed to simplification: this is the key issue upon which democracy's future hinges at a time when democracy seems fatigued. Its outcome will depend, in part, on our ability to clarify its theoretical foundations. This is at present one of the major tasks of the social sciences. More than ever, democracy must define itself as the regime that is constantly questioning itself. It must remain a living and demanding experience, rather than locked into a model in which its most outspoken demands are lost.

---

[4] Pierre Rosanvallon, *Counter-Democracy: Politics in an Age of Distrust* (Cambridge: Cambridge University Press, 2008).

# The Enduring Appeal of the One-Party State

*Anne Applebaum*

It has now been more than a quarter century since the demise of the Soviet Union—nearly thirty years have passed since 1989. In the time that has elapsed since then, wars have begun and ended, governments have come and gone. The European Union expanded, and then, with Brexit, began to contract. For a moment, the United States of America appeared to be a hegemon, but now that moment has definitively passed.

All of that time and all of that change has given us broader perspectives on the state that Lenin created, and that became an imperial power as well as a force for injustice, poverty, and mass murder. In the longer light of history, with the help of archives and scholarship, the extent of the moral, political, economic, and environmental damage inflicted by the Soviet Union on itself and its neighbors has become far easier to describe and evaluate. With more distance, it has also become easier to see how much the Soviet system had in common with the Nazi system, supposedly its polar opposite. Both systems created concentration camps and firing squads for the citizens who did not fit into their ideological framework. Both systems relied upon elaborate lies and false constructs in order to stay in power.

It has also become easier, in the longer light of history, to understand what was truly original about the Bolshevik state. For a long time, we have focused on Marxism as the source of Lenin's brutality and Stalin's tyranny. But while you can certainly find the seeds of Soviet totalitarianism in Marx's work, you can find other things, too. After all, elements of the philosophical thinking of Karl Marx were adopted by social democrats in other countries without the use of bloodshed, violence, or elaborate lies, and sometimes with some positive results.

No, Lenin's real originality lay elsewhere. In the political science textbooks of the future, I am now certain that he will be remembered for something else: as the inventor of the world's first truly enduring, and truly influential, one-party state, predating Hitler's one-party state by fifteen years. This is a form of politics unknown to political scientists before the twentieth century. Monarchy, tyranny, oligarchy, and democracy were familiar to Aristotle more than two thousand years ago. But the illiberal one-party state, which can now be found all over the world—think of China, Venezuela, Zimbabwe—began in the twentieth century.

To be clear: One-party rule is not synonymous with fascism or communism, though of course both of those systems also revolved around a single party. Nor is the one-party state synonymous with absolute tyranny, for there have been one-party states that tolerated the existence of other political parties, at least at long as they remained relatively powerless, and without much access to media or money. Although Lenin did persecute other political parties—and Stalin finished them off—rump opposition parties were allowed to exist, for example, in communist Poland, and even in Stalinist East Germany. In the non-communist world, there was Ben Ali's Tunisia, which was run by a party called, with an Orwellian flourish, the "Rally for the Democratic Constitution," and which tolerated a tiny political opposition so long as that opposition did not become too loud. There was Mugabe's Zimbabwe, where it was possible for opponents of the Zimbabwe African National Union—the party that has ruled the country since 1980—to compete for power, but it was not possible for them to win.

Of course many one-party states, including the one originally created by Lenin, do eventually become absolute tyrannies. In the 1930s, the Soviet Union did employ mass violence to physically eliminate the opposition and to maintain power. Later, in the 1960s, 1970s, and 1980s, the USSR and its satellite states used more targeted violence, arresting people who posed genuine threats to the system and tolerating lower-level dissent. Even more recently, contemporary one-party states have used even more sophisticated, and even more targeted violence—not just the arrest but the online intimidation of dissidents, the manipulation of television and mainstream media, and of course the saturation of social media with trolls and bots on an unprecedented scale. In Zimbabwe, "ghost voters" suddenly appeared on the electoral roles when the ruling party seemed likely to lose. In Venezuela, serious opponents of the regime are chased out of the country.

But it is also very important to note an important feature of this unique political system: in most one-party states, the party itself is not the source of the violence. In the Soviet Union, the KGB was responsible for surveilling and arresting citizens, not the party. In Hitler's Germany, the SS fulfilled that same function, not the Nazi party functionaries themselves. In both of these states, as in many modified modern versions of the same political system, the party's purpose is different: It is not the body that attacks the enemy, but it is rather the body that defines who is ideologically or personally suited to be a member of the nation's governing elite.

If you think about it, it is not surprising that this idea first evolved in Russia. In old-fashioned monarchies—of which pre-revolutionary Russia was most definitely one—the right to rule was granted to the aristocracy, which policed itself according to rigid codes of breeding and inherited wealth. In Western-style democracies, the right to rule is granted by a form of mixed competition, not just voting and campaigning, but also meritocratic tests that determine access to higher education and to the civil service. At least until recently, a dose of the old-fashioned rules and social hierarchies have sometimes been part of the mix—think of the many British aristocrats who took part in democratic politics in the twentieth century—but they too must usually obtain power through some form of competition.

Lenin's revolution of course overthrew the aristocratic order. But, as too many forget, it did not put a competitive model in its place. The Bolshevik state was not merely undemocratic; it was also unmeritocratic. In a certain sense, it was anti-meritocratic. There was no open competition, not for places in universities, or for civil service jobs, or for roles in government and industry. To succeed, it was not good enough to be intelligent or hardworking. One also had to conform to the rules of party membership. Though those rules were different at different times, and though they allowed for exceptions, they were consistent in certain ways. They usually excluded the former ruling elite and their children, as well as certain other categories, for example suspicious ethnic groups. They always demanded a great deal of members, who had to accept the rigid rules of party membership: belief in the creed, attendance at meetings, public displays of enthusiasm, and total conformity to the ideological line of the moment, however nonsensical.

For millions of people in Lenin's, Stalin's, and indeed Khrushchev and Brezhnev's Soviet Union, the ownership of a party card was a ticket to higher education, to jobs in industry, and of course to jobs in government. With very few exceptions, no one could be mayor of a city, or member of the regional government, or boss of a factory without a party card. And this of course is one of the things that the USSR had in common with the shorter-lived Nazi state: party membership in Hitler's Germany was also a ticket to higher things. Though the Nazi party did not last long enough to extend its tentacles all the way into industry and commerce, the possession of a party card was the key to other kinds of power. In both systems, those with "early" party cards—cards with low numbers—had a special kind of prized position. Whatever their other talents, intellectual or personal, their party card was the most important thing about them.

But from the very beginning, this new, ideologically defined one-party elite was anxious: about itself, about its members, about their loyalty. The Italian writer Curzio Malaparte, himself originally a supporter of fascism, brilliantly described this syndrome in his novel, *The Kremlin Ball*. In a hereditary aristocracy, he writes, "the nobility's reserve, their simplicity, their natural decorum, their particular condescension in manner and words" is innate. The manners of a nouveau riche class, by contrast, are loud and vulgar, as they seek to establish their right to behave differently. By contrast, he explains, the chief characteristic of the communist nobility is not "bad taste, vulgarity, or bad manners: it is suspicion." Suspicion and, of course, ideological intransigence.

In other words, from the beginning the leaders of the Soviet communist party—and, later, the leaders of the communist parties in the USSR's European colonies—were insecure. They had good reason to be: as soon as they took power, civil war broke out. But they were also insecure because their claim to power was so fragile. Unlike the czar they replaced, they were not legitimized by centuries of tradition, or by the church and its hierarchy. They could not claim the endorsement of God or point to their ancestors. Nor had they been legally elected, endorsed in a formal way by the law. They had not won by an open competition, either, at least not one conducted according to an agreed set of rules.

Their sole claim to legitimacy lay rather in their ideology: We deserve to rule because our interpretation of Marxist-Leninism says that we deserve to rule. And this, of course, is precisely why they would spend so much time making the members of the party study the party doctrine, write about the party doctrine, and repeat it, repeat it, repeat it. Eventually, party members were expected to celebrate Marx, Lenin, the communist party, and the proletariat in banners and posters, in songs and poems, in speeches and lessons, in academic citations and in virtually every other form of human communication.

They also spent a vast amount of time policing their own ranks, checking and rechecking to see whether their members were truly loyal. At times this paranoia became violent. In the 1930s, what began as a purge of the party, designed to eliminate doubters, devolved into madness—much as it did again here in Hungary and elsewhere in the late 1940s. But violence was never the only tool that that the one-party state used to keep party members in check, and it is a mistake to focus on violence alone. The founders and the leaders of one-party states have historically also sought to eliminate dangerous ideas and the people who think them even *before* they infected the minds of the party, as well as the general public. In harsher eras, this meant physical elimination, arrest, or murder, but throughout much of both Soviet as well as Nazi history, the goal was more often simply to ensure that fewer people were listening. This meant the elimination of organizations through control over funding, venues, access to media, and above all legal status.

In a way, it is easier to see how this process worked not by looking at the history of the Soviet Union, where the one-party state developed organically over time, but in East Central Europe, where Soviet troops imposed it in the aftermath of a devastating war that had weakened all state and civic institutions. We are accustomed to thinking about the imposition of Marxist regimes in the economic categories preferred by Marxist states themselves: the nationalization of industry, the restrictions on private property, the imposition of price controls and quotas. But in fact, long before they fully nationalized industry, the Soviet occupiers of East Central Europe had different priorities. In the immediate aftermath of occupation—years when there were many urgent tasks to carry out—they harassed and disbanded youth groups, forbade the creation of independent sporting organizations, and treated anyone who worked for a religious or even a secular charity with intense suspicion. In Hungary, in 1946, when much of Budapest was still in ruins, the Interior Minister took the trouble to ban, among more than a thousand other groups, the Hungarian Athletic Club, the Count Széchenyi Association of War Veterans, and the Association of Christian Democratic Tobacco Workers. In Poland, in 1949, before the economy had really started to move again, the members of the young communist movement stormed into the Polish YMCA and smashed all the jazz records. In Eastern Germany, in the first months after the war, the occupying Soviet forces, who one would imagine had better things to do, actually spent a good deal of time making lists of organizations that would and would not be tolerated. I note for the record that they were very adamant that hiking clubs be banned at all costs. Why hiking? Maybe because hikers are wont to stray near borders, maybe because the Hitler youth was keen on hiking too. But I don't know.

In the wake of those efforts followed control over the media—radio stations were especially important to them, because these were the mass media of their time—as well as literature, the arts, and academia. These efforts were supplemented, of course, by economic policies, including the redistribution of land, the nationalization of heavy industry and, over time, a creeping state control of retail and small business. But just because they were Marxists, and just because their rhetoric therefore made it sound as if they believed the economy mattered above all else, this does not mean that they always *behaved* as if the economy mattered above all else. On the contrary, they behaved as if they were above all interested in extending control over all aspects of public life, to an unprecedented degree.

Though they did not always succeed, it was certainly the Soviet and the East Central European communists' intention—and, by the way, the Nazis' intention—to create totalitarian one-party states, designed to control not only the economy, not only property, not only the political sphere, but also sports, leisure time, hospitals, universities, summer camps, children's after-school activities, art, music, and museums. That ambition to achieve total control put people in terrible ethical and moral binds, forcing even those who were indifferent to politics to make political choices.  People who wanted to get on with their lives, rebuild their countries, educate their children, feed their families, and stay far away from those in power, had little choice but to collaborate.  Andrzej Panufnik, a Polish composer, had no love for communism, a system he found "artistically and morally dishonest ..." After the war, he wanted nothing except to rebuild his country and compose music. But in order to be allowed to do so, he had to join the Union of Polish Composers. And when all Union members were ordered to compete to compose a new "Song of the United Party," he was forced to do that, too: if he refused, he was told that not only would he lose his post, the whole Union would lose the financial support of the State. Grimly, he wrote a song, he said later, and I quote: "Literally in a few minutes, setting the ridiculous text to the first jumble of notes which came into my head. It was rubbish, and I smiled to myself as I sent it off to the adjudicators."[1] To his eternal embarrassment, he won the first prize.

This of course was an extreme moment, and the request was absurd. Nowadays, the leaders of one-party states rarely feel the need to make either their fellow party members or their fellow citizens go through such extreme hoops, though there are some interesting contemporary parallels. One fascinating study of the Syrian dictator, Haffez al-Assad, the father of the current dictator, noted that his subjects often made absurd statements about him in public—for example that he was, among many other things, the country's "gallant knight" or its "greatest pharmacist." The author of that study concluded that the very absurdity of these compliments was the point: "The regime's power resides in its ability to impose national fictions and to make people say and do what they otherwise would not. This obedience makes people complicit; it entangles them in self-enforcing relations of domination."[2]

But even in non-violent dictatorships—indeed, even in one-party states, or would-be one-party states, with laws guaranteeing freedom of speech, freedom of assembly, and much else—it is still not difficult to find people who will voluntarily say absurd things as proof of their loyalty. Not too far from here, members of the Law and Justice Party in Poland, which aspires to create a one-party state though it has not yet succeeded, know that they must tread carefully when discussing the plane crash that killed Lech Kaczynski, the brother of the party leader. Those who want promotion and advancement inside the party, and now inside the government, know that they have to support the conspiracy theory, for which there is no evidence whatsoever, that the crash was not an accident but the result of a devious plot. Sometimes the perpetrators are the Russians, sometimes the previous government of Donald Tusk. It does not matter, so long as the speaker stays away from the truth—which is that it was an accident, partly caused by the demands of the late president himself.

In Budapest, you would find it similarly difficult to advance in the ranks of Fidesz if you did not subscribe to a different conspiracy theory, namely, that the greatest enemy of the Hungarian state is an 87-year-old man who lives abroad, or that the Hungarian nation is under terrible threat from a

---

[1]  Andrzej Panufnik, *Composing Myself* (London: Methuen Publishing, 1987), 183.

[2]  Lisa. Wedeen, *Ambiguities of Domination: Politics, Rhetoric, and Symbols in Contemporary Syria* (Chicago: University of Chicago Press, 1999).

non-existent horde of migrants—I challenge you to find them on the streets of Budapest. But I am trying to be polite and will not mention any names.

As my examples demonstrate, latter-day one-party states, and nascent one-party states, have learned that they can police their own party members and assure their cooperation in subtler ways than their bloodier, more violent predecessors. As it has turned out that the maintenance of the power of the one-party state in countries with capitalist economies does not even require total control, let alone policemen. Much the same effect can be produced, simply, through the intelligent use of money, through the manipulation of human ambition, and through the power of the state.

If you can alter the legal system so as to make it difficult for civic institutions and organizations to exist, then you do not need to ban them outright. If you can intimidate advertisers so that they are afraid to pay for space in independent newspapers, then you do not need censorship, because the business model of those newspapers collapses. If you can then offer, in turn, government advertising to newspapers that support the ruling party, then you can ensure laudatory coverage. If you can politicize government contracts, and make the companies afraid to lose them, then you can win the support of at least a part of the business class, even if its members live outside your country. I have some friends who run a small Iranian human rights charity, and know something about the difficulties they have raising money even from the Iranian diaspora. Iranians who spend most of their lives in London or Los Angeles are afraid to support political causes in their own country, on the grounds that the state might take revenge, somehow, on their relatives, or find a way to exact revenge on their companies or contacts in Iran.

If you can manipulate the electoral system, then you can even insure that the ruling party remains in power despite being subjected, periodically, to a popular vote—even when that vote is lost. Here I offer the perhaps surprising example of North Carolina, an American state that is bitterly divided. In 2010, the Republican Party took control of the state legislature for the first time, and had the governorship as well. But in 2016, the governor lost to a democrat. Just a couple of weeks before he was due to take office, the Republican-dominated state legislature passed a raft of laws designed to severely limit his authority. I will spare you the details, but you will not have any difficulty imagining them: they involve changes to state electoral law, changes to rules about appointments, and of course hardline gerrymandering that means there is no real competition for many state seats. The point was to ensure that, even in the United States, one of the world's oldest democracies, the minione-party state of North Carolina could continue to restrict the power and influence of anyone who did not accept the ruling party's rigid ideology and loyalty tests.

So what is wrong with that? Why should the people of North Carolina care? Their state government is certainly not violent. Nor has it necessarily broken the law, although there are legal challenges that are now moving through the system and may reverse some of the changes. Even so, I concede that in many modern one-party states it is possible to live in relative safety and within a relatively law-abiding state. The trouble is that to do so, millions of people must either abandon their ambitions, or tailor them to suit the needs of the ever-suspicious, always rigid, ruling party.

For one-party states, even when originally elected by a majority, and even when situated within the European Union, cannot help but evince some of the characteristics that Malaparte observed long ago. Again, they are not, by definition, aristocratic. They contain a new generation of leaders, linked by ideology rather than blood. But nor are they meritocratic. They do not exist in order to promote competition, to find the best outcomes for society, to spread the wealth farthest. They exist in order to promote their own people, and in order to insure that they stay in power. So you do not get to be head of a state company in Poland right now because you are a good manager or have a track record in the relevant business. You get to be head of a state company because you are a friend or relative of the party leader. By the same token, you do not get to remain in your job at a Turkish university, regardless of your scientific achievements or talent, if you are suspected of "disloyalty" to the Erdoğan regime. One decree issued under the state of emergency imposed in 2016 allows any academic to be dismissed on grounds of "supporting terrorism," without proof or elaboration. Anyone working at a Turkish state university risks losing not only their job, but also their housing, as well as having a permanent mark on their records.

Unsurprisingly, that law has created a climate of fear that restricts academic debate at all levels, which suits the state: too much free thinking, after all, could lead the loyal party members to ask dangerous questions.

The damage done to society by this kind of political system is not brutal, but rather subtle. In the climate of the airless, rigid one-party state, mediocrities are promoted; the talented are kept away from areas where they could shine. Because the party is anxious, it requires ever-greater demonstrations of loyalty. Promotions go instead to people who are willing to repeat—and repeat, and repeat—the ideology of the ruling party. The louder, the better, even to the point of absurdity. People who lie on the party's behalf win the greatest rewards of all.

State institutions also grow worse: if the civil service promotes you according to your degree of loyalty, then there is no need to be creative or competent. All you need to do is serve out your time.

Corruption also becomes endemic, not least because it is not even called corruption. The favoring of the ruling party's businessmen is legalized in various ways, and justified as somehow good for the state. It is rare to find a one-party state in which the leader's family has not been somehow enriched, often massively enriched, even if the leader himself appears to be above the fray. Supporters of the ruling party do not object, because if you have defined the party as synonymous with the state and the nation, then it must be good for the state and the nation to enrich the party.

But however mild, and however seemingly popular, the ruling party in the one-party state will always be anxious, and it will always be suspicious. Deep down, the party leaders know that they have bent rules in order to stay in power. They know that their power is sanctioned by their ideology, not by fair rules of competition. They know that their power relies on fear—fear of losing jobs, fear of exclusion—and in some cases fear of violence. They are always insecure. They are always paranoid. They must constantly scramble to find new ways to silence opponents, to uncover new conspiracies, to imagine new enemies, to shut down objectors, to ban institutions like the Central European University, in order to keep people from even imagining political alternatives. And if they do decide to break the law, or if they do decide to use violence, it will be very, very difficult to stop them. The Turkish one-party state has, in the end, resorted to arresting thousands of people as traitors, although they are clearly not all guilty. The Chinese state has returned to older forms of censorship, as I know since my books about the Soviet Union, which were once in print there, are now banned once again.

Still, I would like to conclude by reminding you how the harsh and violent Soviet version of the one party state eventually came to an end. In his brilliant 1978 essay, "The Power of the Powerless," the Czech dissident Václav Havel called upon his countrymen to take advantage of their rulers' obsession with total control. If the state wanted to monopolize every sphere of human activity, he wrote, then every thinking citizen should work to preserve the "independent life of society," which he defined as including everything from "free creative activity and its communication to others" to "independent social self-organization."[3] He also urged them to discard false and meaningless jargon and to "live in truth"—to speak and act, in other words, as if the regime did not exist. In due course, the Czechs formed jazz bands, the Hungarians joined academic discussion clubs. The Poles organized underground scouting troupes and, eventually, independent trade unions. Everywhere, people played rock music, organized poetry readings, set up clandestine businesses, held underground philosophy seminars, sold black market meat, went to church, and told jokes. In a different kind of society, these activities would have been considered apolitical, and even in communist Europe they did not necessarily constitute "opposition" as such. But they created spheres of freedom and free thinking that eventually helped to undermine the system.

I think Havel's advice still stands. Even in the freest and most successful democracies, we still need these kinds of institutions: academic, cultural, religious, philosophical, but above all independent. Even in the wealthiest societies, we need to be constantly vigilant against corruption, nepotism, and the politicization of the civil service, and we need independent bodies to protect against those things too. And of course in democracies whose rulers are seeking to turn themselves into one-party states, independent institutions and independent thinkers are more crucial than ever before. Someone needs to continue to imagine the political alternatives. Someone needs to preserve alternative ideas. And someone needs to help society overcome the deadening, stifling, corrupting hand of the one-party state.

---

[3] Vaclav Havel, "The Power of the Powerless," *Http://www.vaclavhavel.cz*, 1978, Section XV, http://www.vaclavhavel.cz/showtrans.php?cat=eseje&val=2_aj_eseje. html&typ=HTML.

# PART FIVE

# From Transition to Backsliding:
# Did Open Societies Fail?

# After 1989: The Perennial Return of Central Europe Reflections on the Sources of the Illiberal Drift in Central Europe

*Jacques Rupnik*

1989 was celebrated as the return of Central Europe. A liberal-democratic revolution that restored democratic sovereignty along with the language of rights and constitutionalism. A belated "bourgeois revolution" without a bourgeoisie. It was also seen as proof of the resilience of a Central European culture that outlasted the communist structure that had come in from the east. If the "tragedy" of postwar Central Europe was, in Milan Kundera's words, to be "culturally Western, politically in the East and geographically in the centre,"[1] then 1989 meant the reconciliation of politics, culture, and geography. Thus, parallel to the emergence of liberalism associated with the dissident movements of the of the 1970s and 1980s (human rights and civil society) was the rediscovery a Central European cultural identity as the "kidnapped West." The 1989 "return to Europe" entailed the convergence of these two complementary developments: (re)claiming a Western identity and a "conversion" to liberalism. The cultural narrative combined with the liberal narrative, the "Kundera moment" with the "Havel moment." A quarter of a century later, both have been challenged.

---

[1] Milan Kundera, "Un Occident kidnappé ou la tragédie de l'Europe centrale," *Le Débat*, November 1983. The English translation was published as "The Tragedy of Central Europe," *The New York Review of Books*, April 26, 1984.

Postwar "Eastern Europe" reinvented itself in the 1980s as "Central Europe," and, after 1989, was eager to merge with Western Europe.[2] The rapid post-Cold War convergence between the two formerly divided parts of Europe, and EU integration was a success at the expense of the Central European idea, that was demoted to a phase or a fad. In the 2008 financial crisis, which brought about a North/South divide within the European Union, the countries of Central Europe sided resolutely with Germany against the Southern countries rebranded as "PIGS."[3] In dealing with the financial crisis, Radek Sikorsky, then the Polish foreign minister, said, "Poland definitely belongs to Northern Europe."[4] So within a quarter of a century, we moved from Eastern Europe to Central Europe and then to Western or even Northern Europe. The countries had not moved, but the mental geography played havoc with their assumed or imagined identities.

Now Central Europe is back on the European scene, this time in illiberal and nationalist cloth. This current Western rediscovery of Central Europe is rather different from the post-'89 return of the prodigal son; now it is the herald of the nationalist-populist wave that has been gaining momentum across Europe in recent years. The responses of the Visegrád group (Poland, Hungary, Czech Republic, Slovakia) to the migrant crisis that began in 2015 brought back into the open an East/West divide within the EU concerning the definition of national and European identity. Simultaneously, a regression of democracy in several countries, particularly in Poland and Hungary, has brought to power overtly anti-liberal political forces. The combination offers indeed a startling contrast with the 1990s.

Countries that were considered as the "success story" in the transition to and consolidation of liberal democracy (Hungary and Poland) now challenge the institutions of the rule of law. Instead of building a "state of law" (*Rechtsstaat*), Hungarian Prime Minister Viktor Orbán now calls for an "illiberal state."[5]

---

[2] The issue of *Deadalus* published in January 1990 (vol. 119, no. 1) was appropriately entitled: "Eastern Europe ... Central Europe ... Europe."

[3] Portugal, Italy, Greece, and Spain.

[4] Radek Sikorsky, speaking at Harvard University, February 28, 2011.

[5] Full text of Viktor Orbán's speech at Băile Tuşnad (Tusnádfürdő) on 26 July 26, 2014: *The Budapest Beacon*.

Central Europe, unlike the Balkans, in the 1990s avoided the nationalist temptation and developed open societies and open markets eager to join the European Union. To deal with Hungarian minorities in neighbouring states, the government in Budapest opted "in Europe's name" for recognized and open borders with European standards in the recognition of minority rights. "Europe without barriers" was still the motto of the Czech presidency of the European Union at the beginning of 2009. Today, the Czech president Miloš Zeman campaigns on issues such as protecting borders from migrants, while his predecessor, Václav Klaus, appeared as a guest speaker at the March 2016 Conference of the xenophobic Alternativ für Deutschland.

The Visegrád Group, formed in the immediate aftermath of the demise of the old order by presidents Havel, Wałęsa, and Göncz, stood for democratization, overcoming nationalist legacies of the past and the shared goal of joining the process of European integration. At the time, Visegrád meant that Central Europe was leaning to the West. Today, Visegrád asserts itself in opposition to Western Europe, Brussels, and Berlin on the migrant issue, while Orbán and Kaczyński call for a "counter-revolution" in Europe. So how did we get from there to here? What are the main features of Central Europe's illiberal turn? How to account for them? And what are the implications for Europe?

## The Illiberal Turn

"The liberal non-democracy is over. What a day! What a day! What a day!"[6] Thus spoke Hungarian prime minister Viktor Orbán on the morning after Donald Trump's election victory, which happened to be the anniversary of the fall of the Berlin Wall. Brexit was a "knock on the door," he said, and with the election of Donald Trump as President of the United States, we have "crossed the threshold." While the rest of Europe was groggy, Orbán was euphoric. "I feel liberated," he said, from the constraints of the European Union and political correctness. *Vindicated* may be the more appropriate word. Since he

---

[6] "Viktor Orbán interview: Full transcript," Peter Foster, *Daily Telegraph*, November 11, 2016. The Czech président, Miloš Zeman, in his letter of congratulation to the newly elected U.S. president, proudly claimed: "In my country I am known as the Czech Trump." His predecessor, Václav Klaus, after supporting Brexit, saw Trump in the White House as the victory of "common sense of ordinary people." Havel must be turning in his grave.

came to power in 2010, his "regime change" has been criticised by the EU as well as the Obama administration. With the Brexit referendum in the UK ("The greatest act of defiance against the establishment since the coming of universal suffrage"[7]) and Trump in the White House, he feels—rightly so— that the tide has changed.

The specter of populism is haunting Europe. Hofer, narrowly defeated in the Austrian presidential elections, joined a coalition government with the conservative Right; the Northern League and Pepe Grillo's Cinque Stelle formed a coalition government in Italy, and Marine Le Pen's National Front made it into the second round of the presidential elections in France. All these are different incarnations of nativist populist political forces that are challenging liberal democracies, reshaping the political landscape of most member states of the European Union, while threatening the EU with paralysis or even disintegration. Although we face the rise of populist nationalist parties elsewhere in Europe, only in East Central Europe were they the first to seize power. A difference as well as a warning. Brexit and Trump are also changing the picture and with it the dialectic between center and periphery.

For about two decades, the countries of East Central Europe were engaged in imitating Western European political and constitutional models. When signs of "democracy fatigue" appeared in one country or another, it was considered an isolated case and usually attributed to the legacies of the communist past. Post-'89 democratization was based on adopting Western-type institutions of the rule of law and their export was known as "EU enlargement." *Transition* to democracy led to *consolidation* of democracy (where all actors accept the constitutional framework and an election is a choice of government, not a regime change), which in turn was part of the process of European *integration*. This three-phase pattern generated a considerable academic industry under the heading of EU's "transformative power" or "Europeanization," as inadequate a term then (the nations joining had been "European" long before the EU came into existence) as it is ambiguous now (as it is not clear who actually defines what the European model is).

With the rise of populist forces throughout Europe and particularly with the Brexit referendum (sovereignty) and Trump (nationalist xenophobia), the perspective changes. Orbán and Kaczyński clearly understood

---

[7] Nelson Fraser and James Forsyth, "How Teresa May can seize the Brexit revolution," *The Spectator*, July 9, 2016, https://www.spectator.co.uk/2016/07/how-conservatives-can-seize-the-brexit-revolution/.

and exploited the shift in the epicenter of Western liberal democracy: Brexit was used in Central Europe to call for repatriation of powers to the nation-states. Hungary will not be a "colony" and will not "live according to the commands of foreign powers." "Stop Brussels" is the rallying call of the campaign launched in Budapest in the spring of 2017. And Trump, the wall-builder, is seen as a partner by Orbán, the fence-builder.

The Western anchor of the new democracies has been undermined: *deconsolidation* of democracy[8] goes hand in hand with the weakening of a divided European Union. Anti-liberalism and anti-Americanism used to go together. Now, the new U.S. President provides legitimization to the anti-liberal forces in East Central Europe and beyond. In Orbán's words: "Twenty-seven years ago here in Central Europe we believed that Europe was our future; today we feel that we are the future of Europe."[9] An ironic reversal of the post-'89 paradigm, reminiscent of a short story by Marcel Aymé about a cyclist in the Tour de France who lagged so far behind in the race that he found himself leading the peleton the following year!

The main features of the illiberal turn can be summed up as follows: *departure from the rule of law* as the foundation of liberal democracy in the name of the sovereignty of the people. This is a call to the "general will" according to Jean-Jacques Rousseau as opposed to the separation of powers according to Montesquieu. *The rise of nationalism and the hardening of identity politics* corresponds to the shifting axes of legitimation from liberal-technocratic to populist democracy. "A new era of political thought has opened," we are told by Orbán, "because people want democratic societies but not open societies."[10] And finally, *culture wars*: a conservative revolution or, better, a cultural "counter-revolution" in Europe that Kaczyński and Orbán called for at their meeting in Krynica in October 2016. In the old days, that is, before 1989, Czech and Polish dissidents would meet in the mountains at the border to discuss strategies of democratic change. Today, two former dissidents meet in the Tatra mountains calling for a "counter-revolution" against liberal, permis-

---

[8] See Roberto Stefan Foa and Yascha Mounk, "The Signs of Deconsolidation," *Journal of Democracy* 28 (2017).

[9] Viktor Orbán's speech at the 28th Bálványos Summer Open University, July 22, 2017, Tusnádfürdő (Băile Tuşnad, Romania), in *Visegrád Insight*, http://about-hungary.hu/speeches-and-remarks/viktor-orbans-speech-at-the-28th-balvanyos-summer-open-university-and-student-camp.

[10] Orbán's speech of January 28, 2017, quoted in *Le Monde*, January 30, 2017.

sive, decadent Europe in a language not too far from Putin's or that of Russian conservative nationalist ideologues such as Alexander Dugin.[11] In the culture wars, does this mean a Central Europe that leans towards the east? How to account for this reversal of the post-'89 developments? What happened to the liberal project in East Central Europe? Several hypotheses can be proposed.

## Decoupling Liberalism and Democracy

In the early days of 1989, I was asked to introduce an evening conversation in Vienna at the Institute for Human Sciences (IWM) entitled "After Communism What?" Cardinal König and Prince Schwarzenberg were sitting in the first row, so I treaded carefully but eventually raised the unpleasant question: "Would the cultures that proved most resistant to Communism (such as the Polish combination of nationalism and Catholicism) be also conducive or compatible with the introduction of liberal democracy?" Conversely, would the Czech tradition of secularism and a Masarykian version of "social democracy" that proved vulnerable to the postwar Communist project perhaps offer a "usable tradition" for the post-communist transition? I was wrong, and 1989 did bring about liberal democracies precisely in Poland or Hungary, where post-1918 "transitions to democracy" had soon drifted towards nationalist authoritarianism.[12]

Two developments help to account for this. First, the legacies of dissent. In their own different ways, Solidarność, the Democratic Opposition in Hungary, and Charter 77 in Czechoslovakia all stood for reclaiming the language of rights and the autonomy of civil society, as well as for overcoming the partition of Europe. That legacy inspired at least the initial phase of the post-'89 transition.

No less important, major intellectual and political re-alignments in the period between 1968 and 1989 helped overcome some of the old divides in the political cultures in East Central Europe. In Poland, Leszek Kolakowski wrote a memorable essay in the mid-1970s describing himself as a "conservative, liberal, socialist," a sign that old labels and dividing lines no longer

---

[11] For an analysis of Dugin's nationalist and radical critic of the West, adapting for his purposes some of Heidegger's concepts, see Jeff Love and Michael Meng, "Heidegger and Post-Colonial Fascism," *Nationalities Papers* 45, no. 2 (2017): 307–20.

[12] For a comparative survey, see Antony Polonsky, *The Little Dictators: The History of Eastern Europe since 1918* (London: Routledge, 1975).

applied.[13] Adam Michnik wrote two influential essays to illustrate this. *The Church and the Left* (1977)[14] suggested the two historical rivals shared certain values of human dignity and human rights and that their dialogue could help defend liberties suppressed by the Communist regime. The other essay, "The New Evolutionism" (1976) suggested ways to overcome or bypass the old Polish dilemma inherited from the nineteenth century between revolution and accommodation, the traditions of Pilsudski and Dmowski. It reflected that failed past attempts at change called for an alternative strategy: the self-organisation of civil society.

In Czechoslovakia, a 1980 samizdat volume paid tribute to Tomáš Masaryk, the philosopher-king founder of Czechoslovakia as a liberal democracy. The list of contributors read like a "who's who" of Czech intellectual life at the time, ranging from 1968 revisionist Marxists to Christian philosophers or liberals like Václav Havel. A meeting ground had been found, and Havel could later capitalize on this development, stepping, so to speak, into Masaryk's shoes.

In Hungary, the symbolic political point of convergence was István Bibó, the political thinker who came from the populist tradition and who became one of the most original and influential thinkers rediscovered by the democratic opposition.[15] For a while, during the late 1980s, it seemed that the old divide between "urbanists" inspired by Western political and economic models (liberals or social democrats), and populists who saw the peasantry as the depository of true national and democratic values (and who were concerned with the "Hungarian question," i.e. the fate of Hungarian minorities in neighbouring countries) was becoming blurred. This convergence also provided the background to an informal dialogue between the liberal opposition and reformers within the Party concerning the rule of law. Both developments led to a degree of consensus necessary to lay the foundations of liberal democracy in post-'89 Hungary.

---

[13] Leszek Kolakowski, "Comment Être « Socialiste-Conservateur-Libéral »," *Commentaire* Numéro4, no. 4 (1978): 455 (published in English in *Encounter*). The piece opens famously with "'Please, move forward to the back!' This is the approximate translation of a behest once heard in a Warsaw streetcar. I propose to make it the rallying call of a powerful International that will never exist."

[14] Adam Michnik, *Kosciol, Lewica, Dialog* (Paris: Kultura, 1977). Translated as *The Church and the Left* (Chicago: University of Chicago Press, 1993).

[15] Bibó's major work is *Histoire des Petits Etats de l'Europe de l'Est* (Paris: L'Harmattan, 1988, c1944).

What happened to the "liberal moment"? Was it just that—a moment? What became of that intellectual and political convergence that made liberal democracy possible? How to account for the de-coupling of liberalism and democracy in East Central Europe? One explanation is that the above-mentioned convergence was made possible by both the existence of a common enemy (the Communist regime) and the conveniently broad platform offered by movements such as Solidarity. Charter 77 was an "opportunity structure" built on the language of rights and anti-politics. The predictable post-'89 eclipse of ex-dissidents from the political scene was an important factor undermining political liberalism.

Another possibility would chronicle the transformation of a Hungarian movement of promising young '89-ers advocating political, economic, and societal liberalism into a party of nationalist conservatives who embarked on building an "illiberal state" to conquer and preserve political power. Not an "opportunity structure," but rather Fidesz as a structure for political opportunists who ended up identifying with and reproducing some of the nationalist pathologies remarkably analyzed by István Bibó.

Perhaps the best illustrations of the divorce between liberalism and democracy are provided by the itinerary of two Polish former liberals. Marcin Krol, the intellectual historian and editor of a samizdat liberal journal *Respublica*, argued for overcoming another cultural divide, between Catholicism and liberalism, and finding compatibility between them (not an obvious proposition, and not just in Poland). In 2015, he published a short book entitled *We Were Stupid*,[16] which squarely blames the ex-dissident intellectuals' infatuation after 1989 with the advocates of radical free-market reforms. The best known was Leszek Balcerowicz, the promoter of "shock therapy," who, Krol says, "never liked the idea of social solidarity and certainly could not imagine a 'solidarity' economy. He managed to fascinate intellectuals with neoliberal concepts and ideas." Thus, ironically, radical free-market reforms were introduced in Poland under the banner of a trade union called "Solidarity"! The Solidarity ethos on which the alliance of intellectuals and workers had been built in the previous decade disintegrated, and, as Krol points out, "the newcomers—taking control of the economy—were completely alien to the Solidarity tradition and just as ruthless as the budding capitalists of the nineteenth century." In short, and this has broader relevance

---

[16] Marcin Krol, *Bylismy glupi* (Warsaw: Czerwone i Czarne, 2015).

for the region, today's decoupling of liberalism and democracy has a lot to do with the post-'89 confusion or collusion between political and economic liberalism.

To understand how this happened, it is important to recall that just as the above-mentioned recasting of the intellectual-ideological landscape allowed for the emergence of political liberalism, the decay of state socialism favored the rediscovery of economic liberalism. Economists in Poland and Hungary, and later also in Czechoslovakia, who intimately knew the failed reforms of planned economies but precious little about "actually existing capitalism," became strongly influenced by ideas of a "minimal state." They looked for inspiration to the Chicago School adepts of free markets, which—as it turns out—happened to be Central Europeans! Tony Judt fittingly called the economic neoliberalism of the Reagan-Thatcher years "the revenge of the Austrians."[17] And indeed, Friedrich Hayek, Ludwig von Mises, Joseph Schumpeter, Karl Popper, and Peter Drucker were all born in the old empire and "profoundly shaken by the interwar catastrophe that struck their native Austria." The lessons they drew from it about minimal state interference in the economy and society became widely shared by those who designed the economic reforms in post-'89 Central Europe.

It is the roll back of the state that provided the common ground for political liberals (ex-dissidents) defending human rights and the emancipation of society and culture from the grips of the party-state, and economic liberals who wanted to free the markets from the intrusions of the state. This convergence provided the political consensus for radical market-oriented reforms, but it was also based on ambiguities and misunderstandings, which partly account for the current illiberal backlash. Leftist intellectuals had been called "useful idiots" in the post-1945 advent of "socialism with a Stalinist face." Should we now consider liberal ex-dissident intellectuals as the "useful idiots" ("We were stupid," says Krol) of the post-'89 transition to "capitalism with a liberal face"?[18] Have political liberals ignored—at their own peril—the

---

[17]　Tony Judt, *Ill Fares the Land* (New York: Penguin, 2010), 91.

[18]　In the Czech case, the distinction remained at least on a symbolic and political level in the 1990s, with president Václav Havel representing political liberalism and his main political opponent, Prime Minister Václav Klaus, a strident advocate of economic liberalism who, like Mrs. Thatcher, believed there is such a thing as society and scorned "ngoism" and "humanrightism" (two terms he introduced into the Czech language).

social question, or, to put it another way, has post-'89 Central Europe travelled from (economic) neo-liberalism to (political) illiberalism?

No less revealing is the itinerary of a second ex-liberal, the Polish political thinker Ryszard Legutko. A 1989 liberal, he published a book entitled *Demons of Democracy: The Totalitarian Temptation in a Free Society.*[19] What is the "demon of democracy"? It is liberalism—just as it had been communism in the pre-89 period. For the communists' primary obsession with class, the liberals substituted race, gender, and sexual orientation. Yet, Legutko argues, the aim remains the same: the dissolution of traditional family values and institutions such as the church and the nation. For Legutko, it is not the "social question" (as for Krol), but the "societal questions" which matter. A member of the European Parliament, he accuses the EU of promoting this left-liberal agenda of feminism, LGBTQ2 rights, and multiculturalism, which, he believes, conservatives must oppose.

The "culture wars" thus defined are key to understanding the Central European hostility to the migration wave of 2015 and the EU Commission's attempts to establish a quota system for taking in asylum seekers. It also revealed two contrasting European narratives. The first narrative is of Central Europeans (in the Visegrád Group) warning about security risks and threats to their national and European identities. Historically, in the nineteenth century they adopted the German model of nation building (*Kulturnation*, based on a shared culture, language, and religion), which they have now transposed to the European level. Orbán, Kaczyński, and Fico claim to protect European cultural identity and civilization in the face of a Muslim threat, just as they had defended it vis-à-vis Soviet totalitarianism in the past. They considered the opening of the borders as the most important freedom conquered in 1989; now, they advocate the politics of closure. Sharing migrants is seen as a tool used by the European Union to impose on Central Europe a multicultural model of society that has failed in the West.

Ironically, the other European narrative is the narrative that is most explicitly formulated by Germany's chancellor Merkel: acceptance of migrants in the name of "European values" identified with universal human rights. Europe, says Ulrich Beck, stands for "substantial void and radical

---

[19] Ryszard Legutko, *Demons of Democracy: The Totalitarian Temptation in a Free Society* (New York: Encounter Books, 2016) (original Polish edition: *Triumf czlowieka pospolitego*, 2012).

openness." It is not easy to identify with "substantial void," and nothing could be more at odds with the Central European *Zeitgeist* today.

Beyond these two departures from liberalism, the conservative critique of the post-1989 consensus in Central Europe has now become more explicit and more articulate. Among its best illustrations is a collection of essays by conservative thinkers from Poland that focuses on three main failings or blind spots of the now closing liberal era.[20] First, the exclusion of memory in the name of the "end of history" (the European liberal version substituted for the Marxist version). Confronting the communist past was presented as looking backward, an obstacle to future-oriented modernization (a critique of Mazowiecki's "thick line" policy of 1990). Second, the promotion of liberal individualism at the expense of the collective dimension of identity (the nation). Third, the liberal reluctance to consider the state as the sovereign subject of domestic and international affairs in the name of global governance based on dubious assumptions such as Fukuyama's "end of history" or Kantian projects of "perpetual peace."

## The Exhaustion of the Post-'89 Liberal Cycle

Central Europe's return in illiberal cloth has revived perceptions of a European East-West divide and questions about the wisdom and viability of the EU's Eastern enlargement. This indeed misreads the problem and possible responses to it. To be sure, there are specific features of the populist backlash in East Central Europe with distinct political cultures and post-'89 legacies. Yet the crisis of liberalism today and the rise of a variety of populist nationalisms is a trans-European, indeed a transatlantic phenomenon. Anti-liberalism in Europe used to go hand in hand with anti-Americanism. Now it is Trump's America that leads the anti-liberal movement. Trump and Putin converge in their contempt for a decadent and declining Europe. The former thrives on insurgent populism; the latter prefers to manipulate it from afar. The decline of Europe's influence and the rise of authoritarian capitalism in China, Russia, or Turkey have changed the international environment in a direction unfavorable to the liberal ideas of an open society.

---

[20] Maciej Ruczaj, ed., *Pravym okem. Anthologie polskeho politickeho mysleni* (Prague: Prague Centrum pro studium demokracie a kultury, 2010).

The post-'89 liberal cycle has been exhausted. A major reason was that revolutions of 1989 did not offer a new social project but embarked on imitating Western models which themselves were in crisis. In East Central Europe, it meant a triple transition—to democracy, to market economy, to Europe. All three were achieved with the accession to the European Union more than a decade ago. Yet all three are in crisis.[21] New democracies built over two decades ago now face illiberal regression. Integration into the Western market economy was completed just before the global financial crisis of 2008. Accession to the European Union in 2004 was celebrated as the "unification" of Europe, followed only shortly thereafter by the discovery that Europe was divided between "old Europe" versus "new Europe" (as Donald Rumsfeld put it). Now, the very pursuit of European integration itself is questioned by its great beneficiaries in Central Europe. Demise of future-oriented political projects gave way to mere ad hoc responses and the tyranny of immediacy (markets and media), with policies without politics and the language of rights. Europe, the last utopia, became the victim of this shift. Liberal elites in Europe—not just in Central Europe—were retreating because they failed to reformulate the project to make it relevant in the age of glo-balization. Their demise and that of the mainstream parties has created new space for identity politics and anti-European populist movements. After more than two decades of a dominant liberalism "without borders,"[22] there is now a return to border protection, communalism, and nationalism. Instead of a "global civil society"[23], we have a global rise of populist nationalisms. We are familiar with the Central European cohort of Orbán, Kaczyński, Fico, Zeman and their West European soul mates (Farage, Wilders, Strache, Le Pen), but

---

[21] On the 20th anniversary of 1989, I described the exhaustion of the "triple cycle" of post-'89 liberalism in "In Search of A New Model," *Journal of Democracy* 21, no. 1 (2009): 105–12.

[22] Liberal politics "without borders" go back to the legacies of 1968 and Bernard Kouchner's "Médecins sans frontières," leaving the barricades of Paris for the famine in Biafra. It extended in the 1970s thanks to dissidents and the Helsinki process to human rights "without borders" and the right to interfere. It provided and ideology for the post-'89 period translated into "global civil society," global democracy promotion, and global governance. Most of it exists only virtually, on the Internet. The most successful and enduring globalization has been that of markets. Back to the distinction between political and economic liberalism.

[23] Mary Kaldor, "The Idea of Global Civil Society," *International Affairs* 79 (2003): 583–93, https://www.jstor.org/stable/3569364.

the phenomenon is global: from Trump to Erdoğan in Turkey, from Putin to Modi in India.

There may be a different, perhaps complementary, way of understanding the end of this era in light of what Michael Walzer calls the "liberation paradox."[24] Examining the cases of Algeria, India, and Israel, Walzer shows how the legacy of secular, national liberation movements is challenged twenty-five years later by religious backlash: modernizing nation-state builders are replaced by religious conservatives and nationalists. A somewhat similar pattern holds for East Central Europe: a quarter of a century after the Great Transformation, we witness a conservative backlash against the liberal, modernizing, pro-European elites.

Beyond the reflection on modernizing and liberal short cycles, there looms a more pessimistic question as to whether the current populist politics and culture wars are part of the closure not just of the post-'89 era, but of an even longer cycle that began with the Enlightenment and is associated with the idea (liberal or socialist) of progress. Beyond Kaczyński's and Orbán's call for a "cultural counter-revolution" in Europe, the radical populist movements can be seen as a political expression of deeper undercurrents, conservative and outright reactionary, in the age of de-Enlightenment.[25]

The medium-term outcome of the political confrontation between liberals and populists, adepts of an open society versus adepts of the politics of closure, will depend to a large extent on the capacity to bridge the disconnect between liberalism and democracy. This implies restoring the autonomy of political liberalism from economic liberalism. If, as has been suggested, the exhaustion of the liberal cycle is a trans-European phenomenon, then Europe is the obvious forum where these dilemmas can begin to find appropriate answers. National approaches, in this respect, are merely cop-outs. Will the populist tide in Central Europe be contained or find support in the rest of Europe? Containment depends both on institutions, which have a resilience of their own, and on the capacity to offer a credible alternative. Brexit and Trump were a boost to Central European populists; they could also become catalysts for a revitalized European project.

---

[24] Michael Walzer, *The Liberation Paradox, Secular Revolutions and Religious Counter-Revolutions* (New Haven: Yale University Press, 2016).

[25] An important distinction that Mark Lilla revisits in *The Shipwrecked Mind: On Political Reaction* (New York: New York Review Books, 2016).

The rise of nationalism and populism has prompted frequently drawn parallels with the interwar period, from the breakdown of democracies to the rise of fascism in the 1930s. One can indeed look with concern at the erosion of liberal democracies and note similar symptoms while browsing through the proceedings of the German Sociological Society, whose 1926 Congress in Vienna was devoted to the crisis of democracy (!), whose 1928 meeting in Switzerland concerned migrations (!), and whose 1930 conference in Berlin was concerned with the state of the "press and public opinion." Yet parallels with the demise of liberal democracies in the 1930s can be misleading. Today, there is no readily available alternative totalitarian ideology, and contemporary nationalist populists are indeed anti-liberal reactionaries, but not (yet) fascist.

Finally, the great unknown about the current rollback of liberal democracy in East Central Europe concerns the societies, the public sphere, and the citizens. To what extent have they accumulated, during the two decades of their post-'89 transitions to democracy, a sufficient buffer against authoritarian temptation? Is Poland, as in the old days, an exception or a model? In any case, the way Polish society responded to a series of authoritarian moves by the PiS government suggests that a successful *Gleichschaltung* and loyalty are unlikely: voice and exit are the main options. The Hungarian historian and political thinker, Oscar Jászi, used the term *Rückschlag* or regression, a term borrowed from psychoanalysis, to define the Hungarian predicament under the Horthy regime. While Orbán and Kaczyński call for a counter-revolution in Europe, their populations remain overwhelmingly in favor of their membership in the European Union. It seems therefore more likely that Central Europe's regression from liberal democracy will be contained if that is the case in Europe as a whole.

# Perhapsburg: Reflections on the Fragility and Resilience of Europe

*Ivan Krastev*

## Introduction

This essay is based on a book I published in the summer of 2017 that I wanted to call *Perhapsburg*. The publishers said that the title was too poetic, so I called it *After Europe*.[1] Probably the book is not as pessimistic as the title suggests, but Bulgarians can never be blamed for being too optimistic. According to opinion polls, Bulgarians are much unhappier than our GDP suggests. When the pessimists and optimists disagree whether the glass is half full or half empty, we are convinced it is half broken. What I try to do in the following pages is to connect some of the problems the European Union faces today to some of the basic problems open society is facing.

Had I been cryogenically frozen in January 2005, I would have gone to my provisional rest as a happy European resident. Imagine January 2005: The European Union was perceived as a successful conversion machine for decades, the distance between the poorest and the richest members of the Union had been closing. Everybody around the European Union wanted to join. It was simply a question of when this was going to happen. There was a lot of optimism, also on the societal level, due to free travel and the idea of increasing prosperity. Timothy Garton Ash continued saying that if he were unfrozen in 2017, he would have died from shock because everything turned

---

[1] Ivan Krastev, *After Europe* (Philadelphia: University of Pennsylvania Press, 2017).

into crisis and disintegrated. How can we make sense of this crisis and how should we rethink those 25 years to understand what is happening now?

There is a beautiful novel by José Saramago, which I found one of the best ways to understand what is going on. It is called *Death With Interruptions*. The plot of the novel is about a country in which people suddenly stop dying. I am saying this because part of the problem that the European Union is facing today is that it is a dream that turned into a nightmare; the thing we loved most is what we now feel threatened by. Nothing symbolizes this better than the problem of open borders. As an East European, if you go to the opinion polls that were held at the 25th anniversary of 1989, you see that countries like Bulgaria are not happy with how the situation evolved over the past 25 years. There is one major advantage: the opening of borders, the possibility for people to travel. Then suddenly, open borders stopped to mean that East Europeans can go outside, and began to mean that others can come in. As a result, the same open borders that were perceived as a major advantage began to be perceived as the major vulnerability of the European project. I thus believe that if we do not understand that the migration and refugee crisis challenges some of the major assumptions of the notion of open society, we are not frank with ourselves.

## Migration as the Twenty-First Century Revolution

If you read Francis Fukuyama's article *The End of History*,[2] you are going to be surprised that there is a lot of talk about the free flow of ideas, goods, and capitals. There is one word you are not going to find in the article, and this is migration. Ideas are going to travel, goods are going to travel, capital is going to travel, but it was not assumed that people are going to travel. Today we start to realize that it is the travelling of people that is going to change and reshape the world of tomorrow, rather than the free flow of ideas or institutions.

I want to argue that migration is going to be the twenty-first century revolution. It will not be a revolution of revolutionary parties; there will be no manifestos, no revolutionary leaders, no blueprints. It will be the exit revolution of individuals who have realized three things. First, if you want to change your life in one generation, it is better to change your country than to change

---

[2] Francis Fukuyama, "The End of History?," *The National Interest* 16 (1989): 3–18.

your government. Second, globalization changes the frame of comparison. Let me give you one example: In the 1980s, when the *World Values Survey* was initiated by the University of Michigan, they discovered that there was no positive correlation between happiness and wealth. In the 1980s, Nigerians were as happy as West Germans. Twenty years later, this was not the case anymore. Nigerians were as happy as their GDP suggested. What happened in the meantime was that Nigerians got televisions. Now they can see how Germans live, they can see their schools and their hospitals. You are neither comparing with previous generations, nor with your immediate neighbour, but you start to compare with those who are most advanced in the world.

The single biggest factor that determines how much money you are going to earn and spend in your life is not your education, but the place you are born. From this point of view, we end up with a situation in which individuals, because of new technologies and mobility, can change their life radically, simply by moving. Nobody can stop it, because like any other type of revolution it is driven by people's desire to better their lives. Third, if immigration is the revolution of the twenty-first century, Europe is becoming a major counter-revolutionary power, because this is the place where people are coming. If we really want to understand the impact of the migration crisis, we should go beyond the legal and humanitarian talk about people coming, i.e. how many people are coming and how they are going to be integrated. Instead, we should try to look at the migration crisis from two different angles. One is the flow of people everyone has been talking about; the other is related to migration arguments. In the 1970s, the European left defended the position that some indigenous villages have the right to resist development and World Bank projects because they have the right to defend their own way of life. Now, some of the middle classes and conservative parts of our societies say we also have the right to defend our way of life. From this point of view, the same arguments that were put forward by the left are becoming the arguments of the right; it is not accidental that not only arguments migrate, but voters, too. One of the major effects of the refugee crisis is the fact that we see a massive migration of blue-collar voters from the left and center-left to the far right. If you look at the result of Brexit or the Austrian presidential election of 2017, particularly the second round, you are going to see that more than 85 per cent of blue-collar voters in Austria voted for the far right. This demonstrates the end of Marxism as the framing ideology of the working class. The working class is not internationalist; they are economic and cultural protectionists. The very identity of the European political system organized around class conflict and between the left and the right, as we knew it during the Cold War, is in crisis today. As a result of these changes, new political identities and new political forces emerge not only in Europe, but also in the United States, which to a great extent is shaping politics. I call this force the *threatened majorities*.

You have ethnic and religious majorities that are panicking and feeling persecuted in the way minorities normally feel. These are not the losers of today, but the many people who perceive themselves as the losers of tomorrow. From this point of view, one of the major characteristics of these groups is the unleashing of the demographic imagination. You are trying to imagine the world without you and to be honest, for some of the small Central and East European countries, this is a real problem. Let us take some Bulgarian statistics. Now, there are around some 7.5 million people living in Bulgaria or even less. 1.5 million have left the country over the past 25 years, according to some statistics. According to projections of the United Nations, Bulgaria is going to lose 27 per cent of its population in the next thirty years. The idea of ethnic disappearance is becoming one of the major forces that shape the imagination of the future.

We are not dreaming of the future anymore, we fear it. What populist parties promise as a response is to stop time. These are not only demographic but also technological fears. Some analysts argue that around fifty per cent of existing European jobs will go to robots.[3] Now people are facing a choice of what they should fear more: robots or foreigners. Threatened majorities, who perceive globalization as a permanent revolution, are becoming apocalyptic. From this point of view, these are not conservative but reactionary movements. They do not have a dream of how things should be, but believe that radical change can be stopped, ending the dreaded status quo of insecurity and uncertainty.

With threatened majorities, two other very important changes enter our political lives. First, the erosion of any type of argumentative discourse in democratic societies. I do not want to use the notion of fake news—there is something very fake about fake news. People are becoming ahistorical and have forgotten how erosive this kind of news is. During war, spreading rumors was punished by death. Even before new technologies, people knew

---

[3] Compare http://bruegel.org/2014/07/chart-of-the-week-54-of-eu-jobs-at-risk-of-computerisation/.

about the corrosiveness of such news, as it can create huge distrust. Second, conspiracy theories have always existed and people like to believe in them. Coming from the Balkans, for us, conspiracy has been a form of common sense. We tend to believe that people are looking for the truth, but when it comes to power, they are looking for the secret. Thus, I am very sceptical of this idea of falling in love with transparency. There is nothing more suspicious than a government that says it is transparent.

Conspiracy theories are the ideology of the age of mistrust. Let me give you an example. The strongest factor to predict who is going to vote for the "Law and Justice" party in Poland is not age or income, but the belief that the tragic death of President Kaczyński and a hundred more members of the Polish elite was not an accident but an assassination. This assassination hypothesis gives people a political identity. Paradoxically, in politics where conspiracy theories are creating political identities, you cannot hold your leaders accountable. Everyone gives the negative example of Trump, but I would like to give the example of Hillary Clinton. If you believe that the only reason Hillary Clinton lost the election is Russian hacking, then there is no reason to ask what was wrong with the campaign or whether she really was the best candidate. You have a high level of unaccountability going on there because conspiracy theories create victim identities and, paradoxically, the majorities became the major victims. From this point of view, these threatened majorities hate both the elites and the immigrants. They see a conspiracy between the elites and the immigrants—both want to destroy their way of life. This is quite important, because my second argument discloses the relationship between democracy and open society. Open society is based on the assumption that democracy, democratic institutions, and democratic mechanisms include different social groups and different minorities in the political process. But democratic institutions can be institutions of exclusion, too. In the same way, elections can exclude people as they include them. From this point of view, under certain conditions, democracy can be a way of opening societies and closing societies, closing them legitimately through the popular vote.

## The Three Paradoxes of the EU Crisis

I believe that to understand the controversial nature of the crisis of the European Union today, we need to address three paradoxes. First, the East Central European paradox. According to various opinion polls, the two most pro-

European societies in Europe were the Hungarians and the Poles. So why are they voting for openly Eurosceptic governments? Why do societies that distrust politicians do not do more to defend the separation of powers? How can you mistrust politicians and at the same time be ready to give all the power to one politician or to one party? Here is my attempt to explain it.

I do not believe that in East Central Europe we can talk about Euroscepticism in the same way you can talk about it in the United Kingdom. Eurosceptics believe that the European Union is bad and assume that if one's country is outside the EU, it is going to do better. I know many East Europeans who are unhappy with many things in the EU, for legitimate reasons, but I do not know many who believe that their country will prosper if they leave the EU. What you have in East Central Europe is much more Euro-pessimism than Euroscepticism. Part of this Euro-pessimism is based on one major distinction between East Central and Western Europe. We, in the East, have witnessed the collapse of a political system as part of our personal experience. This type of political fragility is creating the pessimistic view that we should hedge. Probably it is better for the EU to survive, but you should behave in a way that if the European Union does not survive, you are not on the losing side. Paradoxically, this hatching is becoming a way of weakening and paralyzing the European Union, because if the EU will collapse, it will not happen because of an anti-EU revolution or because there will be more people in Europe who are against, rather than for, the Union. If it will collapse, then it will be similar to a bank run, i.e. you fear that it will collapse and you start to behave accordingly, to better your position when it does. I do believe this is an important part of understanding the strange behaviour of otherwise pro-EU East Europeans who tolerate EU-unfriendly governments. Some of the sensitivity of these populist governments that were elected is similar to that of second-generation migrants. The first generation consists of people like Václav Havel and Adam Michnik and many people who have studied at Central European University. For them, the integration into European institutions was the definition of collective success, because the truth is that for the past 25 years we have all migrated from the East to the West. Some did so individually, others collectively, with their countries. But what is typical for second-generation migrants is that although they are much more integrated than the first generation, they begin to experience, in a rather painful manner, the limits of integration, i.e. the feeling that you are a second-class citizen.

The second paradox I want to present is the fact that people are not willing to defend the separation of power or neutral institutions like the media, central banks, or courts. My hypothesis is the following. From a liberal point of view, and particularly from the point of view of a theory of open society, the separation of power is the best way to hold elites accountable. But for many people on the street, the separation of power is the way in which elites avoid accountability. The government says it cannot be blamed because courts are not allowing it; it says it cannot change economic policy because the central bank is not allowing it. When this goes on for long periods of time, people begin to suspect that instead of controlling elites, the separation of power is a trick elites play so they can do what they want. As a result, you have this strange situation in which people mistrust their political leaders and believe they are corrupt and incompetent. Then they say that the only way to hold a leader accountable is to give him lots of power, so he has no excuse for what he is doing or not doing.

If you look at the Brexit vote, you will see that age and education made a major difference between *remainers* and *exiters*. After 2008, you see that the younger generation is much more politicized than before, there are a lot of protests, and most of the people on the streets were young people. Why did the political impact of these people, who are theoretically much more pro-European, not increase the chances of the European Union to survive? There are many explanations. One is that the young are becoming minorities in most of our societies, not simply the voting minority but the demographic minority as well, because we have a reversed age structure. But there is also something typical about these movements. They are composed of young people, empowered by new technologies and the fact that they can make a difference, and for making a difference they do not need organizations. This is a very strong constitutional ethos if you think about the idea of horizontal networks or leaderless protests and leaderless revolution. You are not going to end up with 100.000 people on the streets through social media, but you might to end up with 5.000, which can become 10.000. Paradoxically, the same instrument that is empowering people also weakens them. The very fact that you can get 200 people just through Facebook out onto the street makes it much more difficult to create a political organization that stands and that can move. And I do believe that this paradox of the empowered individual, who is so empowered to believe that they can ignore the need for collective action, the need for representation, is one of the reasons we have a powerless youth that is otherwise pro-European and politically active. If you do not believe in political representation, you cannot be part of the European conversation. The European Union cannot exist as a union of direct democracy.

It is too big, there are too many different languages. As a result, the major mistrust of political representation makes these movements ineffective on the European level. And here is the paradox: The two cases in which political parties born out of these movements were quite successful were Podemos in Spain and Syriza in Greece. What is typical for these two parties is that in their structure they are the most traditionally organized parties in Europe. Podemos, which was a leaderless movement, a leaderless party, now has the face of their leader. Syriza is closer to an old-fashioned leftist party than anything close to a horizontal network. From this perspective, the paradox of the younger generation is that their mistrust in organizations weakens their possibility to make change.

The third paradox I want to talk about is probably closer to the heart of some of us, namely, the idea of meritocracy. If you look at European elites— and I am particularly talking about the top bureaucracy in Brussels—they are the most meritocratic elites we have. They are people who made their career through good education. I call them the exam-passing elites. They do it the fair way. They have been competing, they passed exam after exam. So, why do parents who give all their money to send their kids to the best universities do not want to be governed by people who graduated from these universities? From this point of view, I do believe that Mr. Trump is an interesting example. There is one thing that President Trump was hiding in his biography, namely, that he had a very good education. He graduated from Wharton Business School, a well-respected institution. He has talked about his money, but he never allowed people to understand that he graduated from one of the big business schools in the United States. Part of the resentment and mistrust is not against the rich, but against the people who made their money based on good universities and the networks that come with them.

Now, what is so problematic about meritocratic elites? If you read Michael Young's book on meritocracy, which is now almost fifty years old, you will see that we could have expected this.[4] A meritocratic society makes the distinction between winners and losers very clear. The winners have the feeling that they did it the fair way, and they do not have much sympathy for the losers. As a result, we have this paradox of inclusive elites leading to an exclusive society. Universities are becoming more inclusive, but exactly because you see minorities in your class and people from a humble back-

---

[4] Michael Young, *The Rise of the Meritocracy* (London: Thames and Hudson, 1958).

ground, you lose your sympathy and compassion for those who did not make it. It has been argued that it is better to be a loser in a fair society than in an unfair society. This is a very strong philosophical argument, but I do believe there is nothing more depressing than being a loser in a fair society. If you are a loser in an unfair society, you can always blame the system. But if you are a loser in a fair society, you can only blame yourself. Blaming yourself is not very popular and I perfectly understand why. And there is the second important feature of the meritocratic elite—their mobility. You can teach in Budapest but you can also teach in London, you can teach in Buenos Aires, you can go anywhere. But there are people who have nowhere to go. Thus, something so important for the identity of the meritocratic elites became one of the major sources of resentment.

The major message of the populist elites is, yes, we are probably corrupted, we are probably incompetent, but we are going to stay with you until the end because we have nowhere to go. We do not speak foreign languages, we do not have international networks. Unfortunately, this is quite an important message. If fifty years ago, the major change about how the world was going to develop was about the nationalization of assets, factories, and others, now the major message is the nationalization of the elites, perceived as cosmopolitan, meritocratic, and offshore.

## Conclusions: How Pessimistic Should We Be About the European Union?

After putting forward these "optimistic" views, how pessimistic should we be about the European Union? Machiavelli used to say that people should never surrender, for the simple reason that they do not know what the future has prepared for them. I do believe this is very wise, because we are surprised all the time and we can also be surprised for the better. From this perspective, I would like to make a major distinction between the years 2016 and 2017. The major shock of 2016 was not simply Brexit or the election of Trump, but the fact that very few who did not vote for them expected this to happen. As a result, there is the shock that you no longer understand the world in which you are living. This created a kind of depression, which was not simply a depression caused by something bad that happened, but the feeling of being displaced, the feeling of vulnerability because you do not understand anything anymore.

I do believe that the survival of any political project is one of the major sources of legitimacy. We trust things not simply because they are good or bad, but because they survive. "Perhapsburg" is a reference to that. Everyone is now carefully reading books about how the Habsburg Empire collapsed in 1918. But the more interesting question is why the Empire did not collapse in the previous hundred years.

Life has the pleasure to surprise us. And here is my last point: Even if we do not know whether the European Union will be saved, who is going to save it? There is a beautiful book called *Anatomy of a Moment*.[5] It tells the story of the famous failed coup in Spain in 1981. Franco is dead, transition starts. In 1981, a lieutenant, who is a soldier of the National Guards, enters the Parliament and decides to put an end to Spanish democracy. People were not on the streets to protect democracy, probably they were too busy, or too tired, or they were exhausted. The king played a very important role in the failure of the coup. But there was something important that psychologically changed the dynamics of the event, and this happened in Parliament. When the soldiers entered—and this is recorded on film because the plotters forgot to stop the camera—they asked all members of Parliament to lie on the floor. Three people did not obey, they remained standing up. These were the three most unlikely people to remain standing up in defense of democracy. The first was Prime Minister Suarez, a Franco functionary who made his career during the Franco period. He was famous for compromise and not for heroism. The other was the Minister of Defense, a Francista general who made his career fighting the republic. And the third was the leader of the Spanish Communist Party, which for years had been claiming that bourgeois democracy is a scam. They remained standing up, the coup plotters were totally frustrated and lost the initiative. We can expect that the resilience of Europe will come from some unexpected sources.

---

[5] Javier Cercas and Anne McLean, *The Anatomy of a Moment: Thirty-Five Minutes in History and Imagination* (New York: Bloomsbury, 2011).

# Capitalism and Democracy in East Central Europe: A Sequence of Crises

*Dorothee Bohle*

## Introduction: Capitalism and Democracy and East Central Europe

The relationship between capitalism and democracy has always been a problematic one. In a recent book, Wolfgang Streeck has argued that it was only under the exceptional circumstances of the post-World War II period that the tensions between the market logic, with its relentless pursuit of profit and private gains, and the collective logic of democracy, with its concern for safety and security of citizens, could be reconciled.[1] This was because markets were tamed through widespread regulations, and democratic polities were including citizens not only as voters, but also as producers in corporatist settings. Since the crisis of this model in the 1970s, politicians have mostly been "buying time." States took up public debt to finance increasing popular needs for welfare services, or enabled citizens to take up private debt, allowing them in this way to consume more than their meagre wages would allow. The recent global financial crisis has put an end to this, and it is unclear how democratic capitalism will survive.

My essay will explore whether Streeck's arguments travel to East Central Europe. More specifically, I am interested in how capitalist democracies could have been relatively stable for the past two decades, and whether there is a relationship between the recent phase of capitalism—

---

[1] Wolfgang Streeck, *Buying Time: The Delayed Crisis of Democratic Capitalism* (New York: Verso, 2014).

the debt crisis and its aftermath—and the democratic backsliding in some parts of the region. In a nutshell, my argument is that while governments in East Central Europe have been successfully "buying time" through welfare states and identity politics, the recent crisis has transformed social relations of capitalism into relations between debtors and creditors. It is this type of relation that is conducive to democratic backsliding and to populist revolts as debtors' revolts.

# Streeck's Argument:
## A Series of Crises of Democratic Capitalism

Streeck argues that since the end of Fordism in the 1970s, when mass-production, the Keynesian welfare state, and popular democracy came to an end, we have had a series of crises of democratic capitalism and a series of displacements of the tensions between capitalism and democracy. In this context, policy makers have been "buying time," postponing the conflict between capitalism and democracy. Thus, during Fordism, the major location of conflict in capitalist societies was located in the labor markets, pitting capital against labor. When the crisis of Fordism hit, the conflict was smoothened through inflation. Labor could still get wage hikes, while asset owners and capitalists lost due to this. The conflict around inflation was fought in the labor markets, through democratic corporatism, and in the electoral arena.

From the 1980s onward, we have what Streeck and many others call the neoliberal counterrevolution. Reagan and Thatcher were the major proponents of this. It was a revolt of capital against labor. Streeck argues that this resulted in the decline of trade unions and labor as a collective force. As a result, democratic corporatism was dismantled, and the conflict between capital or capitalism and social integration moved entirely into the electoral arena, pitting capital against the voters. Democratic governments now bought time through taking on public debt. This allowed them to maintain (and partly even extend, at least in terms of expenditures) the welfare state, while capital withdrew from financing states through taxes. In the 1980s, we see an important increase of public debt. The political formula at that time was a compromise between conservative forces that wanted some embeddedness of societies, and radical market leaders who wanted to free the market.

This compromise lasted until the late1990s–early 2000s. From then on, public debt was seen increasingly as a problem rather than a solution. This ushered in a new phase of "buying time," dubbed "privatised Keynesianism" by Colin Crouch.[2] There was an increasing indebtedness of private house-holds. While wages stagnated, people got access to cheap credit. This allowed for social peace in a period when public debt had to be consolidated and welfare states were retrenched. Voters now became consumers and indebted mortgage owners. The political force associated with this, interestingly enough, is the left, in the form of third-way social democracy.

The Global Financial Crisis has put an end to privatized Keynesianism. With states coming to the rescue of their banks and getting once again heavily indebted in the process, a new chapter in the consolidation of public debt began. Streeck conceives of the politics of public debt as a "distribu-tional conflict between creditors and citizens," with both of them having "claims on public funds in the form of contractual-commercial and political-social rights, respectively."[3] In Europe, this conflict is being played out at two levels: in national politics, where governments have to restore creditwor-thiness while keeping up their citizens' rights, and on the European level, where international financial diplomacy has installed a system of tight sur-veillance that ties government hands in order to ensure that financial inves-tors are being protected against financial losses. Table 1 summarizes Streeck's argument.

**Table 1**

| Type of capitalism | Institutional location of tensions | Postponing the crisis ("buying time") | Political formula |
|---|---|---|---|
| Crisis of Fordism | Labor market (capital vs. labor) | Inflation | Democratic Corporatism |
| Neoliberalism | Electoral arena (capital vs. voters) | Public Debt | Conservative-Market Radical |

---

[2]  Colin Crouch, "Privatised Keynesianism: An Unacknowledged Policy Regime," *The British Journal of Politics & International Relations* 11, no. 3 (2009): 382–99.

[3]  Streeck, *Buying Time*, 155.

| Type of capitalism | Institutional location of tensions | Postponing the crisis ("buying time") | Political formula |
|---|---|---|---|
| Financialized Capitalism | Financial markets (asset owners vs. indebted consumers) | Private Debt | Third-Way Social Democracy |
| Austerity Capitalism | Within and between states (creditors vs. debtors) | | Technocracy |

Source: Author's summary based on Wolfgang Streeck, *Buying Time: The Delayed Crisis of Democratic Capitalism* (New York: Verso, 2014).

## Applying Streeck's Argument to East Central Europe

Does Streeck's template travel east? I argue that we can see similar phases of a change of capitalism, consequences for labour, public and private debt, and, at the end of it, a debt crisis. As is well known, East Central Europe—for the purpose of this essay I distinguish between the three Baltic States, the four Visegrád states, and Slovenia—all had major transformational recessions after the breakdown of state socialism. This was also the time when a number of authors pointed to the difficulties of creating capitalist democracies in the East. While the agendas of creating capitalist market economies and democratic societies were inextricably linked, they were also mutually contradictory. Creating a market society was a political project, which required popular legitimacy in order to succeed. The social dislocation that marketization would inevitably bring about, would, however, create masses of dissatisfied voters who could use their newly gained democratic rights to obstruct further reforms. Many countries in the region not only had to cope with the challenges of simultaneously introducing democracy and the market; they also had to build up new nation-states. Most East Central European countries thus had to traverse three stages of a process which in Western Europe "were mastered over a centuries-long sequence."[4] Early literature saw a real danger, therefore, that the double or triple transformation would either result in economic backsliding

---

[4] Claus Offe, "Capitalism by Democratic Design? Democratic Theory Facing the Triple Transition in East Central Europe," *Social Research* 58, no. 2 (1991): 865–92, 873.

to "third ways" between socialism and capitalism, or give rise to authoritarian temptations and upsurges of nationalism and xenophobia.[5]

However, the early breakdown theories did not come true. The region developed relatively stable democracies and market economies simultaneously. What accounts for this? First, indeed argued in a similar vein by Wolfgang Streeck for the West, democracy became hollow, that is, labor's collective action capacity and people's voices were relatively low-key. Trade union density dropped dramatically, so that already by the end of the 1990s trade unions in the Baltic States stopped being a major social force. It took much longer in Slovenia, which for a long time was considered a democratic corporatist country, and the Visegrád countries are somewhere in between [Figure 1]. But in all three groups of countries there is a dramatic decline of trade unions. Collective action was basically dismantled.

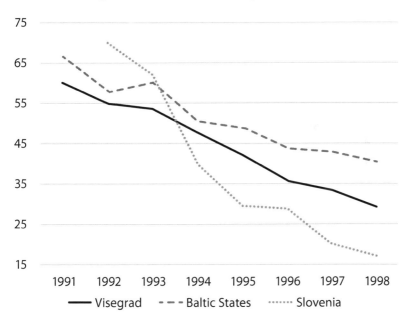

**Figure 1: Trade Union Density, 1991–1998**

Source: J. Visser, ICTWSS Database, version 5.1 (Amsterdam: Amsterdam Institute for Advanced Labour Studies (AIAS)/ University of Amsterdam, September 2016).

---

[5] Ibid.

The same also holds for voter turnout. Figure 2 shows the decline of voter turnout (as a percentage of resident population), which once again is most dramatic in the Baltic States. This is due to the fact that two Baltic countries, Estonia and Latvia, did not grant citizenship rights to sizeable Russian-speaking minorities. But also in the other countries, there is a pretty consistent decline of voter turnout. That means that democracy can get away with a lot, because voters exit rather than use their voice.[6]

### Figure 2: Voter Turnout (1990s)

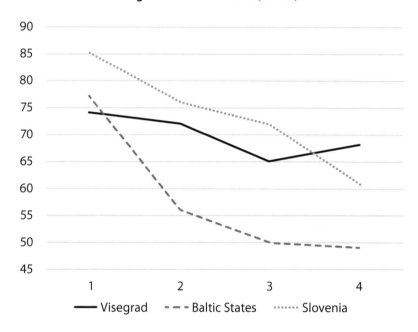

Source: http://www.idea.int/advanced-search?th=Voter%20Turnout%20Database.

But societal demobilization is not all. As Béla Greskovits and I argue in our book *Capitalist Diversity on Europe's Periphery*, leaders in different parts of the region offer their population different forms of compensation for the

---

[6] Béla Greskovits, *The Political Economy of Protest and Patience: East European and Latin American Transformations Compared* (Budapest & New York: Central European University Press, 1998).

losses of transformation.[7] In the Visegrád countries and in Slovenia, we had what we call a "welfarist" social contract. This means that certain groups of the population received social compensation, mostly through early retirements and relatively generous pensions. For Westerners these were not generous pensions, but if we think about the standards of living in the region, these pensions were basically allowing people to make a living and to engage in the informal economy and have a decent income. Pieter Vanhuysse calls this phenomenon the abnormal pensioners' boom.[8] Figure 3 shows how the abnormal pensioners were not people in retirement age, but rather people on early retirement, handicapped, or disability pensions. It was a pacification of the elderly and partly the more skilled workers. Other social programs, such as unemployment benefits or social assistance, were much less generous.

**Figure 3: The growth in the numbers of old age pensioner in Hungary, Poland and the Czech Republic, 1989–1996**

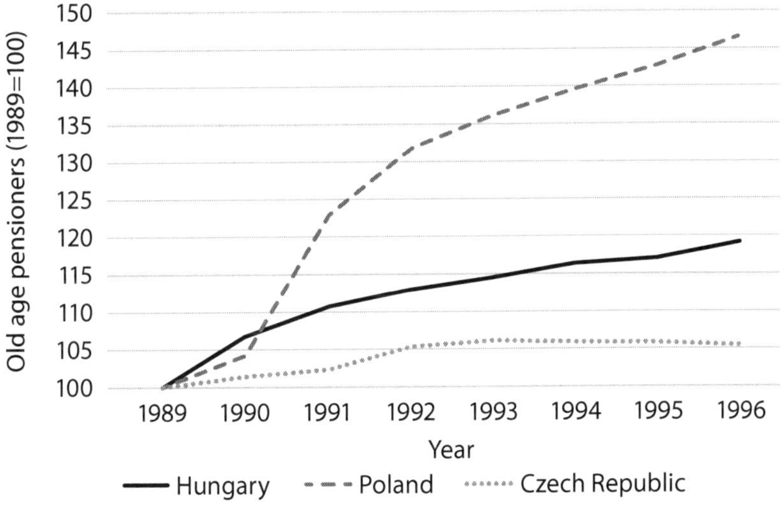

Source: Pieter Vanhuysse, *Divide and Pacify: Strategic Social Policies and Political Protests in Post-Communist Democracies* (Budapest & New York: Central European University Press, 2006).

---

[7]  Dorothee Bohle and Béla Greskovits, *Capitalist Diversity on Europe's Periphery* (Ithaca: Cornell University Press, 2012).

[8]  Pieter Vanhuysse, *Divide and Pacify: Strategic Social Policies and Political Protests in Post-Communist Democracies* (Budapest & New York: Central European University Press, 2006).

In Slovenia, there is a combination of this with democratic corporatism. It lasted throughout the 1990s. This had—if we follow Streeck's argument—consequences, namely, public debt. Especially in Hungary, the tensions around this can be seen from the mid-1990s onward, particularly with the Bokros package.[9] Not dissimilar to what we see in the West, a decrease of the tax base together with increasing social entitlements made public expenditures unsustainable.

In the Baltic States, a different form of compensation took hold, namely identity politics. The issue of state and nation building was very important, and it gave ethnic Balts a sense of belonging and a source of pride. But it also resulted in the marginalization of the Russian-speaking minorities. Given that these people were proportionally stronger affected by de-industrialization and the transformation recession, not giving them citizenship rights also meant the destruction of the losers' collective action capacity. The mobilization of national pride and belonging and the demobilization of Russian-speaking minorities worked for some time to stabilize capitalist democracies in the Baltic States. But it had a downside, and that is the social question. The Baltic States' welfare states were rather meagre. The social question emerged in all three countries around 1990–2000 as the stronger issue, and partly replaced the ethnic question.

By the turn of the millennium, East Central Europe—not unlike the West—entered a new phase in the reconciliation of capitalism and democracy. Figure 4 shows that for the Visegrád countries and Slovenia, public debt had become important, and that from 2000 onwards, private debt has been on the rise as well. In the Baltic States, to the contrary, public debt was very limited. This is an exception in the European landscape. From 2000–2003 and onwards, we see a rapid increase of private mortgage debt and household debt. In both groups of countries, privatized Keynesianism took hold, although to different degrees.

We think that the United States, Great Britain, and Spain had major housing and mortgage booms. But if we compare the annual change in residential loans to GDP and in nominal house prices, we actually see that East Central Europe had the highest increase in both [Figure 5]. Especially in the Baltic States, mortgage lending and housing was at the core of the growth

---

[9]  A series of austerity measures announced in March 1995 by the Gyula Horn Government in Hungary.

### Figure 4 : Public and household debt, Visegrád and Slovenia

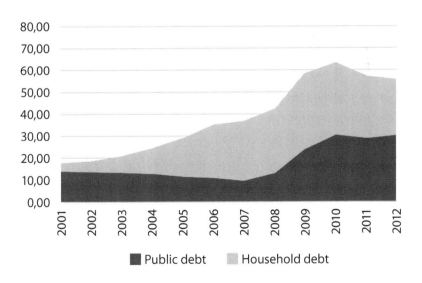

Public and household debt, Baltic States

Source: Public debt Eurostat, household debt. European Mortgage Foundation.

model. This helped to address the social question, as it provided for strong economic growth and rising wages.

### Figure 5: House price and mortgage lending (2002–2006)[10]

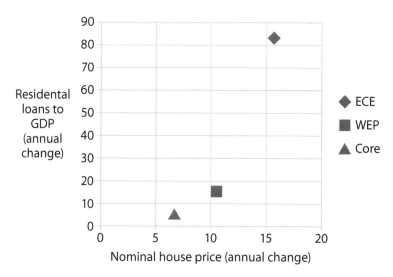

Source: Balázs Égert and Dubravko Mihaljek, "Determinants of House Prices in Central and Eastern Europe," *Comparative Economic Studies* 49, no. 3 (2007): 367–88. European Mortgage Foundation.

One peculiar feature of the mortgage boom in East Central Europe is that it was initiated by foreign banks. In the Baltic States, it was mostly Swedish banks. Swedish and Scandinavian banks had almost ninety per cent of bank assets and were the major mortgage lenders. In the Visegrád countries, it was mostly Austrian banks that unleashed the mortgage boom. In Romania, Bulgaria, and Greece, banks were also very important. Foreign banks introduced mortgage booms and mortgages were issued in foreign currencies, such as the famous Swiss Franc loans in countries like Hungary and Poland, or in Euro in the Baltic States. This was a very risky approach. Taking out mortgages in Swiss Franc, when you have a flexible exchange rate, is extremely dangerous. The reason is simple: interest rates were much lower, and thus

---

[10] ECE = East Central Europe; WEP = West European peripheries: Ireland, Spain, Portugal; Core = Western Europe.

credits were much cheaper. But of course, when the crisis broke out, this was a major issue that countries needed to address, which put a lot of home-owners into unsustainable positions overnight.

## Why the Debt Crisis Can Partly Explain the Populist Backlash

I now come to my core argument that it is this relation, between the debt crisis and the ensuing creditor-debtor relations, which can partly explain the populist backlash and the backsliding of democracy. Let me start with the Hungarian case. There are of course many reasons why Fidesz came to power. I do not want to debate them all. But without this debt crisis and the sig-nificance of austerity capitalism—which was partly imposed on the country because public debt and private debt had gone too far and the previous government was unable to address it—the new government could not have legitimized itself. It could probably not have come to power without its "fight against debt slavery." This was a major part of the legitimation of the govern-ment. Here are a couple of quotes: "In 2011, we are declaring war against gov-ernment debt. We must and will defeat government debt, which is the source of most of our problems and difficulties today. If we do not overcome it, then it will overcome us once and for all."[11] Another issue was the fight with the International Monetary Fund (IMF): "When it is an issue, we put our social rights and social concerns of pensioners against what the IMF wants of us, this leads to conflict, and we have to take up this conflict and this is how we come into conflict with representatives of the IMF."[12]

There was a lot of symbolic politics in the early years of the Fidesz regime, such as staging a major conflict with the IMF, which ended with the Fund having to leave Budapest. This was framed as a debtor's revolt in the name of the people and national sovereignty. The following quotation shows this: "The banks [...] must get used to the new situation. Now we are the stronger ones and they must adapt to the Hungarian people. Nobody is going to gain extra profit at the expense of the Hungarian people ever again. The era of colonization is over."[13] This fight against banks, multinationals, a bullying

---

[11]  Viktor Orbán during his State of the Nation address in February 2011.

[12]  See https://theorangefiles.hu/.

[13]  Viktor Orbán, September 13, 2013, https://theorangefiles.hu/notable-quotes-prime-minister-viktor-orban-by-subject/.

IMF, and Brussels resonates with popular sentiments, as it reacted against the humiliating fact of being indebted and having to go through creditors' surveillance that imposed unpopular austerity policies.

Is there a link between the debt revolt and democratic backsliding? It seems to me that while there is no direct link—after all, as I will show below, debt revolts can also occur in democratic settings—the issue of debt is conducive to populist legitimation strategies. There are a number of reasons for this. First, the debtor-creditor relation pits states against states, rather than addressing social conflicts within countries. It is about Hungary against Brussels, or Germany against Greece. This is conducive to nationalism. Instead of addressing distributional conflicts within a country, they are projected on an international level.

Second, the debt crisis provides the external and internal enemies that can cement the imagined unity of the "real people," which is the basis of populism. The enemies are foreign bankers, international organizations, and the previous government. This is another mechanism how such a situation provides the scaffolding for populist regimes. Third, the debt crisis offers a very welcome opportunity to challenge external checks and balances. As creditors impose conditionality on the debtors, which often seems unjust, it makes it easier to discredit any external condition. Thus, anything that comes from "Brussels" can more easily be rejected. Fourth, the debtor-creditor relation supports what Arlie Russel Hochschild calls a "deep story."[14] She develops this idea in a completely different context in her book *Strangers in their Own Land*, in which she tries to understand why so many people support the Tea Party even if it seems to go against their basic interests. The deep story is a narrative that expresses deeply felt resentments. In Hungary, such a deep story can sounds like this: "We are a small and vulnerable country, and great powers have always taken advantage of us. In the last decades, we have worked hard and sacrificed a lot to become a full and respected member of the European Union. To this aim, we have always played by the EU's rulebook. But we have been—as so often in our history—betrayed. The socialists have betrayed us by selling our country to foreign companies and accumulating debt. The EU, rather than respecting our achievements and rewarding our sacrifices, has enslaved us with its harsh conditions and treats us as

---

[14] Arlie Russell Hochschild, *Strangers in Their Own Land: Anger and Mourning on the American Right* (New York: The New Press, 2016).

second-class citizens. But we will not take this anymore. We demand and deserve respect. We will free ourselves from debt slavery, restore our sovereignty, and regain our dignity. No one will ever meddle with us again." This is a kind of deep story that resonates, and that helps to make sense of what happened: it is the others who are to blame, not us.

These are the reasons why debt crises can be conducive to populist revolts. Now let's look at what happened to debtors' rebellions that were democratic. This is the Greek story. In Greece, Syriza came to power. While many people argued that Syriza is a populist party, it is certainly not an anti-democratic populist party. Syriza has accepted the democratic rules of the game. It came to power with a mandate to renegotiate debt and to end austerity. Their revolt was probably not done very smartly, but there is no denying that this democratic debt revolt was crushed by the creditors, and that the German finance minister did have a particularly strong role in this. As Wolfgang Schäuble told the newly elected and notorious Greek finance minister, "Elections cannot be allowed to change economic policy."[15] An intriguing question here is: Why is it that democratic debt revolts like the one in Greece are crushed and anti-democratic revolts like the one in Hungary are not? There are two plausible answers to this question. First, Greece wanted a debt renegotiation, which Hungary did not. In Hungary, the government has implemented austerity by stealth, and repaid its loans. In contrast, Greece openly challenged the sustainability and fairness of the repayment norm. This was considered especially problematic, as Greece is member of the Eurozone. Second, left wing revolts are more frightening than right wing revolts for the powers that be. As is well known, Hungary has powerful allies among the European People's Party and the German conservatives. Syriza, on the other hand, lacks these allies. The point is: debtors' revolts do not have to be anti-democratic, but if they happen to be carried out by the wrong people, they get crushed. This, however, challenges democracy in yet another way.

Then, of course, there is an alternative to debt revolt, exemplified by the Latvian story. In Latvia, it was not public debt but initially a private debt crisis, which then turned into a sovereign debt crisis, because one of the banks had to be bailed out. The precursor of the troika came in. The Latvian

---

[15]   Wolfgang Schäuble, quoted in Yanis Varoufakis, *Adults in the Room: My Battle with the European and American Deep Establishment* (New York: Farrar, Straus and Giroux, 2017), 236.

story had an interesting twist, because it was the government that insisted on internal rather than external devaluation. Representatives of the IMF thought adjustment for Latvia might be easier if the country devalued. Keeping the currency peg demanded extra harsh austerity measures, which the government willingly administered. As a debtor, Latvia was more Catholic than the Pope. Latvia could do it because of its hollow (and hollowing) democracy. There were protests in 2009, and there was massive exit, that is, migration. Protest waves and discontent led to government changes, but not to policy changes. Policy-wise, Latvia represents the classical "there is no alternative." New governments keep implementing the same policies, and the only party that is critical of austerity, which also repeatedly received most of the votes, was never part of the government because of the ethnic question. Thus debt could be serviced, but at the expense of popular democracy.

## Conclusions

I would like to conclude by making three points. Firstly, similar to advanced capitalist countries, East Central Europe has experienced a sequence of crises of democratic capitalism and has relied on a number of solutions to overcome these crises, but none of these solutions have been sustainable. With each crisis, new fixes had to be found. Secondly, in the current phase of capitalism, democracy's biggest challenge is to cope with multiple debt crises, in an environment where the power lies with creditors. In this situation, the democratic center does not hold. And thirdly, either we have right wing populist revolts against debt in the name of the people, only to later dispense of the people, or we have debt compliance, which is only achieved at the cost of the popular component of democracy.

# Civic Activism, Economic Nationalism, and Welfare for the Better Off: Pillars of Hungary's Illiberal State

*Béla Greskovits*

## Introduction: Double Attack on Liberalism

This essay is motivated by what I regard as a key international development, the double attack on liberalism both as a political and as an economic project, observed in many countries. I analyze this attack in a case study on Hungary, where an illiberal political force moved from the opposition to an enduring political rule. This case study is divided into two parts. The first part shares some findings of my ongoing research on the Civic Circles Movement that played a crucial role in the successful rebuilding of the Hungarian right in 2002–2006. The second part is based on a paper I co-authored with Dorothee Bohle on illiberal politics in power, more specifically on some of the economic and social policies of Premier Viktor Orbán's governments in 2010–2018.

Currently, liberalism is going through hard times. As a political project, it is under attack for its efforts to educate citizens to be willing to recognize and accept their societies' diversity, because its challengers hold that it emancipates the wrong actors: sexual and ethnic minorities, non-whites, or women. Simultaneously, and very often by the same political actors, economic (neo)liberalism is attacked as a force that exacerbates inequality through promoting global capitalism. While both criticisms have been around for some time, their merger into powerful anti-liberal agendas is one of the striking features of the new political context in the wake of the global financial crisis and the Great Recession. These days it seems as if liberalism can do no good: whether it emancipates or creates inequalities, it is always pushed into defense.

The illiberal counterattack is either explained as a cultural backlash, or by economic insecurity and social deprivation, or as a combination of both.[1] The notion of cultural backlash is often traced to the anger of members of social groups who resent that the "silent revolution" of value change, embraced since World War II by the entire western world, led to their decline and a marginalization of their social status. With their traditional attachments to nation, religion, and family hierarchies, they feel looked down upon by the winners of the silent revolution. Their anxiety about their social status is often combined with fears about their deteriorating position in the labor markets, social deprivation, and in many cases a resentment of others, who they consider as competitors for jobs and welfare benefits. What both these explanations have in common is the focus on the grievances of losers, the "have-nots." I suspect this is partly due to a kind of liberal soul-searching, which stems from the discomfort of having betrayed and left behind the white lower middle and working classes, the "small people." Researchers try to understand how these "losers" merge into electoral protest coalitions, which in several countries have proved more successful than ever before. I find these explanations not wrong but incomplete.

Here I see the importance of the Hungarian case. While Prime Minister Orbán's illiberal state building is no longer exceptional, it has a couple of unique features. One of these is its resilience: it is a remarkably successful political project. Whether you like it or not, Orbán's Fidesz party has won seven elections in a row, European, municipal, and national. In the last national elections, in April 2018, Fidesz managed to once again claim a two-third majority in Parliament. Another key feature, which is less known, is that part of the success story of this illiberal project is its strong embeddedness, its roots and its support, in civil society. The Hungarian case illuminates not only the anger and mobilization of ordinary people, the "have-nots," but also the agency of educated middle and upper middle classes, which can play a very important role in challenging liberal regimes and then stabilizing illiberal regimes. It illuminates the dynamics of and the links between building a right-wing civil society before, and an illiberal state after, electoral victory.

---

[1] For a summary of these arguments and an elaboration of the cultural backlash thesis, see Ronald F. Inglehart and Pippa Norris, *Trump, Brexit, and the Rise of Populism: Economic Have-Nots and Cultural Backlash*. Faculty Research Working Paper Series RWP 16-026, Harvard University, John F. Kennedy School of Government, Cambridge, MA, August 2016.

# The Civic Circles Movement

I want to make two arguments here. The first is that the rise of the illiberal right in Hungary is rooted in its superior embeddedness in civil society, which was achieved in opposition. The second argument is that the Civic Circles Movement, founded by Viktor Orbán after he lost in the national elections in 2002, managed to mobilize all fractions of the right and occasionally to even cooperate with non-rightist organizations, such as environmental, peace, and anti-poverty movements, as well as smaller trade unions. Through this all-encompassing effort, the right caught up with the originally better established left and liberals in terms of civil society organization. Simply put, the left and liberals had lost the societal fight before they lost the political one. After eight years in opposition, this accumulated social capital in civil society was transformed into political capital. This goes far in explaining the landslide victory of Fidesz in the 2010 elections, and it is a key factor of social support behind the march of the Orbán regime to illiberal state-building and electoral authoritarianism ever since.

In my research on the Civic Circles Movement I found four features that I consider crucial.[2] First, this was a militant movement in terms of its hegemonic aspirations and collective practices. Second, it was massive in terms of membership and activities: reportedly there were around 150,000 to 160,000 activists, more than 10,000 civil society organizations, and hundreds of large organizations cooperating with the smaller circles. Already in 2002, the movement was densely inter-networked, long before the era of Facebook or Twitter. Third, the bulk of its membership came from middle-class and upper-middle-class backgrounds, including conservative lawyers, teachers, doctors, priests, pastors, entrepreneurs, media people, and artists, as well as their existing or newly founded organizations and associations. The circles were far from being hotbeds of fascist mobs, as they were presented at the time by left-liberal political leaders and the media. Finally, the events (co)organized, advertised, and attended by the circles typically took place in Budapest and the big cities in the countryside. Two-thirds of the around

---

[2] For further details and the empirical sources of my research, see Béla Greskovits, *Rebuilding the Hungarian Right through Civil Organization and Contention: The Civic Circles Movement.* EUI Working Papers, Robert Schuman Centre for Advanced Studies, RSCAS 2017/37.

5,000 events of the movement that I recorded over four years were either metropolitan or organized in large cities in the countryside.

As to the movement's contentious activities, my earlier research with Jason Wittenberg shows that from 2002 onwards the right clearly out-competed the left and the liberals in terms of the frequency, duration, and number of participants in street demonstrations, rallies, marches, strikes, as well as milder instances of protest.[3] Often civic circles were among the organizers. These were not violent events; protesters mainly used "graphomaniac" forms of resistance, petitions, open letters, and public statements. This confirms the presence of educated members and activists. Many of the contentious events were not about economic issues, but issues of identity, such as nation, religion, media contents, and the like.

The Civic Circles Movement was Janus-faced from its birth as it incorporated Tocquevillian as well as Gramscian understandings of civil society.[4] A related interesting detail is that Viktor Orbán had explored some of these ideas long ago in his Master's thesis submitted at Eötvös Loránd University in 1987. The thesis analyzes Polish Solidarity as a massive social movement, which has paved the way to civil society organization in an authoritarian state.[5] Reading the thesis, you may be surprised by the young author's erudition and ample references, among others to Antonio Gramsci, Alain Touraine, and Jürgen Habermas. Orbán clearly knows his Gramsci, perhaps more so than some of his left-wing political opponents do nowadays.

Without making too much of this detail, it is clear to me that by organizing and acting according to Tocquevillian and Gramscian logic simultaneously, the civic circles had found a winning formula.[6] A Tocquevillian civic

[3] Béla Greskovits and Jason Wittenberg, *Civil Society and Democratic Consolidation in Hungary in the 1990s and 2000s* (Budapest and Berkeley: unpublished manuscript, 2016).

[4] Alexis de Tocqueville, *Democracy in America* (New York: Vintage, 1990); Antonio Gramsci, *Selections from the Prison Notebooks* (New York: International Publishers, 1971).

[5] Viktor Orbán, *Társadalmi önszerveződés mozgalom a politikai rendszerben (a lengyel példa)* [Movement of self-organizing society in the political system (The Polish case)] (Budapest: ELTE, 1987), http://2010-2015.miniszterelnok.hu/attachment/0017/szakdolgozat.pdf.

[6] In the distinction between the Tocquevillian and Gramscian approaches to civil society, I follow David Riley, "Civic Associations and Authoritarian Regimes in Interwar Europe: Italy and Spain in Comparative Perspective," *American Sociological Review* 70 (April 2005): 288–310.

logic was central to reorganizing and combining the grassroots networks and different streams of the Hungarian right: the national Christian middle class, the populist national middle class, and initially also the radical right. This was aided by sustained efforts to reinvent traditional holidays, and the heroes, the authentic writers, and other idols and symbols of the right. Much energy was spent on creating the right's own public sphere at the local, regional, and national levels, and on delegitimizing the public and commercial media, allegedly dominated by the left and the liberals. At the same time, a Gramscian hegemonic logic was superimposed on the Tocquevillian civic logic. Ultimately, the circles' civic activism became part and parcel of the right's hegemonic aspirations, about which Orbán was not silent. In his famous speech that can be rightly viewed as the founding document of the movement, he said: "Civic Hungary is not one smaller or larger part of this country. It is the whole. [...] Even if our parties and elected representatives might be in opposition in the Parliament, we, all those present in this square, will not and cannot be in opposition, because it is impossible for the nation to be in opposition. It is only a government that may end up in opposition to its own people if it fails to act in the nation's interest."[7] Declaring that the nation in opposition was an oxymoron, Orbán questioned the power-holders' "true Hungarian" identity, and invited everybody else to join the struggle for reclaiming the nation. With this, he was aiming higher than merely uniting all fractions of the right in a single political community, expressed at the time in another battle cry: "There is one flag, there is one camp."

The cause of fighting for identity and the promise of community proved attractive for many. Reading the statements of people participating in the circles, we find striking revelations of strong attachments: they felt dignity, they felt taken seriously, they felt that their opinions mattered. While some activists were not novices, the movement also attracted large numbers of newcomers, people without any significant prior record in politics, whether in conventional or nonconventional arenas. They were worried that the lost election sentenced them to living in an undemocratic regime ruled by a tyrannical majority, which was unwilling to respect and protect them. They felt left without a fair representation of their values and causes in the public

---

[7] Orbán Viktor beszéde a Dísz téren 2002. május 7-én [Viktor Orbán's speech at Dísz Square on May 7, 2002], http://mkdsz1.freeweb.hu/n22/orban020507.html, translation by Béla Greskovits.

and commercial media. In many ways, they felt much like the supporters of the Hungarian opposition today.

The movement offered remedies by nurturing its members' emotional attachment to some of the most encompassing imagined communities[8]: the nation, Christianity, citizenry, and Europe. These were by no means obsolete categories at the time, just twelve years after the collapse of the socialist system. Thus, rather than being born nationalists or Christians, let alone citizens of Europe, Hungarians were in the midst of a process of re-imagining these communities, and their own ways of belonging to them. There existed a scope for educating people about relevant ideas and practices, which happened through frequent encounters of the civic circle members with each other and with leading activists. Among the latter, the main roles were played by activists of patriotic or nationalist organizations, professional policy makers, politicians, priests, and media pundits.

My inquiry into the manifestations of patriotism and/or nationalism within the Civic Circles Movement sheds light on a complex picture. Offered to different audiences, there are at least four types of national imaginations and related practices, such as local patriotism, Hungary as a nation of fifteen million inhabitants, including the neighboring countries' Hungarian minorities, and Hungary as a European nation. The first Fidesz government (1998–2002) did a lot for Hungary's integration into the European Union. Experts, both politicians and technocrats, went to the civic circles and explained what was likely to happen with Hungarian culture, the legal system, agriculture, industry, and the church, in a united Europe. The civic circles embraced the message: Europe is our future, Hungary is our country—Hungary first, never second. A fourth interesting concept of nationalism came in the form of what I call sacral-medievalism, related to an ancient past that goes back thousands of years. Attachment to this latter imagination was built through lectures, spectacles, thematic summer camps dedicated to ancient Hungarian military arts, and uniform writing to young and adult participants. There were also costumed processions and events related to the cult of the holy Hungarian crown. Instead of going into further details, let me illustrate with a single example that these forms of national imaginations, instead of being mutually exclusive, were compatible.

---

[8] Benedict Anderson, *Imagined Communities: Reflections on the Origin and Spread of Nationalism* (London: Verso, 1983).

**Figure 1**

Source: Népszavazás, December 5, 2004.

Figure 1 replicates a poster, designed by one of Hungary's most renowned and creative visual artists, István Orosz, on the eve of the December 2004 referendum. The ultimately invalid referendum was on whether ethnic Hungarians living outside Hungary, mainly in neighboring countries, should be offered a second, Hungarian citizenship. The poster was circulated across all the civic circles as campaign material. Its symbolism is intriguing: it depicts a slice of bread whose contours are reminiscent of Greater Hungary's borders. This conveys the message that the citizens of Hungary are willing to share their bread, that is, anything they have, with the neighboring countries' Hungarian populations. However, what is really meant to be shared is a European citizenship and a passport with Hungarians living in Romania, Serbia, Croatia, or Ukraine, who, at the time, could not yet enjoy the privileges of early EU-accession. It nurtures the idea of bringing together fifteen million Hungarians in Europe at a time when the basic notion was that Hungarians had a long way to go before their unity as a cultural nation could be re-established.

A further feature of the movement was the strong support it received from the so called "historical" churches, i.e. the Roman Catholic, Lutheran, and Calvinist Churches. Many of the circles' events were organized either in church buildings or in other church-owned properties: monasteries, religious gymnasiums, or denominational homes for the elderly. Many members or supporters of the movement were church-goers: they either belonged to the clergy or were teachers, students and their parents in religious gymnasiums, or representatives of religious professional associations. These activists organized and/or gave lectures at conferences or summer camps and performed at other events involving liturgical practices or other church-related themes and rituals. In the first half of 2003, for instance, 31 per cent of all events were in some way connected to the Church.

A no less important issue for the civic circles was the fight for their own public sphere, i.e. a right-wing media. In their—not quite false—perception, the major printed media forums and TV stations were dominated by the left, by liberal ideas and pundits, or commercial capital. The civic circles deeply distrusted all of these, and fought for equal media representation in several ways. For example, they tried to create a local, small-scale media. There were villages of around 200 inhabitants where civic circle members produced the localities' first-ever printed media about famous people of the village and its historical events. Many circles fought for being featured in the major weeklies, dailies, and the public and commercial media catering to massive audiences. The media-related activities focused on defending the right-wing media outlets and programs; attacking the left-liberal media for lies (in the popular current term "fake news"); and events during which media-pundits met with their audiences. Hundreds of such meetings happened in the civic circles.

These circles do not exist anymore in their original form. Even if some of them still exist, their numbers are a far cry from their strength in the first half of the 2000s. They certainly play a less significant role now than they did in the period when the right was still in opposition. Still, they might very well exist in a new shape. Specifically, some of the civic circles' "spirit" seems to have survived in the so-called Peace Marches organized by the Civic Union (Civil Összefogás Fórum, CÖF), an umbrella organization that claims to be the heir of the movement. So far, the last event organized by CÖF was the pro-government demonstration on March 15, 2018, in Budapest attended by tens of thousands of people. The typical critical view of these marches is that they attract brainwashed pensioners bribed with a sandwich and a free trip to Budapest by the government into rallying for its defense. In my view, while making some valid points, this criticism fails to capture the whole picture. After all, there is empirical research on the mindset of the participants of these marches.[9] It tells us that—no less than those joining anti-government demonstrations—participants in the Peace Marches think that democracy is important. They also feel that their voice counts, and they are ready to identify with and defend what they see as "their own democracy." What crucially distinguishes them from the anti-government demonstrators is that they much more frequently participate in patriotic and/or religious organizations, and tend to get information from right-wing media.

The picture that emerges is essentially that of two Hungaries in one country, whose citizens co-exist in conflict without knowing much about, let alone accepting, members of the other camp. My personal fascination with this research stems from the wish to better understand that half of the country that has found its community and representation in the Civic Circles Movement, including people close to me, such as my own mother.

## Economic Nationalism and Welfare Protection for the Middle Class

On the economic and social policy side of the coin, my argument is the following.[10] In addition to its embeddedness in civil society, the resilience of the anti-liberal right in power is also supported by a hybrid political and policy strategy. In general terms, this strategy can be described as a combination of noisy rhetorics and certain policies of change with the quiet policies of continuity with the previous developmental model. Interestingly, the idea that notwithstanding the radical rhetoric in actual policies there is as much continuity as there is change, is easily accepted neither by friends nor by opponents of the Orbán regime. Instead, both camps tend to share the view that the shift to a new political economic model has been systematic and radical. Let me elaborate why I disagree.

First, there is a contradiction between the Orbán regime's loud rhetorics of breaking with the institutional constraints and "colonizing" powers of neo-

---

[9]  Pál Susánszky, Ákos Kopper and Gergely Tóth, "Pro-Government Demonstrations in Hungary—Citizens' Autonomy and the Role of the Media," *East European Politics* 32, no. 1 (2016): 63–80.

[10]  This section draws on Dorothee Bohle and Béla Greskovits, "Re-Politicizing Embedded Neoliberalism: Shifting Patterns of EU-Integration and Dependency in the Visegrád States," under review for publication in *West European Politics*.

liberal capitalism, such as the International Monetary Fund and the European Union, and the remarkable continuity in the actual institutional setup of the Hungarian economy. Data of the Heritage Foundation show that while after 2010, the index of economic freedom in Hungary declined, it is still close to the average of ten East European newcomers to the EU. Proxied by this index, economic freedom in Hungary in 2016 is roughly at the same level as in 2004, when the country was admitted to the EU. What is visible though is that whereas in 2007 and 2008, the country was the Visegrád group's leader in terms of economic freedom, it is now a laggard.[11] However, while there has been a cutting back on neoliberalism, overall Hungary continues to have a free economy.

Second, one should not take the rhetorics of combating the domination of global corporations at face value. Undoubtedly, the regime supports the emergence of a "friendly" national bourgeoisie in the banking, energy, retail, and media sectors, previously captured by allegedly "bad," unproductive, speculative, and exploitative foreign capital. Yet, the attempts at squeezing out "bad" foreign capitalists via taxation, regulation, and nationalization go hand in hand with the continuation of earlier policies of generously subsidizing "good" foreign investors in the export-oriented manufacturing sector.[12] We also see that compared to GDP, the inflow of FDI in Hungary has not dramatically worsened; rather, in some years it is actually higher than in some of the other Visegrád countries. Multinational firms obviously like it in Hungary. In sum, what we find is that there is economic nationalism, but it is cautious and selective, as it targets some but not all the important sectors, and mainly supports capitalists close to the rulers. The political gains are twofold. Externally, the strategy has managed so far to satisfy veto players such as transnational manufacturing firms and EU-actors. Domestically, the nurtured national bourgeoisie tends to pay with political loyalty or at least neutrality.

---

[11] Economic Freedom Index of the Heritage Foundation, https://www.google.it/sea rch?q=economic+freedom+index+2017&ie=utf-8&oe=utf-8&client=firefox-b-ab&gfe_rd=cr&dcr=0&ei=_AYgWviEOqiZX6mGqPgJ&gws_rd=cr.

[12] See, for example, Andrea Éltető and Katalin Antalóczy, "FDI Promotion of the Visegrád Countries in the Era of Global Value Chains" (Budapest: Institute of World Economics, Centre for Economic and Regional Studies, Hungarian Academy of Sciences, 2017), Working Paper 229, http://real.mtak.hu/54728/1/WP_229_Elteto_Antaloczy_u.pdf.

How exactly should we imagine the contribution of Hungarian businesses to the Orbán regime's political stability? While the loyalty of the regime's favored cronies is unsurprising, what about the rest, i.e. those firms and interest groups outside of the privileged circles, or even close to the opposition? How to make sense of the limited voice of those excluded from the benefits of economic nationalism?[13] While this issue deserves further inquiry, let me propose here a speculative logic.

Few would deny that partisan considerations have played a role in the support offered to national capitalists under *all* the Hungarian governments. However, there is a sense that prior to the Orbán regime, the perks were more equally divided. Rumor has it that before 2010 the share of the government's and the opposition's business friends from public procurement contracts was regulated by a "two-thirds–one third" rule of thumb. Since this rule was largely observed by both political camps, it helped manufacture consent with the power holders in two ways. First, national capitalists were not denied a share in contracts merely on grounds of their links with the opposition. Second, since the fast-changing political fortunes of the time brought about regular alternations of center-right and center-left coalitions in power, businesses in both camps could realistically expect that the next round of alternation would allow them to grab a larger "slice of the cake." The resulting logic of patience is reminiscent of Albert O. Hirschman's famous "tunnel effect." According to Hirschman's concept, those left behind in the course of economic growth may tolerate increasing inequality if they anticipate that their "matters are bound to improve pretty soon."[14]

In contrast, in the Orbán regime the "two-thirds–one third" rule no longer seems to function. Nor is the "tunnel effect" there anymore to make the excluded national capitalists feel hopeful. After all, if the same political camp wins all the elections, it difficult for those outside the privileged circles

---

[13] One notable exception is Lajos Simicska, who amassed his wealth from public contracts under several Orbán governments, and was for a long time among the main financiers of Fidesz, until conflicts over his reckless economic expansion led to his expulsion from the ranks of the regime's grand bourgeoisie. After the incident, his media empire has become critical of the Fidesz government, and he started to support the far-right Jobbik party.

[14] Albert O. Hirschman, "The Changing Tolerance for Income Inequality in the Course of Economic Development," in *Essays in Trespassing: Economics to Politics and Beyond* (Cambridge: Cambridge University Press, 1981), 39–58, 47.

to imagine that "their turn will come in due course."[15] It is puzzling, then, that the business actors permanently left behind refrain from being more vocal about their grievances. And despite certain measures that are beneficial for the business community at large, such as low corporate taxes, there exist many grievances. Protected by anonymity, chief executives and owners of public, private, and domestic (and sometimes even foreign) firms complain about lacking or withheld information about public projects, reveal that since they lost their "friends in court" their voice is no longer heard, or mention instances of political pressure.[16] I suspect that herein lies the source of the weak resistance to the concentration of economic nationalism's benefits to a privileged circle. Exposed to political pressures and/or attracted by the perks of insiders, business opponents may be tempted to convert and change camps—or contribute to regime consolidation with their silence.

In regards to social policies, the Fidesz administration claims to resist external pressures for austerity and to protect living standards primarily through replacing Hungarians' dependence on the wasteful welfare state with their involvement in a new "work-based society." However, Hungary is still far from adopting a meager social model as we can see it in the neoliberal Baltic economies. Instead, data on public welfare spending from the Eurostat database demonstrate that the country is still the largest spender among the Visegrád countries.[17]

On what and how efficiently the sums devoted to social protection are spent is a different issue. The right-wing media use militant rhetorics, occasionally with anti-Roma undertones, that distinguish between "undeserving" and "deserving" beneficiaries of social protection. Actual policies follow suit in that workfare, i.e. badly paid precarious employment in public works programs, is the lot of "have-nots," in contrast to the better-off middle and upper middle classes, whose welfare is protected among others by low personal income taxes and generous family policies.[18] In respect to domestic politics,

---

[15] Ibid., 41.

[16] Dorottya Sallai and Gerhard Schnyder, "The Transformation of Post-Socialist Capitalism—From Developmental State to Clan State?" Greenwich Papers in Political Economy, GPERC57 (London: University of Greenwich, 2018).

[17] Eurostat, http://ec.europa.eu/eurostat/data/browse-statistics-by-theme.

[18] Dorottya Szikra, "Democracy and Welfare in Hard Times: The Social Policy of the Orbán Government in Hungary between 2010 and 2014," *Journal of European Social Policy* 25, no. 5 (2014): 486–500.

this strategy helps mobilize the consent of the middle and upper middle class "haves." Simultaneously, the strategy either silences the "have-nots" through electoral intimidation by local distributors of public works programs, or even buys their loyalty.[19] Both phenomena might have played a role in the surprising outcome of the 2018 elections in the Hungarian countryside.

All this is not meant to say that this new (or, as I indicated, not so new) social model is able to save the middle class from the consequences of austerity. Despite its rhetorics, the model functions through what Dorothee Bohle and I have termed the "depletion without replenishment" of human capital resources through neglecting investments in education and health care.[20] The major critical point in that regard is that while the social model's winners are offered some escape routes from the pressing problems of the present, this happens at the price of cutting back future-oriented social investment and the further erosion of the country's competitive advantages.

The pattern of living in the present while neglecting the future also appears in the context of financing development. To be sure, instead of breaking out of economic dependency, the regime only bought time by diversifying the sources of dependency. Hungary is extremely successful within the Visegrád region in attracting EU Cohesion and Structural Funds. The country also profits from the remittances of migrant labor.[21] These became alternative sources of financing development. Being dependent is not a problem in itself; after all, small countries are typically dependent. The big question, rather, is whether the policies of the Orbán regime help the Hungarian economy to advance in the hierarchy of the international division of labor.

---

[19] Isabela Mares and Lauren E. Young, "The Core Voter's Curse: Clientelistic Threats and Promises in Hungarian Elections," *Comparative Political Studies*, first published online on March 26, 2018, https://doi.org/10.1177/0010414018758754.

[20] OECD 2014, *OECD Economic Surveys: Hungary 2014*. OECD Publishing, https://doi.org/10.1787/eco_surveys-hun-2014-en; OECD 2016, *OECD Economic Surveys: Hungary 2016*. OECD Publishing, https://doi.org/10.1787/eco_surveys-hun-2016-en; Eurostat, http://ec.europa.eu/eurostat/data/browse-statistics-by-theme.

[21] See http://ec.europa.eu/budget/figures/interactive/index_en.cfm and http://www.worldbank.org/en/topic/migrationremittancesdiasporaissues/brief/migration-remittances-data.

## Conclusion: Questions for Friends of the Open Society

I conclude with a few puzzles and questions that friends and advocates of the open society need to solve and answer. Some of these are related to the political economy, others to the civil society foundations of Hungary's illiberal state. Let us start with the former.

There is little doubt that new solutions must be found for the pressing problems of global neoliberal capitalism and its crisis: grave insecurity and social inequality, and dwindling trust in achieving economic growth through welfare or primarily through global markets and corporations. This is why I think that instead of rejecting the current "new-old" model of Hungarian capitalism altogether, it is more constructive to take seriously the problems the Orbán regime has faced, and use the regime's solutions as contrasts or inspiration, as it may be the case, when thinking about alternative and superior strategies.

Viewed from this angle, it is not the case that the priorities of the Orbán regime all lack sense. *Horribile dictu*, I can see some justification for supporting the emergence of a national bourgeoisie. It is sensible to argue that in a country that has left the socialist system without a sizable pool of robust national entrepreneurship and that was immediately exposed to massive inflows of foreign capital, the rise of a domestic capitalist class could have some beneficial effects. In contrast, I find it difficult to imagine how a society in which the important propertied positions are all occupied by foreigners could be healthy and cohesive.

But can corrupt practices remedy such disparity? This concern has frequently and rightly come up in the debates on Hungary's economic situation and prospects.[22] One political thinker close to the government dismissed critics saying that what they called corruption was in fact the government's active policy to support the national bourgeoisie. At first this sounds absurd. How could one ignore that there is a threshold beyond which cronyism and favoritism erode a market society and the performance of national capitalists? At the same time, when you think about it, you are hard-pressed to come up with a single case of a national bourgeoisie that was originally not sup-

---

[22]  See Mihály Fazekas and Lawrence P. King, "Perils of Development Funding? The Tale of EU Funds and Grand Corruption in Central and Eastern Europe," *Regulation & Governance*, ahead of print, 2017, https://doi.org/10.17863/CAM.14169.

ported through a variety of murky protectionist interventions, especially in latecomer developing countries. It is the details that make all the difference.

Or take the social model that fights austerity through a reverse distribution of income to the "haves" from the "have-nots" and through workfare, and that thus exacerbates social exclusion and poverty. There is no doubt that today many Hungarians suffer from poverty and social exclusion, and have virtually no chance for upward mobility. Yet, advocates of a middle class-based welfare policy defend this strategy on the grounds that it is possible to combat poverty not only by helping those who are already poor, but also by protecting the middle class against impoverishment and social decline. In this respect, it is interesting to notice that three indicators of income inequality—the at risk of poverty rate, the Gini coefficient, and the income quintile share ratio—all suggest that in 2017 Hungary was somewhat more equal than in 2006. Considering the same indicators, in 2017 inequality in Hungary was still below the average level of the 27 EU member nations, and far below that of the Baltic States.[23] Similarly, while experts share the view that people involved in public works programs have little chance to ever transfer to the normal labor market, it is also true that in desperate, depressed areas of Hungary, where the public sector is absent and the private sector has moved out, this is the only employment these people have access to. Even these kinds of jobs may make them feel better off than doing nothing. Preferable alternatives to workfare may certainly exist. Nevertheless, extremely low employment was already a grave problem in the Hungarian economy well before Fidesz came to power, and no solution had been found.

Finally, while it is easy to agree that a future-oriented social investment strategy is preferable to the practice of depletion without replenishment of human resources, one big question begs for an answer: Is increasing investment in education, research and development, and healthcare a solution for a country that cannot create attractive conditions for young people to stay rather than to migrate? After all, the Baltic States are viewed as champions of a "social investment welfare state," and yet they have been plagued by the largest population losses through emigration by far over the last decade or so.[24] Should a peripheral country invest more just to train doctors, nurses, social workers, teachers, and scientists for Germany, the U.K., or Austria?

---

[23]  Eurostat, http://ec.europa.eu/eurostat/data/browse-statistics-by-theme.

[24]  Sonja Avlijas, *Revisiting the Baltic Growth Model: From Neoliberalism to the Social Investment Welfare State*. LIEPP Working Paper 2017/66, Sciences Po, Paris.

Again, the problem of a threatening brain drain is obvious, but it is not hard to see the difficulties in finding a solution.

Let me now turn to the questions raised by the case study of rebuilding Hungary's right-wing civil society. What is not yet well understood is the poor response of the left and the liberals to the rise and expansion of the Civic Circles Movement and the parallel weakening of left-liberal positions in civil society. Was the reason pure negligence on the part of power holders? Or is the weak answer to the challenge due to Hungarian or more generally post-communist specificities, especially the stigma left behind by the communist past? Or, finally, do we merely see a local manifestation of a global or European declining trend of forces of renewal of the left and liberals?

While these questions open the field for important and fruitful comparative research projects, as you may have realized, I hardly use the word "populism." This is because I believe that the Hungarian story can be told without using the term. I see something else here: a robust and reactionary elitist regime that has become increasingly nationalist and more and more critical about European integration while enjoying all its fruits. Its rhetoric is highly divisive, and what it has done to democracy is deplorable. But in my view, characterizing it as populist captures so little of its complex character that such classification may become a hindrance to its better understanding.

I conclude with questions that puzzle me in a positive way, even if I cannot answer them. Can friends of the open society holding the rainbow banner of diversity learn from those who rally around the national tricolor and the cross? And if the open society stands for diversity in civil society and for meaningful conversation between various civic groups, is sticking to this approach sufficient for regaining some of its lost influence in sharply divided societies?

# Corruption: The Ultimate Frontier of Open Society

*Alina Mungiu-Pippidi*

King Otto of Greece, a Wittelsbach, debarked from his native Bavaria in 1832 with 3,500 Bavarian troops and three Bavarian advisors aboard the British frigate HMS *Madagascar*. For the next thirty years, he would be set on the business of turning Greeks into Germans. In 1862, he was evacuated from Greece on another warship of the same Majesty. He left behind a constitution, courts, and his creation, the University of Athens, but no different rules of the game. Following its partial liberation from the Ottoman Empire at the beginning of nineteenth century, Greece remained a closed society, a country based on particularism where clan interests did not align well with the interests of the state, despite all institutional and dynastic imports. In other words, the experiment of turning Greece into Bavaria failed. Despite gradual modernization and enrichment, the project remains largely unfulfilled to this day. Why has Greece's governance proven so resilient to change? Why have so few countries succeeded to achieve what the Scandinavians, the British, and a few others managed during their modernization: to build open societies and fair states, where favoritism and corruption are the exception and treating everybody equal (ethical universalism) is the norm? The price of extensive democratization seems to be that corruption, rather than tyranny, has become the number one barrier to open society.

# Why Corruption and Open Society are at Odds

My main argument is that the reason why Greece, alongside many East European, Asian, Latin American, or African countries has not managed to accomplish a modern state similar to Britain or the Scandinavian countries, despite many components of modernity being present (such as the generalization of education or increased urbanization), is due to the difference between its society and the original Western ones, which generated modern states.[1] I do not call these differences "cultural": simply, the patterns of power and cooperation in these societies generate a different type of governance, which entails a democratic deficit and a poor quality of government. I argue that governance—defined as the set of formal and informal institutions determining the outcome of social allocation in a given society—can be observed as a configuration of consistent rules of the game, which proves more difficult to change than political regimes, being grounded in the power distribution of a society (hence the strong correlation between the "power distance" concept of Geert Hofstede and corruption).[2] I call these governance configurations "regimes" or "orders," and work to explain why transitions from one order to another are so rare and difficult, even after the fundamental problem of violence control is solved. Based on the experience of the few countries that succeeded, I look at how a society can transition from a governance norm where public resource distribution is systematically biased in favor of the power-privileged, to one where the state is mainly autonomous from private interests, and where the allocation of public resources is based on ethical universalism, open access, and the pursuit of social welfare (the benefit of the most).

The social norm of particularism that we observe in Greece and the behavior that goes with it are humanity's default condition, and they have

---

[1]  I have developed this argument in Alina Mungiu-Pippidi, et al., "Contextual Choices in Fighting Corruption: Lessons Learned," *Norwegian Agency for Development Cooperation* (2011): 1–165, https://papers.ssrn.com/sol3/papers.cfm?abstract_id=2042021; Alina Mungiu-Pippidi, *The Quest for Good Governance: How Societies Develop Control of Corruption* (2015), doi:10.1017/CBO9781316286937; Alina Mungin–Pippdi, "Learning from Virtuous Circles," *Journal of Democracy* 27, no. 1 (2016): 95–109, doi:10.1353/jod.2016.0000. I am indebted to editors of the *Journal of Democracy* for their permission to draw on the latter article for parts of the present text.

[2]  A point argued at more length in Alina Mungin-Pippidi, *The Quest for Good Governance*, chapters 1 and 4.

overwhelmingly predominated throughout human history. Societies based on open and equal access and public integrity have been very much the exception—fewer than a third of the countries in the world have reached this state of affairs (see Figure 1). This did not deter the promoters of the 2008 United Nations Convention against Corruption. More than 160 countries have signed this pledge of allegiance to the very essence of modernity: ethically universalistic treatment of citizens, delivered impersonally by a state that is not beholden to private interests.

**Figure 1**

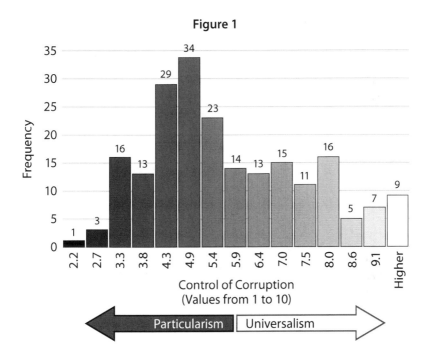

Distribution of countries on a 1-10 recoded scale of control of corruption from the World Bank Institute. The numbers above columns represent numbers of countries.

While most states adopted modern de-jure institutions (constitutions, laws of merit-based civil service, ethical codes, etc.), only in about a third of the world today do we encounter a governance order where open society with universal access to public resources exists. Sixteen countries (the bars on the right in Figure 1) are close to enjoying open access, with a score above nine on a one to ten scale of control of corruption. Most countries cluster around four or five. The competition between formal and informal institutions in the

RETHINKING OPEN SOCIETY

countries under six is an important symptom of uncompleted modernization. The main informal institution subverting modernity is particularism,
the treatment of a person depending on group belonging. Societies where
social allocation is based on particularism have markets that do not manage
to evolve from a state of imperfect competition (merit is supposed to shape
well functioning markets, not connections) and poorly governed states,
making democracy a mere façade even when elections are held, as resources
are systematically spoiled by ruling elites. Particularism can take the form
of clientelism, bribery, patronage, nepotism, and other forms of state favoritism. It limits access to public resources, favoring some applicants while dis-
criminating against others, resulting in unequal access and unfair allocation.
Particularism may coexist with political pluralism, in which case we have an
instance of "competitive particularism"; or it may be joined with a monopoly
of power, in which case we are dealing with some form of patrimonialism,
whether classic or "new" (mixed with appearances of modernization). Whatever form particularism may take, all its varieties produce the same outcome:
a regular pattern of preferentially distributed public goods. Douglass C.
North and his co-authors call this a "limited-access order,"[3] Daron Acemoglu
and James Robinson favor the term "extractive institutions,"[4] and Francis
Fukuyama refers to it as "patrimonialism."[5] They are all talking about roughly
the same social phenomena, and have come to acknowledge that open competition on the basis of equality is key to good governance, the functioning of
markets, and a democratic society.

If we cross-tabulate control of corruption measured by the World Bank
with the existence of free elections measured by Freedom House, we come
up with a distribution reflecting governance regimes as seen in Table 1. Electoral democracies score in the upper tercile of control of corruption, as against
only three autocracies—Qatar, the United Arab Emirates, and Singapore. The
average score of all democracies, corrupt or non-corrupt, is far better than that

---

[3] Douglass C. North, John Joseph Wallis, and Barry R. Weingast, *Violence and Social
Order: A Conceptual Framework for Interpreting Recorded Human History*, Prague
Economic Papers (Cambridge: Cambridge University Press, 2009), doi:10.18267/j.
pep.389.

[4] Daron Acemoglu and James Robinson, "Response to Fukuyama's Review," *WhyNa-
tionsFail Blog*, 2012, http://whynationsfail.com/blog/2012/4/30/response-to-fuku-
yamas-review.html .

[5] Francis Fukuyama, *Political Order and Political Decay: From the Industrial Revolution to the Globalization of Democracy* (New York: MacMillan, 2014).

of non-democracies (5.33 versus 3). Neo-patrimonial regimes (corrupt or very corrupt non-democratic polities) are otherwise almost even in numbers with democratic countries that are either very corrupt or corrupt; in other words, competitive particularism regimes (75 to 79). The worst corruption, however, is to be found in neo-patrimonial countries. Across the three groups, we find—as expected—that the countries which are in the upper tercile of control of corruption (the "universalism" countries) differ significantly from those where particularism is the norm, having almost no bribery, far less (although far from zero) perception of the importance of connections for success, and significantly fewer people who believe that a few big interests run the government (that figure is still far from zero, though it is lower than in particularistic countries). Ethical universalism, then, seems to be more an ideal benchmark than a real governance regime, with only the Scandinavian countries, Australia, New Zealand, Switzerland, the Netherlands, and Luxembourg above nine, and therefore close to Denmark and Norway, the top performers.

### Table 1: Governance Regimes at a Glance

| 2012 | CC lowest tercile | CC mid tercile | CC top tercile | Total | Average CC score |
|---|---|---|---|---|---|
| Non democratic | 51 | 24 | 3 | 78 | 3.06 |
| Electoral democracies | 22 | 57 | 35 | 114 | 5.33 |
| Total | 73 | 81 | 38 | 192 | |

Control of corruption (World Bank Institute, 2012) recoded 1 to 10, with 10 being the best, by electoral democracy as classified by Freedom House.

In a society ruled by particularism, limited access and favoritism create the main social allocation rules of the game, with widespread use of connections of any kind, exchange of favors, and, in their absence, monetary inducements, which are only a minority (see Table 2). Particularism in a society operates mostly to the advantage of those with more power resources, but no simple elite theory type explains it. The weaker have their defenses, resorting to patronage, cheating, bribery, tax evasion, and a variety of other practices to reduce inequality once they perceive that the social contract that is imposed on them is unfair. Elites in societies with a great deal of particularism enjoy a culture of impunity, mirrored by the self-indulgence of the rest of the population, who see the behavior of elites as the best excuse for their own behavior.

By and large, vertical and horizontal exchange networks intersect to create the systemic nature of the problem. As Table 2 shows, most bribe payers (around ninety per cent) come from the group of individuals complaining about the inequality of treatment by various public services. In many situations, bribing is engaged in to get access. In such European countries, bribing is under ten percent on average. The high percentage of people reporting unequal treatment (only in Northern Europe are they in the minority) attribute favoritism to connections and social status, not to bribing, a marginal phenomenon in Europe with the exception of a couple of countries.

**Table 2: Perception of Open Access and Equality of Treatment Comparing General Population with Bribe Givers**

| Region | Equal treatment in the public health care system | | Unequal treatment in the public health care system | |
|---|---|---|---|---|
| | % of citizens who agree that everyone is treated equally in the public health care system | % of bribe payers who perceive equal treatment | % of citizens who think they are treated unequally in the public health care system | % of bribe payers who perceive unequal treatment |
| Northern Europe | 64% | 2% | 36% | 98% |
| Mediter-ranean Europe | 58% | 7% | 42% | 93% |
| New EU Members | 47% | 13% | 53% | 87% |
| Non EU | 53% | 10% | 47% | 90% |

Source: ANTICORRP Survey.[6]

Political pluralism does not necessarily bring about better governance in severely unequal societies, where, despite formal horizontal institutions, informal client-patron relations structure politics in a vertical and particu-

---

[6]  See N. Charron, "European Perceptions of Quality of Government: A Survey of 24 Countries," in *The Anti-Corruption Report, Vol. 1: Controlling Corruption in Europe*, ed. Alina Mungiu-Pippidi (Berlin: Barbara Budrich Publishers, 2013), 99–120.

laristic manner. Voters in such regimes act as clients "selling" their vote for favors. Occasionally, unaffiliated voters manage to elect an uncorrupted president, but that leader then develops a new clientele, as between elections there are insufficient constraints and no horizontal accountability.[7] Under patrimonialism, the rule of law can evolve to "thin" at best (applied predictably, even if not "just" in its essence); under competitive particularism, it will always be interpreted in favor of the group in power (hence, the danger of unleashing anti-corruption campaigns that can be used against political opponents). Power holders are accountable in competitive particularism only when they fall from power; only in open access order regimes are rulers not above the law and answerable to prosecution at any time. Today we find that many democracies remain in the realm of competitive particularism, with a few Southeast Asian and more Eastern European cases evolving to borderline situations. The borders between categories cannot always be well defined, and the exact moment in time when the threshold has been passed from one category to another might prove difficult to identify. But the key message here is that a large participation of society in particularistic distribution is an obstacle to real democratization more difficult to defeat than tyranny. It is the ultimate civil war, as who wins might turn into a profiteer very much like who lost.

## Who Made It in Our Times and Why?

How can open access and ethical universalism be engineered? Simply adopting formal Western institutions was frequently tried. Except for some cases of military occupation—Japan or West Germany, as Sam Huntington famously noted—it did not work,[8] let alone in anti-corruption.[9] The solution of modernizing recipient societies altogether, although obviously a longer term one, was also tried by the development community and is still under

---

[7] Guillermo O'Donnell, "Illusions About Consolidation," *Journal of Democracy* 7, no. 2 (1996): 34–51, doi:10.1353/jod.1996.0034.federalism, judicial review, rule of law

[8] Peter Evans, "Development as Institutional Change: The Pitfalls of Monocropping and the Potentials of Deliberation," *Studies in Comparative International Development* 38, no. 4 (2004): 30–52.

[9] Mungiu-Pippidi, et al., "Contextual Choices in Fighting Corruption: Lessons Learned."

way in many countries, although the engineered transition from traditional societies has so far produced anything but ethical universalism. To the extent that we can measure it, we have had little to no evolution to good governance globally over the past twenty years, though small improvements do exist.[10] Modernization actually explains only about half the variation in control of corruption, with Greece, Argentine, or Russia being negative outliers—with far worse governance than they should have—and countries in Scandinavia being positive ones. More sophisticated panel-regression analyses highlight a complexity of factors accounting for a country's level of success at corruption control. Roughly speaking, this complex includes a society's capacity to place constraints on both those endowed with power and the various "resources" that power holders can exploit (whether natural rents, for instance mineral resources, or simply opportunities that can be turned into rents, such as red tape or foreign aid). Societal constraints are not independent of classic "modernity" factors: autonomous citizens and magistrates are essential in constraining corruption, and the more schooling and development a society has, the more resistance it can provide.

Besides these general statistical models, a few countries exist that managed to change their governance regime in the past fifty years or less. Learning from these "achievers" might prove a way to find solutions. How can they be identified? First, a country must *either* rank in the upper third of all countries on the World Bank's Control of Corruption scale, *or* be performing significantly better than other countries in its neighborhood, *or* set the expectation by its human-development scores. Second, no country can make the list unless it is on Freedom House's roster of "electoral democracies." Third, a country must have compiled the bulk of its corruption-control achievements in the last thirty years, since our oldest corruption indicator dates from 1984. Countries that are "authoritarian achievers," such as Qatar, Singapore, and the United Arab Emirates, are excluded because no place where the rulers are above the law can be said to be governed by ethical universalism, even if it has little bribery, able bureaucrats, and a business-friendly climate. Policy expertise also cannot create enlightened despots: the challenge remains, i.e. taming corruption by means consistent with democracy, which implies solving collective-action dilemmas.

---

[10]  Brian Levy, *Working with the Grain: Integrating Governance and Growth in Development Strategies, Oxford Scholarship Online*, vol. 6 (Oxford: Oxford University Press, 2014), doi:10.1093/acprof.

The group of "achievers" is thus highly varied. It includes Estonia and Georgia in Eastern Europe; Chile, Costa Rica, and Uruguay in Latin America; Botswana in Africa; and South Korea and Taiwan in East Asia. To analyze these cases, I follow a three-step methodology. First, I assess how well each country fits the models that relate corruption control to the level of modernization and to the interaction between resources and constraints in a society.[11] Then I examine the dynamics of change in each country through process tracing in order to understand the context and the drivers of institutional change from "moment zero" (when particularism ruled) to the present.[12] Finally, I compare all these cases with one another.

The contemporary achievers differ from one another in many ways, including the number of years since independence and more recent trends in corruption control (the most advanced among them have been stagnating or even regressing slightly). A brief comparison is summarized in Table 2. Estonia and Georgia made the most rapid transitions (lasting less than twenty years). They had full-fledged revolutions, with political liberalization accompanied by free-market reforms aimed at taking away old elites' rents. In both Estonia and Georgia, there was an alternative elite committed to ethical-universalist ideas. In Estonia, this was the group around the young nationalist historian Mart Laar, who was able to engineer Eastern Europe's most successful transition, even though, at the time he became premier in 1992, he had read only one book on economics—Milton and Rose Friedman's *Free to Choose* (1980). Laar took little Western advice, relying instead on his own knowledge of Estonian society. During his first stint as prime minister (1992–1994), he replaced almost every judge left from Soviet times, and uprooted much of the "resource base" for corruption by passing a flat tax and cutting red tape. When he returned to the premiership, between 1999 and early 2002, he furthered the cause of good governance by giving his country the globe's most advanced e-government system. Under Laar, Estonia made the quickest and most successful good-governance transformation that the contemporary world has ever seen.

The staunch anti-communism of Laar and his group provided an extraordinarily powerful incentive—Laar told me in an interview in April 2015 that he and his colleagues considered communist institutions to be

---

[11]  Mungiu-Pippidi, *The Quest for Good Governance*, chapter 5.
[12]  Mungiu-Pippidi and Michael Johnston, *Transitions to Good Governance: Creating Virtuous Circles of Anti-Corruption* (Cheltenham: Edward Elgar, 2017).

entirely corrupt, so removing them meant removing corruption. But the honesty and wisdom of this group of former Soviet dissidents was extraordinary. From the mistakes that Russian premier Yegor Gaidar had made while following U.S. advice, they learned a key lesson: the rule of law must come first. Grasping that in a post-communist context it matters a great deal who the first capitalists are, they prevented the communist-holdover networks of enterprise managers, secret police bureaucrats, and other nomenklaturists from emerging as the transition's big winners and controllers, thereby sparing Estonia the crony capitalism that has blighted Russia for the past twenty years. More exceptional still, the Laar team was remarkably open to the principle of competition. Its members, while seeking no profit themselves, allowed very young consultants to make decisions about privatization as they thought best. By 1998, Estonia was already edging towards good governance as the dominant norm.

After the Rose Revolution of 2003, Georgia sought to reproduce this pattern, and still holds the record (granted, measurements of this kind of thing have not been around very long) for the greatest positive change in corruption control in the shortest period of time by any country, anywhere. In Georgia, as in Estonia, the keys were the reduction of administrative discretion by a simplification of legislation and an extensive economic liberalization, which reduced resources for corruption. Georgia had the advantage of its own alternative elite, concentrated in universities and NGOs, despite the hardship of Soviet times, with U.S. ties and classical liberal ideas. In Georgia, however, the new elite had a weaker commitment to making sure that its own members did not wind up profiting from rent seeking.

Except for Estonia, which had a ninety per cent literacy rate as long ago as 1900 (thanks mostly to the influence of evangelical Christianity), none of the cases on our list fits the good-governance predictive models. South Korea and Taiwan had undertaken U.S.-sponsored land reform efforts, followed by the rapid spread of education, but remained far from having a modern societal structure. Chile had some favorable conditions for good governance—it lacked the vast landed estates that were so prominent in Argentina and its elite was a merchant class with views close to those of British liberals—while Uruguay was South America's most urbanized society. Yet as of 1945, both countries were still very poor. The desire to alleviate poverty drove the governance reforms of the Chilean Christian Democrat Eduardo Frei, whose career began as the head of the public works ministry in 1945, and culminated in the presidency (1964–1970). Poverty has also had much to do with the success of the urban-Marxist Frente Amplio (Broad Front) movement in Uruguay. Chile had extensive natural resources (chiefly copper) that gave corruption a foothold. Georgia has had to contend with a trio of separatist regions, recent civil wars, and the enmity of Russia, its biggest neighbor.

Despite conditions that were often less than ideal, all these cases came to outshine their modernization levels. A state-society virtuous equilibrium describes much of what we see today, as low administrative discretion coincides with high levels of civil society activism and states that avoid hindering market competition. Formal legal constraints on corruption seem to have followed rather than led changes in the social balance of power and the adoption of good-governance policies. Even in Chile, people do not credit courts with squelching corruption and do not fully trust them.

The institutional equipment available to corruption fighters in these countries is quite varied. Only Botswana has an agency tasked with prosecuting corruption, but is also the only one lacking a freedom-of-information act. Preventive institutions in the form of audit and control organizations carry some weight in Chile, Costa Rica, South Korea, Taiwan, and Uruguay. Having an autonomous, merit-based, and prosperous civil service prior to democratization was helpful everywhere except in the post-Soviet cases, which replaced nearly all their Soviet-holdover public employees. Estonia under Laar stressed prevention, requiring public officials to disclose their assets and conflicts of interest as a way of engaging the public in the work of watchdogging government.

Botswana deserves a separate word, as its achievement differs from the ethical-universalism ideal and from the interaction model. Its path has been more traditional and top-down.[13] We did no process tracing in the Botswanan case, since there is no process to trace, only top-down, state-led modernization. Botswana was put on its positive path by Seretse Khama (1921–1980), its first president and a traditional chief. He was a monarch in all but name, and an enlightened one who founded autonomous courts and an autonomous civil service, protected from widespread politicization. The concentration of power has remained high, and the current president is the founder's grandson, with a cabinet full of relatives. Botswana's achieve-

---

[13] David Sebudubudu, "The Evolving State of Corruption and Anti-Corruption Debates in Botswana: Issues in Good Governance," *EU FP7 ANTICORRP Project*, 2014, http://anticorrp.eu/wp-content/uploads/2014/03/Botswana-Background-Report_final.pdf.

ments are obvious: at the time it gained independence from Britain in 1966, it was one of the world's poorest countries in a very poor region; it has developed steadily ever since. Botswana seems to have traveled a virtuous path in comparison with its neighbor, Zimbabwe, which has slid into social and economic collapse. But then again, the Botswanan model can be a source of inspiration only for countries that have enlightened traditional rulers and limited pluralism.

The sequencing of political reforms and economic growth seems to confirm the presence of virtuous circles. In all our Latin American and East European cases, political reforms that shrank resources for corruption preceded long periods of economic growth. The Asian cases are murkier. South Korea and Taiwan experienced gradual evolutions punctuated by confrontations, leading in each case to a wavering progress curve and growth that benefited from state support as well as better governance. If these cases seem to confirm that good governance promotes growth, how it happens is a complicated story; only in Costa Rica and Estonia were democratic regimes the main achievers. Democratization helped everywhere, but in some places the virtuous circle needed more time to close, with authoritarianism sometimes playing a role by suppressing clientelism or cultivating an effective bureaucracy.

At other times, authoritarian reversions taught democrats hard but useful lessons that made them change their ways; this was the story in Uruguay. There, as in Chile, the alternation of dictatorship and democracy subtly advanced the cause of ethical universalism. Nondiscretionary government has been achieved by both leftists (ex-Marxists in Uruguay) and students of Milton Friedman (not only in Estonia but in Chile and Georgia as well). What matters is that social allocation is based on ethical universalism and not on the ideology of a particular government. A strong central government seems to matter as well: no success story is a federal state. Key individuals had a variety of motives, but human agency mattered a great deal everywhere: no place just drifted into better governance as a secondary effect. In Taiwan, for example, a series of justice ministers willing to impose tough reforms played a big role. Precisely because they all had the stomach for doing hard things, none was in office for long. In a counterfactual Taiwan with no virtuous circle, we would find long-serving ministers with no reforms to their names. Individuals who were willing to reach for a goal and take the heat made a difference.

External factors played an uneven role. The international anti-corruption movement of the past two decades cannot claim credit for any of the success stories that we have listed. South Korea and Taiwan, both on the front lines of the Cold War, received foreign assistance at critical moments, part of it conditional upon reforms, and Americans clearly played a positive role there, starting with the land reform at the end of World War II, which created a middle class. Emulation of foreign models, in particular the Anglo-Saxon liberal model, played a role in Chile, Estonia, and Georgia, where local elites in charge of the economy often had spent time studying in the United States. Uruguay had a Swiss constitutional model and its population descends from immigrants from various European countries, giving it a far more diverse mix than other Latin American countries. A similar dynamic is at play in South Korea, where a considerable number of local elites were educated in Japan. Estonia has benefited from its emulation of the Finnish corruption-control model as well as help from the Scandinavian countries (whose investments in Estonian local media outlets kept post-Soviet oligarchs from buying them up).

## No Prescriptions, But Some Lessons Learned

One cannot reproduce history, although one can always learn from it. Contemporary cases are more rewarding than older historical ones when lessons learned are concerned. Changes in governance order are possible, we learn, but occur only gradually and by a succession of radical actions and disequilibria until a new equilibrium is achieved at superior control of corruption. That explains why so few success stories exist, and why they seem to result more from domestic agency (nobody succeeded without either enlightened leaders or elites) and broad reforms following exceptional circumstances, such as democratization after a dictatorship, rather than from typical internationally assisted anti-corruption strategies focused on civil service and the judiciary.

By and large, countries evolve to good governance and open society in three ways.

First, in the case of traditional monarchies, the path is that of the King of Denmark at the beginning of nineteenth century, namely, enlightened despotism: top-down reforms, strong control agencies, the build-up of a merit-based, solid bureaucracy, and the mobilization of lower ranked social groups in the effort to reduce the rents of the privileged class. We do have Qatar, the United Arab Emirates, and Bhutan, which seem to move in this direction by themselves. Even Saudi Arabia has budged. Jordan and Morocco are certainly well placed for such gradual evolution.

In the case of neo-patrimonial systems, the situation is different. Their leaders and cliques are generally far more predatory and authoritarian than traditional monarchs. Assisting them in "anti-corruption" hardly results in credibility transfer from the donor to the ruler. It risks being both useless and immoral. Entrusting them with anti-corruption tough legislation and agencies (which they will control) is dangerous for their opponents. What is behind this reasoning, i.e. hoping they will reduce the administrative discretion they profit from? Solutions should therefore be sought in the area of building demand for good governance, empowering citizens, and fostering collective action, and if such programming risks being too political, it is always a good backup plan to invest in alternative (new) media, the development of civil society (regardless of area), and citizen empowerment. A village with an Internet café is connected to the news and other people, so it has far better potential to contribute to good governance than a village without an Internet café. The strategy to build an enlightened citizenry and the capacity for collective action is a long term one. This is the basis of sustainable development, though few donors pursue this path presently.

Often, even this strategy is not realistic and political barriers exist, preventing this sort of programming. The best strategies for such situations—if a donor needs to engage in a country—is to ensure some form of direct provision of aid through charities that work directly at grassroots level in cooperation with targeted recipient communities and apply both external and community-based mechanisms of audit and control (with the great advantage of also developing local organization and collective action capacity). Pre-modern community-based mechanisms that are described in chapter 3 of my book *The Quest for Good Governance: How Societies Develop Control of Corruption* (2015) can hopefully be a source of inspiration here: downsizing aid on sector and community can allow building participatory audit and oversight mechanisms even in pre-modern societies and contexts. Direct organization of aid procurement by donors themselves could also be a solution where evidence exists that spoiling would otherwise be dramatic and aid would only increase resources for corruption.

Finally, in the case of competitive particularism, the United States are the classic success story, where free elections preceded the autonomy of the state, and politicization of bureaucracy and corruption of municipal government were fought over for many decades. It is a story of gradual evolution and buildup of a critical mass of magistrates, journalists, and clean politicians. Identifying such agents of ethical universalism should be the primary task of donors who want to contribute to good governance, if they could also succeed in the usually elusive goal of uniting their efforts. Countries of this type have pluralism and freedom: what they miss is the capacity of collective action, the sort of social organization allowing permanent accountability of the government, not only at elections. Magistrates, clerks, policemen, and voters all need to become far more autonomous and change oriented. Nobody can organize them from outside—donor sponsored coalitions, like in the early nineties in Albania by USAID, are frail and disappear once the financing is gone. But genuine, organically grown coalitions need support and encouragement. External conditionality or selectivity might not succeed in building good governance directly, as is shown in most of my work (or that of others), but any form of international pressure can be conceived to work in a piecemeal way, leading to the gradual adoption of institutional weapons the domestic civil society can use: e-government, freedom of information, fiscal transparency, red tape reduction, participatory budgeting, and auditing (see Table 3). The success mechanism is building an interaction that cuts across state and society, proposing some mechanism to affect the equilibrium: FOIA and a civil society using it actively, tax simplification and tax collection outsourced to private collectors (as in Uruguay), e-government and media watchdogs, or Ombudsmen from civil society watching government sites. Participation and social accountability have great potential, as shown in some famous experiments (for instance, in municipal budgeting in Brazil). Attempts in the Czech Republic and India to build anti-corruption parties have shown in recent years that Facebook is a great means to gather people at a protest rally, but building stable alternative organizations on the basis of ethical universalism and ideology to compete in elections against client-based party machines remains a daunting task. However, parties may reform at a faster pace if challenged by alternative political formations with an integrity building agenda: both countries cited are evolving case studies worth watching in this respect.

There are also those situations where the international community is very strong in a country for one reason or another: from the Balkans to Taiwan or Namibia. Such cases do surface now and then. When violence is not the paramount problem, as in Iraq or Afghanistan, donors can take advantage of their privileged position to intervene in institution building. They can do this by correcting the initial institutional endowment, as in the case of U.S. sponsored land reforms in South Korea and Taiwan; greater accountability, as in the case of a general controller in Chile (an American-inspired advice); or the radical reform and socialization of judiciaries and magistrates involved; i.e. lawyers trained in British, American, or Japanese law schools made a difference in Botswana, Chile, India, and various other places.

Borderline countries (where the past norm, particularism, and the new norm, ethical universalism, compete for supremacy) present the best opportunity for the international anti-corruption industry to make a serious impact, as they already have the necessary societal preconditions, in other words, a critical mass that demands good governance. And here is where the current strategies of just adopting fail: too many laws in countries where nobody follows laws, existing mostly to create rents, are a poor anti-corruption strategy. In other words, a sound good governance program in countries where sufficient conditions exist for an intervention should be built on the lines of this classic elementary strategy: to reduce opportunities and increase constraints for corruption (see Table 3). Rather than monitoring a rather insensitive CoC or Transparency International's Corruption Perception Index (CPI), or doing general population surveys, agencies promoting good governance can monitor indicators on a number of robust independent variables, which I put together in a deeply researched index for public integrity.[14] These variables include time to pay taxes, red tape for external trade, fiscal transparency, e-services offered by government and used by citizens, and the independence of top judges and prosecutors. All these are statistically proven contributions of good governance.

The policy menu in Table 3 does not overlap well with the ordinary toolkit of consultants, who sell an endless list of "must-adapt" laws and agencies with no evidence of their utility, or against the evidence that they do not make any difference. Francis Fukuyama insightfully warned the domestic state-builders to beware of "foreigners bearing gifts of institutions," as the industry of transforming other countries has taken serious proportions in recent years.[15] The above more or less extensive list is tested and as such robustly significant. We know that it matters in affecting control over corrup-

---

[14] See www.integrity-index.eu.
[15] Francis Fukuyama, *Political Order and Political Decay: From the Industrial Revolution to the Globalization of Democracy* (New York: Farrar, Straus and Giroux, 2014).

## Table 3: What Worked in Successful Countries

| | Action | Indicator | Benchmark country |
|---|---|---|---|
| **Reduce opportunity** | | | |
| Natural resources | Private management with public share of proceeds established by broad consultation and transparently spent | Public report on spending revenues from natural resources | Botswana (EITI) |
| Administrative discretion | Reduce red tape and enforce equal treatment Ombudsman as auditor and controller Make resources transparent through e-government | Ease of doing business; indicators of equal treatment Cases solved administratively/ cases solved through prosecution E-services as % as total public services | Georgia Chile Estonia |
| Public spending | Public spending concentrated on areas such as health, education, research, and innovation with infrastructure funded mostly through private-public partnerships (FDI) | Existence of e-portal on online tracking expenses for national and local government procurement | Uruguay |
| Formalization | Tax simplification Tax collection by private agents E-payments facilitation | Time of paying taxes % increase in collection rate yearly | Uruguay |
| **Increase constraints** | | | |
| Judicial independence | Tenure, appointment, and sanctioning of magistrates entrusted to magistrates' bodies only with validation by two-thirds of upper chamber | WEF Judiciary independence (perception of businessmen) Successful litigations against government | Chile Botswana Taiwan |
| Civil society | Ease of registering, "sunshine" laws for public consultations, civil society component in every donor program, separate or combined with assistance to government, conditions on participatory budgeting, auditing, or evaluations | Number of NGOs % public consultations from total new legal drafts or policies Existence and traffic of watchdog websites Facebook users per country | Estonia |

| | Action | Indicator | Benchmark country |
|---|---|---|---|
| **Increase constraints** | | | |
| Freedom of the media | No government regulation for media except anti-trust or cartel legislation Political conditionality from international community related to media freedom | Media sustainability indicators News readership/audience | Estonia |
| Empowered citizens | IT investment in education, training for educators Freedom of Internet | Internet connections per household Facebook users per country % citizens using e-services | South Korea Estonia |

Source: Updated from Alina Mungiu-Pippidi, *The Quest for Good Governance: How Societies Develop Control of Corruption* (2015), 219–20.

tion in a context with all relevant controls. Second, each strategy or policy action was tried in some previously borderline country, and worked. On the weak side, administrative and judicial reforms depend too much on the government—so if no genuine domestic agency exists, it is unlikely that reforms will prove lasting, even if pushed as part of a conditionality package. The table should not be seen or used as a universal recipe. Rather, it is an evidence-based checklist of previously successful reforms delivered with the indicators to measure progress on what should finally be an optimal equilibrium. It cannot solve political economic problems, like the absence of a strong part of society that is competitive and wants to eliminate rents, not just inherit them; it comes after the "who" question has been solved, in other words, when a credible alliance in favor of open society and ethical universalism exists. In the absence of sufficient domestic agency, it is an illusion that external actors, irrespective of their benevolence, can build clean government and open societies in other people's countries, and the contemporary attempts, from Afghanistan to Kosovo, have been anything but successful.

# Conclusions:
# The Future of the Open Society Ideal

*Michael Ignatieff*

All contributors to this volume pose a number of sharp questions that cut to the core of the open society ideal. When Mark Lilla asks whether open society might not be a contradiction in terms, he is arguing that any society must have moral boundaries, territorial borders, and civic allegiances that include citizens while excluding strangers. In an era of migration, terrorism, and economic uncertainty, citizens of all political persuasions want borders, boundaries, and a state that protects them. Small wonder, then, that defenders of open society find themselves on the defensive. Other contributors echo this theme. Béla Greskovits, for example, asks: "Can friends of the open society holding the rainbow banner of diversity learn from those who rally around the national tricolor and the cross?" This reminds us how much religious beliefs and national attachments contribute to the political cohesion of even the most open society. These were binding forces that the open society advocates of the 1940s only understood as nationalist dangers to avoid or as religious legacies fated to disappear. But Greskovits's question can also be turned around: if national belonging matters, if diversity only works when all citizens share a common emotional attachment to a political order, how should modern societies lay down rules that strengthen belonging and attachment without increasing coercion and exclusion? If advocates of open society need to ask themselves these questions, so do the ideologists of the current wave of national and conservative counter-revolution. Since 1945, these nationalists and conservatives have accepted the liberal constitutional order and the international obligations towards human rights, migrants, and refugees that go with it. In the face of competition from the anti-liberal, anti-constitutional radical right, they will have to choose which side they are on: democracy or authoritarianism. How these choices will be made—who will have the power to make them politically—will determine whether the political systems of European and North American societies will remain open in the generations ahead.

The central question, posed by the contributors in this volume, is why the transitions in East Central Europe have veered away from the open society path that opened in 1989. Jacques Rupnik asks us to remember that in 1989, the new and untried political elites of East Central Europe had to master three simultaneous and convulsive changes: the creation of democracy, the establishment of a market economy, and the entry into Europe. It is hardly surprising that they could not surmount all of these challenges. The open society model of transition was supposed to result in a pluralistic political and economic system, with political parties alternating in power and a competitive market system empowering a broad-based, economically independent middle class. Dorothee Bohle's essay demonstrates that the liberal constitutional orders created after 1989 proved unable to control the market forces—of instability and inequality—that were unleashed when the communist system was dismantled. What has taken shape instead—in response to the shocks of economic integration and the inter-elite struggle for power—is the consolidation of what Anne Applebaum calls the single party state.

As both János Kis and Jan-Werner Müller point out, what is novel about these single party states is the astute way their rulers have used the rhetoric of democracy to undermine democracy. They are masters at manipulating majoritarian consent of "the people" in order to undermine the checks and balances of liberal constitutional rule. The regimes in Poland and Hungary create societies that give the illusion of openness and maintain a surface appearance of freedom—they allow citizens to exit and to express their voice, and they do not impose loyalty, to use Albert Hirschman's typology, but as András Sajó demonstrates, their constitutional order is closed, gerrymandered to ensure that power remains in the control of ruling parties. The unanswered question is how far these new single party regimes in East Central Europe will go, whether illiberalism will turn into the overt authoritarianism of Russia and China. At present, neither Hungary nor Poland has resorted to state repression or political imprisonment. Both remain within the European

Union and NATO. Yet these alliance structures have failed to exert any meaningful check on the slow slide towards authoritarian single party rule.

What is clear, however, from the anti-NGO legislation introduced in Hungary and elsewhere, is that open society advocates will have to rethink a change model based on foreign or external funding of domestic civil society organizations. There are two mistakes here, namely, the illusion that you can do politics without politics, by mobilizing non-partisan civil society NGO's rather than political parties, and the failure to counteract the populist narrative that characterizes foreign funding as an assault on domestic political sovereignty. Here, too, authoritarian populists have been skillful in using the language of democracy to assault a key principle of democracy: freedom of civil society and freedom of association.

Yet it would be premature to pronounce the death of open society in East Central Europe. The urban populations of the region are still so attracted to the freedom and opportunity of open societies that, as Ivan Krastev points out, they are emigrating in droves. They may have given up, temporarily, on building them at home, but the appeal of pluralist open society models remains and awaits a new wave of internally generated domestic political expression. Those who have emigrated within the Schengen area will have a decision to make: whether to remain bystanders in the politics of the open societies they have adopted as their home, or to return and build an open society where they were born. We do not know what they will decide, but the future of East Central Europe depends on their choices.

The political tides in 2018, the date these essays appear, may be running against the pluralist and liberal values of an open society, so it is all the more important to remember that open societies have strengths. They emancipate, they empower, and sometimes they even inspire their citizens. Their freedom makes economic and scientific dynamism possible while, as Alina Mungiu-Pippidi's contribution illuminates, single party states have structural weaknesses—progressive ideological exhaustion, demographic decline, and increasing corruption—that may eventually prove their downfall.

Open societies cannot prevail in this new battle of ideas with the new illiberal and authoritarian regimes, Pierre Rosanvallon argues, unless those who believe in them are prepared to rethink democracy itself. If populist authoritarians seek to appropriate "the people" and speak in their name, democrats will have to offer the aggrieved and excluded more than representative democracy by elites and a transparent and accountable bureaucracy run by functionaries. A reimagined open society has to restore a sense of agency and

participation in individual citizens, affirmed in new institutions of consultation and direct democracy that re-engage citizens from the bottom up and
give them the power to speak in their own name.

If the open society advocates of the 1990s underestimated nationalism
and failed to predict the single party rule, if their vision of democracy left
the people behind, they also were naively rationalist in their understanding of
how democratic public opinion is formed and shaped. Erica Benner's contribution to this volume reminds us that Popper and his generation of Cold War
liberals neglected to emphasize what Machiavelli understood only too well:
that pretense, artifice, demagoguery, deception, and outright lying are incor-
rigible features of civic discourse, especially in open societies. So the open
society ideal of rational argument based on shared facts can easily appear to
be pious and naïve. But we do not have better alternatives. As Thomas Christiano shows in his contribution, citizens are being bombarded with political
propositions that they have little way to assess critically. But that does not
leave them as helpless pawns of demagogues. Facts are stubborn things, even
in politics, and sooner or later, facts can be pressed into service to dispel illusion. Citizens can help each other to find out whether promises are kept or
not. With easily available public information, citizens can establish whether
political programs work or don't. Thanks to the increasing sophistication of
digital techniques of manipulation, we can all be fooled once or twice, but
not indefinitely. Eventually the very digital technologies that allow the manipulators to spread deception will also empower counter-narratives. What
remains resonantly democratic and optimistic about the open society vision
is the idea that all of us remain open to rational persuasion. None of us is
so rational that we are fully sovereign in our judgment, but none of us is so
deluded that we cannot figure out when we have been fooled. András Sajó's
contribution shows that the liberal constitutional architecture of an open
society is fragile and easily manipulated, but its resilience resides in the fact
that an open society empowers the sovereign judgment of citizens. An open
society enables all its institutions—media, courts, review bodies, universities,
civil society, parties, unions, and associations—to join in the debate about
what constitutes reality and what counts as truth. This debate, fractious and
unending as it may be, helps to protect citizens from succumbing to organized illusion.

An open society's political culture, like its institutional matrix, has to
be pluralistic if it is to be truly free, but it need not be relativistic. As Tim
Crane makes clear in his contribution, tolerance is a cardinal open society

virtue, but toleration does not require acceptance or endorsement of all opinions. In fact, it is often the case that what citizens feel obliged to tolerate, as a condition of a free society, is a doctrine or belief they actively dislike or have good grounds to reject. An open society must find a way to accommodate, incorporate, and include the widest possible variable of religious and secular beliefs, but toleration is not an obligation to respect all opinions and beliefs equally, but rather an obligation to accord equal respect to persons. This ideal of equality of respect remains an open society's most appealing feature, even when, in reality, such societies inevitably fall short of the ideal.

Traditional conservatives, as opposed to the authoritarian and "alt-right" variety, concede the attractiveness of open society as an ideal, as Roger Scruton does in his contribution, but they go on to claim that the liberalism that dominates political discourse in open society is neither so tolerant nor so open as it claims. In fact, conservatives claim that in liberal-dominated universities, liberal toleration has curdled into coercive and self-righteous political correctness. There is an unfortunate degree of truth in this, as far as the academy goes. In regards to society as a whole, it is a curious claim given the rude health of conservative and anti-liberal discourses everywhere and the political ascendancy that conservative parties have enjoyed in Western democracies, not only since Margaret Thatcher and Ronald Reagan but throughout the entire postwar period. Conservative complaints about political correctness may exaggerate the victim's status of conservative discourse, but some liberals and some liberal institutions, especially the university, have restricted debate when they should have opened themselves up to challenge. Timothy Garton Ash's contribution warns fellow liberals against these temptations, reminding us that the liberal spirit is one that is not too sure of itself, one whose self-doubt and self-questioning is the necessary condition for its own renewal.

The contributions in this volume make the important point that the history of open society since World War II and its future in the twenty-first century are closely dependent upon shifting configurations of global power. Margaret MacMillan provides a striking historical account of how Western victory in the world wars fostered the spread of open society values through the creation of liberal international institutions like the European Union and the United Nations. At the same time, MacMillan warns us that if societies embrace closed borders, protectionism, and exclusionary domestic policies, the fragile but robust international order, based on rules, co-operation, and state consent, may be unable to survive. Stephen Walt warns us that liberal democracies have fractured domestic consensus at home and caused chaos abroad by aggressively promoting their own values overseas, often by force of arms. Instead of trying to spread liberal democracy abroad, the most important task ahead is to create good examples of robust and resilient civility at home. Robert D. Kaplan worries aloud that the postwar international order that provided the basic security to maintain open society at home is now breaking up. A new age of state rivalry is emerging with uncertain implications for the postwar peace and the American hegemony that made open society possible. While the United States is retreating from its position as the leader of the free world and the main defender of open society values, many look to Germany to take its place. Daniela Schwarzer points out that Germany can only play this role if it leads a European Union that is stable and speaks with one voice. Yet the European Union itself is struggling to maintain itself as a union of open societies, as single party states consolidate on its periphery. Open society ideals cannot be defended nation by nation and state by state: their survival depends on democratic alliances of like-minded societies, united in their determination to defend a common core of pluralistic values.

New technology is empowering and accelerating the forces of disruption that the open societies of the twenty-first century will have to master if they are to survive. Niall Ferguson draws our attention to the radical challenge that new technologies pose to the hierarchical top-down, statist orders that delivered justice and growth in the open societies of the postwar era. New technologies disrupt hierarchy, overturn deference to authority, and empower disaffiliated citizens. The tacit trust that has held open society together and kept it civil is breaking apart. At the same time, the technologies vest network owners with immense power and these imbalances of power threaten the basic equality before the law that open societies require if they are to hold together. Open societies are struggling now to subject the new information oligopolies to regulation, without strangling the explosive potential of new technologies. They will also have to find ways to guarantee the integrity of their democratic systems in an age when new technology enables democracy's authoritarian competitors to engage in highly sophisticated and deniable forms of manipulation and disinformation.

The final challenge to open society lies in our own heads. Those who believe in such ideals once thought, in 1989, that history was on our side. Triumphalist narratives took hold of many of us. History had ended with victory and we had won. Even then, this seemed a hubristic and delusional fable to anyone who, for example, watched the democratic transition in the former

Yugoslavia in the early 1990s collapse into a ferocious civil war.[1] Today, in 2018, it is not triumphalist historical determinism that is the enemy of clear thought, but its pessimistic equivalent: a determinism that confidently pronounces the democratic recession to be permanent; that announces that "the West has lost it"[2]; that the authoritarian ascendancy of single party states is the wave of the future and will sweep all before it; that the European Union is facing a terminal crisis of cohesion and confidence. A similar pessimism overtook liberal democrats and progressive forces in the 1930s, as Mussolini, Hitler, and Stalin demonstrated with ruthless determination what single party states, backed by terror and aggression, could accomplish. It became fashionable in the thirties to doubt the capacity of liberal democracies to compete or even endure. Yet we know how the story turned out.

It is important to derive the right lessons from the 1930s. Today, open society does not face a totalitarian threat, backed by violence and state terror. It faces a new adversary: authoritarian single party states that are actually parasitic on our freedoms. They are not the closed societies of the past. They are not in the grip of messianic, totalizing ideologies like Fascism or Communism. They are rent-seeking machines whose goals are the preservation of power and the reward of their elites. They trade their goods and resources in an open international economy; they secure capital on international markets; their citizens travel to and from free societies; they share global information. Free societies are in a deeply collusive relationship with their authoritarian competitors, but this collusion and interpenetration confers levers of influence and counter-power that free societies can use to their own advantage.

We need to co-exist with these regimes and keep the peace. We may not be able to inflect, influence, or change their domestic political orders. Externally funded or supported attempts to change regimes or even to mobilize domestic political opposition seem bound to fail or play into the hands of these regimes. Changing these regimes, ultimately, is a matter for their own citizens. But the governments of actually existing open societies do not have to collude, empower, or enable authoritarian single party states and their cronies. The European Union does not have to provide structural subsidies to regimes that manifestly violate basic norms of academic freedom, rule of law, freedom of association, and freedom of speech. The United Nations

---

[1]  Michael Ignatieff, *Blood and Belonging: Journeys into the New Nationalism* (London: Farrar, Straus and Giroux, 1993).

[2]  Kishore Mahbubani, *Has the West Lost It? A Provocation* (London: Penguin, 2018).

and its agencies do not have to remain silent when single party states—or open society democracies, too, for that matter—violate the obligations that their countries have accepted towards refugees and migrants. Democracies should not be selling weapons to regimes that imprison or oppress their people. Banks and commercial institutions in free societies should not allow their facilities to be used to offshore rents and profits extracted by single party regimes and their local elites. Free media in open societies should not repeat the mistake of the 1930s, which was to suppose that countries where freedom is being extinguished are far-off places "of which we know little." For here the lesson of history is relatively clear. Democracies—open societies—tend to keep peace with each other. Authoritarian single party states do not always do so.[3] They need enemies. Once they have vanquished the domestic foes of their own invention—foreigners, dissenters, political opponents—they will invent external enemies. If they are sufficiently powerful or can ally with those who are, they will endanger the freedom of their neighbors.

The conclusion that needs to be drawn is not that authoritarian single party states necessarily constitute a clear and present danger, still less a justification for aggression or war, but simply that we need to defend ourselves, with force of arms, but above all, with the force of argument. When we are told that single party illiberal democracies are democratic, we need to point out that an illiberal democracy is a contradiction in terms. When we are told that authoritarian regimes are the wave of the future, we need to repeat, with the wise men of the nineteenth century, that history has no libretto. History is on no one's side, not theirs, not ours. History will be made by those who defend their ideals with the most determination, guile, and wisdom. In addition, and at a practical policy level, we need to address open society's deep collusion with these regimes. Our banks and companies have no business propping up the rent extraction systems or offshoring the ill-gotten gains of authoritarian rulers; we should stand together to defend the integrity of our domestic institutions against external digital subversion; we should not allow states to violate the basic norms of the clubs—the United Nations, NATO, or the European Union—that they have joined; and when such regimes do violate these norms, we need to rally alliances of democratic peoples and their leaders to say: this far and no further.

---

[3] Michael W. Doyle, "Liberalism and World Politics," *The American Political Science Review* 80, no. 4 (1986): 1151–69.

# About the Contributors

Anne Applebaum is a *Washington Post* columnist, a Pulitzer-Prize winning historian and Professor of Practice at the Institute of Global Affairs at the London School of Economics.

Erica Benner is a Fellow in Political Philosophy at Yale University.

Dorothee Bohle holds a Chair in Social and Political Change at the Department of Political and Social Sciences at the European University Institute in Florence.

Thomas Christiano is Professor of Philosophy and Law at the University of Arizona and a Fellow at the Institute for Advanced Studies in Toulouse.

Tim Crane is Professor of Philosophy at Central European University.

Niall Ferguson is the Milbank Family Senior Fellow at the Hoover Institution at Stanford University and a Senior Fellow of the Center for European Studies at Harvard University.

Timothy Garton Ash is Professor of European Studies at the University of Oxford and a Senior Fellow of the Hoover institution, Stanford University

Béla Greskovits is University Professor at the Department of International Relations and the Department of Political Science at Central European University.

Michael Ignatieff is President and Rector of Central European University.

Robert D. Kaplan is a bestselling author, Senior Fellow at the Center for a New American Security and Senior Advisor at the Eurasia Group.

János Kis is University Professor of Political Science and Philosophy at Central European University.

Ivan Krastev is Chairman of the Centre for Liberal Strategies in Sofia and a Permanent Fellow at the Institute for Human Sciences in Vienna (IWM).

Mark Lilla is Professor of Humanities at Columbia University.

Margaret MacMillan is Professor of History at the University of Toronto.

Jan-Werner Müller is Professor of Politics at Princeton University.

Alina Mungiu-Pippidi is Professor of Democracy Studies at the Hertie School of Governance in Berlin and Director of the European Research Centre for Anticorruption and State-Building.

Stefan Roch is a Postdoctoral Researcher at the Rectorate of Central European University.

Pierre Rosanvallon is Professor and Chair of Modern and Contemporary History of Politics at the Collège de France.

Jacques Rupnik is Research Professor and Senior/Fellow at Sciences Po (Paris) and at the College of Europe (Bruges).

András Sajó is University Professor at the Department of Legal Studies at Central European University.

Daniela Schwarzer is the Director of the German Council on Foreign Relations.

Sir Roger Scruton is a writer and philosopher and Fellow at the Ethics and Public Policy Center in Washington D.C.

Stephen M. Walt is Professor of International Affairs at the Harvard Kennedy School of Government.

# Index